KEYWORDS IN YOUTH STUDIES

WITHDRAWAL

With recent attention to issues such as youth social exclusion, poverty, school underachievement, school violence, gang activity, sexuality, and youth's interactions with media and the internet, youth studies has emerged as a significant interdisciplinary field. It has moved beyond its roots in subcultural studies to encompass a diverse array of disciplines, subfields, and theoretical orientations. Yet no volume exists that systematically presents and puts into dialogue the field's areas of focus and approaches to research.

As a unique blend of reference guide, conceptual dictionary, and critical assessment, *Keywords in Youth Studies* presents and historicizes the "state of the field." It offers theoretically informed analysis of key concepts, and points to possibilities for youth studies' reconstruction. Contributors include internationally-renowned scholars who trace the origins, movements, and uses and meanings of "keywords" such as resistance, youth violence, surveillance, and more. The blending of section essays with focused keywords offers beginning and advanced readers multiple points of entry into the text and connections across concepts. A must-read for graduate students, faculty, and researchers across a range of disciplines, this extraordinary new book promotes new interdisciplinary approaches to youth research and advocacy.

Nancy Lesko is Professor of Education and Maxine Greene Chair at Teachers College, Columbia University.

Susan Talburt is Director and Associate Professor of Women's Studies at Georgia State University.

KEYWORDS IN YOUTH STUDIES

Tracing Affects, Movements, Knowledges

Edited by Nancy Lesko and Susan Talburt

Routledge
Taylor & Francis Group

NEW YORK AND LONDON

First published 2012
by Routledge
711 Third Avenue, New York, NY 10017

Simultaneously published in the UK
by Routledge
2 Park Square, Milton Park, Abingdon, Oxon OX14 4RN

Routledge is an imprint of the Taylor & Francis Group, an informa business

© 2012 Taylor & Francis

Library of Congress Cataloging in Publication Data
Keywords in youth studies: tracing affects, movements, knowledges/
edited by Nancy Lesko and Susan Talburt.
p. cm.
1. Youth—Study and teaching. I. Lesko, Nancy. II. Talburt, Susan.
HQ796.K425 2011
305.235072—dc22
2011006342

ISBN: 978–0–415–87411–3 (hbk)
ISBN: 978–0–415–87412–0 (pbk)
ISBN: 978–0–203–80590–9 (ebk)

Typeset in Bembo
by Book Now Ltd, London
Printed and bound in the United States of America on acid-free paper
by Edwards Brothers, Inc

CONTENTS

ACKNOWLEDGMENTS

This book spanned a long arc from initial idea to publication, and many folks contributed along the way. First of all, Nancy and Susan wish to thank all the contributors to this book, who were willing to explore undefined keyword territories. Without their creative and original scholarship, this volume would not exist. We are also most grateful to our students, at Teachers College, Georgia State University, Teachers College in Tokyo, and the University of Oslo, whose perspectives, insights, and passions "called for" this book. We also imagine many future conversations in response to it. We are sincerely grateful to Catherine Bernard at RoutledgeFalmer for her belief in the book and to Georgette Enriquez for her assistance.

In addition, Susan wishes to thank students in Women's Studies at Georgia State University for their assistance at different stages of the creation of this book: Tahereh Aghdasifar, Dylan McCarthy Blackston, Alex Venegas-Steele, and Whit Young. In addition to some friends and colleagues who have been present in important ways, she particularly thanks people (and creatures) who have accompanied her throughout: Elizabeth Beck, Debra Moore, Steve Johnson, Francie the black dog, and always, her parents, Hollis and Thomas Talburt.

Nancy also thanks Mary Ann Chacko and Becky Stanko, who provided editorial assistance at crucial times, her mother, Virginia Lesko, Leonard the pug, and most importantly, Tama, pack-leader, whose humor and surrealism keep the world livable.

AN INTRODUCTION TO SEVEN TECHNOLOGIES OF YOUTH STUDIES

Susan Talburt and Nancy Lesko

We begin this book with some questions: What imaginings of youth exist? How do they work? What do they produce? What do they make possible or impossible? In what forms have youth been imagined, endowed with meaning, and problematized? And how do these imaginings relate to or revitalize other imaginings about, say, society, community, the future, or progress? Our questions direct us to consider the proliferation of social, cultural, economic, institutional, material, and linguistic practices that operate across multiple locations, such as the media, national governments, psychologized advice literature, and international organizations, about problems of youth and how to solve them. Problems can include issues of youth social exclusion, poverty, school underachievement, school violence, gang activity, sexuality, health, or youth's interactions with and uses of media and the internet, and so on. These interconnected practices, familiar but always shifting, sediment and are sedimented by certain ideas of who youth are, who they could or should be, and who they could or should become, especially given the "right" circumstances and opportunities. Consider the following, rather typical, depiction of the "state of affairs" for youth, who are said to face rapid and threatening changes in the context of social and institutional disintegration:

> For youth today, change is the name of the game and they are forced to adapt to a rapidly mutating and crisis-ridden world characterized by novel information, computer, and genetic technologies; a complex and fragile global economy; and a frightening era of war and terrorism. According to dominant discourses in the media, politics, and academic research, the everyday life of growing segments of youth is increasingly unstable, violent, and dangerous. The situation of youth is today marked by the dissolution of the family; growing child abuse and domestic conflict; drug and alcohol abuse; sexually transmitted diseases; poor education and crumbling schools;

and escalating criminalization, imprisonment, and even state execution. These alarming assaults on youth are combined with massive federal cutbacks of programs that might give youth a chance to succeed in an increasingly difficult world.

(Best & Kellner, 2003, p. 75)

In this construction, "youth" is a universal, stable category whose adaptations and successes are disrupted only by the rapid transitions of an increasingly complex world. Embedded in this imagining of youth, like most, is a construction of the category youth as "transitional subjects," neither child nor adult, but "in the making." As subjects-in-process, they must acquire knowledge, skills, and dispositions that will enable them to function in society. The meanings of youths' transitions are uncertain and dangerous, subject to constant rewriting, a construction that makes youth a particularly malleable category, neither this nor that, but always in-between, becoming.

Demonstrating the politics of this precarious development, Valerie Walkerdine (1984, p. 173) has traced how "the rational, the savage, the animal, the human, the degenerate, [and] the normal" were scaffolded into the normalized and regulated child. The youth, like the child, is a particular species; yet the youth differs from the child in terms of its problems, possibilities, and needs. For example, in contrasts made between "child" and "youth," the child is cast as innocent and the youth as "out of control," with children's play depicted as intrinsically creative and constructive and youth "leisure" as potentially "threatening and disturbing" (Nayak & Kehily, 2008, p. 7). Thus, to develop these subjects-in-process, adults, those who are "already made," must provide social, institutional, and emotional support and guidance for youth to become future workers, citizens, homeowners, consumers, parents, and so on. Because youth are seemingly "everywhere," and thus always available as a "cultural resource" (Castañeda, 2002, p. 1), youth is a productive category that regulates both youth and adults.[1] Imaginings of youth often invoke a past to orient us to a future based on particular ideas about family, community, nation, responsibility, morality, and progress.

While "youth" invokes a universal category of transitional beings on their way to productive, responsible, and legal adulthood, deviance and exceptions haunt particular youth. The effects of youth discourses mark some young people as exclusions, as failures, as freaks (Ramlow, 2005) and thereby unable to take up the position of awkward-yet-worthy teens. Some young people's raced, classed, sexualized bodies are read as disabled, violent, or pathetic; for example, Anita Harris (2004) distinguishes girls who live up to contemporary opportunities to achieve, consume, and exercise a voice as "can-do" girls and those who fail the new markers of success as "at-risk." Cindy Patton (1996) deciphered how policy makers deemed White middle-class youth as not needing protective HIV/AIDS curricula which "other" youth had a responsibility to learn. Tom Popkewitz (1998) emphasizes the system of reasoning of Teach for America, which despite its rhetoric and intentions, produces classroom teaching practices in which urban and rural youth underachieve. Scaffolded discourses about urban and rural youth generate principles for new teachers' understanding, participation, and intervention. Scaffolded discourses offer ways of reasoning about abstract "youth" and about particular, marked youth.

Thinking, Feeling, Diagnosing, and Ameliorating: Retheorizing Youth Problems, Knowledge, and Specialists

This book explores connections among a range of anxieties, inducements, satisfactions, problems, knowledges, solutions, methods, and institutions that assemble to produce the figure "youth," to govern youth and adults, and to constitute a field of "youth studies." Our goal is to create a history of the present of youth and youth studies that questions the logic of the present time as inevitable by interrogating the orders and knowledges that direct us to think about and act toward youth in particular ways. Histories of the present, or genealogies, point to the possibility of an otherwise by examining "the historically sedimented underpinnings of particular 'problematizations' that have a salience for our contemporary experience" (Barry, Osborne, & Rose, 1996, p. 5). The logic of the present has constructed youth as a population with emergent problems and created an attendant variety of knowledges to understand and administer them.

Historicizing the present of youth studies' discourses and approaches locates them as interdisciplinary constructions with firm ties to economics, politics, and social relations, national and international. As a field, youth studies has moved beyond its roots in subcultural studies of the Birmingham School, psychological developmental research, and sociological studies of socialization and deviance to encompass a diverse array of disciplines and subfields. Interdisciplinary formations that engage Marxism, psychoanalysis, postcolonialism, feminism, queer studies, and race and ethnic studies open the field to new configurations even as they carry traces of its pasts. This book interrogates how these knowledges at once (re)produce the subject of youth studies and question it. In the rest of this introduction, we present ways of thinking about the regulation of youth and adults through expert and popular knowledge, positioning this book as an intervention that analyzes dominant rationalities and technologies of youth.

Our initial thinking about youth studies is inspired by a Foucauldian understanding of political rationalities as "ways of thinking about and acting upon one another and ourselves" (Barry et al., 1996, p. 5) that obscures the cultural politics of the creation of problems, ideals, and goals through systems of expertise. Rationalities create and justify the forms by which reality can be represented, analyzed, and rectified. Rationalities ask us to think in particular ways about who youth are, what they need, and how "we" can help them. Following Rose (1996), we argue that rationalities of the government of youth have a moral, or normative, form that identifies ideals and distributes tasks among various authorities (the psychologist, the NGO worker, the after-school program administrator); an epistemological form that embodies the subjects to be governed (the pregnant teen, the obese youth, or the underachieving Latina student); and particular styles of reasoning that render problems and realities thinkable or unthinkable, reformable or not reformable (developmental theory, sex education, zero tolerance) (p. 42). Rationalities create techniques, or technologies, that employ a variety of procedures, strategies, and actors to construct and enact ends and means. Foucault's (1991) phrase to describe governmentality, "the conduct of conduct," refers to the art of acting on the actions of individuals in order to correct, guide, develop, or shape their behaviors. The conduct of conduct is "made thinkable under certain rationalizations and practicable through the assembling of technologies," (Barry et al., 1996, p. 12).

Our use of the term rationalities does not elide affect's contributions to modern conceptions of youth. Young people are defined as fundamentally emotional, moody, and defiant, traits that are linked to hormonal surges (Lesko, 2001). Youth is said to involve an intensification of self-reflexivity, or turning inward, and affective capacities, such as "emotional intelligence," must be analyzed, diagnosed, and developed. But affect also circulates in how sturdy images and narratives, say of "problem youth" or awkward youth, hook adults. Part of the operation of rationalities and technologies is affective, evoking an almost-automatic response to stock representations of gang members, innocent teens, or gangling geeks. Thus, educators', youth workers', and researchers' investments in particular rationalities and technologies are often felt ones.

As ways of doing things, technologies have particular purposes and develop in relation to a "practicable object" (O'Malley, 1996, p. 193), shaping subjectivities. Constituted as a practicable object, the category "youth" mobilizes actors, both youth and not-youth, to behave in certain ways. Young people encounter an array of institutions and knowledges that would incite them to develop proper habits of hygiene and diet, material and moral responsibility, cognitive awareness, chaste sexual behavior, and so on. Adults—the mother, the father, the relative, the teacher, the social worker, the activist, the judge—take particular positions to support this proper development. By this, we do not mean to suggest that what constitutes proper development is uncontested but that the idea of development itself is uncontested.

The assembling of rationalities and technologies occurs in shifting configurations at "macro" levels, such as the government department or ministry or the transnational organization, and "micro" levels, such as the school, the juvenile courtroom, the detention center, the mall, the family, or the TV show. "Youthscapes" often confound standard macro and micro analyses as hybrid forms of music, fashion, language, and technology, as well as old and new practices of movement and containment, mix in local, national, and international registers (Maira & Soep, 2005; Nilan & Feixa, 2006). Yet even in globalized youth culture, technologies of government—an array of "strategies, techniques and procedures through which different authorities seek to enact programmes of government in relation to the materials and forces at hand" (Rose, 1996, p. 42)—can be identified. To analyze rationalities and technologies is to uncover the ways they have been produced and have been productive of particular subjectivities, imaginings, logics, institutions, and actions. For example, socialization, a seemingly innocent term employed by the social sciences and popular culture, typically describes how young people are affected by and become functioning members of the society in which they live. Yet socialization must be understood as a historical process of shifting assemblages of rationalities, technologies, practices, institutions, and individuals. Similarly, the idea of stages or transitions popularized by developmentalists creates seemingly objective norms for youths' physical, cognitive, and moral progression to mature adulthood, enabling a range of ever-shifting technologies "by which and in which it is proposed that we work on, divide, make whole, sculpt, cultivate, pacify, contain, empower, and optimize" (Dean, 1996, p. 217) youth and those incited to support their development.

We are particularly concerned with interrogating youth studies' naturalization of certain youth imaginings, many of which, like socialization and developmental stages, are popularizations of "expert knowledge." Expertise, or "authority arising out of a claim to knowledge, to neutrality and to efficacy" (Rose, 1996, p. 39), has been significant to the invention and administration of youth. Referring to what he calls "a swarm of experts, specialists, advisers and empowerers," Dean (1996) has written of the diffuse locations of expertise:

> These "authorities of truth" operate within and outside local, regional, national and transnational State bodies, demanding they take on or withdraw from their functions, act in new and different ways, form new relations with other bodies and other States, divide, compose and assemble themselves differently, and position themselves in certain networks and relays.
>
> (p. 211)

Expertise functions as an affective apparatus. It appears to support the interests of social order, whether it governs youth through the state, through society and its institutions, or through "the regulated choices of individual citizens" (Rose, 1996, p. 41) who become aligned with its goals through "persuasion, education and seduction rather than coercion" (p. 50).

This book, then, examines various locations at which expertise and the popular, the seemingly rational and the affective, the past and the future, assemble and reassemble to produce the logic of the present. It interrogates how various imaginings of youth, their development, and their potential problems naturalize and are naturalized by an array of perceived social problems and solutions. Taking up the sedimentation and intensification of rationalities and technologies across locations, the book emphasizes the ways in which affective apparatuses incite both youth and adults to govern themselves.

The Book as Event

What does this book do? In traditional terms, this book is a blend of reference guide, dictionary, textbook, and critical assessment that presents and historicizes the "state of the field" of youth studies, offers theoretically informed analysis of key concepts, and points to possibilities for the field's reconstruction. Indeed, the book does the following: (1) it introduces and analyzes the development and present status of the topics and methods of youth studies across its subfields; (2) it historicizes and interrogates key concepts in the field and their relations across youth studies' subfields; (3) it introduces "submerged" concepts that have shaped and continue to shape research in the field; and (4) it offers directions for the creation of new theoretical and methodological approaches and new substantive areas of research. But as our introduction suggests, we wish not simply to present ideas about youth studies' development, discourses, focal areas of attention, and methods—and to offer a linear solution that will "improve" the field and incite readers, whether researchers or youth workers, to conduct themselves in the "right" ways.

We have thus chosen an unusual format for this book: sections introduced by longer conceptual essays followed by shorter keyword essays that create multiple dialogues within the text and between the text and readers. Not only do we place researchers across subfields in dialogue to counter narrow ideas of expertise, but we create unusual juxtapositions of ideas and institutions in order to enact an interrogation of the field's common sense. Our purpose is to create an active text to which readers must bring their own imaginings and through which they might create other imaginings. The seven sections, which we think of as "technologies of youth studies," present and analyze the field's ways of accomplishing certain purposes following particular systems of reasoning. Each section includes an introductory essay that presents theoretical, interdisciplinary interrogations of the field's assumptions, practices, purposes, and possibilities. The essay is followed by shorter "keyword" essays that explore significant analytical terms, themes, or categories for youth studies through the lens of that particular technology.

In selecting technologies and keywords, we have drawn from what we consider to be both "stuck places" and "open places" in conceptualizations within and across a range of disciplines and subdisciplines, including anthropology, criminology, education, psychology, sociology, social work, and women's studies. Our choice of the technologies and keywords strikes a balance in representing some traditional approaches and issues (such as resistance, subculture, and citizenship) and some more recent approaches and concerns (such as transnational governance organizations, hijab, and musicking)—keeping these concepts in constant dialogue. The seven technologies offer something of a structure, in which the first three sections—A History of the Present of Youth Studies, Research and Regulation of Knowledge, and Populational Reasoning—offer a history and overview of the field of youth studies, in particular how knowledge in the field has been constituted and institutionalized. The next three sections— Citizenship Stories, Mobilities and the Transnationalization of Youth Cultures, and Everyday Exceptions: Geographies of Social Imaginaries—shift the focus to specific social, political, national, and global dimensions of youth studies that are increasingly salient in the field. The final section, Enchantment, represents what we identify as a dominant mode of address in the field in perpetuating particular representations of youth and youth development to researchers and practitioners.

Following these entries are "keywords," an idea we borrow from Raymond Williams' (1976) classic *Keywords: A Vocabulary of Culture and Society* and Bruce Burgett and Glenn Hendler's (2007) *Keywords for American Cultural Studies*. A keyword is neither a dictionary nor a glossary but, according to Williams, a "record of an inquiry into a *vocabulary*" (p. 15) that emphasizes the ways in which meanings are made and altered over time through contestations among diverse social groups or constituencies. A focus on youth studies' keywords creates a method of mapping the presence and transformations of words, ideas, practices, and institutions within a particular domain. As Desai, Bouchard, and Detournay (2010) suggest in their analysis of enduring concepts in transnational feminist studies, to center on keywords effects "a shift in emphasis away from the individual scholar's or feminist's capacity for self-reflexivity and toward the enabling structures, paradigms, and assumptions of the concepts that many of us working in this area of inquiry use" (p. 48).

We selected keywords for each section that represent concepts that have been central to youth studies or that have a peripheral, repressed presence in the field's thought. The keywords are in dialogue with the multiple disciplines and subdisciplines in youth studies, youth-related policies and institutions, and the material conditions of youths' lives. At the same time, these keyword essays bring analytical strategies from fields outside youth studies to foster a revisioning of the field's past, present, and future. Like Williams' (1976) desire for inquiry to remain open, we make no claim that we offer *the definitive* keywords or that we can map their relations with certainty. Rather, as Burgett and Hendler (2007) say, the keywords

> provide a counterpoint to the discourse of expertise. They treat knowledge not as a product of research that can be validated only in established disciplines and by credentialing institutions, but as a process that is responsive to the diverse constituencies that use and revise the meanings of the keywords that govern our understandings of the present, the future, and the past.
>
> (p. 3)

The process of selecting keywords entailed developing lists of terms and concepts based on our readings in youth studies, followed by an iterative process of adding, eliminating, and placing keywords in relation to the sections, or technologies. The groupings of the words are quite intentional, as the position of an entry changes its meanings, interrupting usual connections in order to open up spaces for critique or reconstruction. To foster questioning of naturalized imaginings and systems of reasoning, rather than placing keywords in "obvious" sections, we shift their seemingly natural placement in order to demonstrate linkages across technologies and concepts and to invite readers to think differently about their roles and frameworks in the field. The keywords deliberately interrupt a narrow idea of "expertise" and promote creative, idiosyncratic, and unpredictable approaches to the use and *revision* of keywords that regulate imaginings of youth and understandings of youth studies' present, past, and future. To this end, we asked authors to design keyword essays that address the following questions in relation to (but not limited by) the "technology" in which the keywords were placed: Where does the term come from? What have been its uses and meanings over time? What effects have those uses produced? What knowledge or ways of thinking has it enabled? What has it obfuscated? What might be some alternatives?

In choosing and placing terms, our goal was to balance "classical" and "newer" work in the field, placing those keywords in such a way that neither writers nor readers would fall into traditional chains of reasoning (such as identifying a problem, describing the theoretical and/or material conditions of that problem, and then moving to propose a correction or solution to the problem). We include unusual terms to highlight subordinated categories and to bring concepts from different subfields into dialogue. As we worked through keywords, we found that using certain terms salient in youth studies literature would only repeat the field's common sense, rather than asking readers to engage alternatives. A significant example lies in "identity categories," such as Black, Asian, Latino/a, gay, straight, male, female, and so on. This set of terms could have filled the third section, Populational Reasoning, in very predictable ways. Rather than simply repeat the field's proliferation of social categories, we included one "identity" term, "trans," in this section, intentionally choosing a keyword that receives less analysis in youth studies literature and allowing it to "trans" any reasoning based on stable populations. At the same time, we included "classic" youth studies words, such as "resistance," "subculture," "style," or "culture," not only to highlight their importance in the field, but to open them to new readings. Readers will note that many of these terms could be grouped in other sections. That is precisely our point—by interrupting the usual chains of reasoning we seek to call attention to the thinking and reading that the positioning of these concepts demands. We wish for readers to ask themselves how concepts become ossified in chains of reasoning and what might happen if their usual associations were to be disrupted. For example, the placement of "subculture" under Populational Reasoning invites critique of ideas of a fixed, discrete group (youth) entering into an Oedipal conflict with a parent culture and calls for a reconceptualization of subculture. Alternatively, if it were placed in a section such as Mobilities and the Transnationalization of Youth Cultures, "subculture" might suggest dual processes of the creation of new forms of critique and commodification.

The blending of introductory essays to the technologies and focused keywords creates a rhizomatic approach to youth studies that works against linearity, inviting readers to enter the text through multiple points and to create their own unique connections across concepts. Deleuze and Guattari (1987) argue against understanding books as closed systems that have a meaning that imitates the world, reflects nature, or represents ready-made meanings and hierarchies. They compare such a book to a tree or a root, which "plots a point, fixes an order" (p. 7). If a tree-book "composed of chapters has culmination and termination points" (p. 22), a rhizomatic book is not based on foundations, beginnings, and endings. It is comprised of multiple connections in which "any point of a rhizome can be connected to anything other, and must be" (p. 7). A rhizome is always in the middle. The blending of conceptual essays and disruptively placed keywords functions as rhizomatic representations "entirely oriented toward an experimentation in contact with the real" (p. 12). We hope that readers will enter the text with this openness to creating connections, perhaps keeping in mind Deleuze and Guattari's words:

We will never ask what a book means, as signified or signifier; we will not look for anything to understand in it. We will ask what it functions with, in connection with what other things it does or does not transmit intensities.

(p. 4)

Our hope is that readers will move between familiar concepts and ideas, germane to their work in, for example, sociology of youth cultures or adolescent literacies, and unfamiliar ideas, terms of analysis, and theories, say, from geography, history, or sexuality studies. This juxtaposition of familiar and strange, common and uncommon, is what we seek to offer readers, thereby promoting novel or original readings through a movement of content and form.

As readers engage with individual contributions and the linkages and disjunctures among them, we hope they will question what the present urges us is necessary to think and to do. Our goal is to invite readers to move across essays and keywords, asking questions of the text and of themselves, making connections that are at once obvious and not, evaluating the implications of the present, and inventing new possibilities for thought and action.

Note

1   We extrapolate from the child to the youth as we draw on Edelman's (2004) theorization of the political uses of the child to regulate the present and naturalize "reproductive futurism" (p. 11) and Castañeda's (2002) theorization of the ways in which "each figuration of the child not only condenses particular material-semiotic practices, but also brings a particular version of the world into being" (p. 4).

References

Barry, A., Osborne, T., & Rose, N. (1996). Introduction. In A. Barry, T. Osborne, & N. Rose (Eds.), *Foucault and political reason: Liberalism, neo-liberalism, and rationalities of government* (pp. 1–17). Chicago: University of Chicago Press.

Best, S., & Kellner, D. (2003). Contemporary youth and the postmodern adventure. *The Review of Education, Pedagogy, and Cultural Studies, 25*, 75–93.

Burgett, B., & Hendler, G. (Eds.). (2007). *Keywords for American cultural studies.* New York: New York University Press.

Castañeda, C. (2002). *Figurations: Child, bodies, worlds.* Durham, NC: Duke University Press.

Dean, M. (1996). Foucault, government, and the enfolding of authority. In A. Barry, T. Osborne, & N. Rose (Eds.), *Foucault and political reason: Liberalism, neo-liberalism, and rationalities of government* (pp. 209–229). Chicago: University of Chicago Press.

Deleuze, G., & Guattari, F. (1987). *A thousand plateaus: Capitalism and schizophrenia.* Minneapolis: University of Minnesota Press.

Desai, J., Bouchard, D., & Detournay, D. (2010). Disavowed legacies and honorable thievery: The work of the "transnational" in feminist and LGBTQ studies. In A. Lock Swarr, & R. Nagar (Eds.), *Critical transnational feminist praxis* (pp. 46–62). Albany, NY: SUNY Press.

Edelman, L. (2004). *No future: Queer theory and the death drive.* Durham, NC: Duke University Press.

Foucault, M. (1991). Governmentality. In G. Burchell, C. Gordon, & P. Miller (Eds.), *The Foucault effect: Studies in governmentality* (pp. 87–104). Chicago: University of Chicago Press.

Harris, A. (2004). *Future girl.* New York: Routledge.

Lesko, N. (2001). *Act your age! A cultural construction of adolescence.* New York: Routledge.

Maira, S., & Soep, E. (Eds.). (2005). *Youthscapes: The popular, the national, the global.* Philadelphia: University of Pennsylvania Press.

Nayak, A., & Kehily, M. J. (2008). *Gender, youth, and culture: Young masculinities and femininities.* New York: Palgrave Macmillan.

Nilan, P., & Feixa, C. (Eds.). (2006). *Global youth? Hybrid identities, plural worlds.* London: Routledge.

O'Malley, P. (1996). Risk and responsibility. In A. Barry, T. Osborne, & N. Rose (Eds.), *Foucault and political reason: Liberalism, neo-liberalism, and rationalities of government* (pp. 189–207). Chicago: University of Chicago Press.

Patton, C. (1996). *Fatal advice: How safe sex education went wrong.* Durham, NC: Duke University Press.

Popkewitz, T. S. (1998). *Struggling for the soul: The politics of schooling and the construction of the teacher.* New York: Teachers College Press.

Ramlow, T. (2005). Bad boys: Abstractions of difference and the politics of youth "deviance." In S. Maira, & E. Soep (Eds.), *Youthscapes: The popular, the national, the global* (pp. 192–214). Philadelphia: University of Pennsylvania Press.

Rose, N. (1996). Governing "advanced" liberal democracies. In A. Barry, T. Osborne, & N. Rose (Eds.), *Foucault and political reason: Liberalism, neo-liberalism, and rationalities of government* (pp. 37–64). Chicago: University of Chicago Press.

Walkerdine, V. (1984). Developmental psychology and the child-centred pedagogy: The insertion of Piaget into early education. In J. Henriques, W. Hollway, C. Urwin, C. Venn, & V. Walkerdine (Eds.), *Changing the subject: Psychology, social regulation, and subjectivity* (pp. 153–202). London: Methuen.

Williams, R. (1976). *Keywords: A vocabulary of culture and society.* New York: Oxford University Press.

SECTION I

A History of the Present of Youth Studies

Susan Talburt and Nancy Lesko

> Young people have not been enfranchised by the research conducted on their lives. The history of youth cultural studies of the last four decades tells us more about the politics of academic research than it does about young people.
>
> (Valentine, Skelton, & Chambers, 1998, pp. 21–22)

This section of the book initiates a partial *history of the present* of youth studies. By *history of the present* we mean a method of historical analysis that problematizes the very terms and concepts through which we know and understand a topic. A history of the present starts with questions around categories and discourses in use and interrogates how, where, when, and why they emerged and became popular. Therefore, we ask: Who are the youth that youth studies examines? What are the systems of reasoning youth studies draws on to know and engage youth? How might we imagine youth and youth studies differently? In creating a history of the present, we do not assume "youth" as a biological reality or age-based category. Rather, we emphasize systems of reasoning, or discourses, that circulate across sites and times to create the concepts that produce "youth" as a category to administer through such social and institutional locations as schools, families, the labor market, correctional institutions, popular culture, and scientific expertise (see Tait, 2000, p. 11; Wyn & White, 1997, p. 8). We name three historical moments and their sedimented discourses that define the boundaries of what can be thought or said within youth studies: (1) the "mental hygiene" movement's use of pastoral power to regulate youths' mental and physical health at the end of the 19th century; (2) the popularization of psychological developmental stages and sociological studies of adolescent society and deviance of the 1950s and 1960s; and (3) the Birmingham Centre for Contemporary Cultural Studies' (CCCS) turn to subcultural studies of youth in the 1970s. Discourses produced within these moments assemble in the present to construct youth as defined by age: in a transitional moment to adulthood, they are "at-risk" for deviations from proper development for adult work and family roles; they serve as barometers of societies' and nations' social and economic well-being and future potential; they are enmeshed in peer culture, yet developable through adult administration in formal and informal institutions, such as schooling, scouting, sports, and families.

These discourses incite adults and institutions to orient themselves to youth through systems of reasoning that universalize youth as a unitary category with particular needs at the same time that they differentiate youth according to their alignment with desired developmental norms. An incitement to know and help youth progress and succeed demands a "forgetting" of the dismantled social, political, cultural, institutional, and economic resources that could support their well-being (Duggan, 2003; Quinn & Meiners, 2009). We return to this "forgetting" of diminishing resources and supports after first sketching dominant rationalities that animate thought and action in the present.

Creating Systems of Reasoning: Three Historical Moments

Pastoral Power, 1880s–1890s

Dramatic changes in the United States in the 1880s and 1890s, including industrialization, immigration, urbanization, the rise of science, women's entry into the labor force, and the emergence of consumerism, created changes in family and social life, and accompanying anxieties. Adolescence emerged in this context as scientists and social reformers offered prescriptions for raising the next generation of American boys and girls in an uncertain future. Adolescence became a way of talking about the future of the nation and developing modern citizens who were rational and self-disciplined (Lesko, 2001). Modernization entailed measuring, monitoring, and standardizing time, a zeitgeist applied to civilization and development. As Lesko and Mitschele (2011) point out, "Modern ideas of adolescence came into being as clock time became the central way of ordering past, present, and future events and their meaning" (p. 7). With adolescence understood to be a turbulent time, development-in-time became a dominant way of ordering the adolescent. G. Stanley Hall argued that, as they develop, individual children recapitulate the same evolutionary steps as do human groups as they reach toward higher, civilized stages. The job of science was to measure and guide this development.

Systems of reasoning cobbled together in this era emphasized youth as a distinct population, a universal adolescent who was nevertheless gendered, raced, and classed, and whose body proclaimed a healthy, moral status or its dangerous specter, social degeneration. The playground movement, scouting, and the YMCA governed developing bodies to support self-improvement, respectability, and productivity. Central to these practices was the expertise of the "boyologists," who collected data from young people. Their pastoral power merged scientific techniques of knowledge production, an understanding of the importance of peer relations, and an ability to act like a friend (Hunter, 1994; Laqueur, 1976). Teachers were, in turn, admonished to become more like peers and confidants: sensitive, honest, and tactful as they instilled "self-doubt and self-correction" (Hunter, 1994, p. 81).This pastoral power distributed discipline among adult authorities and youthful subjects who internalized regulations to monitor the self.

Teenage Markets, 1950s–1960s

In the 1950s, an increasing emphasis on consumption, style, and leisure and an array of goods and services aimed at a new market, youth, inaugurated the "teenager" and, with that invention, the incessant crossing of images between youth-as-fun and youth-as-potential-offender (Valentine et al., 1998, p. 4). As young men were gaining financial independence and cultural spaces apart from their families, moral panics about delinquency and urban gang activity fueled academic study, born in criminology, of youth (Cohen, 2002 [1972, 1987]). Teenage popular culture, especially music and comics, became a target for censors who rallied against the moral corruption of bad uses of leisure (Gilbert, 1986). Rock and roll music, with its clear African American origins and explicit sexuality, was another frightening indicator of wayward and/or rebellious youth. John Waters parodied the hysteria linking racial integration, rock and roll, sexuality, and marijuana in his film *Hairspray* (1988), in which a psychologist is consulted to brainwash Tracy, the central character, into dating White boys.The 1960s free schools and student-centered pedagogy (Cuban, 1984/1993; Graubard, 1972; Neill, 1960) offered reassurances that the "kids were alright" if schools, adults, and textbooks would get out of their way. Romantic ideas of youth—for example, youth was a creative and generative time—gained ascendancy in these practices, which also dovetailed with marketing spins on the teens as the "best years of one's life."

In a context of anxiety about youth behavior in changing times, legions of psychologists and sociologists were recruited to identify and solve youth problems. Erik Erikson (1950/1985, 1968), for example, focused on youth commitment within social change and called for a moratorium of responsibilities for young people, which would allow them to work through the developmental challenges of identity consolidation that he considered an essential task of youth. Lawrence Kohlberg and Rochelle Mayer (1972) championed moral development through guided discussions of cases in which values were in conflict; for example, in the Heinz dilemma, students debated whether Heinz should steal money in order to save his wife's life. These stage-oriented measures of youth progress intensified earlier iterations of development-in-time.

The Adolescent Society (1961) positioned James Coleman as the preeminent youth sociologist, and his research portrayed youth as preferring to spend time chatting with friends rather than studying for a test.Youth, even those identified as middle class and college-bound, were choosing leisure activities over achievement-oriented ones. Coleman (1974) later focused on reintegrating youth into a society that was in transition, thereby linking psychology and sociology as centers of expertise about youth problems and possibilities.

Youth Subcultures, 1970s–1980s

With antecedents in sociologists' studies of deviance and delinquency from the 1920s to the 1960s, the Birmingham CCCS continued a stage-of-life approach to studying youth (Tait, 2000) in a context of social change. Their Marxist approach to ethnographic and semiotic research of youth subcultures centered a class analysis of how youth resisted, subverted, or appropriated dominant cultures and ideologies as they created their own meanings, styles, and practices. The CCCS positioned youth subcultures' counterhegemonic practices as reasonable responses to their material conditions. At the same time, researchers' "neglect of the young people who conform in many ways to social expectations" (Valentine et al., 1998, p. 24) perpetuated a construction of youth as potentially disruptive, locating youth subculture somewhere between delinquency and normalcy (Tait, 2000, p. 45). Whether conceptualizing youth as a mediated version of or an Oedipal conflict with a parent culture (Halberstam, 2005, p. 160), the emphasis on generational distinction to characterize subculture recirculates ideas of youth as "different" from adults. Moreover, the centering of age to define subculture downplays the significance of popular culture and style in constituting youth as a category (Bennett and Kahn-Harris, 2004, p. 10).

Youth studies surged as mass market commodity and new scientific specialization in the later decades of the 20th century. *Reviving Ophelia* (Pipher, 1994) and *Real Boys* (Pollack, 1998) are two examples of cross-over books that are read by parents, social scientists, physicians, and Oprah. Part-voyeurism, part-social science, and part-therapy, the books reaffirm youth as an endangered "separate tribe." Another swath of books focuses on analyzing and curbing violent young men and women (e.g., Garbarino, 1999, 2007); one such book, *Queen Bees and Wannabes* (Wiseman, 2002), crossed quickly from the bookshelf to the comic film, *Mean Girls* (Michaels & Waters, 2004). Finally, neurology has recently discovered the "teenage brain" and its hidden vulnerabilities; medical doctors in white lab coats on YouTube discuss the undeveloped frontal lobe of the teenage brain, thereby reworking the age-based, biological difference of youth in new language (see http://www.youtube.com/watch?v=RpMG7vS9pfw).

In sum, the systems of reasoning identified here continue to produce youth in certain ways. Youth are trapped in "becoming," and their bodies, actions, and emotions are read as evidence of their immaturity. Condensed phrases, such as "raging hormones" or "peer pressure," efficiently telegraph their position. The developmental framework, consumed at-a-glance in age, requires youth's "less than" status. Researchers, activists, and educators strive to help young people, but on the established terms, which reduce and homogenize them while forgetting the play of power and resources in these representations.

"New" Conditions and "New" Responses

There is a circularity in which universal discourses of youth and their needs perpetuate a "forgetting" of the diminishing social and economic resources available to them; in turn, this "forgetting" of social dislocations and inequitable material relations perpetuates the sedimentation of systems of reasoning that individualize youth in relation to supposed universals in order to make their lives better. For example, the present logic of high-stakes testing adopts a discourse of youth empowerment that seeks to ensure that young people have skills and knowledge to succeed in a global economy and contribute to society.Yet, as the inevitable and inequitable failures and successes created by high-stakes testing reveal, not all youth, particularly poor youth and youth of color, are offered equal institutional resources or are equally empowered (Su, 2009). This individualizing empowerment discourse intensifies a neoliberal "can-do" attitude, or a "belief in [young people's] capacity to invent themselves and succeed" (Harris, 2004, p. 14) that erases the cultural politics of school achievement.

In a context of economic change accompanied by diminishing state and institutional supports and collective social ties, success and risk are individualized.This shift to a privatized, neoliberal present is "forgotten" when experts and popular culture mobilize sedimented systems of reasoning to help youth. As Harris (2004) argues,

> In the modern period of the late nineteenth century, youth were disciplined directly by the state and its agents so that they would develop slowly, under close supervision, to serve a unified and progressive nation. Late modern times, however, are characterized by dislocation, flux, and globalization, and demand citizens who are flexible and self-realizing . . . direct interventions and guidance by institutions have been replaced by self-governance; power has devolved onto individuals to regulate themselves through the right choices.
>
> (p. 2)

Self-governing citizens must

> make choices and create life trajectories for themselves without traditional patterns or support structures to guide them.They must develop individual strategies and take personal responsibility for their success, happiness, and livelihood by making the right choices in an uncertain and changeable environment.
>
> (p. 4)

Youth become individually accountable for being able to adapt, conform, be innovative, be flexible, and be successful—all the while monitoring their own progress toward their future trajectories.

Youth studies offers means of measuring young people's self-government and progress by drawing on familiar developmental discourses. For example, in the guise of attending to socioeconomic changes related to increased educational demands in the information economy, Tanner and Arnett (2009) confidently assign individuals aged 18–25 years to a "new," distinct developmental period, "emerging adulthood," a stage characterized by "identity explorations, feeling 'in-between,' instability, self-focus, and possibilities" (p. 9). Emerging adults' three-stage process of "recentering" is reminiscent of the identity crisis, role confusion, and developmental tasks Erikson (1950/1985, 1968) attributed to adolescence half a century ago. Emerging adults move from dependence to mutual responsibility, explore romantic and career roles and opportunities, and end by "making commitments to enduring roles and responsibilities of adulthood (e.g., careers, marriages, and partnerships, commitments to the parental role)" (p. 40). Like development-in-time a century ago, or the middle-school movement that identified specific needs of 10- to 15-year-olds in the 1980s, the young person is inserted into ever more fine-grained segments of *panoptical time* through which to be understood. Panoptical time

> emphasizes the endings toward which youth are to progress and places individual adolescents into a temporal narrative that demands a moratorium of responsibility yet expects them at the same time to act as if each moment of the present is consequential.
>
> (Lesko, 2001, p. 107)

In this prolonged moratorium, the individual continues to be responsible for monitoring and directing her movement forward.

In turning to the present, rather than joining talk of the contemporary "war on kids" (Grossberg, 2005, p. 5) or the "assault on youth" (Giroux, 2000, p. 10) that identifies commercialization and commodification of youth, failed institutional policies and practices, and dwindling spaces and resources to foster youth creativity, we turn to three programs intended to make young people's lives better: teaching emotional resilience, bullying prevention, and "Slumdog Basketball." These programs, which circulate globally, appear to combine "new" psychological and sociological expertise to approach contemporary problems youth face in changing socioeconomic and cultural contexts.

Emotional Resilience: "You Can Do It!"

Following the popularization of Goleman's (1995) *Emotional Intelligence*, schools in the United Kingdom, the United States, Australia, and other countries began to employ curricula to teach emotional resilience to young people to develop their internal strengths and social skills. Justified by "recognition that in the current climate of social, political and economic upheaval young people need to be resilient more than ever" (Leach, n.d., para. 34), teaching emotional resilience is said to level the proverbial playing field for young people to develop into healthy, productive—and self-governing—adults. Leach explains,

> There is increasing global awareness of the need to improve life chances for all young people. Life chances relate to having autonomy, engaging in positive social and community networks, accessing education and employment opportunities, being economically stable, experiencing health and well-being and living in a safe environment.
>
> (para. 1–2)

Rather than pathologizing youth, emotional resilience training claims to mark a shift "from simply fixing what is seen to be wrong with them, to promoting their strengths and potential contribution to society" (para. 4).

Psychologists typically define resilience as individuals' or groups' capacity to cope in the face of risk or adversity (such as poverty, crime, substance abuse, natural disaster); resilience is fostered by "protective factors," such as social or family support, a sense of belonging, and community involvement (Luther, Cicchetti, & Becker, 2000). Yet "emotional resilience" represents a stripped-down, individualized version of how young people can cope that ignores the social. Emotional resilience curricula, such as "You Can Do It!," teach a "social-emotional competence called emotional regulation" (Bernard, n.d., p. 1), or "toughness," based on an idea that "with emotional control, one has the calmness to make rational behavioural decisions that are in one's best interest" (p. 5). Because angry students are said to be underachievers (p. 1), young people learn through "You Can Do It!" to control how anxious or angry they become, moderate behavioral impulses, and calm down quickly when upset. The University of Pennsylvania's Penn Resiliency Program, dubbed "Emotional Health 101" in at least one New York City KIPP (Knowledge Is Power Program) Charter School, helps youth to control their reactions to situations by "replac[ing] negative thinking with more realistic and flexible thinking" (Aubrey, 2010, n.p.). The curriculum teaches late elementary and middle-school students "to detect inaccurate thoughts, to evaluate the accuracy of those thoughts, and to challenge negative beliefs by considering alternative interpretations" (Resilience Research in Children, n.d., para. 1). A school administrator using this curriculum explained the need for students to develop tools to manage their emotions: "'They're constantly looking for fairness in the world, and they're spotting unfairness in the world'...This can lead to a lot of hurt feelings, sadness, stress" (Aubrey, 2010, para. 9).

Forgetting the conditions that create "perceptions" of unfairness teaches youth docility and acceptance and diminishes possibilities for constructive action against injustice. Moreover, teaching emotional resilience as adaptive behavior recirculates discourses of "cultural deficits of inner-city children and/or families rather than the real-life conditions plaguing schools in inner cities" (Su, 2009, p. 22). It is worth noting that KIPP schools have been portrayed as "successful in improving the educational attainment of poor children because of their emphasis on teaching middle-class mores and aspirations" (Theoharis, 2009, p. 202). An emotionally resilient mantra of "You Can Do It!" forgets, and quite possibly supports, the social and material relations underpinning inequitable access and outcomes in stratifying institutions by placing the focus of "corrective" action on youth.

In a reiteration of the mental hygiene movement's construction of the good student, youths' academic achievement and developing emotional control are measured and monitored. Emotional resilience follows the late 19th and early 20th centuries' blending of morality, or obedience to rule-based discipline, with a science of skills and utility to promote efficiency and mental health and to reduce social conflict (Boler, 1999, pp. xxii, 31). As a form of pastoral power, emotional resilience individualizes governance so that young people "internalize rules of self-control and discipline" (p. 21). Social science can harness this emotional technology to identify types of young people to develop in desirable directions and to address social problems, such as bullying.

Bullying

After the 1999 school shootings at Columbine High School, and a series of publicized shootings in Europe and North America, public concern with school violence stimulated interest in bullying as a potential cause of such violence. A proliferation of research, school programs, and parenting manuals related to bullying ensued, focusing on creating types of youth and means for adults to administer them.

A best-selling popularization of bullying discourses that addresses parents, Coloroso's (2003) *The Bully, the Bullied, and the Bystander*, positions all young people as potentially one of these "three characters in a tragic play performed daily in our homes, schools, playgrounds, and streets" (p. 3). The book warns of future risks: the bully will continue to have poor social skills and respond aggressively to others; the bullied is at risk of violence against self or others, such as a "rampage" (p. 9); and the bystander risks growing up guilt-ridden or desensitized to violence (pp. 8–9). Concerned that youth have "no opportunity to develop more constructive social skills" (p. 5), Coloroso urges parental interventions:

> We can re-channel the governing or controlling behavior of the bully positively into leadership activities. The nonaggressive behaviors of the bullied can be acknowledged and developed as strengths. The role of bystander can be transformed into that of a witness: someone willing to stand up, speak out, and act against injustice.
>
> (p. 5)

Parents can identify these characters through "assessment tools listing warning signs of possible violent juvenile behavior" (p. 56) and help them to develop skills aligned with emotional intelligence. Not only is the child individualized, but so is the responsible parent who must listen to his or her child and become more aware of what is happening in the school and playground (see Baez & Talburt, 2008). The text is silent about the social, political, and material contexts of competition, evaluation, and narrowing acceptable social roles that feed school cultures that encourage the formation of exclusionary peer groups. Thus, in another act of forgetting, the individual parent, armed with expert advice, is responsible for monitoring their child and creating the healthy families, caring schools, and community involvement said to be necessary for their children's success.

Slumdog Basketball

The last approach to improving young people's lives that we turn to is Gamechangers, a partnership between Architecture for Humanity and Nike Inc. designed to "encourage community organizations to empower youth through sports by proposing programs that spur social and economic development in a community" (About Gamechangers, 2008). Bearing the same name as Nike's Jordan Game Changer shoe, Gamechangers awards grants for the construction of facilities that offer youth access to sports and play spaces, improve physical activity, develop social cohesion, and create opportunities for social and economic empowerment in communities lacking resources. The Gamechangers' website announces a featured program: "Slumdog Basketball aiding in the psycho-rehabilitation of slum dwelling youth in Mumbai thru sports!" Slumdog Basketball will bring four basketball courts and a space for computer training to "fill two voids, recreation and education . . . This program will create dynamic social change and life long learning by arranging daily sports and life training for at-risk slum dwelling children" (Gamechangers, n.d., para. 1). Slumdog Basketball promotes well-worn discourses of "healthy lifestyles" and "job skills" as resources for youth to move successfully from a life of poverty to self-determination. How the program is to be sustained beyond facilities construction, not to mention how the success of the young people beyond a few rounds of hoops or some internet surfing will be sustained, is unclear. What is clear is that this global program follows an established system of reasoning that incites adults through the discourse of the underdog who will make it in the world: "Beat Anything. Change Anything" (Nike Gamechangers, 2009). This incitement blends sports and the swoosh logo with enthusiastic humanitarianism to create a collective forgetting that little sustained scaffolding is available to young people to change the conditions of their lives.

Each intervention—emotional resilience, bullying prevention, and Slumdog Basketball—names itself as a response to cultural worlds and material relations, yet recirculates discourses that universalize youth categorically, employing pastoral power to individualize them as responsible for overcoming obstacles to succeed. Each support incites adults to clear a space for young people, only to position them more firmly in panoptical time where they must govern the self as they develop skills for successful transition to adulthood. The intensification of the ideal of a youthful "can-do" attitude ensures that some youth will not succeed on the terms laid out for them.

Alternative Spatiotemporalities in the Present

In considering the possibilities of a youth studies that refuses present neoliberal discourses that reframe a public sphere in terms of personal responsibility and moves beyond systems of reasoning that delimit youth in terms of problems and solutions, we draw on several projects that attend to the sociopolitical and material realities of young people's lives in the present. These projects suggest reworked relations of adults and youth along with glimmers of counterdiscourses.

Our Schools Suck (Alonso, Anderson, Su, & Theoharis, 2009) centers youth voices in order to counter the dominant public discourse of a "culture of failure," offering "an intervention into the adult-driven debates on inner-city youth" (p. 5). The text's emphasis on young people's affect and activism connects their anger, their seemingly "poor choices," and their work against injustices to "the conditions in which they live, work, and attend school rather than essentialized 'cool pose' values" (p. 6). It offers a powerful antidote to emotionally resilient neoliberal "can-do" discourses by attending to youth's awareness of and struggles against their positioning via incoherent messages of personal responsibility in the face of systemic material inequalities in their lives: "Despite living in an urban center with a small employment base for low-skilled young workers, attending under-resourced schools, and facing discrimination in their job searches, they were repeatedly told that success rested on their motivation" (p. 25).

Chávez and Soep (2005) present an analysis of Youth Radio, in which adults and youth coproduce media products, a project that pushes against the romanticizing of youth voice as intrinsically emancipatory, a deficit model of youth, or an authoritative role for adults. Youth media projects often position young people as sources for intimate details of their lives but not as editors or as compensated contributors. But youth media production, they argue, "can provide a resource for young people to rewrite the stories that are told about them, against them, or supposedly on their behalf" (p. 410). In what they call a "pedagogy of collegiality," adults and youth depend on each other's skills and knowledges to communicate to an audience, which acts as witness, mediating the dialectical power dynamics between students and teacher. Like the authors of *Our Schools Suck*, Chávez and Soep refuse to invoke "youth voice" divorced from political, social, and relational contexts or in order to establish their own progressive credentials (p. 413). Youth Radio intentionally puts "youth development considerations" first, but this policy of "collegial pedagogy" has "baked in" generative tensions (pp. 418–419) that they discuss as "joint framing, youth-led inquiry, mediated intervention, and distributed accountability" (p. 421). The authors note: "Participating as an adult in collegial pedagogy means always searching for that shifting balance between sufficient mentorship and excessive intervention" (p. 424). And the program's "distributed accountability" refuses the individualized accountability of most pedagogical contexts and "functions as an iterative process of forming and weighing judgments about the work being produced as it relates to a series of criteria—including those shaped by considerations of accuracy, originality, aesthetics, rigor, and matters of social impact" (p. 430). Chávez and Soep offer a multifaceted portrait of the pedagogy of collegiality that consciously avoids romanticizing, forgetting inequalities, and erasing power differentials. Youths and adults take on many roles and characteristics, and while no one *saves* anyone else, together they produce award-winning programs.

These authors construct youth within social, political, and relational contexts, not as always-already figured by biology, age, and difference. We understand these "breaks" with conventional youth figurations as operating in distinctive temporal imaginaries. While conventional youth studies focuses relentlessly on the future and on "becoming," these authors emphasize the present with its inequalities, limitations, and lines of action in relation to past and future. The temporal imaginary is a dynamic one that not only keeps past, present, and future in relation but also takes into account space. In other words, this is a spatiotemporal imaginary that does not figure only time as the active figure, but space as well. This is a significant reconceptualization, for time has been the privileged term in conceptualizing adolescence. But time and space are mutually constitutive and are constitutive of our imaginings of the social world and the human. In relation to the child and the adult, youth "defines a moment of disturbance: a space *in between*" (Oswell, 1998, p. 38).

A more supple youth studies attends to youth–adult relations of research or pedagogy in specific, material spaces as well as attending to imaginings of space. For example, at Youth Radio, external audiences and criteria shape the radio stories and the collaborations of youth, peer educators, and adults. Each collaborator interprets the "external" criteria, such as originality or social impact, differently and the product and process must be negotiated in relation to those interpretations. Alonso et al. (2009) also locate themselves with youth in specific urban school spaces, refusing the usual discourses and affects of such locations and working, instead, to establish a good urban school. Yet their work gestures to a more metaphorical understanding of spaces as an effect of relations and connections that represent "*constellations of temporary coherence*" (Massey, 1998, p. 125). This is a political view of space, in which it is not static but dynamic. Space is not a container where youth action takes place (Ruddick, 1998, p. 346) but, like time, is integral to producing youth as a social category. At the same time, space itself is produced through action and interaction. To organize youth spatially, whether by mandating their presence in schools or prohibiting it in malls after dark, is a strategy of "spatial organization [that is] deeply bound up with the social production of identities" (Massey, 1998, p. 127). And this production of identities, imaginations, and actions has much to tell us. For example, Dillabough and Kennelly (2010) explore "the role that particular spatial landscapes and their symbolic assemblages play in framing" the moral-inflected identities of youth groups as "'disgusting,' 'superior' and/ or 'shameful'" (p. 72). Their ethnography of youths' relational and emotional geographies in Toronto and Vancouver neighborhoods offers phenomenological portraits of shifting urban landscapes, identities, and symbolic resources, as well as the production of discourses of "lost youth." Youth are making themselves and also being made within sedimented and changing locations, economies, and discourses.

These explicit uses of temporality and spatialization, or different spatiotemporal imaginaries, in studies of youth offer counternarratives to the biological, developing, and othered youth. They suggest a politics of making explicit both youth studies' and youths' spatiotemporal imaginings and actions in the production of knowledges, identities, and practices. Whether these theoretical orientations can interrupt conventional progressive practices and the relations of adults and youths in research is an open question.

References

About Gamechangers. (2008). Retrieved from http://gamechangers.architectureforhumanity. org/about

Alonso, G., Anderson, N. S., Su, C., & Theoharis, J. (2009). *Our schools suck: Students talk back to a segregated nation on the failures of urban education.* New York: New York University Press.

Aubrey, A. (2010, January 18). Emotional training helps kids fight depression. Retrieved from http://www.npr.org/templates/story/story.php?storyId=122526518&ps=cprs

Baez, B., & Talburt, S. (2008). Governing for responsibility and with love: Parents and children between home and school. *Educational Theory, 58,* 25–43.

Bennett, A., & Kahn-Harris, K. (2004). Introduction. In A. Bennett, & K. Kahn-Harris (Eds.), *After subculture: Critical studies in contemporary youth culture* (pp. 1–18). New York: Palgrave Macmillan.

Bernard, M. E. (n.d.). Emotional resilience: Implications for You Can Do It! Education theory and practice. Retrieved from http://www.youcandoiteducation.com/reflections onemotional_files/ReflectionsOnEmotional.pdf

Boler, M. (1999). *Feeling power: Emotions and education.* New York: Routledge.

Chávez, V., & Soep, E. (2005). Youth Radio and the pedagogy of collegiality. *Harvard Educational Review, 75*(4), 409–488.

Cohen, S. (2002 [1972, 1987]). *Folk devils and moral panics: The creation of the Mods and Rockers.* New York: Routledge.

Coleman, J. S. (1961). *The adolescent society: The social life of the teenager and its impact on education.* Westport, CT: Greenwood Press.

Coleman, J. S. (1974). *Youth: Transition to adulthood. Report of the panel on youth of the President's Science Advisory Committee.* Chicago: University of Chicago Press.

Coloroso, B. (2003). *The bully, the bullied, and the bystander: From preschool to high school—How parents and teachers can help break the cycle of violence.* New York: HarperCollins.

Cuban, L. (1984/1993). *How teachers taught: Constancy and change in American classrooms, 1880–1990* (2nd ed.). New York: Teachers College Press.

Dillabough, J., & Kennelly, J. (2010). *Lost youth in the global city.* New York: Routledge.

Duggan, L. (2003). *The twilight of equality? Neoliberalism, cultural politics, and the attack on democracy.* Boston: Beacon Press.

Erikson, E. H. (1950/1985). *Childhood and society.* New York: W. W. Norton.

Erikson, E. H. (1968). *Identity: Youth and crisis.* New York: W. W. Norton.

Gamechangers. (n.d.). Slumdog Basketball aiding in the psycho-rehabilitation of slum dwelling youth in Mumbai thru sports! Retrieved from http://gamechangers.architecturefor humanity.org/proposals/slumdog_basketball_aiding_in_the_psycho_rehabilitation_of_slum_dwelling_youth_in_mumbai_th

Garbarino, J. (1999). *Lost boys: Why our sons turn violent and how we can save them.* New York: Knopf.

Garbarino, J. (2007). *See Jane hit: Why girls are growing more violent and what we can do about it.* New York: Penguin Group.

Gilbert, J. (1986). *A cycle of outrage: America's reaction to the juvenile delinquent in the 1950s.* New York: Oxford University Press.

Giroux, H. (2000). *Stealing innocence: Youth, corporate power, and the politics of culture.* New York: St. Martin's Press.

Goleman, D. (1995). *Emotional intelligence: Why it can matter more than IQ.* New York: Bantam.

Graubard, A. (1972). *Free the children: Radical reform and the free school movement.* New York: Pantheon Books.

Grossberg, L. (2005). *Caught in the crossfire: Kids, politics, and America's future.* Boulder, CO: Paradigm.

Halberstam, J. (2005). *In a queer time and place: Transgender bodies, subcultural lives*. New York: New York University Press.

Harris, A. (2004). *Future girl: Young women in the twenty-first century*. New York: Routledge.

Hunter, I. (1994). *Rethinking the school: Subjectivity, bureaucracy, criticism*. New York: St. Martin's Press.

Kohlberg, L., & Mayer, R. (1972). Development as the aim of education. *Harvard Educational Review, 42*(4), 449–496.

Laqueur, T. W. (1976). *Religion and respectability: Sunday schools and working class culture, 1780–1850*. New Haven, CT: Yale University Press.

Leach, C. (n.d.). Resilient and resourceful young people: A national youth strategy? Retrieved from http://wa.psnews.com.au/BooksFeaturesWApsn0175.html

Lesko, N. (2001). *Act your age! A cultural construction of adolescence*. New York: RoutledgeFalmer.

Lesko, N., & Mitschele, K. (2011). Rethinking adolescence. In G. Andrews (Ed.), *What research says to the middle grades practitioner*. Athens, GA: National Middle School Association.

Luther, S. S., Cicchetti, D., & Becker, B. (2000). The construct of resilience: A critical evaluation and guidelines for future work. *Child Development, 71*, 543–562.

Massey, D. (1998). The spatial construction of youth cultures. In T. Skelton, & G. Valentine (Eds.), *Cool places: Geographies of youth cultures* (pp. 121–129). London: Routledge.

Michaels, L. (Producer), & Waters, M. (Director). (2004). *Mean girls* [Motion picture]. United States: Paramount Pictures.

Neill, A. S. (1960). *Summerhill: A radical approach to child rearing*. New York: Hart Publishing Co.

Nike Gamechangers. (2009, June 15). Nike Gamechangers. Retrieved from http://www.youtube.com/watch?v=VoVVfCfqcUo

Oswell, D. (1998). A question of belonging: Television, youth, and the domestic. In T. Skelton, & G. Valentine (Eds.), *Cool places: Geographies of youth cultures* (pp. 35–49). London: Routledge.

Pipher, M. B. (1994). *Reviving Ophelia: Saving the selves of adolescent girls*. New York: Putnam.

Pollack, W. S. (1998). *Real boys: Rescuing our sons from the myths of boyhood*. New York: Henry Holt & Co.

Quinn, T., & Meiners, E. R. (2009). *Flaunt it! Queers organizing for public education and justice*. New York: Peter Lang.

Resilience Research in Children. (n.d.). Retrieved from http://www.ppc.sas.upenn.edu/prpsum.htm

Ruddick, S. (1998). Modernism and resistance: How "homeless" youth subcultures make a difference. In T. Skelton, & G. Valentine (Eds.), *Cool places: Geographies of youth cultures* (pp. 343–360). London: Routledge.

Su, C. (2009). Introduction. In G. Alonso, N. S. Anderson, C. Su, & J. Theoharis, *Our schools suck: Students talk back to a segregated nation on the failures of urban education* (pp. 1–30). New York: New York University Press.

Tait, G. (2000). *Youth, sex, and government*. New York: Peter Lang.

Tanner, J. L., & Arnett, J. J. (2009). The emergence of "emerging adulthood": The new life stage between adolescence and young adulthood. In A. Furlong (Ed.), *Handbook of youth and young adulthood: New perspectives and agendas* (pp. 39–45). London: Routledge.

Theoharis, J. (2009). Conclusion. In G. Alonso, N. S. Anderson, C. Su, & J. Theoharis, *Our schools suck: Students talk back to a segregated nation on the failures of urban education* (pp. 177–214). New York: New York University Press.

Valentine, G., Skelton, T., & Chambers, D. (1998). An introduction to youth and youth culture. In T. Skelton, & G. Valentine (Eds.), *Cool places: Geographies of youth cultures* (pp. 1–32). London: Routledge.

Waters, J. (Producer and Director). (1988). *Hairspray* [Motion picture]. United States: New Line Home Video.

Wiseman, R. (2002). *Queen bees and wannabes: Helping your daughter survive cliques, gossip, boyfriends, and other realities of adolescence*. New York: Crown Publishing Group.

Wyn, J., & White, R. (1997). *Rethinking youth*. London: Sage.

1

BIOLOGY/NATURE

Elizabeth Seaton

The words *nature* and *biology* are two primary means by which the category of youth is "put into discourse" (Foucault, 1990, p. 11). In fact, for the Western world, the very term "youth" immediately connotes a biological reality. Young people (both children and adolescents) are foremost defined by their age and physiological development (or their "stage in the life-course"). Processes of biological and behavioral change are seen as germane to youth: so much so that their particular qualities are said to comprise their essential nature. Such processes of change must not only be monitored and understood, but managed in order to cultivate the best adult human possible. In this respect, our very idea of youth rests upon a dialectic: youth is both a "natural" and universal state of difference and a process of physiological change and development; youth is not only a time of freedom and experiment, but it is also a period of strict regimen and discipline in the biologically and socially guided activity of becoming an adult.

Torn between the ontological and the teleological, this idea of youth is reflected in our understanding of nature as both a quality and a process. Raymond Williams has famously written that "*Nature* is perhaps the most complex word in the [English] language" (1983, p. 219). In its general usages, the word may mean either "i) the essential quality and character of something; ii) the inherent force which directs either the world or human beings or both; and iii) the material world itself, taken as including or not human beings" (p. 219). In this variability, *nature* describes both a quality (the nature of things, or life itself) and a process (that abstract inherent force which directs them). Nature as a quality of something is derived from its original uses in both the Latin and old French "natura" or "nasci," meaning "to be born" or that which is native or innate. The second connotation of nature as an essential force or process which directs all life came later (14th century). This latter notion was, as Williams describes it, impelled by "the assumption of a single prime cause," a singular, universal nature which is "structurally and historically cognate with the emergence of God from a god or 'the gods'" (p. 220). This shift from a multiplicity of qualities (the nature of things; "the gods") to an abstract singularity (a universal and inherent force which directs all things; God) was to further change in the 18th and 19th centuries with the development of Enlightenment sciences. Here, as Williams puts it, nature "was altered from an absolute monarch to a constitutional lawyer, with a new type of emphasis on natural laws" (p. 222).

While Williams' use of "natural law" is more commonly associated with juridical common law, it is clear that he is referring to the development of modern biology as a means to understand the "laws of nature." Supported by techniques of classification (e.g., Linnaeus' 1735 taxonomy of the natural world), and advancements in visual technology (e.g., Anton van Leeuwenhoek's [1632–1723] development of the microscope, which later allowed for the early 19th century discovery by the German biologists Schleiden and Schwann of the cell as the basic organism of life), biology has lent validity to the universal "laws of nature." Inspired by the Greek words for life (bios) and its study (logia), biology's methods of empirical observation are designed to discover and illustrate consistencies of pattern, growth, and behavior of all living things. This project was to advance considerably with the development of evolutionary thought initially forwarded by Comte de Buffon and later, and more famously, in the theories of Jean-Baptiste Lamarck (1744–1802) and Charles Darwin (1859). The concept of evolutionary change is central to biology, in its assertion that all life stems from a common origin, and that life evolves through historical response (or adaptation) to its environment. These underlying laws of nature—its regularities of qualities and processes—may then become accepted as conditional and yet universal truths.

By the 20th century, most biological scientists had abandoned the theist view that attributed the universal order of nature to God's design. Nature was found to have its own design: in the development of species through natural selection, in the regularities of the life process, and the conditional structures of evolution. And yet, "the laws of nature" are often utilized as rhetorical devices calculated to insist upon normalized or orthodox truths (e.g., in the claim that same-sex marriage is counter to the "laws of nature"). In these instances, biology as a science loses its grasp of empirical authority and is made a servant to ideology. Thus, the pseudo-science of social-Darwinism, with its perversion of theories of genetic branching and natural selection, has been used as a popular apologist for the racist excesses of imperialism and the continuation of White privilege. Such occurrences remind us that the history of biological science is as much sociopolitical context as it is transcendent discovery.

The Science of "Natural" Development

Uses of evolutionary theory in the aid of modern scholarship on child and youth development often suggest such sociopolitical influence. Industrial modernity brought with it an emphasis on the idea of "development" and "progress" as universal and positive goals. This mandate for a new age was influenced not only by Charles Darwin's *Origin of the Species* in 1859, but the ideas found in Herbert Spencer's *Social Statistics* (1850/1888), which held that development and progress for modern civilization was not only a certainty, but also a necessity. In this respect, as Emily Cahan (2008) writes, "The child's development served to demonstrate the connection between development in evolution and the development of civilization. The child became a lynchpin—a link between natural and human history" (para. 8).

Such conceptual linkages were developed in the work of G. Stanley Hall—often called "the father of adolescence"—whose two-volume work, *Adolescence: Its Psychology and Its Relations to Physiology, Anthropology, Sociology, Sex, Crime, Religion and Education* (1904), sought to establish the nature of progress in human civilization via the adolescent as object of empirical study. Hall based his ideas of adolescent development on a Lamarckian theory of evolution, which, in line with dominant beliefs of the early 20th century, emphasized Lamarck's (1809/1984) proposal that the "acquired characteristics" of a species are inherited through accumulated experience (p. 113). This allowed Hall to propose his well-known view that adolescence is inherently a time of "storm and stress" due to the accumulated generational memory of a moment in human evolution marked by turmoil and disruption. For Hall, then, the practice of challenging parents, the flights of temper and the depressions of mood, and the propensity for risk and sensation seeking are all aspects of a "recapitulated" memory, now manifest in the storm and stress of modern adolescent development.

Hall's work has lent a number of key axioms that continue to structure and define the discourse of adolescence today (Sercombe, 2010, p. 41). The legacy of his development thesis can be found in our common understanding that a young person's life is temporally and spatially organized into "stages and scripts" (Kovarick, 1994, p. 103), with each progressive stage (toddler, preschooler, school-aged, teenage, etc.) assigning qualitatively different scripts of conduct. This process of development is dutifully recorded in the archives of growth charts, school records, psychological reports, vaccination histories, and family photo albums, each providing a means by which to discipline the necessary progress of young people.

The Discipline of Natural Bodies

"Storm and stress" also remains discursively operative, if only in its more popular vestiges. Yet, today we tend to understand it in biological, rather than psychological, terms (even if the psychological is recapitulated as physiological and evolutionary memory). There are ancient precepts to the biologized understanding of young people, as evidenced in Aristotle's statement that youth are "heated by Nature as drunken men by wine" (as cited in Arnett, 1999, p. 317). Such "heats of Nature" are now understood as the epidemiological changes taking place within young bodies during puberty.

Puberty is known as the process of physical change in which a child's body begins to mature into one capable of reproduction. While puberty involves a number of psychosocial, cultural, and physical changes, it is primarily based upon the hormonal stimulation of growth in a young person's body which then initiates the appearance of secondary sexual characteristics. Yet, because puberty is premised upon the emergence of a sexually reproductive body, the understanding of puberty as a physiological process becomes tempered by social connotations of an emerging adult sexuality. An example of this discursive currency of puberty can be found in the aftermath of the publication of a 1997 nationwide study on early puberty or "precocious sexual development" in girls in the United States (Hermann-Giddens et al., 1997).[1] While the study found that, on the mean, girls were experiencing the onset of puberty a year earlier than the previous standard (set in 1969),[2] media reaction to this research was quick to capitalize on the difference a year makes, with particular focus upon the scientific term "precocious sexual development" used to describe early puberty. Most fortuitously for the manufacturers and marketers of girls clothing and goods, there was now a biological veracity lent to what remains an invention of marketing and cultural representation: the sexually precocious "tween" girl.

The human body has long served as evidentiary or "essentialist" ground for any number of social ideologies, however arbitrary the constructed equation of body and "truth" may be. As "natural" material of flesh, bone, and blood, the body is seen as independent of social influence. But the universal truths of the body are also beholden to the productions of scientific and social epistemologies. As Thomas Laqueur (1990) has shown, the sexually dimorphous body was the creation of late 17th century Enlightenment sciences and practices of anatomy. Today, this body is so naturalized that, when variable bodies appear, they may be dealt with swiftly and with surgical correction. The "abnormal" appearance of an infant with ambiguous genitalia must be restored to its "normal" state—despite the possibility that such restorative work might just deny the chromosomal identity of the infant. It is an action of signification in which the "normative" (as either unambiguously male or female) is constructed (Kessler, 1990). As Laqueur writes, "Sex, in both the one-sex and the two-sex worlds, is *situational*; it is explicable only within the context of battles over gender and power" (1990, p. 11). In this regards, compulsory heterosexuality—premised as it is on the sexually dimorphous reproductive body— also acts to strongly situate the transitional process of adolescence.

More recently, another part of the body has been claimed to offer biological evidence of generational (and gendered) differences in behavior.[3] Aided by the technology of magnetic resonance imaging, cognitive neurological studies have found differences in the brain structure and function of young people and adults. One conclusion that has been publicly drawn from these studies is that young people are more prone to risk behavior, due to the possibility of a greater reliance upon amygdala of the brain. The amygdala is said to both occupy the "primitive or crocodile-like brain area" (Strauch, 2004, p. 67, as cited in Males, 2009, p. 5) and, paradoxically, to "inhibit . . . midbrain aggressive patterns of behavior" (Petri, 1990, p. 122, as cited in Males, 2009, p. 5). Thus, the psychologist Laurence Steinberg has argued that "heightened risk taking during adolescence is likely to be normative, biologically-driven and to some extent, inevitable" (as cited in Males, 2009, p. 4). As Mike Males points out, this response to the research risks promoting a biodeterminist construct of youth as "innately limited by [their] unalterable biology" (p. 5) and has dire consequences for the legal and social repression of young people.

The Dialectic of Nature and Culture

As Raymond Williams writes in his genealogy of the word *nature*, the two dominant connotations of quality and process which define it are not at all opposed to one another. Instead, they act in dialectic fashion in their ability to shape our understandings of the nonhuman and human worlds. In this respect too, *nature* is closely aligned to its opposite *culture*, which Williams also describes as "one of the two or three most complicated words in the English language" (1983, p. 87). Like one aspect of *nature*, *culture* is a "noun of process"; the cultivation or development of growth.

Much of our understanding of young people is shaped by this dialectic of nature and culture as qualities and processes. The two are especially confused when we attempt to ascribe a process of cultural behavior to an observed biological quality of youth. And yet, recent neurological studies of the brains of teenagers also indicate a particular reciprocity of culture and nature. As Howard Sercombe argues,

> One of the first breakthroughs in the research [of brain science] . . . was that the brain as a structure is not only shaped by genetics, by biology, but also by environment, by experience. The brain does not only determine experience. Experience also determines the brain.
>
> (2010, p. 34)

In this respect, the phenomenon of youth must be understood as involving the mutual plasticities of the body and its environment. Each structures the other; each are covariables which, however inadvertently, gesture to the ways that "nature" and "culture" have long been wedded to one another—not just in terms of the semiotic productions of a binarism—but as a necessary relation of reciprocity which guides the processes of all life.

Notes

1 Conducted via the American Academy of Pediatrics Research on Office Settings Network, the goal of this research was to describe the prevalence of secondary sex characteristics in American girls aged 3–12 years as seen in pediatric office practice. Data were collected from July 1992 to September 1993 from 17,077 girls.
2 Until Hermann-Giddens et al. (1997) published their national data, most clinicians relied upon Marshall and Tanner's classic study on pubertal changes in girls published in 1969.
3 This most recent finding is a recurrence of biodeterminist practices of gendering or racializing the human brain. See for instance Brizendine (2006).

References

Arnett, J. (1999). Adolescent storm and stress, reconsidered. *American Psychologist, 54*, 317–326.
Brizendine, L. (2006). *The female brain*. New York: Broadway Books.
Cahan, E. (2008). History of the concept of child development. Encyclopedia of children and childhood in history and society. Retrieved from http://www.faqs.org/childhood/Bo-Ch/Child-Development-History-of-the-Concept-of.html
Darwin, C. (1859). *On the origin of the species by means of natural selection, or the preservation of favoured races in the struggle for life*. London: John Murray.

Foucault, M. (1990). *The history of sexuality, Volume 1: An introduction.* New York: Vintage Books.

Hall, G. S. (1904). *Adolescence: Its psychology and its relations to physiology, anthropology, sociology, sex, crime, religion and education* (vols. I & II). New York: Appleton.

Hermann-Giddens, M., Slora, E., Wasserman, R., Bourdony, C. J., Bhapkar, M. V., Koch, G., & Hasemeier, C. M. (1997). Secondary sexual characteristics and menses in young girls seen in office practice: A study from the pediatric research in office settings network. *Pediatrics, 99,* 505–512.

Kessler, S. (1990). The medical construction of gender: Case management of inter-sexed infants. *Signs, 6,* 3–26.

Kovarick, J. (1994). The space and time of children at the interface of psychology and sociology. In J. Qvortrup, M. Bandy, G. Sgritta, & H. Wintersberger (Eds.), *Childhood matters: Social theory, practice and politics* (pp. 101–122). Aldershot: Avebury Press.

Lamarck, J. (1809/1984). *Zoological philosophy: An exposition with regards to the natural history of animals.* Chicago: University of Chicago Press.

Laqueur, T. (1990). *Making sex: Body and gender from the Greeks to Freud.* Cambridge, MA: Harvard University Press.

Males, M. (2009). Does the adolescent brain make risk taking inevitable? A skeptical appraisal. *Journal of Adolescent Research, 24,* 3–20.

Marshall, W. A., & Tanner, J. M. (1969). Variations in the patterns of pubertal changes in girls. *Archives of Diseased Child, 44,* 291–303.

Sercombe, H. (2010). The gift and the trap: Working the "teen brain" into our concept of youth. *Journal of Adolescent Research, 25,* 31–47.

Spencer, H. (1850/1888). *Social statistics.* New York: Appleton.

Williams, R. (1983). *Keywords: A vocabulary of culture and society* (Rev. ed.). New York: Oxford University Press.

2

(DIS)ABILITY

Beth A. Ferri

To talk of ability is not to speak of a biological "fact," but rather to call forth a socially produced system of norms that construct and regulate the boundaries between ability and disability. Indeed, it is difficult to conjure ability without simultaneously bringing disability to the fore. The very category of "youth" relies upon normative notions that produce categories of ability, distinguishing at-risk and deviant students from those of promise. In other words, normalcy creates the "problem" of disability (Davis, 2006, p. 3). Moreover, such ideas are reified by the labels used to sort students into categories of regular, special, and gifted. Once divided into types, specialized curriculum, teacher certification, special classes, and so on further cement these differences. But, when and where should we begin to tell the story of "(dis)ability" and what are some of the ways of talking and thinking that engender our present ideas about (dis)ability?

The Emergence of Norm(al)

First, there is the issue of discourse. When speaking of ability we invoke a host of ideas and images that rely on systems of norms to demarcate the line between ability and disability. Although ubiquitous, the notion of normal(cy) emerged relatively recently with "political arithmetic" or statistics (p. 26). According to Davis (1995), the words "'normal,' 'normalcy,' 'norm,' 'average,' 'abnormal,'—all entered the European languages" in the mid-1800s (p. 3). Once we had ways of talking and thinking about norms, traits could then be divided into standard and nonstandard, normal and abnormal. The emergence of these terms also coincided with the first institutions and asylums for children and youth deemed "feebleminded," a precursor to labels such as mental retardation and intellectual disability. Individuals who were considered to be emotionally disturbed or physically disabled (crippled) faced similar treatment. Moreover, these ways of talking about student difference continue to inform present-day categories of general (or "regular") and special education. Likewise, treatment of those who fall outside norms of behavior or ability evolve from the very same discourses of care and control passed down from institutions to special schools and group homes to segregated special education classrooms. Normalcy, however ubiquitous, is not a static category, but rather a social obligation that must be enforced (Davis, 1995, 2006) and protected.

Compulsory Able-Bodiness[1]

Enforcing normalcy, as viewed through the emerging understanding of genetics, quickly translated into eugenic[2] desires, obsessions even, to root out populations or traits that did not or could not conform to an ever-widening system of norms. Not surprisingly, those who were most likely to be targeted as unfit or subnormal were those who could not claim White middle-class status. As an elastic category, the "unfit" included a host of marginalized individuals, including, among others, immigrants, racial and ethnic minorities, the poor, disabled people, epileptics, alcoholics, as well as unwed mothers and prostitutes, and their children. Policies and practices to contain those considered unfit included immigration and marriage restrictions, segregation, sterilization, and, taken to its most extreme iteration in the Nazi T4 program,[3] eradication (Selden, 1999, 2000). Steeped in deficit thinking and conflating disability with depravity, eugenic practices were part of a far-reaching Progressive Era experiment in social engineering, designed to rid the larger society of those considered mentally and morally defective. Advocates of eugenics,[4] who were influenced by social Darwinism, sought to rid the nation of diseased and defective populations in what amounted to a form of genetic cleansing. From its inception, the line between those considered normal and abnormal was a contested space, caught up in webs of race and class bias with far-reaching implications for those who were deemed unfit. Conversely, those who could claim normalcy, often by virtue of social class or racial privilege, shared a social status that conferred a host of advantages. In this way normalcy or ability, like whiteness, manifests as a form of property (Harris, 1993). Harris (1993) argues that whiteness is experienced as an identity, but also functions as property, conferring rights and privileges to those who can claim its status. Ability functions in a similar way—conferring both rights and privileges. Likewise, ability can be deployed in ways that subjugate others via ableism.

With the advent of intelligence testing,[5] norms for ability became ever more abstract and malleable and even more deeply legitimized by the emerging science of mental measurement. No longer was normalcy tied to embodied or physical difference, but even subtle and imperceptible differences could be located in and on the body. New labels emerged to talk about differences in ability that were not obvious and required clinical expertise to diagnose. Cognitive ability or intelligence, for example, became understood as something that could be measured, quantified, and ranked. Not wanting the United States to be "defined by the mediocre middle" (Davis, 2006, p. 8), Progressive Era reformers pushed for intelligence testing to be used as a way to root out feeblemindedness (a catch-all term for perceived intellectual difference) in children and adults. Scores on intelligence tests would come to be seen as a person's intelligence quotient (IQ), a score that could be compared and ranked and that, taken collectively, would represent a measure of the nation's fitness. Because ability (or "fitness") was viewed as a fixed and inherited trait, progress required perfecting the gene pool by eliminating deviance from the population (Davis). Of course, grounded in biological determinism, eugenics simply provided scientific legitimacy to the already "existing social, institutional, and political" inequalities operating in American society at the time (Selden, 1999, p. 85).

Institutions and practices to ferret out, contain, and restrain those who were deemed unfit, deficient, or disabled proliferated. Institutions and asylums, conceived, at least at first, as humanitarian, were charged with warehousing the feebleminded. As the category of the feebleminded grew, however, institutions could no longer contain the expanding numbers of society's others. Thus, immigration restrictions were passed to tide the flow of "undesirables" coming into the country. The Immigration Act of 1924 reflected eugenic ideas about race and mental fitness. The act sought to limit immigration from Southern and Eastern Europe and to bar immigration of those from the Asia-Pacific region. Believing in a racial hierarchy, these policies were aimed at racial and ethnic groups who were seen as diluting the "higher classes" of Nordic and western European populations (Selden, 1999). Likewise, marriage restrictions and involuntary sterilization laws[6] were passed to help curb the possibility of feebleminded women passing on defective genes to their offspring. Taken together these measures were designed to rid the society and the streets of those who were perceived as defective or abnormal.

Schooling Difference

Schools, too, had a pivotal role to play in rooting out difference, particularly among youth. Enacting a form of "ability profiling" (Collins, 2003), schools were entrusted with the task of developing the nation's talent pool by sorting students according to normative notions of ability and teaching them accordingly. Armed with an expanding array of psychometric and achievement tests, a new set of "helping" and clinical professions emerged to help identify and sort students according to perceived ability. Informed by the Social Efficiency Movement, schools were entrusted with the task of diagnosing and sorting students into tracks (Baker, 2002; Valencia, 1997). Each track was then assigned a curriculum—from functional, life-skills curriculum for students in special classes to vocational education for students on lower tracks to advanced and academic curriculum for those on higher tracks (Baker, 2002; Valencia, 1997). Running parallel to the creation of segregated special classes for students who were seen as intellectually deficient or emotionally disturbed, which were disproportionately serving the children of working class and immigrant populations, were classes for the gifted and talented, serving students of the wealthy. Students of color were, and continue to be, overrepresented in special education and in remedial tracks and special education, whereas White students are represented disproportionally in advanced placement, honors, and gifted classes.[7] Thus, school practices continue to reinforce systemic inequalities operating in the society.

Unfortunately, conceptions about student ability have become completely naturalized. So ubiquitous are our ideas about ability (and disability) that they seem to be without a historical trajectory. We define and sort youth according to perceived notions of ability, as if these categories were self-evident and located in the bodies and brains of students. Normalcy continues to narrow as categories of disability proliferate, as do the number of students who are placed in special education. Because we perceive differences in ability as meaningful, we train and certify some teachers to work with students who are labeled as disabled and others to teach those who are deemed normal or regular. We organize the geography of our schools around perceived student differences—often placing students with disabilities off the beaten track in segregated spaces within (or even outside) the school building. At the same time, we mistakenly perceive these practices as benevolent and rational ways to deal with student difference. Yet, special education is less a service to students with disabilities than a system of supports that serve general education by removing unwanted students, similar to ways that earlier institutions served to rid society (and the streets) of unwanted individuals. Thus, rather than taking notions of ability or the systems set up to deal with those who are perceived as disabled for granted, we must historicize and contextualize their origins. In other words, our ways of thinking about student ability and our educational practices with regard to perceived differences must account for the ways that ability is socially, culturally, spatially, and temporally located.

Notes

1 See Kafer (2003) and McRuer (2006).
2 See http://www.eugenicsarchive.org/eugenics/
3 See Mitchell and Snyder (2003) and Selden (1999, 2000). The Nazi "euthanasia" program targeted institutionalized and disabled adults and children. Viewed as a financial drain on Germany, 240,000 disabled people were killed by the Nazis between 1939 and the end of the war. The progression from "eugenics, to euthanasia, to full-scale genocide" (Ferri & Connor, 2006, p. 27) illustrates the dangers of deficit thinking taken to the extreme.
4 Along with early architects, Sir Francis Dalton, Charles Davenport, and Francis Galton, many influential people supported eugenics: Alexander Graham Bell; Oliver Wendell Holmes; John D. Rockefeller; Theodore Roosevelt; Margaret Sanger; as well as Educationalists, Edward Thorndike and Leta Hollingsworth (Selden, 1999).
5 The first IQ tests were developed in the early 1900s as a way to screen students who were having academic difficulty. Henry Goddard and Lewis Terman believed that the IQ test could predict "thinking capacity" (Danforth, 2009, p. 3).
6 *Buck v. Bell*, upheld by the Supreme Court in 1927, affirmed Virginia's right to sterilize Carrie Buck, considered feebleminded, against her will. Sixty thousand sterilizations were subsequently performed in the United States and the Buck decision was cited at the Nuremberg trials to defend Nazi-era sterilizations and medical "experiments" (Lombardo, 2008).
7 Early advocates of gifted education drew on discourses of eugenics, biological determinism, and "racial meritocracy." These ideas continue to hold sway, as evidenced by texts such as *The Bell Curve* (Hernstein & Murray, 1994).

References

Baker, B. (2002). The hunt for disability: The new eugenics and the normalization of school children. *Teachers College Record, 104,* 663–703.

Collins, K. (2003). *Ability profiling and school failure: One child's struggle to be seen as competent.* New York: Routledge.

Danforth, S. (2009). *The incomplete child: An intellectual history of learning disabilities.* New York: Peter Lang.

Davis, L. J. (1995). *Enforcing normalcy: Disability, deafness, and the body.* New York: Verso.

Davis, L. J. (2006). Constructing normalcy: The bell curve, the novel, and the invention of the disabled body. In L. J. Davis (Ed.), *The disability studies reader* (2nd ed., pp. 3–16). New York: Routledge.

Ferri, B. A., & Connor, D. J. (2006). *Reading resistance: Discourses of exclusion in desegregation and inclusion debates.* New York: Peter Lang.

Harris, C. L. (1993). Critical characteristics of whiteness as property. *Harvard Law Review.* Retrieved August 10, 2010, from http://academic.udayton.edu/race/01race/white02.htm

Hernstein, R. J., & Murray, C. (1994). *The bell curve: Intelligence and class structure in American life.* New York: The Free Press.

Kafer, A. (2003). Compulsory bodies: Reflection on heterosexuality and able-bodiness. *Journal of Women's History, 15,* 77–89.

Lombardo, P. (2008). *Three generations, no imbeciles: Eugenics, the Supreme Court, and Buck v. Bell.* Baltimore: The Johns Hopkins University Press.

McRuer, R. (2006). *Crip theory: Cultural signs of queerness and disability.* New York: New York University Press.

Mitchell, D. T., & Snyder, S. L. (2003). The eugenic Atlantic: Race, disability, and the making of an international eugenic science, 1800–1945. *Disability & Society, 18*, 843–864.

Selden, S. (1999). *Inheriting shame: The story of eugenics and racism in America*. New York: Teachers College Press.

Selden, S. (2000). Eugenics and the social construction of merit, race, and disability. *Journal of Curriculum Studies, 32*, 235–252.

Valencia, R. R. (1997). *The evolution of deficit thinking*. London: Falmer.

3

JUVENILE JUSTICE

Erica R. Meiners

The collision of two shifting artifacts and corresponding institutions, *juvenile justice* is simultaneously a tactic, a symptom of failures, and a longing. Pointing to the underlying functions and values of the U.S. justice system, and naming how the production of the category—juvenile—expands a dynamic of protectionism, this essay seeks to trouble taxonomies and to imagine and build other futures.

Failures of Justice

Thinking through the juvenile justice system requires denaturalizing justice. Not a neutral or a priori practice, justice is a constructed system, a social contract that frames and naturalizes how harm is recognized, prioritized, and addressed. The contemporary justice system in the United States circulates around four central theories about "why people decide they should lock people up by locking them in": retribution, deterrence, rehabilitation, or incapacitation (Gilmore, 2007, p. 14). With no evidence that incarceration and punishment act as a deterrent, and as programs inside institutions (education, healthcare, and employment) have steadily eroded since the 1980s (Mauer, 1999; Mauer & Chesney-Lind, 2003), the principles shaping contemporary U.S. justice are retribution and, most centrally, incapacitation.

With the largest prison population in the world, over two million and counting, the number of people incapacitated in the United States has grown since the 1970s, not because of any increase in violence or harm, but rather because of policies, most notably *three strikes and you are out* legislation, mandatory minimum sentencing, and the war on drugs (Gilmore, 2007; Mauer, 1999; Pew

Center on the States Public Safety Performance Project, 2008).The most current data suggest that approximately 93,000 youth (Petteruti, Walsh, & Velázquez, 2009, p. 1) are held in juvenile justice institutions every day.This incapacitation is not arbitrary; people are warehoused because they are poor, mentally ill, under- or uneducated, framed as superfluous in the workforce, or their lives are evidence of White supremacy, colonialization, and gender repression.The function of the justice system has long been to scaffold oppressive ideologies, to shape labor for the economy and legitimatize the state's abandonment of communities.

Prison expansion and the carceral state also traffic in affect—fear, anger, alienation—and carceral logic legitimates containers for these public feelings. For example, the archetype of the defenseless vulnerable child (and woman), available to those with White, heterosexual, socioeconomic, and other privileges, necessitates increased surveillance and protection in the form of a security or "daddy" state (Berlant, 2004; Young, 2003). Sexual violence against children requires registries that carefully track all the "stranger danger" bad men, but these state responses do not challenge the violence from patriarchy, poverty, White supremacy, or heteronormativity. Instead "law and order" public safety narratives translate into building bigger borders and more prisons to keep out/ lock up the bad people (who are never those denying access to healthcare or living wages).

A symptom of this commitment to incarceration in the United States, the first juvenile justice court was established in 1899 to wrest "better" treatment for a small class: another court, alternative institutions, confidentiality, and fewer "rights" (including initially no right to due process or representation) (Feld, 1999; Krisberg, 2005). A progressive era, child saving reform, juvenile justice created a class where "protection" necessitated surveillance, containment, management, and the erasure of rights. Science, specifically the new discipline of psychology, legitimated this defense of diminished capacity (Krisberg, 2005), suggesting that select juveniles could be eligible for rehabilitation rather than solely retribution or incapacitation. Legitimately scientific principles include (and in many contexts still *are*) eugenics, compulsory heteronormativity, and misogyny, and these taxonomies and practices still shape core state institutions from immigration to child welfare (Canaday, 2009; Roberts, 1997; Stern, 2005).

In addition to (sometimes) differential treatment for specific kinds of crimes— murder, theft, rape—the juvenile justice system has historically *produced* categories of crime and illegality—truant, delinquent, runaway—or status offenses that are *only* applied to those framed as juveniles. Status violations are created in direct concert with public anxieties, and for young women this involves the control of sexuality. A 1912 Chicago study of the juvenile court's first decade identified that 80% of the 2,440 girls who went before the juvenile court during this time did so because "their virtue is in peril, if it has not already been lost" (as cited in Schaffner, 2006, p. 39). In the last decade narrow "baggy pants" bills, antiloitering laws, and zero tolerance school policies sought to control bodies, movement, and assembly for low-income urban youth of color. According to a 2009 Justice Policy Institute report, 66% of all juveniles are locked up for non-violent offenses, including "drugs (8.6 percent), technical violations [breaking parole or probation regulations] (13.3 percent) and status offenses (6.6 percent)" (Petteruti et al., 2009, p. 3).While the number of youth locked up has stayed relatively static over the last 15 years (Office of Juvenile Justice and Delinquency Prevention, 2008), "the caseload of the juvenile justice system has increased by over half a million cases in the last 20 years" (Petteruti et al., 2009, p. 1). Expanding and contracting in concert with the nation's anxieties about what juveniles represent, the questionable protection afforded select juveniles arrives with a sizeable cost.

Developmental Symptoms

Juvenile, adolescent, teenager, youth, minor, and *young adult* are categories that hover between childhood and adulthood, create buffer populations, and offer more insight into adult longings surrounding life, death, and purity, than information about the body in question. This categorization further stalls (beyond childhood) entry into key capital producing institutions: workforce, political participation, marriage, military. Legally, childhood is a kind of "legal strangeness" (Stockton, 2009, p. 16) and juvenile is the transition between this artifact, the child, and adulthood, yet, like the "strangeness" of the child, there is no consensus about the boundaries of this transition.

Definitions of adolescent and juvenile continue to be publically inflamed and remade, offering insights into cultural and political anxieties. While those who are 15 can be culpable and accountable for crimes as adults, the state protects that same age cohort through the enactment of laws that stipulate that a 15-year-old is not able to consent to heterosexual acts (except in, some states, with her parents' consent, she could get married). Innocence, the defining characteristic of childhood, is "a lot like the air in your tires: there is not a lot you can do with it but lose it" (Kincaid, 1998, p. 53).While there is no agreement around how or when childhood "evolves" into youth, or how or when youth transition to adulthood, the precise legal, political, and social meanings attached to these categories are never produced in isolation of race, sexuality, gender, ability, geography, socioeconomics, and more (Lesko, 2001). Black boys are perceived as dangerous in elementary school by some White female teachers (Ferguson, 2001), the care and needs of the children of immigrant domestic childcare workers are erased (Salazar-Parrenas, 2001), and institutional and interpersonal violence against queer and gender nonconforming youth is naturalized (Kosciw & Diaz, 2006).These bodies are all too often not afforded association with the protections affiliated with innocence.

Debates about where to draw the chronological (and culpable) line repeatedly surface in mainstream media; less visible yet equally important is the evidence used to rationalize any boundary by the media, "child savers," psychological experts, and other parties across the political spectrum. Frequently experience and science are deployed and these can obscure deep ideological tentacles and naturalize constructed artifacts. Psychology, experience, and neurology legitimate "delay," and are organized as evidence that juveniles need protection and should not receive the death penalty, or that 26-year-olds ("emerging adults") should be able to continue to access their parents' health insurance and remain dependent on state or parental management and intervention (American Bar Association, 2004; Cohen, 2010).Yet, the inverse names those with fully developed brains, or those who start work, sex, or parenting at age 13 years, as culpable. Rehabilitation, transformation, and protection are available because of adults' longings, our curious investments in the delayed, temporal status of select juveniles. In particular, for youth, experience becomes a double bind. Remaining innocent (the defining category of childhood) requires the negation of experience (sexual, life, and other), and therefore knowledge becomes tricky for children. For example, it is nearly impossible to name child sexual agency and pleasure, particularly *within* a culture of persistent sexual violence that targets women and children.

Longing for Just Futures

Built with the tools at their disposal that would be later used to expand the prison nation in the United States, juvenile justice was started in Chicago by justice workers, including women such as Jane Addams who were intent on building a new world—fighting for child labor laws, unionization, and healthcare. Juvenile justice was, and still is, a tactic produced from this temporal moment—a fragile possibility and unfinished business. This tactic created longer-term problems and has historically obscured the array of technologies and actors—the mobilization of a bureaucratic and professional army of social welfare policies and workers, juvenile detention centers, truancy officers, child development experts, education professors, and more—that produce, manage, and are *sustained by* this artifact.

Yet, deconstructing juvenile justice offers windows into thinking about some of the most central questions in justice work today, for example the tensions between reform work and structural, systematic changes. If select juveniles are "becoming" and can access rehabilitation, does that require adults to be static and only eligible for incapacitation? Does rehabilitation require the reification of normativities—sexual, developmental, economic? But, most centrally, for organizers and workers, if we cannot separate out juvenile justice from histories and practices of child saving that create expanding punitive surveillance systems, what are the local, narrow moves that are possible for those that work in schools, detention centers, and in courts? What are the possible movements that create better life pathways for all, and not simply the temporally privileged few?

If childhood, a repository for all of the accumulated anxieties of adults, gets all of us into trouble, one response, as Stockton (2009) writes, is to abandon the category altogether. "Given that we cannot know the contours of children, who they are to themselves, should we stop talking of children altogether? Should all talk of the child subside, beyond our critique of the bad effects of looking back nostalgically?" (p. 5).

But, in an expanding prison nation, all bodies matter. As Black and Brown youth are transferred to adult court, seven- and eight-year-olds are moved into juvenile detention, and female, queer, and nongender conforming youth are still targeted for containment and sexual surveillance, it matters, desperately, who is viewed (or not) as innocent or disposable. Rather than this categorical abandonment, impossible as there are no pure places for organizing, research, and movement building, the work requires at least a doubled practice. As tactics are deployed, the parallel labor is to meticulously understand their meanings in particular contexts. Or, as queer theorist Eve Sedgwick (1990) asks in relation to the creation of the homosexual, when a category is engaged it is central to also ask *who benefits?*, *how is this category possible?*, *what is obscured through these practices?*, and *why?* (p. 27). Building just futures pushes us "to ask questions that see beyond the given" (Davis, 2005, p. 23) but simultaneously to use the tools, always partial, in our hands.

References

American Bar Association (Juvenile Justice Center). (2004, January). *Cruel and unusual punishment: The juvenile death penalty: Adolescence, brain development and legal culpability.* Washington, DC: ABA. Retrieved from http://www.abanet.org/crimjust/juvjus/Adolescence.pdf

Berlant, L. (Ed.). (2004). *Compassion: The culture and politics of an emotion.* New York: Routledge.

Canaday, M. (2009). *The straight state: Sexuality and citizenship in twentieth century America.* Princeton, NJ: Princeton University Press.

Cohen, P. (2010, June 11). Long road to adulthood is growing even longer. *New York Times.* Retrieved from http://www.nytimes.com/2010/06/13/us/13generations.html

Davis, A. (2005). *Abolition democracy: Prisons, democracy, and empire.* New York: Seven Stories Press.

Feld, B. (1999). *Bad kids: Race and the transformation of the juvenile court.* New York: Oxford University Press.

Ferguson, A. (2001). *Bad boys: Public schools and the making of black masculinity.* Ann Arbor: University of Michigan Press.

Gilmore, R. W. (2007). *Golden gulag: Prisons, surplus, crisis, and opposition in globalizing California.* Berkeley: University of California Press.

Kincaid, J. (1998). *Erotic innocence: The culture of child molesting.* Durham, NC: Duke University Press.

Kosciw, J. G., & Diaz, E. D. (2006). *The 2005 National School Climate Survey: The experiences of lesbian, gay, bisexual and transgender youth in our nation's schools.* New York: GLSEN.

Krisberg, B. (2005). *Redeeming our children.* Thousand Oaks, CA: Sage.

Lesko, N. (2001). *Act your age! A cultural construction of adolescence.* New York: RoutledgeFalmer.

Mauer, M. (1999). *Race to incarcerate.* New York: New Press.

Mauer, M., & Chesney-Lind, M. (Eds.). (2003). *Invisible punishment: The collateral consequences of mass imprisonment.* New York: New Press.

Office of Juvenile Justice and Delinquency Prevention. (2008). *Census of juveniles in residential placement 1997, 1999, 2001, 2003, and 2006.* Washington, DC: OJJDP. Retrieved from http://ojjdp.ncjrs.gov/ojstatbb/corrections/qa08201.asp?qaDate=2006

Petteruti, A., Walsh, N., & Velázquez, T. (2009). *The costs of confinement: Why good juvenile justice policies make good fiscal sense.* Washington, DC: Justice Policy Institute. Retrieved from http://www.justicepolicy.org/images/upload/09_05_REP_CostsOfConfinement_JJ_PS.pdf

Pew Center on the States Public Safety Performance Project. (2008). One in 100: Behind bars in America 2008. Pew Center on the States. Retrieved from http://www.pewcenter onthestates.org/uploadedFiles/One%20in%20100.pdf

Roberts, D. (1997). *Killing the black body: Race, reproduction, and the meaning of liberty.* New York: Vintage Books.

Salazar-Parrenas, R. (2001). *Servants of globalization: Women, migration and domestic work.* Palo Alto, CA: Stanford University Press.

Schaffner, L. (2006). *Girls in trouble with the law*. New York: Rutgers University Press.

Sedgwick, E. (1990). *Epistemology of the closet*. Berkeley: University of California Press.

Stern, A. M. (2005). *Eugenic nation: Faults and frontiers of better breeding in modern America*. Berkeley: University of California Press.

Stockton, K. B. (2009). *The queer child: Or, growing sideways in the twentieth century*. Durham, NC: Duke University Press.

Young, I. M. (2003). The logic of masculinist protection: Reflections on the current security state. *Signs, 29*, 1–25.

4

LEISURE

Carles Feixa

Youth and leisure are two concepts closely linked in contemporary history and in social research. The "scientific" discovery of youth and recreation occurs in the transition from the 19th to the 20th century: Thorsten Veblen published *The Theory of the Leisure Class* in 1899 and G. Stanley Hall published *Adolescence* in 1904. In the first third of the 20th century were born the major youth organizations aimed at educating children and youth in/from the free time: summer camps, boy scouts, and Wandervögel.

After World War II, the consolidation of consumer society was expressed in the emergence of leisure spaces devoted to young people. The welfare state created the conditions for sustained economic growth and for the social protection of dependent groups. The emergence of the *teenage market* offered, for the first time, a specific space for consumption aimed at youngsters, a group with an increasing power of purchase: fashion, garments, leisure centers, music, magazines, and so on. It was a specific segment of the market of adolescent products for adolescent consumers, without going into much class distinction. At the same time, the emergence of mass communication media allowed the creation of a true international-popular youth culture that was articulating a universal language through the media, radio, records, and cinema.

To understand how this process was reflected in youth studies, we focus on three important moments: (a) the discovery of *youth culture*, articulated around free time, by structural-functionalist studies, coinciding with the take off of the consumer society in the 1950s; (b) the critical analysis of class differences in youth subcultures and their potential resistance, by cultural studies, coinciding with the crisis of the welfare state in the 1970s; and (c) the mechanisms of *social distinction* through leisure articulated by post- and cybercultural studies, coinciding with the transition to an information society in the 1990s.

Leisure as Consumption

> There are reasons to think that youth culture has important positive functions as it enables the transition from the security of childhood in the family to adult marriage and occupational status.
>
> (Parsons, 1963, p. 102)

The appearance of the term "youth culture" in the social sciences is related to the development of consumer society between the two world wars (Featherstone, 1991). In their classical urban ethnography, *Middletown*, Robert Lynd and Helen Lynd (1929/1957) observed the emergence of a college culture in urban society. The authors started by highlighting the increasing relevance of the generation gap within North American culture: The delay in professional insertion, the increasing importance of the school as an institution, and the emergence of leisure were widening the generational breach between young people and adults. High school had become the center of young people's social life: The school was not only offering academic culture, but also a space for sociability made up of sports, clubs, sisterhoods and brotherhoods, dances, and parties; a world with a logic of its own that generates "a city within the city" just for the use of the young generation. In this context, age is more important than class; scholars share more with their mates than they do with their parents (Lynd & Lynd, 1929/1957, p. 211).

But it was Talcott Parsons (1963) and structural-functionalist sociology which gave scientific legitimacy to the emergence of a youth culture. For Parsons, the development of age groups was the expression of a new generational awareness that crystallized in an autonomous interclass culture focused on hedonist consumption. Youth culture—analyzed as a homogeneous whole—was produced by a generation that consumed without producing, and by remaining in educational institutions not only was moving away from work, but also from the class structure. The nominal access to "leisure time" seemed to cancel social differences and to create a "new leisure class" personified by young people. Parsons' analysis focused on middle-class boys (and girls), who spent their youth in high schools: the *college boys*. In the 1940s and 1950s these young people generated a microculture of their own expressed by brotherhoods, parties, dances, graduations, fashion, bars, and music. Unlike *street corner boys*, their identity was constructed at school, not in the street, and their rebelliousness without a cause never surpassed the limits imposed by adults.

James Coleman (1961) gave strength to these statements in a classical study about ten high schools in Illinois. School segregation created a real adolescent society "with their own language, symbols and, even more important, value systems . . . different from those established in the wider society" (p. 9). According to this line of thinking, a culture tended to become uniform, as the youth consumers market made social and ethnic differences irrelevant. In the beginning of the 1960s, Parsons (1963) had reached the conclusion that, if young people had their complaints, these came more from excessive expectations about the future than from any injustice lived:

> The general orientation of youth seems to be an aim to learn, to accept the high responsibilities and to "adapt," not in a sense of passive unconformity, but in a sense of their readiness to work within the system, rather than against it.
>
> (p. 115)

The outbreak of the juvenile protest in the mid-decade—brewed in the classroom—was to contradict those expectations (Mead, 1970).

Leisure as Resistance

> Youth culture was identified only by its most epiphenomenal aspects—music, styles, leisure consumption.
>
> (Hall & Jefferson, 1983, p. 15)

In the postwar years different theories that supported the emergence of a homogeneous and interclass youth culture became popular. These theories suggested that age and generation were substitutive factors of class in the explanation of social conflict and social change. In western countries some tendencies appeared to justify these theories (mass schooling, consumer democracy and fashion, the generational taste for rock and roll). But what the notion was masking—class differences between young people, the social basis of youth cultures, their relationship with the dominant culture—was more important than what it showed. For the authors of the Birmingham School, for example, the structuring factor of postwar British youth cultures is not age but class, both working class (ted, mod, skin) and middle class (hippies, freaks) (Hall & Jefferson, 1983). For these authors who try to introduce cultural Marxism, youth cultures can be interpreted as attempts to confront the unsolved contradictions in parental culture, as symbolic elaborations of class identities, generated by the young people in their biographical transition to adult life, which collectively means them joining the class. The changing relations between young cultures and parental and dominant cultures can explain the coexistence of different youth styles in every historical moment, which broadly speaking build social boundaries, but which can also be present in an oblique way. In this sense, processes of cultural circulation, appropriation, and syncretism across different class and social strata are important, since they prevent the mechanical correspondence between youth cultures and class.

The relationship between youth culture and class is expressed basically in the relationship that young people keep with parental cultures. Young people, like their parents, live inside a specific social and family environment that plays the role of primary socialization. Through direct interaction with relatives and older neighbors, young people learn some basic cultural features (sexual roles, language, manners at the table, esthetic taste). While middle-class parental cultures tend to concentrate these functions within the family nucleus, working-class families give more importance to the extended family and the local community. These intimate contexts also tie young people to the outer world: the perception of the labor world for young workers, the university for middle-class young people, views of the police and the authorities, how they interpret communication media, and so on. Although they may identify with other members of the same age group, young people cannot ignore the fundamental aspects that they share with adults of their own social class (educational opportunities, labor itineraries, town problems, leisure spaces, etc.). Most of the literature about youth cultures has focused on working-class young people. The middle-class young have only been taken into account when they joined in dissident or countercultural movements. Although their identity is not expressed as fervently as their working-class coevals, middle-class young people share certain trends, music, focal interests, leisure spaces, and garments that often become labels of daily social interaction: "Middle class young people may not be a problematic group for the whole of society, but this doesn't mean that they don't experience problems as the young people they are. They may be privileged, but they're not always pleased" (Roberts, 1983, p. 159).

Leisure as Distinction

A *hacker* (or a *raver*) moves through and against any national geo-political distinction; any subcultural definition is seen as inadequate, old-fashioned, even a little ridiculous.
(Canevacci, 2000, p. 20)

In the two last decades different authors have developed and questioned the Birmingham School postulates, replacing the concept *subculture* by other terms more in tune with the information era, like *club cultures* (Thornton, 1996), *post-subcultures* (Muggleton & Weinzierl, 2003), *scenes* (Hesmondhalgh, 2005), *global youth culture* (Nilan & Feixa, 2006), and so on. One focus of these approaches has been moving from the *external* differences between youth and adult lifestyles to the *internal* differences between different subcultures, analyzed as strategies of "distinction" through leisure.

In *Club Cultures* (1996), Sarah Thornton introduces Bourdieu's (1979/1991) theories about distinction, and the concept of "subcultural capital." The author analyzed the British electronic scene (*clubbers* and *ravers*) as leisure places used by young people to distinguish themselves from adults and other youths. She suggests that we look into the internal hierarchies within the youth scenario that the Birmingham authors had put in a secondary stage, behind the external hierarchies with parent and hegemonic cultures. Clubs are semipublic spaces that host, in the free time, groups organized around a common affinity: "club cultures are linked to cultural hierarchies . . . what's 'authentic' versus what's 'vulgar,' what's '*hip*' versus what's '*mainstream*,' what's 'underground' versus what's 'mediatic'" (pp. 3–4). Research is shifting toward how youth cultures are internally stratified and gather goods and experience: "the social arrangement of these structures shows them as a *subcultural capital* through which the young people negotiate and acquire a status within a social world of their own" (p. 163). That is, youth cultures are looking for distinction through pleasure.

In *Culture eXtreme* (2000), Massimo Canevacci suggests a reconceptualization of youth in the global city through various ethnographic explorations of electronic scenes in Rome and Sao Paulo. On the one hand, the concepts that had "built" youth as a self-aware group in the 1960s enter a crisis (end of countercultures, end of subcultures). On the other hand, there is an enlargement in the youth concept (end of youth classes, end of generational passages) and a restriction of young people as social subjects (end of labor, end of the body). This experiment "deconstructs" fragments of images, oral speeches, hypertexts, and polyphonic narrations about ravers, cyborgs, hackers, squatters, and other youth that reject labeling: "Through the mobile flows of youth cultures—plural, fragmented, disjunctive—identities cease being unitary, equal, compact" (p. 18). The author acknowledges that the Anglo-Saxon success in the term "subculture" is based on a biased and partial reading of Gramsci, which has led to the development of a type of Marxism that pays attention to the autonomy of culture. But such a term stops making sense when there is no longer a "general unitary culture in front of which a subculture is defined as a *sub*" (p. 19). That is, the walls between consumption and production (between adulthood and youth) collapsed, and leisure time/spaces (real and virtual) became the *non-places* of (post)modernity.

Final Remarks

The three moments reviewed point out different kinds of relationships between youth and leisure. The first moment explored the "marriage by interest" of those two partners, celebrated in the cathedral of consumption by modern society. The second moment explored a "consensual union" between an extended youth and a deregulated leisure, celebrated in urban peripheries and in night subcultures by postmodern society. In the third moment, the partnership between youth and leisure enters into a kind of "identity crisis," breaking down in the global city and in cyberspaces by information society. Youth is no more a transition phase where free time plays the role of a "rite of passage." It became an "intransitive space" where free time is the basis of "rites of impasse" to a juvenilized adulthood. At the beginning of the 21st century, the research on youth culture and the research on leisure culture are both confronted by the same paradox: how to investigate something that can die of success?

References

Bourdieu, P. (1979/1991). *Distinction*. London: Routledge.

Canevacci, M. (2000). *Culture Extreme. Mutazione giovanili tra i corpi delle metropoli*. Roma: Meltemi.

Coleman, J. S. (1961). *The adolescent society*. New York: The Free Press.

Featherstone, M. (1991). *Consumer culture and postmodernism*. London: Sage.

Hall, G. S. (1904/1915). *Adolescence: Its psychology and its relations to physiology, anthropology, sociology, sex, crime, religion and education* (vols. 1–2). New York: Appleton Century Crofts.

Hall, S., & Jefferson, T. (Eds.). (1983). *Resistance through rituals: Youth subcultures in post-war Britain*. London: Hutchinson.

Hesmondhalgh, D. (2005). Subcultures, scenes or tribes? *Journal of Youth Studies, 8*, 21–40. doi:10.1080/13676260500063652

Lynd, R., & Lynd, H. (1929/1957). *Middletown: A study in modern American culture.* San Diego, CA: Harvest.

Mead, M. (1970). *Culture and commitment: A study of the generation gap.* New York: Natural History Press.

Muggleton, D., & Weinzierl, R. (Eds.). (2003). *The post-subcultures reader.* London: Berg.

Nilan, P., & Feixa, C. (Eds.). (2006). *Global youth: Hybrid identities and plural worlds.* New York: Routledge.

Parsons, T. (1963). Youth in the context of American society. In E. H. Erikson (Ed.), *Youth: Change and challenge* (pp. 93–119). New York: Basic Books.

Roberts, K. (1983). *Youth and leisure.* London: George Allen and Unwin.

Thornton, S. (1996). *Club cultures: Music, media and subcultural capital.* Middletown, CT: Wesleyan University Press.

Veblen, T. (1899). *The theory of the leisure class.* London: Allen and Unwin.

5

MIDDLE SCHOOL

Julie McLeod

Middle school is a spatial and temporal phenomenon. It is located as a bridge between elementary or primary school and the senior years of schooling, offering passage from childhood into adolescence. It refers to a site and a period of transition, often characterized by separate institutional arrangements and pedagogies that help organize the movement of young people through school. National systems have adopted different forms of middle schooling, from special programs within secondary schools, to curriculum innovations, to physically and institutionally separate sites (Knipe, 2007). Although the model of separate middle schools is common across the United States, it is by no means universal. Nevertheless, since the 1970s, the middle-school years have commanded increasing attention among education systems, researchers, parents, and teachers (Carrington, 2006), constructed as a time of need and a place of intervention, promising solutions to perceived challenges in educating adolescents.

A consistent theme across middle-school initiatives is that early adolescence is a distinct phase with special emotional, social, and learning needs. Within this temporal logic, three dominant strands can be identified. One strand focuses on the developmental and socioemotional needs and problems of early adolescence, drawing on a variety of psychological frameworks (Roeser, Eccles, & Sameroff, 1998); the second is more sociological, emphasizing the potential of social and institutional arrangements either to alienate or re-engage young people (Prosser, 2008); and the third examines the implications of the middle-school phase for curriculum and pedagogical practice (Groundwater-Smith, Mitchell, & Mockler, 2007). The significance of social class, gender, and ethnic/racial differences in shaping middle-school experience and provision is acknowledged to varying degrees, but is more pronounced in the sociological and curriculum/pedagogy strands. These two emphasize the transformative potential of schooling, drawing on radical and critical traditions to underline the opportunities middle school offers for enhancing student voice and student-led learning. In contrast, psychologically framed discussions more commonly focus on developmental patterns and norms, often addressing things that go awry—good middle schooling is positioned as a prophylactic against any early adolescent cognitive and emotional difficulties. A unifying assumption, however, is that this is an especially vulnerable and risky time, a biographical phase to which school structures and pedagogies should respond (Stevens et al., 2007), by offering developmentally appropriate learning and support structures (Anfara, Mertens, & Caskey, 2007), or reforming the ways schools connect with young lives (Yates & Holt, 2009).

Yet the term "middle school" functions as more than a description of structural, pedagogical, or physical arrangements of schooling. Operating as both noun and adjective, it can describe a type of student and youthful identity, a type of teacher, a type of curriculum and pedagogy, a type of educational problem, and a time and place of schooling. Such diverse uses of the descriptor suggest the extent to which the idea of the "middle" infiltrates the imagination of contemporary schooling and what it means to be an adolescent. It could be argued that the organizational structure of middle schooling produced the identity of middle-school student, but this can be inverted to consider how the invention of the middle-school student—the early adolescent—helped create the need for middle schools. Middle schooling is thus about governance and types of educational provision and also about inscribing forms of youth subjectivity.

Middle-School Identity

The "middle" is a mobile signifier, generating distinctions between middle years, middle schools, and middle schooling. Early adolescence is classified as the middle years, with students usually aged between 10 and 15 years; middle schools denote a separate organizational unit; and middle schooling implies a constructivist educational philosophy that promotes collaborative learning, relationship building, and community links (Chadbourne, 2001). Together, these definitions delineate a middle space/time and a middle-years identity, underpinned by psychological concepts of need and development.

Erikson's influential stage model of identity haunts many middle-school interventions, evident in formal programs and popular discourse. Healthy development requires the resolution of key dilemmas at each stage: adolescence represents the fifth stage, during which young people experience an "identity crisis" as they seek to resolve "identity versus role confusion," work out their relationships with others, and confront the question of "who am I?" (Erikson, 1968). Building strong peer connections, promoting resilience, addressing bullying, and fostering self-reliance and self-esteem are common foci of middle-school initiatives. "With respect to interpersonal relationships and social adjustment, these changes reflect a growing psychological and emotional independence from adults and a corresponding dependence on peer relationships to establish and maintain positive perceptions of the self" (Wentzel, 1998, p. 202). One effect of this developmental framework is the illusion of a common middle-school identity or problems, which obscures how middle-school experience is mediated by many factors, including cultural differences, gender, social class, and school location.

The designation of the middle years as inherently troubling has further consequences. Programs addressing bullying or social isolation, for example, can also produce normative expectations of crises and pathologies—such as low self-esteem or poor adjustment—inciting and constituting the very problem they seek to ameliorate. They also deliver mixed messages to students identified as culturally marginalized, "at risk," or facing a difficult middle-school period. At the same time as promising to include or help these students, the proliferation of interventions marks them out as lacking, negatively underscoring their difference. The problems middle school governs, such as teen sexuality, self-harm, low self-esteem, and body image, are profoundly gendered, with young women typically the implied subject of address. Middle-school debates accentuate the maturational and hormonal discourses of youth and gender differences, from claims that "girls mature earlier" to boys as more naturally rambunctious, more led by their drives and impulses, and more in need of unconfined space. Psychologist Carol Gilligan and colleagues argue that early adolescence is a crucial transition for young women, marked by a "loss of voice" and agency. The tension between self and others is amplified for girls, they propose, because of the intersection of cultural norms of femininity, which encourage an orientation to relationships and others, with developmental imperatives which stress greater independence and autonomy in the trajectory toward adulthood (Gilligan, Lyons, & Hanmer, 1990). This counters the apparently gender-neutral models of development, but also feeds into the stigmatizing of middle-school femininity as an uneasy, troublesome, and needy subject position that requires special attention.

The Invention of the Middle

Middle schooling occupies an ambiguous status. It is a place of potential chaos, a period which requires special intervention, particularly for some groups, and it harbors disruption and pathology, yet good middle schooling is redemptive, promising to rescue from or buttress young people against the troubles of early adolescence or to (re)engage them in learning. A key part of this mission is successful transition, yet paradoxically, the invention of a phase to ease transition establishes even more transition points and potential crises, and more deeply inscribes a normative model of linear development. Transition programs between schooling stages are now part of accepted "best practice," with double-edged effects. Such programs foster a therapeutic focus on the care of students, yet also enable closer scrutiny of achievement and interpersonal relations—common proxies for adjustment and transition—producing new forms of measurement to assess and monitor the quality of transition and the making of adolescence. The classificatory regimes of middle schooling are a form of biopolitics (Rose, 1996): they name and regulate a particular population group and stage of adolescence, attributing characteristics—emotional turbulence, vulnerability, role confusion—and plotting the movement of normative adolescent subjectivities.

Middle-school experience is immersed in the language of mobility but within a circumscribed space. The further classification of adolescence into early, middle, and late amplifies the in-process trajectory of adolescent identity. To designate a middle period of schooling simultaneously calls forth a provisional beginning and endpoint of normative school pathways, and a corresponding middle point. The finer calibrations of the middle promote a false sense of its stability as an a priori category, as a necessary and fixed feature of school provision. They lend force to the authority of temporal grids of development through which normative youth identities are invented and regulated, allowing more occasions for micromanagement to ensure proper conduct and prevent dysfunction. Such stage models emphasize the temporality of identity, suggesting perhaps the cumulative process of self-making. Simultaneously, they entrench lock-step conceptions of identity formation that mask the messy dynamics and desires of subjectivity and make nonnormative youth pathways problematic. The impact of these classificatory systems of the "middle" extends beyond the realm of schooling to become a new marker, a new staging post in youth identity formation.

In yet other ways, the time of middle schooling is invented. The perceived need for middle schools arose from a conjunction of social changes across the 20th century (Cuban, 1992). This included shifting views on the purposes of school—for academic or whole-of-life preparation—demand for increasing availability and length of compulsory secondary schooling, concerns about how to manage the work, leisure, and citizenship formation of young people, and the spread of psychological expertise about adolescence. In the present, however, the idea of middle school has taken on a self-evident, ahistorical character, as if it has always existed as a phase in the collective, organizational, and biographical trajectory of adolescence. Yet, as noun and adjective, middle school is historically contingent and situated, constitutive of new categories and understandings of youth identity and educational work.

The Promise of Middle School

As a site, a time, and an identity, middle school is enmeshed in utopian discourses—of becoming someone, of hopeful intervention, of movement beyond. As the link between one stage of life and another, it promises to redeem the alienated and excluded, to smooth transition, to foster well-adjusted future adults and be a haven before the demands of senior schooling. The redemptive power of middle schooling is evident in recent calls for a "reframing" or "rethinking" of middle school, where the utopian hopes of personal and social transformation are reflected in a greater focus on alternative pedagogies and ways of being than on developmental problems. These include withdrawal programs within mainstream secondary schools that combine community-based and outdoor activities with personal development programs that promote self-reliance. Successful transition to resourceful independence, enabled by responsive middle schooling, becomes a marker of good development, but it frequently rests upon a type of middle-school experience not equally available to all. It risks conflating desirable transition with a particular privileged educational experience, one that depends upon and enhances the accrual of highly valued cultural and social capital, and, in its idealization of the resourceful middle-school student, bestows the subject positions of failed, out-of-control, and aspiring youth.

Adolescents have historically occupied an in-between time, and this is amplified in the construction of a middle-school identity. Above all, middle school is a liminal time: a time out, a time of not-child, and most definitely not-adult, a time signifying the very confusion of identity that surrounds adolescence and the seemingly perennial (yet paradoxical) quest to delimit and pin down the different stages of fleeting youthful identity. Conceptually, middle-school and adolescent identities confound simple binary frameworks. They are the quintessential subject in-process, the celebratory figure of becoming (McLeod & Yates, 2006), *and* they are the regulated, scrutinized, calibrated subject of neo-liberal biopolitics (Rose, 1996). But middle-school identity is more than an abstract emblem for the contradictions of contemporary subjectivity. It is embodied, lived practically and problematically, vagrant, incomplete, lost, mobile, and a source of hope and difference. Middle school is more than institutional arrangements for meeting the needs of adolescence or improving engagement; it is simultaneously a time, place, and subjectivity. And it is a key site for the construction of the youth studies field, its objects of enquiry, and its claims to truth.

References

Anfara, V. A., Mertens, S. B., & Caskey, M. M. (2007). Introduction: The young adolescent and the middle school. In S. B. Mertens, V. A. Anfara, & M. M. Caskey (Eds.), *The young adolescent and the middle school* (pp. ix–xxxiii). Charlotte, NC: Information Age Publishing.

Carrington, V. (2006). *Rethinking middle years: Early adolescents, schooling and digital culture.* Crows Nest, Australia: Allen & Unwin.

Chadbourne, R. (2001). *Middle schooling for the middle years: What might the jury be considering?* Southbank, Australia: Australian Education Union.

Cuban, L. (1992). What happens to reforms that last? The case of the junior high school. *American Education Research Journal, 29*, 227–251.

Erikson, E. (1968). *Identity: Youth and crisis.* New York: W. W. Norton.

Gilligan, C., Lyons, N. P., & Hanmer, T. J. (Eds.). (1990). *Making connections: The relational worlds of adolescent girls at Emma Willard School.* Cambridge, MA: Harvard University Press.

Groundwater-Smith, S., Mitchell, J., & Mockler, N. (Eds.). (2007). *Learning in the middle years: More than a transition.* South Melbourne, Australia: Thomson.

Knipe, S. (Ed.). (2007). *Middle years schooling: Reframing adolescence.* Frenchs Forrest, Australia: Pearson Education Australia.

McLeod, J., & Yates, L. (2006). *Making modern lives: Subjectivity, schooling and social change.* Albany, NY: SUNY.

Prosser, B. (2008). Unfinished but not yet exhausted: A review of Australian middle schooling. *Australian Journal of Education, 52*, 151–167.

Roeser, R. W., Eccles, J. S., & Sameroff, A. J. (1998). Academic and emotional functioning in early adolescence: Longitudinal relations, patterns, and prediction by experience in middle school. *Development and Psychopathology, 10*, 321–352.

Rose, N. (1996). *Inventing ourselves: Psychology, power and personhood.* Cambridge: Cambridge University Press.

Stevens, L. P., Hunter, L., Pendergast, D., Carrington, V., Bahr, N., Kapitzke, C., & Mitchell, J. (2007). Reconceptualising the possible narratives of adolescence. *The Australian Educational Researcher, 34*, 107–127.

Wentzel, K. R. (1998). Social relationships and motivation in middle school: The role of parents, teachers, and peers. *Journal of Educational Psychology, 90*, 202–209.

Yates, L., & Holt, B. (2009). "Under pressure I fall back to being a teacher..." Confronting contending desires for schooling and teaching in a middle school reform project. *The Australian Educational Researcher, 36*, 27–42.

6

SCHOOL-TO-WORK TRANSITIONS

Meg Maguire and Stephen J. Ball

The complex relations between youth, work, and education have been a recurring focus of moral panic in England since the beginning of state education in the mid-19th century. Neither schools nor industry have ever sought to address the needs for education and training of all young people, and yet at the same time young people Not in Education, Employment or Training (NEETs) have been consistently constituted as a social problem requiring policy attention. The way that policy conceptualizes the "problem" of young people moving between education, employment, and training is currently rendered as "school-to-work transitions." In this short essay, drawing on a series of funded research projects which "followed" a diverse cohort of young people from one part of London from age 15 to 19 years, we want to make problematic some of the policy "rationalities"—the normative logics and assumptions—that are embedded in school-to-work transitions.

School-to-work transitions have always been classed and gendered, as well as racialized, in the English setting (Ball, Maguire, & Macrae, 2000). Up until the 1970s, over 70% of all young people left school at 15 years for full-time work. There was an actual school-to-work transition. A small elite (mainly males) obtained apprenticeships and an even smaller, mainly middle-class elite attended university. In a work-rich environment, school-to-work transitions were the unproblematic norm. By the 1980s, with widespread youth unemployment, many of these young people now had to be "warehoused" in courses and colleges or on training schemes (with no work) until they could obtain a job or until the labor market picked up. This "rupture" in school-to-work transitions has persisted (although in different ways at different times) and has become a key arena for policy work.

One additional way of "managing" the social problem of youth unemployment in the 1980s was through the expansion of further and higher education—although this was justified in different ways, particularly through the alleged "need" for a high skills labor force in a competitive globalizing economy (Brown & Lauder, 2004). Even so, for many young people these programs were of lesser value than "proper" work. For those young people who did undertake some work-related preparation, the approach in England was (and still is) that they would abandon any training if a "real" job became available. Gradually from the late 1980s onward, more young people were able to attend universities but, despite policies to include more "nontraditional" applicants, the growth in student numbers has been driven by the enlarged English middle classes—working-class young people are still much less likely to attend higher education (Leathwood & Reed, 2009; Reay, David, & Ball, 2005). In a labor market where there are increasing numbers of graduates, jobs that previously would have been open to nongraduates are now classed as graduate employment (Brown & Hesketh, 2004). In consequence, the labor market situation for those young people with limited certification and no/low skills has been deteriorating and the global fiscal crisis has made things worse (Redwood, 2009). So, while the discourse of school-to-work transitions still persists in policy rhetorics, the reality of what happens to young people when compulsory schooling formally ends at age 16 years is more fragmented and unstable.

More young people in the United Kingdom are staying on in education and training beyond the compulsory leaving age, although a cohort of between 20% and 25% still leave school at the first available opportunity (Archer, Hollingsworth, & Mendick, 2010; Department for Children, Schools and Families [DCSF], 2008). While some are "staying on," who may have left school had there been available work and are picking up qualifications that are "needed" in the expanding service sector, or in areas of new technology, there is still a stubborn rump of young people who are variously positioned in English policy discourses as being "marginalized," "at risk," as being "NEETs." These are young people for whom, in public policy terms, there has been a "faulty" school-to-work transition (Wyn, 2004). These are young people who, in psychologistic terms, have low motivations, low aspirations, and low self-esteem (Ball, 2004), who are seen as potentially being a "drain" on society—they are a public policy "problem." They do not "transition" from school to work. From their perspectives, their "rationalities," they may simply have had enough of a system that has repeatedly positioned them as "lacking." They may also be seeking work that is engaging, that sits with who they feel they are and who they want to be. The experience of school life as difficult and humiliating is a flawed preparation for the demands of the world of work.

> Nobody really enjoys school, especially if they are in special needs like me. School work is hard and I can't do it a lot of the time so I get fed up with it and I wish I wasn't here, and I bunk and that [skip school] because I find the work hard and boring.
>
> (Debra, aged 16 years; data from our projects)

Policy rationalities treat the "ends" of transition, school and work, as given, and as essentially the same for all young people and as uncluttered by affectivity— for most young people these moments of beginning and ending are daunting and sometimes traumatic, in part as a consequence of being positioned as "failing." They symbolize the entry into some form of adulthood, and yet in practice now usually involve a period of "post-adolescence"—a period of liminality between worlds of uncertainty.

Unpacking Some of the "Rationalities" at Play

Taking a step back, what we now want to do is ask some questions about the way in which school-to-work transitions are being produced and presented within policy. Let us start with the notion of "transition." The normative version of "transition" in English policy (policy discourse) is of a progression, a turning point, a break with the old and a point of change; a transmutation. However, for some young people in our research (Ball et al., 2000), school is not the social arena in which their identity and their future is made (Maguire, 2009). Policies disregard the social relations of these young people—friends and family—in which their lives are primarily invested, where their sense of self is being made up, and where opportunities for work (of one kind or another) arise.

A significant minority of young people are avoiding the future as it is constructed in policy texts and are tied into their immediate "horizons for action" (Hodkinson, Sparkes, & Hodkinson, 1996); that is, they are locked into local and short-term possibilities (see also Archer et al., 2010). They are not the rational "choosers" so often depicted in the normative school-to-work discourses and policy texts who select a logical next-step forward; these young people rely on managing and coping through local contacts and their families. For example, Fiona (aged 17 years) talks about her social life that revolves around her home and her housing estate (social housing): "just sort of hang around and that, go to their place [her friends], meet in the park and that ... the lady I used to baby-sit for, she knew someone who needed help in the mornings." The point of, pace of, and meaning of "transition" is different for different young people, and often different from policy norms.

Some young people do not want to deal with the "responsibilities" of young adulthood—they do not want to "transition" anywhere, they just want some freedom and some fun for a while.

> Long ago people had to grow up like really early and go to work and pay money into the house and whatever. But now you might as well have fun this age . . . I'm not ready to be a grown up yet. I just want to enjoy myself.
>
> (Lucy, aged 17 years)

Others have complex and sometimes disrupted social lives that mean that school-to-work transitions are just not on their agenda. "I don't think very much about the future because it's hard enough living just now, never mind thinking about next week, next month" (Ayesha, aged 17 years). Hall, Coffey, and Lashua (2009, p. 556) have argued that, for some young people, life is characterized by "the mundane present . . . speaking from that moment."Thus, some young people's lives will be more characterized by continuities, or repetitions, rather than transitions.

Some of the students in our studies are heavily invested in their social worlds and experience the ending of compulsion to attend school as a time of liminality—where they are sometimes distressed by the compulsion to choose, the compulsion to act. Others are located in identities that celebrate style, fashion, music, and "youth culture"—identities that have very little to do with schooling (Archer, Hollingsworth, & Halsall, 2007; Ball, 2004).

> I have been thinking about it since I was 11. My mum used to make clothes and everything and I used to help her. I just had an interest in clothes. I knitted myself a cardigan, and jeans, loads of clothes I made myself . . . I like jewelry, fashion, hair.
>
> (Michael, aged 18 years)

For these young people, the potency of policy discourses of school-to-work transitions lack any immediacy—in striking contrast with the rhetoric of normative educational discourses.

But "transition" is a problematic construct in a different way for other cohorts of young people. Many of the middle-class young people in our studies have a "disposition" to stay in the system and part of "being people like us" involves staying in education and training until the early-to-mid-1920s (Reay et al., 2005). For this group, "transition" does not occur in the same way—they simply move through the "normal" courses of events that people like themselves traverse. While there is, to some extent, a process of "choice" involved in where to study, and which university to choose, the underlying premise is that they will all go to "uni"; this is a nonnegotiable part of being a member of their family, their class, their social world (Brown & Hesketh, 2004). For this group, "transitions to work" start much later than the end of school (Bradley & Devadason, 2008). While some young graduates move into well-established professions that often follow on from their first degree, Bradley and Devadason (2008, p. 129) found that others take "time out" after graduating or take up unpaid internships; they characterize these young adults as "shifters" who rely on "lengthened and fragmented transitions" and who depend on their families for support.

The Irrationalities of School-to-Work Transitions

In the English context, then, school-to-work transitions are uneven, fragmented, and extended processes—certainly not the one-off events that seem to be imagined in the policy rhetoric that surrounds this phenomenon. One of the complexities relates to the way in which "youth" itself is being constructed. In the recent past in England, it has been low-certificated working-class youth who have been constructed as having a "problem" at the point of the ending of compulsory schooling. Thus, attention has tended to focus on them from about age 14 to 17 years. However, those young people who are more likely to be attempting to transition into work after university may be having a prolonged "youth" forced upon them. In this situation, age-related policies (such as the 14–19 curriculum) might be less than adequate in terms of what is actually taking place. The panic about school-to-work transitions is what it has always been—a panic about working-class youth. And, as Bynner (2001, p. 19) says, "It is still implicitly believed that the transition to adulthood for them is primarily about entry to manual work."

To a great extent, the "rationalities" of school-to-work transitions embedded in policy seem to belong to a past era and not to the current times of insecurity and the "specter" of unemployment. The "rationalities" of providing working-class youth with "more of the same" experiences, with yet more "deficit" positionings, and the movement of parts of unemployment to the postgraduate level, misread and ignore the diverse social locations and axes of identities of contemporary young people. The consequence is a "naive conception within policy of the centrality of education and work to the lives and identities of all young people" (Ball, 2004, p. 8).

References

Archer, L., Hollingsworth, S., & Halsall, A. (2007). University's not for me—I'm a Nike person: Urban working class young people's negotiations of "style," identity and educational engagement. *Sociology, 41,* 219–237.

Archer, L., Hollingsworth, S., & Mendick, H. (2010). *Urban youth and schooling: The experiences and identities of educationally "at risk" young people.* Maidenhead: Open University Press/ McGraw Hill.

Ball, S. J. (2004). *Participation and progression in education and training 14–19: Continuity, futurity and life in the "real" economy—"That's about it really."* Unpublished discussion paper for Nuffield Review of 14–19 Education and Training.

Ball, S. J., Maguire, M., & Macrae, S. (2000). *Choice, pathways and transitions post-16: New youth, new economies in the global city.* London: RoutledgeFalmer.

Bradley, H., & Devadason, R. (2008). Fractured transitions: Young adults' pathways into contemporary labour markets. *Sociology, 42,* 119–136.

Brown, P., & Hesketh, A. (2004). *The mismanagement of talent: Employability and jobs in the knowledge economy.* Oxford: Oxford University Press.

Brown, P., & Lauder, H. (2004). Education, globalization and economic development. In S. J. Ball (Ed.), *The RoutledgeFalmer reader in sociology of education* (pp. 47–71). Abingdon, UK: RoutledgeFalmer.

Bynner, J. (2001). British youth transitions in comparative perspective. *Journal of Youth Studies, 4*, 5–23.

Department for Children, Schools and Families (DCSF). (2008). *The extra mile: How schools succeed in raising aspirations in deprived communities.* London: HMSO.

Hall, T., Coffey, A., & Lashua, B. (2009). Steps and stages: Rethinking transitions in youth and place. *Journal of Youth Studies, 12*, 547–561.

Hodkinson, P., Sparkes, A. C., & Hodkinson, H. (1996). *Triumphs and tears: Young people, markets and the transition from school to work.* London: David Fulton.

Leathwood, C., & Reed, B. (2009). *Gender and the changing face of higher education: A feminized future.* Maidenhead: Open University Press.

Maguire, M. (2009). New adulthood, youth and identity. In K. te Riele (Ed.), *Making schools different: Alternative approaches to educating young people* (pp. 31–39). Sydney, Australia: Sage.

Reay, D., David, M., & Ball, S. J. (2005). *Degrees of choice: Social class, race and gender in higher education.* Stoke: Trentham Books.

Redwood, J. (2009). *Credit crunch: The anatomy of a crisis.* London: ASI.

Wyn, J. (2004). *Beyond the mainstream: Diversity and education for the 21st century.* Unpublished paper, University of Melbourne.

7

SURVEILLANCE

Rachel Oppenheim

According to a report released by the New York Civil Liberties Union (Mukherjee, 2007), on February 3, 2005, at Bronx Guild High School, a school security officer barged into a classroom to arrest a young female student for cursing in the hallway. When the principal asked him to leave, the officer grabbed the student, at which point the principal physically intervened to help her. The officer arrested the principal and the student and pressed criminal charges against both. The principal was removed from his position for 2 months until the charges were dropped and the student was encouraged to transfer schools. However, because she could not get a new placement, she missed several months of classroom time.

This incident points to a complex set of discourses that produce today's students in often contradictory ways. The fact that many urban schools are equipped with various instruments of "safety" and surveillance, including security cameras, metal detectors, and police officers (Casella, 2003), suggests that students are vulnerable. And yet, as the arrest of the young woman reveals, certain students—by and large poor students and students of color—are considered the very "danger" from which their peers must be protected. They are positioned as the perpetrators rather than the victims of school violence, even as officers manhandle them and arrest them for the most trivial of infractions.

In this essay, I describe the place that surveillance occupies in the lives and upon the bodies of today's youth and I outline the ways in which discourses of security and punishment coexist alongside discourses of protectionism and empathy. I describe the ways in which cultural anxiety shapes beliefs about who must be watched and who we should attempt to "know better," and I ask whom systems of surveillance are designed to benefit. Moreover, I argue that even those methods of surveillance that are believed to be well meaning must be viewed with skepticism, their tendency toward voyeurism both acknowledged and scrutinized.

Surveillance and Cultural Anxiety

In *Discipline and Punish*, Foucault (1977) explained the ways in which surveillance is deployed as a disciplinary tactic that—while avoiding physical torture—is undeniably corporeal. He pointed out, "even while they use 'lenient' methods . . . it is always the body that is at issue—the body and its forces, their utility and their docility, their distribution and their submission" (p. 25). The body that is "intelligible" (p. 136) is one that can be made docile and the gaze is therefore a powerful apparatus of control and normalization.

Surveillance has long been a mainstay in the lives of youth, in systems that have sought to sort and stratify them, and specifically in their encounters with school. Indeed, a number of authors have argued that the advent of universal public schooling had as much to do with containing and monitoring youth as with providing educational opportunities for all (Kliebard, 2004; Noguera, 1995; Spring, 2011; Tyack, 1974). Many early reformers perceived a crisis in society and hoped that the common school would mitigate that crisis by keeping "truant" children off of the streets and under the watchful eye of school officials (Casella, 2001; Spring, 2011; Tyack, 1974).

Moreover, even in these early years of public schooling, lines were being drawn between those students whose education was seen as paramount and those who were perceived to be disruptive to their fellow students and to the prevailing social order. Spring (2011) maintained that the charity school movement, while ostensibly created to provide educational opportunities for all children, was also "a result of concerns about urban street children who plagued city dwellers with constant begging and theft" (p. 60). These schools were a part of a stratified educational structure in which poor and immigrant children were sorted into a separate system of schooling whose purpose was in part to monitor them.

Ramlow (2002) argued that we have long positioned youth as straddling this tenuous boundary, marking them "as objects of both discipline . . . and of pity and social concern" (p. 199). He explained that cultural anxieties are mapped upon youth by those who perceive them as both potential protectors of a normative social order and potential threats to that order. It is most often the cultural "other" who is positioned as disruptive. Yet, if the other is made visible—intelligible—his disruptive power might be defused, restoring order and safety to society (Ramlow, 2002). Of course, the push to monitor and regulate young people has always extended well beyond the school walls, as practices such as mandatory curfews, truancy laws, and the recent filtering of "offensive" internet content for children clearly indicate. Yet, school has historically represented a space uniquely qualified to contain, survey, and indoctrinate youth.

A number of authors have drawn parallels between the systems of surveillance deployed in modern-day prisons and those utilized upon today's youth, particularly in the realm of schooling (Casella, 2006; Mukherjee, 2007; Noguera, 1995). Stoked by media coverage of what are in fact rare instances of student violence (Advancement Project, 2005), schools—particularly those in poor, urban areas—increasingly rely upon police personnel, as well as a variety of surveillance technologies, in order to closely monitor youth, positioning them as criminals rather than students.

However, in spite of the illusion of security that these apparatuses appear to offer, we must ask whom such systems of surveillance are in fact protecting. By fixing an intense gaze upon today's youth, are we indeed keeping those youth safe? Furthermore, do "school safety" practices, as some purport, free teachers from safety concerns, ensuring that learning can take place? As a report by the Advancement Project (2005) noted, "While these measures produce a perception of safety, there is no evidence that they create safer learning environments or change detrimental behaviors. There is, however, evidence that these tactics unnecessarily thrust more youths into an unforgiving penal system" (p. 17).

Ironically, those youth who are subjected to such punitive, isolationist forms of surveillance are often neglected in other aspects of education. They are frequently "pushed out" of school (Fine, 1986), placed in lower or segregated academic tracks (Brantlinger, 2006), and otherwise isolated from their peers (Casella, 2003). On the one hand, they are constantly visible, their comings and goings monitored by an ever-present battalion of surveillance personnel and technologies. However, in spite of this relentless scrutiny, they are also remarkably invisible, their distinct selves erased as they are pigeonholed and subjected to reductive stereotypes. This emphasis on pushing "delinquent" students out of school and ignoring their individuality represents a departure from the systems of regulation present at the advent of public schooling. Whereas early reformers hoped that education would alter individuals in part by separating them from their corrupt homes and communities, in their current tendency to isolate and expel, today's officials seem to have abandoned the possibility of indoctrination—implying that some students are simply not capable of change.

Culturally Responsive Pedagogy as Another Tool of Surveillance

Yet, even those educational practices that seem "responsive," that seek to understand and empathize with youth, can be understood as part of the technology of surveillance. There have been calls by students, teachers, and scholars alike to highlight the "voices" of youth who are too often scrutinized and defined by others. Many teachers strive toward "culturally responsive" pedagogies (Ladson-Billings & Tate, 1995), working to know their students better so that they may draw upon their particular histories and backgrounds when designing curricula.

However, these attempts by educators to mine their students' identities and facilitate their self-expression can be seen as another—albeit well-meaning—form of surveillance. While not an overtly disciplinary tactic, asking young people to express themselves and reveal their innermost thoughts nonetheless continues to position them as "objects of knowledge" (Foucault, 1977, p. 24) and can be seen as intrusive, voyeuristic, and regulatory. Jones (2004) argued that, "paradoxically, progressive teachers' call for dialogue may be in danger of reproducing the very power relations they seek to critique" (p. 64). Knowing the "other" and being privy to her intimate thoughts and experiences can be a potent means of maintaining power over her, rather than an avenue toward her "liberation." Moreover, in encouraging particular types of narratives—those that appear "empowering," that reveal suffering, that strive toward personal change, that highlight "redemption"—educators might once again be using their work with students to uphold the normative social order and quell their own anxieties.

By maintaining skepticism toward calls for student voice and by questioning educators' desire to promote dialogue, I do not mean to imply that marginalized students should be encouraged to remain silent, nor that dialogue is an unimportant facet of any classroom. My purpose, rather, is to caution against the assumption that a classroom in which student voices are forefronted is necessarily a space free from surveillance and exempt from the unequal relations of power that have always plagued educational settings. Instead, educators must acknowledge their own ability to suppress and marginalize, even as they attempt to establish progressive practices and enact "liberatory" pedagogies.

Today's youth, perhaps more than any previous generation, have access to a multitude of technologies through which to craft narratives and communicate beyond the watchful eye of adults, even as methods of monitoring such media are rapidly gaining traction. As adults—motivated by cultural anxieties—debate the need to restrict such forms of communication, to prevent "cyber-bullying," to protect teens from online predators, to limit "mature" content, familiar tropes surface: youth are positioned as both innocent and threatening, and surveillance is held up as a method of protecting some and ferreting out others. So too, educators have begun to utilize media such as blogs and online social forums as a way to better "reach" students and encourage their unique forms of self-expression. Today, as in the past, there is a powerful temptation to monitor youth, an impulse that stems at once from fear and from empathy. It is crucial that we continue to scrutinize surveillance in all its forms and to recognize when it may serve to further objectify youth, exploit their experiences, and heighten their alienation.

References

Advancement Project. (2005). Education on lockdown: The schoolhouse to jailhouse track. Retrieved from http://www.advancementproject.org/sites/default/files/publications/FINALEOLrep.pdf

Brantlinger, E. A. (2006). *Who benefits from special education? Remediating (fixing) other people's children*. London: Lawrence Erlbaum.

Casella, R. (2001). *Being down: Challenging violence in urban schools*. New York: Teachers College Press.

Casella, R. (2003). Punishing dangerousness through preventive detention: Illustrating the institutional link between school and prison. *New Directions for Youth Development, 99*, 55–70.

Casella, R. (2006). *Selling us the fortress: The promotion of techno-security equipment for schools*. New York: Routledge.

Fine, M. (1986). Why urban adolescents drop into and out of public high school. *Teachers College Record, 87*, 393–409.

Foucault, M. (1977). *Discipline and punish: The birth of the prison*. New York: Vintage Books.

Jones, A. (2004). Talking cure: The desire for dialogue. In M. Boler (Ed.), *Democratic dialogue in education: Troubling speech, disturbing silence* (pp. 57–67). New York: Peter Lang.

Kliebard, H. M. (2004). *The struggle for the American curriculum 1893–1958* (3rd ed.). New York: Routledge.

Ladson-Billings, G., & Tate, W. F. (1995). Toward a critical race theory of education. *Teachers College Record, 97*, 47–68.

Mukherjee, E. (2007). *Criminalizing the classroom: The over-policing of New York City schools*. New York: New York Civil Liberties Union.

Noguera, P. A. (1995). Preventing and producing violence: A critical analysis of responses to school violence. *Harvard Educational Review, 65*(2), 189–212.

Ramlow, T. R. (2002). Bad boys: Abstractions of difference and the politics of youth "deviance." In R. McRuer, E. Samuels, & A. L. Wilkerson (Eds.), *Desiring disability: Queer theory meets disability studies* (pp. 192–213). Durham, NC: Duke University Press.

Spring, J. (2011). *The American school: From the puritans to no child left behind* (8th ed.). New York: McGraw Hill.

Tyack, D. B. (1974). *The one best system: A history of American urban education*. Cambridge, MA: Harvard University Press.

Research and Regulation of Knowledge

Thomas S. Popkewitz

In what might seem obvious to those steeped in biology and culture: Youth is not a given category about an age group whereby researchers identify its "nature" and then find how to effect changes that ease children into adulthood. Historically, the classification of youth is a social practice about how to think about kinds of people, a way of acting on particular populations, and a way that people are to act for themselves. Adolescence is a case in point. Brought into scientific psychology at the beginning of the 20th century, it organizes thought about who youth are, should be, and who does not "fit" its inscriptions of growth and development.

Regulation, in the sense of this essay, is the making of youth as a human kind that "acts" as the autonomous subject of research. The subject of youth is not merely to describe particular kinds of people. Youth is a subject given an independent space in which the social and psychological sciences order and organize the study of schooling, crime, family, and community, among others. It is a determinant category whose system of reason generates cultural theses about the possibilities of life itself—principles about how people are to think and act. The regulation of research is also thus the political. The rules and standards order the (im)possibilities of what is thought, acted on, and hoped for.

My interest in the category of youth is an exemplar of the social sciences as fabricating human kinds. Fabrication has a double nuance: the autonomous subjects of research are responses to the (ontic) world by creating fictions to act on that world and "fix" its problems. *And*, fabrication entails the simultaneously making of kinds of people such as embodied in the category of "youth." Youth as a subject and object of research embodies these two nuances of fabrication. Fabrication thus is an analytic tool in which to consider the issue of regulation and the political of research.

Youth studies are methodologically considered as an "event," focusing on the conditions that make it observable and historically locatable. The first section focuses on the notion of fabrication of human kinds as a technology of governing. Notions of agency, freedom, empowerment, and "voice" that order youth studies, for example, are never merely about the subject but a method of making the subject calculable and administrable. The second section explores the historical inscriptions of comparative rules and standards in the making of youth as a human kind. That style of reason, I argue, produces difference, divisions, and inequality in the name of governing for equality. The categories and distinctions of research generate cultural theses about the possibilities of life that simultaneously include and abject in casting out of its Others into unlivable spaces.

Two conditions frame this discussion of social science and regulation. First is to place youth as fabrication in the practices of research.[1] Second, that kind of human is produced through a historical assemblage of practices. These practices, I argue, generate cultural theses about youth as modes of living. The modes of living are inscribed in the social and psychological sciences as principles to link notions of human agency with those of collective belonging. The section following explores the youth as a human kind that entails double gestures of differentiating and dividing conduct in a continuum of values.

Methodologically, attention is directed to youth as an event in order to focus on the historical conditions that make it possible to "see" and act on as an object of research (see, e.g., Foucault, 1979). To speak about youth as an event is a counter strategy to the positivism that assigns youth with a given identity from which to search for the origin of its development and the management of its conduct. It is through the double nuances of fabrication that it is possible to challenge the dualism of nominalism and realism in what might be called "the new materialism."

Fabricating Human Kinds: Youth Studies

As argued above, fabrication brings into consideration two nuances in thinking about research. Fabrication is simultaneously a fiction that responds to "things" happening in the world and the making or manufacturing of "things." G. Stanley Hall (1928), for example, proposed adolescence to think about children as a response to the issues arising from the changing social and psychological conditions of urban life at the turn of the 20th century. Scientific psychology, he argued, would identify patterns of intervention in the child's growth, development, and morality that no longer seemed sufficient if left alone. "The momentum of heredity often seems insufficient to enable the child to achieve this great revolution and come to complete maturity, so that every step is strewn with wreckage of body, mind, and morals" (Hall, 1928, p. xiv). The fiction of adolescence, however, was not merely of the researcher's "imagination." Adolescence responded to changes in the world that required attention. Over time, it assumed its own independent existence and ontological qualities. Programs were installed to control the adolescent's "proper development" and rectify moral disorders, such as sexual promiscuity and juvenile delinquency.

The notion of fabricating human kinds provides a strategy to historicize the problem of regulation in youth studies. At one layer, it gives visibility to the rules and standards that order the subject of youth as an object of research. At a different layer, the double nuance of fabrication, as fiction and as manufacturing, brings to the surface the epistemological limits of contemporary research. These limits are in the opposition between, for example, nominalism (discourse) and realism, which differentiate texts (discourse and theory) as different from and not as important as the "real" practices and "lived experience" of children and schooling. The dualisms elide the ways in which "lived experiences" and its corollary assumption about "useful" knowledge are historically instantiated, act on people, and have a materiality in constituting what is and what should be. The productions of human kinds are effects of power through the principles generated to order and classify the objects seen and acted on as "practice."

Assembling Youth as a Human Kind: The Calculation of Reason and the Reasonable Person

Youth as a category of a human kind is made possible and intelligible through a grid of historical practices that is analogous to the making of a cake. The fabrication of youth and the cake are produced through the mixing of different ingredients that come together and form the objects seen and acted on. The objects are given an independent existence or ontological status. The cake is seen as a particular class of food and youth is what the child is! The analogy, though, is limited. At a simple level, the making of the cake involves intentionality in what ingredients to mix. Youth as a classification of people has no single origin or essence to study and map. Different, uneven historical processes overlap to produce it as an object of thought and action. Adolescence is one such example discussed below.

Further, the fabrication of human kinds instantiates cultural theses about modes of life. Lesko (2001), for example, historically examines adolescence as theses about modes of living that change over time; such as coming of age, being hormonally driven, and peer orientation. Brown (2011) examines narratives in the social science about the Black male youth as a particular human kind differentiated and divided from its "other." The Black male was envisioned as "absent and wandering" from the 1930s to the 1950s; as "impotent and powerless" in the 1960s; and then in the 1980s as the prototype "absent father," who is psychologically powerless and with a common cultural pattern of speech and social interactions. Recently the narratives stress the positive "soulful" and "adaptive" Black male. The different themes about the Black male, Brown continues, maintain a resemblance through a populational reasoning that normalizes a particular commonsense about an independent subject different from "others," who are silently present to indicate what Black youth are not.

This historical observation goes against the logic of much of contemporary studies of youth. Youth stands as a unified category whose ontological quality is given as the source of knowledge. Youth is inscribed with an identity and as the origin of the "data," such as in social structural and phenomenological theories of the subject. Research is to effect the development of youth through making teaching more efficient, finding better theories of learning, and identifying the "value-added" qualities that produce higher school achievement. Yet these strategies to act on youth are not natural to the child, descriptions about working of the mind, or the pure logic of thought. The notions of childhood are formed through different historical trajectories.[2]

One trajectory in the making of youth as an autonomous object is associated with Northern European and North American enlightenments' cosmopolitanism.[3] Child studies, the modern school curriculum, and the pedagogical sciences, with different variations in the distinctions about childhood, gave the subject of youth as an expression to the enlightenments' notion of cosmopolitanism. Youth became a site to develop the human "reason" of the child as the source of liberty and freedom. The assumed principles of reason are given as universal qualities, true for *all humanity*, and thus what schooling needed to calculate and develop in order for the child to be a productive citizen—today called the lifelong learner.

That universality given as the principles of reason, however, was never universal. The autonomy of the cosmopolitan citizen historically intersected with, for example, political and cultural principles about the making of the citizen whose participation was necessary for government. The political project connected with Protestant (Calvinist) notions of salvation about the individual good works as serving to provide for happiness and contributing to the community's progress in American schooling and certain European contexts (see Tröhler, 2011).

I speak of youth in this way to suggest that youth as a category exists with a grid of practices that give intelligibility to the objects "seen" and acted on. These practices generate cultural theses about modes of life. They instantiate distinctions and classifications about individuals as agents of change through which happiness and progress were to occur. That agent of change connects with particular notions of the individual living in a rationally ordered and planned mode of life. One lives through planning one's life as a calculated series of events to produce happiness and satisfaction. Biography if planned properly through motivation and proper judgments ordered by the exercise of reason will bring pleasure and satisfaction.

That planning, however, was not merely the implementation of rational systems. The new social and psychological theories secularized Protestant reform salvation themes in American Progressive political theories and sciences (Popkewitz, 2008; Tröhler, Popkewitz, & Labaree, 2011).[4] The psychology of adolescence, for example, embodied the hope of Progressivism's cosmopolitan values that would bring to youth "reason, true morality, religion, sympathy, love, and aesthetic enjoyment" (Hall, 1928, p. xiii). The University of Chicago urban community sociology connected puritan notions of "community of believers" to the social relations and patterns of interaction found in turn-of-the-20th-century urban contexts. The sociological concept of "primary group" and the symbolic interactionism of George Herbert Mead, for example, carried this grid of practices in the ordering of the self and the other. The pragmatism of Dewey's notions of problem solving and "intelligent action," as well, instantiated an enlightenment's hope of the cosmopolitan individual that was linked to Protestant reformism and notions of republican civic virtue. Each was connected with other social and cultural practices that (re)visioned the nation as a secular thesis of the puritan notion of "the city on the hill."[5]

The Agency of Reason as a Principle in the Governing of Human Kinds

Youth is a fabrication that historically entails science as a technology to change social conditions by changing people. Science as planning people traverses ideological distinctions. It is given expression in utilitarian notions about "useful knowledge" and critical theories to challenge the status quo by calling for research to serve for "social reconstruction." While the commitments are different, the notion of planning people circulated in the emergence of the welfare state, the institutionalization of social science, and the formation of the modern school.

This observation about governing of youth has two further points. First, the cosmopolitan notion of "reason" was made into an observable object to study and administrate. If I return to the notions of fabrication and human kinds, the theories and methods of modern social sciences were material practices. "Reason" was a principle of change that focused on the rational ordering of the processes of thought and action. The focus on "reason" as a technology of change expressed different European enlightenments' hopes about the future. Reason became something to calculate, to order, classify, and differentiate "the reasonable person" from its "others."

The cosmopolitan notions of "reason" and the reasonable person are taken for granted in youth studies. Research assumes that individuals have or can be given "reason" in order to produce human happiness and social progress. Research identifies how that reason is ordered, its conditions of realization, and the restraints and constraints that prevent the development of the "reasonable person." This rescuing of the child to become "reasonable" is found in discussions about children's misconceptions and lack of motivation. If I take an article about eight graders learning to generalize through mathematical modeling, the focus on children learning to "reason" is through social interactions and activities. The social psychology of "situated learning" provides the interpretive frame for describing how students think about the "real world" through mathematical modeling (Jurow, 2004).

While this article about mathematics education is thoughtful about the social context influencing children's learning, my interest is in the principles generated about thought and acting. Traveling in the pedagogical project is a particular enlightenment attitude about reason, happiness, and progress. The mode of living is expressed as the child's rationally ordering phenomena through learning solutions to "real-world" problems. The "real-world" problems, however, are not things natural to the world.

The significance of the mathematical modeling inscribes, at one level, the enlightenment's making of the mind (reason) as an equal agent with nature.

This thesis of human agency, an assumption of modern social theory, was a radical innovation. The medieval church, for example, looked at "reason" as a way to find God and as a method to differentiate the soul of the savage to be saved. The European and North American enlightenments separated nature and reason yet connected them through the mind accessing principles of the structure of the cosmos and enunciating them systematically through mathematics (Cassirer, 1932/1951). The "real-world" problems solved by mathematics are given further intelligibility in a grid of Calvinist notions of community and liberal theories of participation that mutate into contemporary theories of situated learning.[6] What constitutes the "real world" is not naturally there but historically given its ontological status.

Second, the idea of the human "reason" as an agent of change brought together two registers normally placed in opposition: registers of freedom with registers of social administration.[7] The discussion of the child's problem solving and innovation, for example, by mathematical modeling is shaped and fashioned within the social rules. These rules relate individual participation to interaction patterns, communication systems, and learning communities.

In the mathematical modeling, the individuality and the social are placed as part of the same phenomenon. There is no individual without some norms of the social. Prior to the 18th century in Europe, for example, society was a word to describe an association or guild of people. Society later came to refer to anonymous forces and structures that gave organization to human life. The joining of notions of society and individuality is evident in the Englishman John Locke's political theory that connected the consciousness of the self to the knowledge gained through the experiences of society. The Swiss Jean-Jacques Rousseau's notion of the *social* contract placed the relation of government and individuality as central in determining "the general will." Adam Smith's notion of the invisible hand of markets gave focus to the abstract forces through which the individual pursued self-interest in the promotion of the good of society.

Irreversible Time and Science in Changing and Making People

The salvation themes about happiness and progress that circulate within social theory embody a "modern" sense of the self in irreversible, secular time. While time prior to the enlightenments was universal and "owned" by God, the notion of progress that became visible in the enlightenments linked the past/present/future. This notion of time marked the political calculations that served as a humanist project to plan for the future (Koselleck, 1979/1985).[8] Secular time makes possible modern historicism that traces the movement of people across a linear temporal sequence. It also entailed the study of the interior of the child during the 18th century through notions of development and growth. Linear time links the actions of individuality and notions of planning for the future with the idea of progress.

The notion of time in ordering life can be contrasted to the Greek Stoics' "reason." The latter embodied a particular cultural thesis about "reason" as acts of memory that liberated one's own being. Knowing oneself meant knowing the past that is drawn from the wisdom given by the gods (Foucault, 2005, p. 468).[9] The mind preoccupied with the future was considered as consumed by forgetting and incapable of action. Claiming knowledge of the future was hubris as the future did not exist for people but for the gods.

The regularizing of time is central to the making of youth as a subject of research. The "reason" of cosmopolitanism brought the question of history as the past that is to be overcome through present "actions." Such actions would enable the progress of the future (Commager, 1950). G. Stanley Hall's (1928) study of adolescence, for example, spoke about youth as existing in a world of irreversible time.

> Old moorings are constantly broken; adaptive plasticity to new environments— somatic, economic, industrial, social, oral and religious—was never so great. All this suggests that man is not a permanent type, but an organism in a very active stage of evolution, toward a more permanent form.
>
> (p. vii)

Dewey's sanction of action ordered through "scientific habit" was to order the future by shedding unwarranted traditions identified with dogma and ignorance. "The old culture is doomed for us because it was built upon an alliance of political and spiritual powers, an equilibrium of governing and leisure classes, which no longer exists" (Dewey, 1929, pp. 501–502).

The irreversibility of a progressive time remains in contemporary studies. To return to the student mathematical modeling, its subject was to study and generalize about populational changes in guppies through organizing time into sequences for comparisons. The "reason" of the modeling is to prepare the child for the world through learning to "reason" by observing and interpreting changes in sequences of time. Time is a determinant and operative in learning what is "sensible" in "real-world" situations through "opportunities for identifying patterns" of differences (Jurow, 2004, pp. 265–267). The learning in the lesson, then, is not only about guppies. It is about what constitutes the conditions of thought that govern the present and its actions about the future.

Although briefly, there are contemporary strands of research that seek to disrupt notions of time as a continuous and regularized movement of past/ present/future and the givenness of the subject and its identities. The French historical school of the Annales, for example, engages in different notions of discontinuous time as a method of history (Braudel, 1980). There are also concerns in geography and architecture of the fluid boundaries of "time/space" (Rajchman, 1997; Soja, 1989) that overlap with postmodern feminist theories about the construction of gender (Stone, 1994) and postcolonial studies. The destabilizing of the givenness of identities in fixed space and time also finds its way to the sociology of youth, viewed as "scapes" that consider shifts and movements (Maira & Soep, 2005).

Comparativeness and the Making of Divisions/Exclusions

The invention of human actors (and agency) as human kinds is given intelligibility within a particular comparative style of thought that differentiated and divided the capabilities of people. The early 20th-century sociologies and psychologies of the family and childhood, for example, were formed as responses to The Social Question. That Question was generated as part of Protestant (Congregationalism) reformism in North Europe and North America concerned with the perceived immorality of the city and its urban populations. American progressive social sciences was directed to The Social Question, asking about the causes of decay indicated by alcoholism, family disintegration, delinquency among youth, and prostitution in the cities' immigrant and racial populations. G. Stanley Hall, in the context of The Social Question, spoke of the danger of "loss" in "our urbanized hothouse" that "tends to ripen everything before its time" where "[t]here is not only arrest, but perversion, at every stage, and hoodlumism, juvenile crime, and secret vice seem not only increasing, but develop in earlier years in every civilized land" (Hall, 1928, p. xiv).

The "urban" problem of The Social Question embodied a comparative style of thought that still preoccupies the study of youth. Today that human kind is called the urban youth, defined through a populational reasoning about the African American male discussed earlier, the Chicano/a, and pregnant teenager, among others. The urban youth as a "kind of people" is inscribed in policy and science as requiring rescue and remediation because of the "achievement gap," dropout rates, and delinquency.

The urban child is a human kind that has little to do with geographical place (Popkewitz, 1998). The urban child may live in the city but also lives in suburbia and rural areas. The urban child is narrated as lacking the qualities to find the reason and agency for pursuing happiness.[10] That lack of capability is (re) visioned in a grid that includes psychological distinctions about poor communication skills, poor self-concept, the lack of self-esteem, and low expectations and motivation. The psychological distinctions overlap with sociological characteristics of poverty, socially disadvantaged, broken families or single parent households and what are called "fragile" and "dysfunctional families."

The urban child is a space of comparison. It is the child who does not fit into the spaces reserved for "all children." The phrase *all* children, at one layer, articulates the commitment to equity. The *all*, however, assumes the unity from which the urban and disadvantaged child is divided. The urban child is different from the unspoken but present qualities of "all children," with the former "targeted," to use the language of U.S. policy, for remediation and rescue. The distinctions that recognize difference for inclusion generate principles about the child whose qualities belong to the spaces outside of those assigned to the category of "all children."

The unity of the qualities of the child who belongs in the space of "all children" in contemporary literature is the particular kind of person who is "the lifelong learner." The social and psychological qualities of the lifelong learner are what the urban child lacks. The cultural thesis of the lifelong learner is of an individuality that entails the never-ending processes of making choices, innovation, and collaboration (see, e.g., Fejes & Nicoll, 2007; Popkewitz, 2008). The reason that orders the agency of the lifelong learner is the life of choices that maximize happiness through continual processes of planning. Choice is sanctioned by acts of working collaboratively in community. The only thing that is not a choice is making choices!

The relation and comparative divide of human kinds is expressed in research about developmentally appropriate instruction for middle-school children. Manning (2002) argues, for example, that curriculum and instructional activities are to develop cosmopolitan values of the lifelong learner who is independent, free, and thinks through higher levels of abstractions. While the narrative of the adolescent child is spoken about as universal qualities of all youth, the distinctions quickly morph into the qualities of urban youth represented as racially and ethnically different and living in poverty. The developmentally appropriate instruction is to rectify the problems and redeem the dangerous populations. "Early adolescence years may be the best time to provide intervention strategies that," in the language of hope and fear, "help youngsters avoid academic failure and behavior problems" (Manning, 2002, p. 52). Traveling against the cosmopolitan lifelong learner are the qualities and characteristics of youths, who experiment "with sexual activity, often leading to sexually transmitted diseases and early pregnancy, use of cigarettes and/or marijuana and other illicit drugs; lower school grades and dropping out, and delinquency and criminal offenses" (p. 52).

The comparative style of thought has a particular quality that subordinates difference to identity and places science as the technology to plan and redeem people. The comparative qualities of nature were given social significance in, for example, the late 17th-century "quarrel of the ancients and the moderns." Europe and North America were generalized as advanced civilizations that superseded others who lacked the capacities, habits, and abilities to reason. The latter were abjected as backward, savage, and barbarians. At its social extremes and ironically, the comparative style of thought made possible the eugenics movements in the 19th and 20th centuries that linked biology and the body to social "fitness" and intelligence.

Historically, the style of comparison that constructs and regulates difference is exemplified in Todorov's (1982/1999) examination of the Mexican conquest by the Spanish conquistadors. He asks, how is it possible for a few men to conquer such a large population? Drawing on a semantic analysis, he explores that possibility as not merely in the cunning and arms of a few men. Todorov discursively differentiates Columbus from Cortes a century later. Columbus, he argues, "saw" the Caribbean Indians and Mexicans through a medieval concept of knowledge. The knowledge acted on was given and predicted by the formulas extracted from sacred books. The concrete experience of Columbus illustrated the truth already possessed about the assignment of place and value to the order given by God. For Columbus, there was no linguistic diversity of meaning and anthropological understanding of the Other. Cortes, in contrast, had a different consciousness that served as a precursor to what now is associated with the enlightenment and modernity. Cortes could think about a plurality of worlds and the practical utility of interpersonal communication to manipulate the Other. This comparativeness differentiated the modes of living and characteristics of the Aztecs on a continuum of values, and enabled the devising of pragmatic strategies for the conquest of the Other.

The comparative style of thought brings into focus gestures of inclusion, exclusion, and abjections in the modern social science. It is embodied in its particular styles of reason and the manner and conditions in which human kinds are produced. If I return to the urban child, it is a human kind that is inscribed in a system of reason that recognizes the child for inclusion by establishing difference. The "urban" child is discursively different and can never be "of the average" to plan life that secures future success.

The Political: Research as Planning for Society and Other Possibilities of Enacting Social Commitments

My concern about the regulation of research echoes that of this volume. It is to think about the ways in which youth are imagined, concretely work, and produce "things." I pursued that argument through viewing youth studies as practices that fabricate human kinds. The principles generated embody cultural theses about modes of life. The regulation functions as the political of research through inscribing the rules and standards that govern what is seen, talked about, and acted on.

The approach historically and epistemologically considers the norms of rationality that order and classify the notion of youth as historical "events." Youth as an object of study, I argued, is formed through a grid of historical practices that gives intelligibility to its object as a subject and agent. Further, my concern was with how the principles generated to produce human kinds for inclusion simultaneously inscribe processes of exclusion and abjection.

This approach gives a different layer of analysis than that posited in ideological arguments. The latter, typically drawing on the philosophy of representation embedded in structural theories, for example, inscribe the subject of change from which divisions are framed and action directed. The assumption is important to "the politics of representation" that shapes public strategies related to inclusion as social access and opportunity.

The limits of this politics, as explored here, is its elision of the inscriptions of a comparative system of reason through which identities and divisions are produced. The focus on ideology (a) leaves unscrutinized concrete practices that fabricate, in its two nuances, youth as a human kind; (b) obscures the complex relations between discourse and knowledge and context; and (c) leaves unproblematic the very framework of its contemporaneity that needs to be made visible in addressing social wrongs. The systems of reason that make the subject as a site of intervention, I argued, is the political through the partition of the sensible and sensibilities.

The regulation of research points to a paradox of the contemporary sciences as planning human kinds. Whether in liberal or critical traditions tied to structuralism, the projects of youth studies begin with an assumption that research will rectify social wrongs that produce inequality. That assumption, the socialist political theorist Rancière (1983/2004) argues, proceeds as the potentiality to compensate for inequality by devising well-placed strategies of change. That strategy paradoxically, he continues, instantiates inequality as the very effort to achieve equality. That paradox is through the inscription of inequality as the starting point of policy and research. That insertion of inequality inserts the precondition of difference in its object of research which instantiates the divisions to be erased. This strategy inscribes a hierarchy, Rancière argues, that places the philosopher and social scientists as the shepherds of the rules and standards of recognition and participation.

This observation about the limits of studies of youth should not be read as the removal of social commitments from the practices of research. The mode of inquiry that orders this essay is bound to the need for conditional foundations to address wrongs through its choice of questions and approach to interrogate the issue of regulation in the notion of youth. Such commitments, found in the writings of Arendt, Deleuze, Derrida, Foucault, Hacking, Latour, Rancière, and Serres, among others, recognizes that philosophy, social theories, and research are not merely epiphenomena to structural forces but have material effects. The different literatures can be read as efforts to find alternatives to the style of comparative thought that inserts identities and divisions that I discussed.

While these projects are without guarantees and embody possibilities of regulation, they maintain social obligations to right social wrongs that, paradoxically, express enlightenment commitments to human reason and agency but in ways that do not subordinate difference to identity. Again without guarantees, they provide alternative systems of reason which do not articulate the comparative style of thought that expresses cultural anxieties about the "other" who is inscribed as threatening the envisioned future. With different nuances in the questions they ask and the methods proposed, the intellectual programs forgo the inscriptions of research as planning the future through planning the subject.

Notes

1 The notion of making human kinds is drawn from Hacking (1986).
2 Much of the discussion related to this observation is explored in the historicizing cosmopolitanism as principles ordering and classifying schooling in Popkewitz (2008).
3 I use the plural to recognize multiple enlightenments related to, for example, German, British, English, and American fields of thought. While both the American and French revolutions transmogrified enlightenment thought into the formation of the nation as a republic, there were differences. The French were anticlerical and focused on questions

of social solidarity. The American Revolution, in contrast, began with sermons from the Protestant churches about the rights of the citizen and incorporated puritan notions of individualism with collective norms of the nation as "the city on the hill."

4 I use this phrase to emphasize the uneven historical practices that came together between the late 1700s and early 20th century and which become visible in both the formation of the welfare state "in care of people" and the social sciences as a particular form of knowledge for assessing and planning that "care." I discuss this in Popkewitz (2008).

5 I discuss this in Popkewitz (2008, 2010); also see Tröhler (2011).

6 For discussion of community as a particular religious cultural narrative in education, see Tröhler (2009).

7 My focus is on the social science but the joining of these two registers is embodied in the welfare state and schooling as well.

8 The idea of progress was thought of before, but becomes visible in its "modern" configuration related to particular principles of "reason" and rationality linked to notions of society, individuality, and human-organized change.

9 As someone who studied Greek art, I recognize that I am merging historical nuances to make the general points.

10 To consider the social and historical location of such categories about human kinds, consider that for youth to produce graffiti is not considered as having agency and then consider what are the rules and standards that differentiate agency from other acts not constituted as "reason" and the reasonable person.

References

Braudel, F. (1980). *On history*. Chicago: University of Chicago Press.

Brown, A. (2011). Same old stories: The Black male in social science and educational literature, 1930s to present. *Teachers College Record, 113*(6).

Cassirer, E. (1932/1951). *The philosophy of the enlightenment* (F. Koelln & J. Pettegrove, Trans.). Princeton, NJ: Princeton University Press.

Commager, H. S. (1950). *The American mind: An interpretation of American thought and character since the 1880s*. New Haven, CT: Yale University Press.

Dewey, J. (1929). *The sources of a science of education*. New York: Horace Liveright.

Fejes, A., & Nicoll, K. (2007). *Foucault and lifelong learning: Governing the subject*. London: Routledge.

Foucault, M. (1979). Governmentality. *Ideology and Consciousness, 6*, 5–22.

Foucault, M. (2005). The hermeneutics of the subject (G. Burchell, Trans.). In F. Gros (Ed.), *Lectures at the Collège de France, 1981–1982*. New York: Picador.

Hacking, I. (1986). Making up people. In T. C. Heller, M. Sosna, & D. E. Wellbery (Eds.), *Reconstructing individualism: Autonomy, individuality, and the self in Western thought* (pp. 222–236, 347–348). Stanford, CA: Stanford University Press.

Hall, G. S. (1928). *Adolescence: Its psychology and its relation to physiology, anthropology, sociology, sex, crime, religion, and education* (Vol. 1). New York: Arno Press and *New York Times*.

Jurow, A. S. (2004). Generalizing in interaction: Middle school mathematics students making mathematical generalizations in a population-modeling project. *Mind, Culture, and Activity, 11*, 279–300.

Koselleck, R. (1979/1985). *Futures past: On the semantics of historical time* (K. Tribe, Trans.). Cambridge, MA: The MIT Press.

Lesko, N. (2001). *Act your age! A cultural construction of adolescence*. New York: Routledge.

Maira, S., & Soep, E. (Eds.). (2005). *Youthscapes: The popular, the national, the global*. Philadelphia: University of Pennsylvania Press.

Manning, M. L. (2002). *Developmentally appropriate middle level schools* (2nd ed.). Olney, MD: Association of Childhood Education International.

Popkewitz, T. S. (1998). *Struggling for the soul: The politics of schooling and the construction of the teacher*. New York: Teachers College Press.

Popkewitz, T. S. (2008). *Cosmopolitanism and the age of school reform: Science, education, and making society by making the child*. New York: Routledge.

Popkewitz, T. S. (2010). The university as prophet, science as its messenger, and democracy as its revelation: John Dewey, University of Chicago President William Rainey Harper, and Colonel Francis Parker. In D. Tröhler, T. Schlag, & F. Osterwalder (Eds.), *Pragmatism and modernities* (pp. 99–122). Rotterdam: Sense Publishers.

Rajchman, J. (1997). *Constructions*. Cambridge, MA: MIT Press.

Rancière, J. (1983/2004). *The philosopher and his poor* (J. Drury, C. Oster, & A. Parker, Trans.). Durham, NC: Duke University Press.

Soja, E. (1989). *Postmodern geographies: The reassertion of space in critical social theory*. London:Verso.

Stone, L. (Ed.). (1994). *The education feminism reader*. New York: Routledge.

Todorov, T. (1982/1999). *The conquest of America: The question of the other* (R. Howard, Trans.). Norman, OK: University of Oklahoma Press and Copenhagen Business School.

Tröhler, D. (2009). Globalizing globalization: The neo-institutional concept of a world culture. In T. S. Popkewitz, & F. Rizvi (Eds.), *Globalization and the study of education. Yearbook of the National Society for the Study of Education* (Vol. 108, pp. 29–48). Chicago: National Society for the Study of Education.

Tröhler, D. (2011). *Languages of education: Protestant legacies in educationalization of the world, national identities, and global aspirations*. New York: Routledge.

Tröhler, D., Popkewitz, T., & Labaree, D. (2011). *Schooling and the making of citizens in the long nineteenth century: Comparative visions*. New York: Routledge.

8

COMMODIFICATION

Lisa Weems

Karl Marx (1976) introduced the term "commodity" to describe a good or service that "enters" the (capitalist) economic system. Marx distinguished between the "use value" of an object/good versus its "exchange value."[1] Whereas the use value of an object (e.g., a doll) is dependent on the costs associated with its production and distribution, its exchange value is variably influenced by the particular cultural desires and wishes (or fetish, if you will) associated with (owning) the object (doll). Hence, Marx utilized the terms commodification and commodity fetishism to characterize the complex dynamics of both subjectification and objectification in processes of "consumption" of goods and services in capitalist economies.

Subjectification occurs as the role of individual and cultural symbolic attachments to objects define the exchange value rather than the object's use value. In other words, the (mostly stable economic) use value of a commodity becomes simultaneously erased and overdetermined by sociocultural factors that are by definition relative. Keeping with the example of the doll, consider how the price of the object depends not only on its production costs, but also on the specific "markets" where the doll is targeted for sale (say New York City vs. rural China). Now imagine that doll is a replication of a New York Fire Department (NYFD) fireman; certainly residents of New York City have a different relationship with the object "NYFD doll."[2] The connotation of NYFD (in this case perhaps signifying U.S. national pride post–September 11, 2001) infuses the commodity with symbolic meaning and in turn shapes the exchange value of the doll. Thus, the doll becomes a commodity fetish, in that it not only relates to the physical use of the doll, but also to a child's semiotic associations of what the doll represents.

The process of objectification comes into play when the commodities in exchange are not material goods, but rather services, ideas, or other intangible products.[3] Thus, we might consider how the labor (today often done by youth) that goes into the production of the doll is also commodified as multinational corporations profit from global asymmetries in wages for workers. Marx worried that "man" would suffer from "alienation" as a result of having to exchange "his" labor in general, and that the working class was particularly susceptible to alienation as a result of the inequitable market values placed upon their labor.

European social theorists elaborated Marx's principle of commodity fetishism to outline a framework of commodity culture or what Adorno and Horkheimer referred to as "the culture industry." Adorno and Horkheimer (and others) applied Marx's notion of commodification to describe the burgeoning "mystifying" effects of mass media including newspapers, stage theater, film, and radio. These theorists (often grouped together as the Frankfurt School of critical theory) argued that authoritarian Nazi political and bourgeois economic interests were disseminated through the medium of mass culture, thus producing a citizenry that confused propaganda with education and entertainment with enlightenment.

Commodifying Youth Identities and Difference

Theorizing commodification took center stage among U.S., British, and French social theorists after World War II with attention to the disparate yet interrelated systems of knowledge production of popular and mass culture (Barthes, 1957; Bourdieu, 1984; Fiske, 1989; Johnson, 1956; Shiach, 1989; Williams, 1980). This scholarship analyzed how popular media (film, television, and advertising) became a key socializing agent in inventing and constructing individual and group identities. For example, Giroux (1999) analyzed the role of the commercialization of popular culture and its effects on youth. Giroux argued that the Disney corporation manufactures "youthful innocence" as an epistemological place of "magic" that stands outside of time/space and politics. Disney, according to Giroux, sells the nostalgia of youth innocence to both youth and adults in order to create Disney consumers. Furthermore, Giroux warned researchers and the public not to buy into the mystifying effects of corporate consumer culture that conflates representations of youth with the lives, conditions, and identities of actual youth.

Feminists and race scholars extended the concept of commodification of culture to analyze how specific elements of youth identities (such as race, ethnicity, gender, and sexuality) are highly mediated through the culture industry (Bernardi, 2009; Hall, 1997; hooks, 1996). Such scholars provided useful critiques of the commodification of youth culture by illustrating how art (Wallace & Dent, 1998), music (Forman & Neal, 2004; Kearney, 2006; McCarthy, Hudak, Miklaucic, & Saukko, 1999), and fashion (McRobbie, 1999) contributed to the fetishism of gender and multiculturalism. For example, DuCille (1994) illustrated how "Black Barbie" went through various transformations to attract an African American market. At first, the only difference between the "Black" and "White" Barbie was simply darkening the skin color. Then, as an attempt to represent a more "authentic" Black Barbie, marketers changed, exaggerated, and/or invented other racially coded markers of biological difference. Thus, "multicultural Barbie" illustrates the point that youth identities are not only commodified, but so too are the relationships between them. In effect, "difference" itself becomes a commodity on the marketplace for youth to produce and consume through objects of style (Black, 2009; Cameron, 2000). Yet, as Rand (1995) argues, cultural consumption among youth demonstrates how youth use these identities of difference to produce alternative and/or subversive readings such as "queering Barbie." These dynamic processes of identification imply that the commodification of identities (facilitated through the media) is neither a passive nor disempowering practice.

Global Youthscapes and the Commodification of Resistance

Within and among every society, youth participate in practices of cultural production and consumption, interpretation, and distribution (Johnson, Chambers, Raghuram, & Tincknell, 2004). However, transnational and feminist scholars have both critiqued and/or provided alternatives to Euro-American critical theorists' framework of commodification. These scholars are still interested in analyzing the "politics of culture," but argue that globalized capitalism and neocolonialism, as well as subjective processes of identification, require more nuanced understanding of the ways in which commodified culture is neither homogeneous nor universally produced and consumed.

Maira and Soep (2005) use the term "global youthscape" to describe a "site that is not just geographic or temporal, but social and political as well, as 'place' that is bound up with questions of power and materiality" (p. xv). Contemporary studies of youth and commodification illustrate how cultural productions are influenced by sociocultural, mediated forms of style and representation that take place inside, outside, and between national boundaries (Dolby & Rizvi, 2008; Livingstone & Drotner, 2008). These scholars investigate the symbiotic relationships between different translocal economic and political discourses on stratification, knowledge production, and practices of youth popular culture (Fernandes, 2003; Kachru, 2006; Maira, 2008). Although each context produces locally specific initiatives, a common thread is the recognition of the role of Western imperialism, colonization, and racial/ethnic struggles as interconnected to processes of "domestic" economic stratification (Lukose, 2008). Lukose's analysis of the "Miss Kerala" pageants in India and abroad illustrates how geographically specific forms of "Keralaness" are a function of marketing ethnic authenticity for the sake of creating a diasporic collective consciousness. Furthermore, gendered representations of beauty (traditional vs. modern) are strategically deployed and purposefully consumed as a tactic of resistance to Americanization.

Similarly, Inderpal Grewal (2005) illuminates how the production and consumption of "Indian Barbie" travels among and brokers real and imaginary transnational consumer subjectivities, which in turn allows for neoliberal recognition as "modern" youth in the global marketplace. According to Grewal, "Indian Barbie" both challenges and reinforces specific ideologies among differentiated audiences rather than having a totalizing effect of mystification on a mass population. As feminist transnational scholars argue, "Culture, understood in this way, constitutes a site in which the reproduction of contemporary capitalist social relations may be continually contested" (Lowe & Lloyd, 1997, p. 32). This suggests that the effects of commodification and consumerism (both symbolic and material) cannot be easily categorized as oppressive or empowering. Indeed, it is not uncommon for (some) youth to articulate and manipulate commodity fetishism and consumerism in ways that appear more politically savvy than economically alienated (Weems, 2009). Thus, specific analyses of particular youth-related cultural productions might allow for an appreciation of how youth negotiate their complicity in and resistance to the commodification of transnational youth culture.

Notes

1   "Youth" do not "enter" the discourse on commodification until after World War II as a result of two factors: (1) the institutionalization of the category of "adolescence" at the turn of the 20th century (Lesko, 2001); and (2) the construction of youth as a potential "market" via consumerism and advertising. Thus, because none of these early conceptions included explicit discussion of children or youth, my use of examples regarding contemporary youth in this section is somewhat anachronistic. Nonetheless, I use the example of the doll as a commodity fetish because it has been a central object in cultural studies of youth culture (DuCille, 1994; Grewal, 2005; Grigsby, 1999; Rand, 1995).

2   In addition, the subjective associations of the doll are also mediated by the NYC residents' situated relationship to the related signifiers in 9/11 and U.S. discourses of patriotism (Maira, 2008). I will explore the question of differentiated consumption later in this essay.

3   Examples of the objectification of "services" as part of the economy include music (Neal, 1999) and sex work (Weems, 2009). Examples of ideas that become commodified include identities (DuCille, 1994) and ideologies (Jhally, 2003).

References

Barthes, R. (1957). *Mythologies*. Paris: Éditions du Seuil.

Bernardi, D. (Ed.). (2009). *Filming difference: Actors, directors, producers, and writers on gender, race, and sexuality in film*. Austin: University of Texas Press.

Black, D. (2009). Wearing out racial discourse: Tokyo street fashion and race as style. *Journal of Popular Culture, 42*, 239–256.

Bourdieu, P. (1984). *Distinction: A social critique of the judgment of taste*. Cambridge, MA: Harvard University Press.

Cameron, D. (2000). Off-the-rack identities: Japanese street fashion magazines and the commodification of style. *Japanese Studies, 20*, 179–187.

Dolby, N., & Rizvi, F. (2008). *Youth moves: Identities and education in global perspective*. New York: Routledge.

DuCille, A. (1994). Dyes and dolls: Multicultural Barbie and the marketing of difference. *Differences, 6*, 46–68.

Fernandes, S. (2003). Island paradise, revolutionary utopia or hustler's haven? Consumerism and socialism in contemporary Cuban rap. *Journal of Latin American Cultural Studies, 12*, 359–375.

Fiske, J. (1989). *Understanding popular culture*. Boston: Unwin Hyman.

Forman, M., & Neal, M. A. (Eds.). (2004). *That's the joint! The hip-hop studies reader*. New York: Routledge.

Giroux, H. A. (1999). *The mouse that roared: Disney and the end of innocence*. Lanham, MD: Rowman & Littlefield.

Grewal, I. (2005). *Transnational America: Feminisms, diasporas, neoliberalisms*. Durham, NC: Duke University Press.

Grigsby, M. (1999). Sailormoon: Manga (comics) and anime (cartoon) superheroine meets Barbie: Global entertainment commodity comes to the United States. *Journal of Popular Culture, 32*, 59–80.

Hall, S. (1997). *Representation: Cultural representations and signifying practices*. London: Sage.

hooks, b. (1996). *Reel to real: Race, sex, and class at the movies*. New York: Routledge.

Jhally, S. (2003). *Wrestling with manhood: Boys, bullying and battering* (R. Ridberg, Producer). Northampton, MA: Media Education Foundation.

Johnson, J. R. (1956). *Television, how it works*. New York: J. F. Rider.

Johnson, R., Chambers, D., Raghuram, P., & Tincknell, E. (2004). *The practice of cultural studies*. London: Sage.

Kachru, Y. (2006). Mixers lyricizing Hinglish: Blending and fusion in Indian pop culture. *World Englishes, 25*, 223–233.

Kearney, M. C. (2006). *Girls make media*. New York: Routledge.

Lesko, N. (2001). *Act your age! A cultural construction of adolescence*. New York: Routledge.

Livingstone, S., & Drotner, K. (Eds.). (2008). *The international handbook of children, media and culture*. Los Angeles: Sage.

Lowe, L., & Lloyd, D. (Eds.). (1997). *The politics of culture in the shadow of capital*. Durham, NC: Duke University Press.

Lukose, R. (2008). *Children of liberalization: Youth agency and globalization in India*. New York: Routledge.

Maira, S. (2008). Flexible citizenship/flexible empire: South Asian youth in post-9/11 America. *American Quarterly, 60*, 697–720.

Maira, S., & Soep, E. (Eds.). (2005). *Youthscapes: The popular, the national, the global*. Philadelphia: University of Pennsylvania Press.

Marx, K. (1976). *Capital: A critique of political economy*. New York: Vintage Books.

McCarthy, C., Hudak, G., Miklaucic, S., & Saukko, P. (Eds.). (1999). *Sound identities: Popular music and the cultural politics of education*. New York: Peter Lang.

McRobbie, A. (1999). *In the culture society: Art, fashion, and popular music*. London: Routledge.

Neal, M. A. (1999). *What the music said: Black popular music and Black public culture*. New York: Routledge.

Rand, E. (1995). *Barbie's queer accessories*. Durham, NC: Duke University Press.

Shiach, M. (1989). *Discourse on popular culture: Class, gender and history in cultural analysis, 1730 to the present*. Stanford, CA: Stanford University Press.

Wallace, M., & Dent, G. (Eds.). (1998). *Black popular culture*. New York: The New Press.

Weems, L. (2009). M.I.A. in the global youthscape: Rethinking girls' resistance and agency in postcolonial contexts. *Journal of Girlhood Studies, 2*(2), 55–75.

Williams, R. (1980). *Problems in materialism and culture*. London: Verso.

9

CULTURE

Mikko Salasuo and Tommi Hoikkala

We begin with a scene to frame our discussion of youth and culture: A gangsta rapper from northern Finland dresses up like his New York kinsman but draws his lyrics from his own cultural sphere. His interpretation scheme resembles that of his role model on the other side of the Atlantic but he uses a very different knowledge reserve as his raw material. Certainly, the northern Finnish rapper's knowledge reserve has "shifted" in a global direction through the impact of the virtual world and has led to a new socialization influenced by information technology. His context, the physical surroundings, is given and different from that of the streets of New York. The Finnish rapper represents, in all likelihood, the middle class of the Nordic welfare state and his ethnic origin is that of the majority of the population.

Notions of "youth" and "culture" are usually interconnected in two ways. In colloquial language, "youth culture" refers to youth phenomena arisen at the end of the 1950s/beginning of the 1960s, such as hippie, punk, heavy, and techno cultures. From an academic viewpoint, the link between "youth" and "culture" dates from the Chicago School of (urban) sociology in the 1920s when sociologists became interested in youth phenomena within urban cultures and in gangs, in particular. Thrasher (1927) was the first to note the social structures of youth gangs and the influence of physical surroundings. His *The Gang* provided a basis for a new generation of youth research. Thrasher defined gangs by the process they go through to form a group:

The gang is an interstitial group originally formed spontaneously, and then integrated through conflict. It is characterized by the following types of behavior: meeting face to face, milling, movement through space as a unit, conflict, and planning. The result of this collective behavior is the development of tradition, unreflective internal structure, esprit de corps, solidarity, morale, group awareness, and attachment to a local territory.

(p. 46)

Whyte's *Street Corner Society* (1943) and Hollingshead's *Elmtown's Youth* (1949) carried on the new approach in youth culture research. Hollingshead's key argument was that

adolescent behaviour is a type of transitional behaviour which is dependent upon the society, and more particularly upon the position the individual occupies in the social structure, rather than upon the bio-psychological phenomena connected with this age, such as puberty, or the assumed psycho-organic conditions variously referred to as drives, urges, and tensions in psychological, educational, and lay use.

(p. 7)

The first systematic theorization of youth (sub)cultures was Cohen's *Delinquent Boys: The Culture of the Gang* (1955), which defined subculture as a distinctive culture within a culture. Hebdige (1993) later wrote that Cohen "sought to supply the missing theoretical perspective by tracing the continuities and breaks between dominant and subordinate value systems" (p. 443).

The Birmingham Centre for Contemporary Cultural Studies, established in 1964, followed the approach of the Chicago School and Cohen. Through its studies, notions of subculture, youth culture, and popular culture reached a wider audience (Schulman, 1993) and is still influential in youth culture research. The Birmingham School's theoretical framework enables us to understand, for example, the Finnish gangsta rapper's communal and symbolic engagements with the larger system of late industrial culture, or what he expresses in his creation of a certain style.

Since the early 1980s, several postmodern research approaches have arisen, such as postsubcultural studies. Postsubcultural studies explore changing relationships between youth cultural tastes, politics, and music in today's postmodern world: "how we could retheorize and conceptualize youth (sub)cultural phenomena of shifting social terrain of the new millennium, where global mainstreams and local substreams are rearticulated and reconstructed in complex and uneven ways to produce new, hybrid cultural constellation" (Weinzierl & Muggleton, 2003, p. 1). The Birmingham legacy of subcultural studies is still fruitful when approaching individual youth groups tied together by, for example, a certain style. On the other hand, when the viewpoint widens to more collective, and diffuse, levels, postsubcultural studies offer a useful starting point. We find it problematic, however, that researchers often adopt these approaches without question. The notions of "youth" and "culture" are, as if spontaneously, combined to form a functional group, subculture, that is separate from the rest of the society.

In this essay, we wish to bring back to discussion the fact that cultural definitions used in youth studies often originate from philosophical discussions. We have chosen a perspective that applies Jürgen Habermas's (1984, 1987) definition of culture, leading us to examine youth and culture from a slightly unusual viewpoint in which culture is conceptualized as a product of an individual's knowledge reserve and interpretation scheme. We do not aim to suggest a competing point of view to subcultural studies, but rather to inspire deliberation and search for new approaches to the notion of culture in order to understand more fully the diversity of youth's lives.

Culture as Knowledge Reserve

Youth researchers like us, drawing extensively on social sciences (Hoikkala & Suurpää, 2005), understand culture as a knowledge reserve (Habermas, 1984, 1987). Communicative actors rely on it to obtain an interpretation scheme when trying to agree on an issue in the world. Researchers ask how culture, or a knowledge reserve, has been generated and distributed to different individuals at different times and what kind of interpretation scheme it creates (e.g., Cohen, 1955; Giddens, 1991; Hollingshead, 1949; Mannheim, 1952 [1927]; Musgrove, 1965; Thrasher, 1927; Weinzierl & Muggleton, 2003; Whyte, 1943; Willis, 1978; Ziehe, 1978).

Habermas (1984) uses the term *Lebenswelt* to refer to the sum total of all immediate phenomena which constitute the world of an individual or of a life-world. The elements of the life-world are culture, personality, and society. Meanings are conveyed through the process of linguistic communication. Individuals need to have a consensus on meanings in order to understand each other and to function in the same culture.

When freely interpreting Habermas (1984), one can define youth cultures as knowledge reserves and their various interpretation schemes. This way, a given local youth culture refers to a group of young people drawing on a shared knowledge reserve but interpreting the world through an interpretation scheme generated by the group's specific physical context (see Geertz, 1973). The rapid change of contemporary culture, particularly with processes of globalization, challenges not only shared national or generational interpretation schemes but also actual knowledge reserves. According to Habermas (1984), modernization challenges processes of cultural renewal and interferes with them. These interferences are the disappearance of legitimation, collective identity crisis, and the breakdown of traditions. Globalization and information technology enable a new distribution of young people's shared interpretation schemes. As old elements "leak out" from the shared national knowledge reserve, youth "fill it in" with new contents. Although the rapper from northern Finland has been socialized to knowledge reserves in Finnish society, the first generation of Finnish rappers from the 1980s does not share the same knowledge reserves or interpretation schemes. Even though they appear to be members of the same cultural group, they do not necessarily emphasize the same symbols, meanings, or even music. The knowledge reserve of the older generation has the roots of its meanings linked to actual street life and the younger ones fill their knowledge reserves from the internet-mediated global sphere. This is what Bennett (2000) means by glocalization: how individuals reshape existing social and economic limitations and create something else, something meaningful—culture (see Lalander & Salasuo, 2005).

Generations and Culture

We can understand the diverging meanings of culture of different generations by applying Habermas's (1984) notion of culture. Habermas (1984), Mead (1967), and Mannheim (1952 [1927]) have all written on the transfer of cultural heritage. Mannheim (1952 [1927]) suggests that the relationship of new generations to cultural heritage is created by "fresh contact." According to Habermas, new generations always create a fresh relationship to the knowledge reserve and its emerging interpretation scheme. In this way, new generations both renew the old culture and shape a new one. Modernization and rapid change challenge the conception of culture of different generations.

In contemporary culture, the knowledge reserve has quickly shifted in a new direction. Older generations do not automatically possess the new interpretation scheme required by the new knowledge reserve. Meanwhile, "Young people wander information networks, urban environments and consumer culture as much as fish wander water" (Hoikkala & Paju, 2008, p. 287). Young generations, or the internet generations, have grown into a landscape and structure characterized by a media explosion which has closely followed the triumph of consumer culture. The example of the northern Finnish gangster rapper illustrates the change in knowledge reserve and interpretation schemes that has taken place between generations. For example, many people born in the 1940s or earlier have found it difficult to understand subcultures as a phenomenon. In their youth, most were socialized to the values and conventions of agrarian society, where there was limited space for self-expression. In their generation's knowledge reserve, there simply is no place for a phenomenon such as rap, so their interpretation schemes label 1980s rap music a ridiculous imitation of American street culture that at times can also appear frightening and threatening. Such rapid change resulting in an unfamiliar knowledge reserve can lead to uncertainty concerning social order. An increasing response to this has been monitoring and control of youth, such as camera surveillance and numerous prohibitions. One way to understand youth culture and to narrow cultural gaps between generations is to try to accumulate knowledge reserves and, thus, to uncover a shared interpretation scheme.

Now, Anything New on Culture?

It is premature to estimate whether the accelerating modernization started in the 1990s constitutes a turning point in the passing on of cultural heritage. The 1960s youth rebellion saw a similar collision of knowledge reserve and interpretation schemes that led to a process where different generations had to accept the fact that culture is not a monolith. In 2010, we again live at a time that requires a fundamental resetting of our knowledge reserve and our interpretation scheme. Ignoring this will leave us longing for the past culture and losing touch with the present one.

Can we social scientists understand the multiplicity of today's youth culture by using "old tools," such as classic cultural theories of the Birmingham School or even postsubcultural studies? Or should we rather go back to the starting point of the Chicago School? Bringing back the Chicago School's methodology would mean a new wave of ethnographic studies followed by serious analytical procedures and rethinking the social dynamics of contemporary youth.

Instead of circulating and mixing ideas created to understand youth cultures and subcultures of the modern era, we could try to create theories that have explanatory strength for contemporary youth cultures that seem to have atomized to millions of individual knowledge reserves and interpretation schemes. Simon During (1993) writes,

> Subcultures cobble together (or hybridize) styles out of the images and material culture available to them in the effort to construct identities which will confer on them "relative autonomy" within a social order fractured by class, generational differences, work etc.
>
> (p. 441)

This comes back to our main point about shifting analysis from the (sub)cultural group to multiple processes. What actually are the images and material culture available (knowledge reserves) and through what kind of interpretation schemes do youth "read" them to construct identities within social orders fractured by new information technology, generational difference, socioeconomical polarization, globalization, glocalization, neo-liberalism, multiculturalism, consumerism, and so on? How is culture seen and created by a gangsta rapper from northern Finland living in a world of continuously transforming knowledge reserves and reshaping interpretation schemes?

References

Bennett, A. (2000). *Popular music and youth culture: Music, identity and place*. New York: Palgrave Macmillan.
Cohen, A. (1955). *Delinquent boys: The culture of the gang*. New York: Collier/Macmillan.
During, S. (1993). Editors' introduction [to Dick Hebdige]. In S. During (Ed.), *The cultural studies reader* (p. 441). New York: Routledge.
Geertz, C. (1973). *The interpretation of cultures: Selected essays*. New York: Basic Books.
Giddens, A. (1991). *Modernity and self-identity: Self and society in the late modern age*. Cambridge: Polity Press.
Habermas, J. (1984). *The theory of communicative action. Volume 1: Reason and the rationalisation of society*. Boston: Beacon Press.
Habermas, J. (1987). *The theory of communicative action. Volume 2: System and lifeworld: A critique of functionalist reason*. Boston: Beacon Press.
Hebdige, D. (1993). The function of subculture. In S. During (Ed.), *The cultural studies reader* (pp. 441–450). New York: Routledge.
Hoikkala, T., & Paju, P. (2008). Entä nuoremmat sukupolvet? Sukupolvitutkimus ja nuoriso-politiikka [What about the Younger Generations?]. In S. Purhonen, T. Hoikkala, & J. P. Roos (Eds.), *Kenen sukupolveen kuulut? Suurten ikäluokkien tarina* (pp. 270–295). Helsinki: Gaudeamus.

Hoikkala, T., & Suurpää, L. (2005). Finnish youth cultural research and its relevance to youth policy. *Young Nordic Journal of Youth Research, 13*, 285–312.

Hollingshead, A. (1949). *Elmtown's youth: The impact of social classes on adolescents.* New York: John Wiley & Sons.

Lalander, P., & Salasuo, M. (2005). Problems of credibility. In P. Lalander, & M. Salasuo (Eds.), *Drugs & youth culture: Global and local expressions* (pp. 5–12). Helsinki: Hakapaino.

Mannheim, K. (1952 [1927]). The problem of generations. In P. Kecskemeti (Ed.), *Essays on the sociology of knowledge: By Karl Mannheim* (pp. 267–320). London: Routledge & Kegan Paul.

Mead, M. (1967). *The changing cultural patterns of work and leisure.* Washington, DC: U.S. Department of Labor, Manpower Administration.

Musgrove, F. (1965). *Youth and the social order.* Bloomington: Indiana University Press.

Schulman, N. (1993). Conditions of their own making: An intellectual history of the Centre for Contemporary Cultural Studies at the University of Birmingham. *Canadian Journal of Communication, 18*, 51–73.

Thrasher, F. (1927). *The gang: A study of 1313 gangs in Chicago.* Chicago: University of Chicago Press.

Weinzierl, R., & Muggleton, R. (Eds.). (2003). *The post-subcultures reader.* Oxford: Berg.

Whyte, W. (1943). *Street corner society: The social structure of an Italian slum.* Chicago: University of Chicago Press.

Willis, P. (1978). *Profane culture.* London: Routledge & Kegan Paul.

Ziehe, T. (1978). *Pubertät und narzissmus. Sind Jugendliche entpolitisiert?* Frankfurt am Main: EVA.

10

ETHNOGRAPHY

Wanda S. Pillow

Ethnography has been central as a social science research method since the early 20th century. Based upon observation and interviews in the field, whether a street, school classroom, or factory line, ethnographers provide thickly written descriptions and interpretations of culture (Geertz, 1973). First ethnographies read like travel narratives depicting foreign lands, peoples, and customs. While these early works were complicit with a colonial gaze directed toward "the other," ethnography as a way of knowing remains significant in the fields of anthropology, education, and sociology and has played an integral role in the development of youth studies.

Ethnography is particularly suited to address questions across the inter-disciplinary arena of youth studies: How do youth construct identities through media? How do youth define civic engagement? How do youth understand race/ethnicity/nationhood? Ethnography has contributed to a vocabulary of youth studies, mapping out meanings and understandings and shaping definitions of youth and youth cultures. This essay explores three major "moments"[1] in youth studies ethnography and considers where ethnography and youth may be mobilized in the future.

Moment I: Mapping Corner Boys and Subcultures

The emergence of youth studies was tied to a growing interest in urban research and influenced by "Chicago School" new sociology in the 1920s and 1930s. Contrary to prevalent beliefs that human behavior was driven by genetic or individual personality characteristics, Chicago School scholars theorized that environment played a major role in shaping human behavior. Thus, social problems such as criminal behavior or homelessness could best be addressed by studying the environments in which these conditions existed. Ethnography, with its focus on analyzing culture in natural settings, was key to this new movement, yielding now classic ethnographies like William Foote Whyte's (1981/1943) *Street Corner Society*, an in-depth portrait of an impoverished Boston Italian American neighborhood.

Ethnographic work like Whyte's created rich portraits of differential experiences within the same city detailing the culture of "corner boys," "gangs," or "race men" (Drake & Cayton, 1945; Hollingshead, 1949). This work influenced thinking about "subcultures," a group sharing common characteristics existing on the margins of normative dominant culture, and by the 1970s researchers in the United States and the United Kingdom applied this lens of analysis to youth. Paul Willis's (1977) groundbreaking study of working-class youth set the stage for research that followed by emphasizing the need to study and understand youth culture: its location; its difference from adult cultures; and its economic, educational, and political structures. Willis demonstrated "how working-class kids get working-class jobs," highlighting public school's role in class reproduction. Willis rearticulated theories of agency and resistance, arguing that the forms of resistance the "lads" engaged in reinforced structures that led to factory work. Willis notes, "When the lad reaches the factory there is not shock, only recognition" (p. 193).

Willis's ethnography highlighted the need for and potential of youth studies research and established youth as a viable subculture of study. Research locations expanded to include both formal (school, church, work) and informal settings (streets, parks, recreational facilities) as ethnographers explored where and how to observe and understand youth.

Moment II: Mapping Multiple Youth Identities

Initial ethnographies of youth formed a vocabulary of youth subcultures but at the same time these foundations were questioned for their dependency and taken-for-granted focus on males and whiteness, which placed the lives of girls and racial minority youth as either on the periphery or absent (McRobbie &

Garber, 1977). In response, "girl studies" formed, specifically tracing and identifying how girls create and experience identities, relationships, aspirations, and so on (Campbell, 1984; Griffin, 1985; Harris, 2004; Hey, 1987; Lee, 1986; Lesko, 1995; McRobbie, 1976; Tolman, 2002; Walkerdine, 1990). These works filled previous absences, identified the unique regulation of girls' identities, specifically around issues of gender roles, sexuality, and desire, and began to map how girls take up and resist such regularities.

Additional focus on how youth negotiate race (Jones, 1988; Valenzuela, 1999) as well as sexuality (Mac an Ghaill, 1988) provided new conceptualizations of youth and debates about agency and resistance. These ethnographies significantly impacted youth studies and ethnography by expanding locations and methods of research; challenging existing characterizations of youth; working against deviancy and social deficit models; continuing to demonstrate regulatory and reproductive roles of institutions like schools; and raising questions of power in research relationships and representations (Fine, 1991; Pillow, 2004; Weis, 2000).

These expansions raised challenges for youth studies and ethnography. For example, as ethnographers moved into "girl" spaces—bathrooms, bedrooms, diaries—questions rose over who should study girls' culture. Are female ethnographers best suited for this work? Can a male ethnographer gain access to and understand girls' culture? Similar questions arose over the study of youth sexual and race subcultures and led to increased reflexivity about the "politics of the ethnographic gaze" and how representations are produced (Pillow, 2003). Concurrently, the limits of identifying youth subcultures via adult presupposed categories of male/female, White/Black, hetero/homosexual were exposed. While these categories remain in use, ethnographers confronted with shifting behaviors and discourses of youth ask, what might be missing or masked by assuming and looking for identities based on certain traits?

Moment III: Remapping Youth Cultures

The challenges of studying youth have remapped conceptualizations of youth from fixed to fluid and hybrid. As Harris (2004) states, "The category of 'girl' is constantly being constructed and deconstructed" (p. xxiv). This understanding yields ethnographies that resist binary categories and acknowledge the multiplicity of identities that youth (re)constitute in shifting discursive clusters across gender and masculinities (Lesko, 2000; Mac an Ghaill, 1997), race, gender, and globalization (Nayak, 2003; Taft, 2010), and sexualities (Gilbert, 2006; Hackford-Peer, 2010; Mayo, 2004). Additionally, technological advancements and creation of online communities, like Facebook, situate youth as "active agents who participate, albeit unequally, in the global economy. They are cultural innovators and consumers involved in a complex negotiation with social transformations" (Nayak, 2003, p. 4).

Youth culture can no longer be simply located or theorized in one place as lines between identity categories and formal and informal settings are blurred.

Despite a turn to analytical lenses and research that speak to hybridity and mobility, some ethnographers have noted a trend restricting ethnographic access to youth, particularly around "sensitive" research issues like sexuality (Kendall, 2010). At present, Institutional Review Board (IRB) approval, necessary for all human subjects research, does not have guidelines to address methodological questions and ethnical concerns about doing research in the "new" places youth culture occupies. Such trends and gaps may limit what gets studied and whom researchers have access to and how.

"Reality" Ethnography

As youth cultures are (re)made and ethnography faces complications of being similarly mobile, reality television, which increasingly depicts youth culture, raises interesting comparisons. Like ethnographies, reality television purports to provide in-depth access to subjects in natural settings (or a "natural" setting invented by the show producers) using similar methods as ethnography: observations, interviews, and subject self-representations through video or other forms of expression. Certainly the merits of these programs are debatable. They often portray stereotypical depictions and employ voyeuristic viewing models that situate certain youth as spectacle. Like ethnographies, voices and representations of subjects are *always* mediated by the author/producer. However, unlike ethnographies, which are explicit about methods, ethics, and constructions of representations, reality shows are silent on these issues and are clearly about entertainment.

For example, *Teen Mom* is a highly popular show documenting the lives of mothering teen girls (Freeman & Gateley, 2010; Naduad, 2010). Each show follows a documentary format featuring six girls; each girl has a self-narrated, 1-hour episode tracing her experiences. "The goal was for them to tell their own stories, to narrate their lives and their feelings in a way that felt organic," says producer Morgan J. Freeman (as cited in Benfer, 2009). *Teen Mom* utilizes techniques familiar in youth studies research, placing audio and video tools in the hands of subjects to record thoughts. The girls were given small flip cameras they could use as "video diaries" to talk about their feelings in private whenever they liked. Some of the show's most revealing scenes were captured on these small cameras.

Watching *Teen Mom* it is easy to get swept up in the narratives and feel you are really getting inside each girl's life. However, the methods of the show, while seemingly "organic," are highly stylized, edited for dramatic intent, and perpetuate images of teen mothers as either victims or bad girls. While ethnography would critically engage and place representations in larger social contexts, *Teen Mom* focuses on individual or family dramas, allowing the viewer to disengage from any role except one of voyeur.

Yet, I also wonder if reality television has taken us where IRB and ethnography have been slow to go. I am interested in the possibilities and perhaps necessity to view reality television as a new ethnographic landscape, not as places of the "real" but as examples of shifting, mass mediated spaces to see and understand constructions of youth. Reality shows' popularity is not limited to viewing;

discussion boards, blogs, and fan pages offer complex locations to engage with and identify how youth cultures are understood and (re)constructed. Herein lies the trial for youth ethnography: can ethnography find and follow the movement and hybridity of youth cultures? Can ethnographic methods work in these new research landscapes and what ethical and methodological questions will arise?

Ethnography as a method of understanding continues to provide opportunity for key insights into youth studies at the same time that youth studies ethnography pushes the limits of ethnographic practices. As constructions of "youth" and sites of youth cultures continue to evolve, shift, and resist, challenges remain for the adult ethnographer to trace the mobility of youth culture and to practice ethnography that is equally mobile while remaining attuned to questions of power and ethics.

Note

1 Denzin and Lincoln (2005) identify "eight moments" of research. Each contains shifts in thinking about voice, validity, subjectivity, reflexivity, representation, ethics, and roles and relationships between researcher and researched.

References

Benfer, A. (2009, July 23). *I actually was 16 and pregnant*. Retrieved from http://www.salon.com/life/feature/2009/07/23/16_pregnant

Campbell, A. (1984). *The girls in the gang*. Oxford: Blackwell.

Denzin, N., & Lincoln, Y. S. (Eds.). (2005). *The Sage handbook of qualitative research*. Thousand Oaks, CA: Sage.

Drake, S. F., & Cayton, H. R. (1945). *Black metropolis*. New York: Harcourt Brace.

Fine, M. (1991). *Framing dropouts: Notes on the politics of an urban high school*. Albany, NY: SUNY Press.

Freeman, M. J., & Gateley, L. (Producers). (2010). *Teen mom* [Television series]. Hollywood: MTV.

Geertz, C. (1973). *The interpretation of cultures*. New York: Basic Books.

Gilbert, J. (2006). Imagining sex. *Journal of Curriculum and Pedagogy, 3*, 38–42.

Griffin, C. (1985). *Typical girls*. London: Routledge.

Hackford-Peer, K. (2010). *Mentoring the imagination: Lesbian, gay, bisexual, transgender, queer and questioning youth engaging and expanding mentoring in Utah*. Salt Lake City: University of Utah Press.

Harris, A. (Ed.). (2004). *All about the girl*. New York: Routledge.

Hey, V. (1987). *The company she keeps: An ethnography of girls' friendship*. Buckingham: Open University Press.

Hollingshead, A. B. (1949). *Elmtown's youth*. New York: Wiley.

Jones, S. (1988). *Black culture, white youth: The reggae tradition from JA to UK*. Basingstoke: Macmillan.

Kendall, N. (2010). *The dilemmas of doing sex research in schools*. Paper presented at annual meeting of the American Educational Studies Association. Denver, CO.

Lee, S. (1986). *Losing out: Sexuality and adolescent girls*. London: Hutchinson.

Lesko, N. (1995). The "leaky needs" of school-aged mothers: An examination of US programs and policies. *Curriculum Inquiry, 25*, 25–40.

Lesko, N. (Ed.). (2000). *Masculinities at school*. Thousand Oaks, CA: Sage.

Mac an Ghaill, M. (1988). *Young, gifted, and black*. Milton Keynes: Open University Press.

Mac an Ghaill, M. (1997). *The making of men: Masculinities, sexualities and schooling*. Milton Keynes: Open University Press.

Mayo, C. (2004). *Disputing the subject of sex: Sexuality and public school controversies.* Lanham, MD: Rowan & Littlefield.

McRobbie, A. (1976). *Feminism and youth culture: From Jackie to Just Seventeen.* London: Macmillan.

McRobbie, A., & Garber, J. (1977). Girls and subcultures: An exploration. In S. Hall, & T. Jefferson (Eds.), *Resistance through rituals* (pp. 208–222). London: Hutchinson Centre for Contemporary Cultural Studies, University of Birmingham.

Naduad, A. (2010, December 23). "Teen Mom" helps give MTV biggest ratings gain in a decade—More to come. Retrieved from http://www.examiner.com/mtv-in-national/teen-mom-helps-give-mtv-biggest-ratings-gain-a-decade-more-to-come

Nayak, A. (2003). *Race, place and globalization: Youth culture in a changing world.* Oxford: Berg.

Pillow, W. S. (2003). Confession, catharsis, or cure: The use of reflexivity as methodological power in qualitative research. *International Journal of Qualitative Studies in Education, 16,* 175–196.

Pillow, W. S. (2004). *Unfit bodies: Educational policy and the teen mother.* New York: Routledge.

Taft, J. (2010). *Rebel girls: Youth activism and social change across the Americas.* New York: New York University Press.

Tolman, D. L. (2002). *Dilemmas of desire: Teenage girls talk about sexuality.* Cambridge, MA: Harvard University Press.

Valenzuela, A. (1999). *Subtractive schooling: U.S. Mexican youth and the politics of caring.* Albany, NY: SUNY.

Walkerdine, V. (1990). *Schoolgirl fictions.* London: Verso.

Weis, L. (2000). Race and gender work in an urban magnet school. *Teachers College Record, 102,* 620–650.

Whyte, W. F. (1981/1943). *Street corner society: The social structure of an Italian slum.* Chicago: University of Chicago Press.

Willis, P. (1977). *Learning to labour.* London: Saxon House.

11

HISTORIES

Andrew J. Reisinger

History is a capacious term used to denote all things past, narratives and chronological orderings describing the past, inquiries leading to some sort of knowledge, and the specialized area of study that takes the past as its subject (Oxford English Dictionary Online, n.d., para. 1, 4, 7). Thus, it makes sense to conceive of historical renderings as "histories" when identifying and imagining the many things that histories have been, are, and can be. Histories can be epistemologies, means by which to form and maintain identities, methods of explanation, and tools for asserting truth claims. They can be stories, imaginings, and forms of entertainment; cautionary devices forewarning people to avoid certain ways of thinking and acting; fonts of inspiration spurring people to clamor for change; teleologies explaining the past and signposting the present and future; catalogs, archives, and systems of organization that can simplify and complicate understandings of the present; commemorations of what came before; well-springs for nostalgia and disgust; and heralds announcing what is present. In regard to youth, histories are of critical importance in that, depending on the historian's perspective, they can explain the ways "youth" as a life stage and identity came into being, the ways adult experts and laypersons have thought of and regulated young persons over time, the roles youth have played in their own constitution, and the historical forces that affect what youth can be at particular times, among other things.

Before turning attention to histories of youth, it is useful to chart the general direction of Western historical studies over time because the history of youth has in many ways paralleled this larger trajectory. Williams recounts that the word "history" came into the English language from the French "histoire," which derived from the Latin "historia" and the earlier Greek "istoria," which connoted an inquiry and the resulting creation of knowledge. Until the 15th century, this notion of history was applied to accounts professedly true *or* fictitious. Although the term continued to convey the idea of "organized knowledge of the past," Williams points out that beginning in the 18th century, and part and parcel of Enlightenment philosophy, it also came to stand for a *process* of "human self-development" that encapsulates past, present, and future. Here the term becomes linear, teleological, and future oriented in that it discerns an historical trajectory, often conceived as independent of human action, that explains and forecasts how human history unfolds in a certain direction and according to a specific logic (Schwarz, 2005, p. 157; Williams, 1983, pp. 146–147).

History took on yet other permutations in the 19th century, driven largely by the forces of Romanticism and professionalization. Beginning in Germany and quickly ascending throughout the West, a movement called historicism demanded recognition of "the autonomy of the past." Historicists asserted that any study of history must approach its subject impartially without imposing contemporary understandings, knowledge, and values onto the past; moreover, historians must recognize that the past is fundamentally different from the present, that historical context is crucial for accurately understanding any historical phenomenon, and that history is an aggregative and relational process allowing one to discern continuity and change over time (Tosh, 2002, pp. 6–12). Incorporating many of the historicists' dictates, the study of history became thematically and temporally precise and professionalized in the second half of the 19th century. Despite these progressive developments, most historical inquiry remained concerned with "significant events" like the history of "kings and armies, nation building, the doings of geniuses, international conflicts, and creation of great works of art." Historians generally overlooked youth as a subject worthy of attention. Indeed, the idea of youth and adolescence as a distinct life stage did not exist until the late 19th and early 20th centuries when emergent social science brought it into being.[1]

Beginning in the 1960s and in response to the limited perspective of most historians, a new generation influenced by the era's social movements demanded a new type of history, "history from the bottom up," or the new social history. These histories focused on the up-until-then-ignored "ordinary people" of the past, including, among others, workers, women, racial and ethnic "minorities," gay and lesbian people, and youth (Appleby, 2005, pp. 2–3, 137–139; Schwarz, 2005, pp. 157–158).

Reflecting on this development, Gillis recounts how "youth" did not become a subject of historical investigation until the 1960s when the youthful generation of the era challenged hegemonic political, social, and cultural structures of their societies, thus forcing a recognition of "youth" and their ability to act on the world, rather than just being acted upon. He claims that, from the dawn of the 20th century and into the 1960s, a facile, ahistorical idea of youth, propagated by objectivist sociologists, psychologists, and anthropologists, dominated thinking about youth and their history. From these expert perspectives, youth or adolescence comprised a distinct and critical life stage bridging childhood and adulthood wherein the subject transitions from the innocence of childhood and security of the family to responsibilities and restrictions imposed by adulthood, marriage, and career. He asserts that this universalizing theory of youth failed to take into account the ways that youth identity was shaped by "the values of the class, gender, and ethnic cultures of which they were a part." He states, "[Y]outh's role was defined for it. The plurality of youth cultures, and the history thereof, was ignored. Deprived of a past, youth became the prisoner of the present, subject to those agencies that claimed the young as their clients." But by the 1960s, youth refused narrow definition, as witnessed by the era's youth upheavals (and other social struggles) (Gillis, 1981, pp. 211–217). One can discern at this juncture how history responds to social change both in terms of its method and content, in large measure because many of the historians undertaking the study of youth themselves identified generationally with their subject.

The study of youth thus burgeoned within the heady days of the new social history. Building on Aries' foundational work, which argued for the social construction of childhood (as distinct from a notion of a timeless, universal, and uniform childhood) (1962, pp. 47, 128–133), scholars like Gillis and Springhall turned their attention to the ideological expectations of youth as instituted through the home, schools, and youth organizations overseen by adults as well as to the social groups and movements controlled exclusively by young people in Europe and the United States. Here the intellectual framework for investigating the history of youth centered largely on questions of how youth were acted upon by society as well as the neglected question of how youth acted to influence society. These histories took care to provide class, ethnic, racial, and (to a lesser extent) gender contextualization; they sought to situate youth within the wider economic, demographic, and political settings in which these histories unfolded—critical contexts ignored by most historians up until this time. This new youth history was a departure from earlier histories in that it emphasized young people's agency and the discontinuity and heterogeneity of youth cultures over time. Still, Gillis noted in 1981 that further work integrating the study of youth with that of gender, sexuality, and locality remained necessary. With an air of gloom, he also presciently observed that the vogue for studying the history of youth or of "age relations," more generally, seemed to be passing, a supposition confirmed by Hawes and Hiner who express concern over the field of youth history's idleness during the past few decades (Gillis, 1981, pp. ix–xii, 217–230; Hawes & Hiner, 2005, pp. 23–29; Springhall, 1977, pp. 13–19, 121–126).

Beginning in the 1970s and accelerating through the 1990s, while histories devoted to the study of youth diminished, another wave of historical inquiry further pluralized the concept of history. Employing theoretical perspectives subsequently encapsulated by the term postmodernism, researchers challenged

> the objectivity of Western science, the stability of language, and the credibility of the individual consciousness, maintaining instead that objectivity was but a convenient fiction of Western culture, language a slippery medium of communication, and the heroic self a socially constructed "subject."
>
> (Appleby, 2005, p. 13)

Postmodern historians continued the social history project of bringing previously neglected histories to the fore. But these investigators parted company with the well-established dictate of history to objectively "recreate the past" and represent its different perspectives and meanings accurately; rather, given their recognition of the implausibility of objectivity and the inseparability of a questioner's personal perspective from the subject under investigation, their aim centered on engaging with the past on the terms of the present (Appleby, 2005, pp. 13–14).

Despite the apparent malaise within the field of youth history, much has been written about the history of youth in the last few decades; however, it is often subsumed within other fields of historical scholarship, notably within histories of social movements, countercultures, schooling, family, childhood, and juvenile justice. These more recent histories simultaneously recapitulate and complicate the ways in which youth identities are socially constructed and regulated by adults, yet they also open new vistas into understanding the history of youth by privileging the perspectives of youth, demonstrating the influence on and allure of youth cultures to older generations, foregrounding the ways in which youth contributes to and creates ideologies, and indicating the dynamic, reciprocal, and often cooperative encounters between youth and adults.[2] A further trend noted by Fass draws attention to how historians of children and youth contribute to the larger postmodern project of "disassembling [the notion] of a coherent life" (2010, p. 161). She points to the ways in which historians of childhood and youth contribute to the intellectual assault on Enlightenment conceptions of a unified self that is static over time, or that teleologically progresses from childhood and youth into coherent, stable, and rational adulthood.

As a whole, the history of youth has in many ways paralleled the larger trajectory of historical studies. If one looks for historical accounts specifically about youth prior to the 1960s, one is hard-pressed to locate anything substantive because history up until this time largely remained the domain of "great men" and "significant" events in national histories; youth were generally absent. However, with the advent of the new social and post-modern histories, previously "hidden" histories of youth received attention from professional historians, and the concept of a history that accounted for everything in the past fractured into the pluralized notion of histories that recognize the multiplicity of perspectives through which one can create knowledge and meaning from the past. Yet despite the emergence of "youth history" as a specialized field, the scholarship has remained stuck in several regards. First, much of the histories of youth still tend to have a populational focus on specific youth classes, subcultures, and gendered experiences. Youth too often are pigeonholed into specific roles as students, workers, children of parents, future citizens, consumers, delinquents, activists, and "the hope for the future" without recognizing the intersections among these identities or imagining alternative ways to make sense of youthful being. Second, histories tend to be extremely place-based, specifically through nation-centered studies of youth. Third, these histories contribute to ghettoizing youth by separating them from other age cohorts with which they coexist and by privileging the perspectives of adults rather than the voices of youth. Fourth, the history of youth remains conflated with the history of childhood, so much so that it is hard to discern what, if anything, makes histories of youth distinct from those of childhood.[3] While these third and fourth criticisms stand individually as valid criticisms of histories of youth, when put together, they suggest a paradox: the problematic separation of youth from others and the simultaneous search for distinct youth histories. This seeming contradiction points to the importance of the historian's task of attending to their participation in recirculating categories and boundaries that adults have defined as they have policed and regulated young people. Finally, the creation of histories of youth continues to be dominated by adult professional historians whereby youth have no voice in creating and interpreting histories of youth past; their singular role within present configurations is to live lives from which future adult historians, memoirists, and biographers will create knowledge and meaning.

Still, what exists in the past and present does not account for all possibilities. Rather than calling for an abandonment of youth as a subject of historical inquiry, historians, professional or otherwise, adult or youth, can consciously move histories of youth beyond the confines of populational, place-based, ghettoized histories that are often indistinct from histories of childhood and toward a conception and practice where historical youth speak for themselves, where contemporary youth interpret and publish studies of youth past (both by themselves and in collaboration with "adult" historians), where questions of youth are studied comparatively and transnationally, where youth is not reduced into a life stage between childhood and the supposed apogee of adulthood, where histories of youth harken back to the fluid understanding of history as fact-based and fictional, and where youth can be imagined outside the structures through which they are historically and presently constructed.

Notes

1 I restrict my attention to the scholarship of professional historians, thus glossing over influential sociological, anthropological, and criminological youth studies from the first half of the 20th century, notably Lynd and Lynd's (1929) work on *Middletown*, the scholarship of the Chicago School of sociologists, Hollingshead's (1949) research on Elmtown, and Whyte's (1943) studies of "streetcorner" youth.

2 Noteworthy examples include Bailey (1999), Braunstein (2002), Brumberg (1998), and Gosse (2005). Fass (2010) also highlights promising new directions evident in several recent texts.

3 Many of the works mentioned in the previous note begin to move beyond these pitfalls.

References

Appleby, J. (2005). *A restless past: History and the American public*. New York: Rowman & Littlefield.

Aries, P. (1962). *Centuries of childhood: A social history of family life* (R. Baldick, Trans.). New York: Alfred A. Knopf.

Bailey, B. (1999). *Sex in the heartland*. Cambridge, MA: Harvard University Press.

Braunstein, P. (2002). Forever young: Insurgent youth and the sixties culture of rejuvenation. In P. Braunstein, & M. Doyle (Eds.), *Imagine nation: The American counterculture of the 1960s & 1970s* (pp. 243–273). New York: Routledge.

Brumberg, J. (1998). *The body project: An intimate history of American girls*. New York: Vintage.

Fass, P. (2010). Childhood and memory. *Journal of the History of Childhood and Youth, 3*, 155–164.

Gillis, J. (1981). *Youth and history: Tradition and change in European age relations, 1770–present* (Expanded student edition). New York: Academic Press.

Gosse, V. (2005). *Rethinking the new left: An interpretive history*. New York: Palgrave Macmillan.

Hawes, J., & Hiner, N. R. (2005). Reflections on the history of children and childhood in the postmodern era. In A. Jabour (Ed.), *Major problems in the history of American families and children* (pp. 23–31). Boston: Houghton Mifflin.

Hollingshead, A. (1949). *Elmtown's youth: The impact of social classes on adolescents*. New York: John Wiley & Sons.

Lynd, R. S., & Lynd, H. M. (1929). *Middletown: A study in American culture*. New York: Harcourt, Brace, and Co.

Oxford English Dictionary Online. (n.d.). History. Retrieved from http://dictionary.oed. com/cgi/entry/50106603?query_type=word&;queryword=history&first=1&max_to_ show=10&sort_type=alpha&result_place=1&search_id=TdI4-li9SIU-14951&hilite=50106603

Schwarz, B. (2005). History. In T. Bennet, L. Grossberg, & M. Morris (Eds.), *New keywords: A revised vocabulary of culture and society* (pp. 156–159). Malden, MA: Blackwell.

Springhall, J. (1977). *Youth, empire, and society: British youth movements, 1883–1940*. Hamden, CT: Archon Books.

Tosh, J. (2002). *The pursuit of history: Aims, methods, and new directions in the study of modern history* (Rev. 3rd ed.). New York: Longman/Pearson Education.

Whyte, W. (1943). *Street corner society: The social structure of an Italian slum*. Chicago: University of Chicago Press.

Williams, R. (1983). *Keywords: A vocabulary of culture and society* (Rev. ed.). New York: Oxford University Press.

12

PEER GROUPS

Johanna Wyn

Peer group is a ubiquitous concept in youth research, imbued with very different meanings. I use Bourdieu's concept of field to make sense of these divergent meanings and uses, following Lingard, Rawolle, and Taylor (2005) who point out that Bourdieu's concept of field can be used as a tool for analyzing academic domains. Bourdieu (1998) sees a field as a structured space which is relatively autonomous, with its own logics and practices. His notion of field opens up a consideration of the internal structures of fields and how they connect with and affect other fields as well as orienting us to the patterns of power relations and hierarchies that exist within and between them.

The concept of the peer group plays a pivotal role within the field of developmental psychology, where it is closely related to the concept of identity. The concept of the peer group is also widely used within sociological approaches to youth research where it tends to be linked to the concepts of culture and subjectivities as well as to identity. In the following discussion I outline significant elements of the concept of peer group within each field, and discuss the influence of developmental psychology across fields.

In developmental psychology, the concept of the peer group occurs within a tightly structured conceptual framework, the centerpiece of which is a concept of identity that sees young people as adults in the making. Within sociological approaches, the peer group is mostly a trope, or cliché—a convenient but largely under-theorized reference to the existence of either significant others (which can be of any age, particularly in an era of digital, "virtual" communication) but mostly referring to same-aged peers. The influence of the field of psychological development on sociological research on young people is seen in the use of the idea of the peer group as a tool for understanding "becoming adult," drawing on the idea that identity is fixed. However, the field of sociological youth research also illustrates the emergence of new approaches to the use of peer groups. This is evident in the focus on collective rather than individual practices of identity, which are seen as relatively fluid and contextual.

The Field of Developmental Psychological Youth Studies

The idea of peer groups is a central concept within developmental psychological research on young people. It provides a tool for researching the stages of identity development leading to the formation of an adult identity. Within this field peers are a necessary, but dangerous, influence on the developmental process. Peer groups are integral because becoming adult involves a process of becoming autonomous and independent from the family, and peers are the main source of this extra-familial influence. Peer groups are dangerous because they have the power to divert individuals away from (positive) family influences on the development of the mature identity. Within this approach, these are the kinds of research questions that are very likely to be fostered: "Do peers constitute a supportive social environment that fosters identity and helps to socialize youth into adult roles, or do they form an arena for frivolous and delinquent activity with patterns of interaction that undermine autonomy and self esteem?" (Brown, 2004, p. 363).

The peer group is a social site for experimenting with different possible identities, before settling on an adult self. This approach is illustrated in Northcote's research on young people and clubbing. He argues that clubbing is an example of peer group activity that inevitably gives way as the young person fixes on an adult identity:

> Specifically, through their clubbing practices, young adults are seen to affirm the structural identity associated with adulthood through experimenting with an independent identity forged through categorical relationships and with personal relationships that characterise adult-type partnerships. The emphasis that young adults place on personal relationships in their peer group is viewed as a provisional safety net for avoiding any loneliness and awkwardness associated with these wider interactions. Over the long term, these liminal flirtations with an adult identity will, for most participants, give way to a more durable identity rooted in the structural "adult" roles of partners, careers and parents, at which point the appeal of clubbing will lose its importance.
>
> (Northcote, 2006, p. 6)

Young people are conceptualized as subjects in the making, a liberal humanist conception of the subject that sees identity formation as synonymous with physical maturation. Identity is inherently unstable until adulthood is reached. This logic is illustrated in Brown's question above and also in research by Lehdonvirta and Räsänen (2010) on the impact of online peer groups. Like Northcote, they conclude: "The finding is consistent with earlier literature concerning the formation of self-identity and social roles throughout adolescence. As a young person begins to assert their independence and individuality, dependence on and identification with peer groups lessens" (p. 13).

The idea of youth as a process of becoming adult, mirrored by the achievement of a stable and unitary identity, and of the peer group as a significant source of influence in this process (alongside family), has had a powerful impact on youth research. It has driven a research focus on peer relations almost to the exclusion of family within youth research (Gillies, 2000) and it has exerted a strong influence on other fields within youth research, particularly in relation to the conceptualization of identity. The field of psychological development has bequeathed a legacy of normative assumptions about stages of development culminating in the achievement of adulthood, including the idea that family is the "natural" site for positive development.

The Field of Sociological Youth Studies

Sociological research on youth also constitutes a distinctive field in Bourdieu's terms, with its own sets of assumptions, internal logics, and structures. Here, the idea of peer group is loosely linked to concepts of culture, subjectivity, and identity. Indeed, the idea of peer group within this field has the qualities of a trope—a figure of speech—rather than being a term that gains its meaning from a clearly articulated conceptual framework. It appears within a range of sociological perspectives, including traditional approaches to socialization (Handel, Cahill, & Elkin, 2007) and poststructuralist approaches to identity (Butler, 1990, 2000; Davies, 2004, 2006). Socialization theories draw on the linear models proposed by theories of psychological development as a backdrop against which to describe ways in which social institutions (families, schools) contribute to the achievement of normative identities. By contrast, in more contemporary sociological research, poststructuralist approaches argue that identity as a fixed characteristic of individuals is a fiction, maintained through repetitive performances (Hey, 2006), and that identity only exists at the point of action (Nayak & Kehily, 2006). Within this field, identity is performed and practiced, recognized and denied in social settings and is forged within the limited, possible subject positions that are historically and locationally specific. This conceptualization of identity locates it within social relations and practices rather than within individuals. The peer group is an important reference point for these performances, but other kinds of social relations are also seen to be significant, including interactions with others in institutional settings such as schools (Youdell, 2006) and workplaces (Stokes & Wyn, 2007). Here, peer groups are only one medium through which preexisting subject positions are practiced and modified.

Because peer groups are framed within conceptual frameworks that contradict the notion of a fixed identity, research questions focus on understanding social mediations and constructions of social and cultural life and on their expressions in different contexts. It has been "borrowed" from the field of developmental psychology, yet within the field of youth sociology it has a very different meaning and use.

I draw on Kehily and Nayak's (2008) comparative exploration of the ways in which different groups of young people appropriate global cultural symbols to illustrate the nature of research questions and approaches within this field. Their work asks, how do young people draw on global cultural commodities to construct new identity performances?—in this case, femininities. This involves exploring the process of subjectification through which subjecthood is made possible (Davies, 2006). Researching young women's relationship to global popular culture icons such as Madonna, they say:

Embracing and repelling characters can be viewed as a gender display intended to purvey a particular femininity in dialogue with commercially produced forms but shaped by local norms and values. In discussion with young women we found that popular tropes of the romance genre are juxtaposed with their own experiences of intimate relationships. The romantic gestures of the form and the promise of future happiness are exposed as "tricks" that do not retain their illusory power in real life.

(2008, p. 333)

Their work illustrates how the concept of peer group provides a short-hand for young women's social relationships with their friends and little more. Their research is framed by the idea that these interactions provide a space within which young women can construct locally relevant and personally grounded performances of gender identity based on their sense of "moral order" (Kehily & Nayak, 2008, p. 336).

It is also important to recognize the patterns of influence across fields, revealing the power of concepts of peer group and identity that derive from the field of developmental psychology, in youth research. Echoing the assumption that peer groups constitute a danger to successful and healthy transition processes to adulthood, sociological approaches regularly invoke the influence of the peer group to explain choices made by young people that may have negative consequences for them. For example, Gilbert (2007) proposes that the desire to affirm status within their peer group is an explanation for young women taking up smoking. Bassani (2007) argues that a focus on peer groups is needed to make better sense of the relationship between behavior and well-being for young people. These references to the peer group draw on a form of authority provided by the field of developmental psychology.

Conclusion

Drawing on Bourdieu's concept of field to interrogate the concept of peer group within youth research makes visible the different conceptual structures and logics associated with this concept, as well as illuminating its lines of influence and departures across and within fields. This approach reveals the different "work" that the idea of peer group does to frame research questions. Within both fields, the peer group is implicated in understandings of the constitution of the subject—the young person—and in both it gains its meaning through theories of identity. The power of developmental psychological approaches is illustrated through the ubiquitous use of the idea of peer group across fields. The idea of the peer group is borrowed from and, in some sociological research, gains authority from its powerful role in developmental psychology. Following Bourdieu's notion that fields involve power relations and the defense of conceptual territory, my analysis highlights the work that the idea of the peer group does in support of conceptions of identity as fixed, of the young person as an adult in the making, and in perpetuating normative conceptions of "good" and "bad" processes and outcomes for young people. This idea of the peer group continues to have currency in research that is designed to create "interventions" that will ensure normative outcomes. This approach is challenged by develop-ments in some sociological research, in particular research that is influenced by poststructuralist approaches that view the young person through the process of ongoing subjectification, exploring the paradoxical conditions through which the accomplishment of subjecthood is made possible. The focus here is not on how subjects are made but on how peer group practices create the fiction that there is a fixed identity to be made.

Contemporary sociological research has highlighted the blurring of boundaries between youth and adulthood and the destandardization of the life course (Wyn, 2009a, 2009b). Because this approach makes visible the unstable nature of identi-ties and the necessity to enact identity performances throughout life, it provides a framework for understanding the changing meaning of adulthood within local and global contexts. This link to changing social contexts encourages awareness of "new" identities in an era where peers can be global and virtual as well as local (Kehily & Nayak, 2008). Poststructuralist approaches refuse three key elements of the developmental psychological approach to peer groups: the unified, liberal humanist conception of identity; functionalist approaches to the family as the site of "positive" identity development which positions peers as a threat; and norma-tive assumptions about "good" and "bad" outcomes. The refusal of these elements opens up new possibilities for research about young people, including a critical focus on the life course, the ongoing relevance of peer relationships, and a fresh focus on family as intergenerational relationships take on new meanings.

References

Bassani, C. (2007). Five dimensions of social capital theory as they pertain to youth studies. *Journal of Youth Studies, 10,* 17–34.

Bourdieu, P. (1998). *On television.* New York: The New Press.

Brown, B. B. (2004). Adolescents' relationships with peers. In R. M. Lerner, & L. Steinberg (Eds.), *Handbook of adolescent psychology* (2nd ed., pp. 363–394). New York: John Wiley & Sons Inc.

Butler, J. (1990). *Gender trouble: Feminism and the subversion of identity.* New York: Routledge.

Butler, J. (2000). Critically queer. In P. Du Gay, J. Evans, & P. Redman (Eds.), *Identity: A reader* (pp. 108–118). London: Sage/Open University Press.

Davies, B. (2004). Identity, abjection and otherness: Creating the self, creating difference. *International Journal for Equity and Innovation in Early Childhood, 2,* 58–80.

Davies, B. (2006). Subjectification: The relevance of Butler's analysis for education [Special issue]. *British Journal of Sociology of Education, 27,* 425–438.

Gilbert, E. (2007). Constructing "fashionable" youth identities: Australian young women cigarette smokers. *Journal of Youth Studies, 10,* 1–16.

Gillies, V. (2000). Young people and family life: Analysing and comparing disciplinary discourses. *Journal of Youth Studies, 3,* 211–228.

Handel, G., Cahill, S. E., & Elkin, F. (2007). *Children and society: The sociology of children and childhood socialization.* Los Angeles, CA: Roxbury.

Hey, V. (2006). The politics of performative resignification: Translating Judith Butler's theoretical discourse and its potential for a sociology of education. *British Journal of Sociology of Education, 27*(4), 439–457.

Kehily, M. J., & Nayak, A. (2008). Global femininities: Consumption, culture and the significance of place. *Discourse: Studies in the Cultural Politics of Education, 29*(3), 325–342.

Lehdonvirta, V., & Räsänen, P. (2010). How do young people identify with online and offline peer groups? A comparison between UK, Spain and Japan. *Journal of Youth Studies, 13*, 1–18.

Lingard, B., Rawolle, S., & Taylor, S. (2005). Globalizing policy sociology in education: Working with Bourdieu. *Journal of Education Policy, 20*(6), 759–777.

Nayak, A., & Kehily, M. J. (2006). Gender undone: Subversion, regulation and embodiment in the work of Judith Butler [Special issue]. *British Journal of Sociology of Education, 27*(4), 459–472.

Northcote, J. (2006). Nightclubbing and the search for identity: Making the transition from childhood to adulthood in an urban milieu. *Journal of Youth Studies, 9*, 1–16.

Stokes, H., & Wyn, J. (2007). Young people's identities and making careers: Young people's perspectives on work and learning. *International Journal of Lifelong Education, 26*, 495–511.

Wyn, J. (2009a). *Youth health and welfare: The cultural politics of education and well-being.* Melbourne: Oxford University Press.

Wyn, J. (2009b). Touching the future: Building skills for life and work. *Australian Education Review*, 55. Retrieved from http://research.acer.edu.au/aer/9/

Youdell, D. (2006). *Impossible bodies, impossible selves: Exclusions and student subjectivities.* Dordrecht: Springer.

13

TRANSNATIONAL GOVERNANCE

Noah W. Sobe

The United Nations (U.N.) has declared the 12 months from August 2010 to July 2011 to be the "International Year of Youth (IYY)." Since declaring December 2, 1949, the "Day for the Abolition of Slavery," the global community the U.N. represents has expressed its interest in particular causes through the dedication of ceremonial "Days" and "Years" that are intended to focus international attention and mobilize resources to address the issues in question. This essay uses the 2010–2011 IYY as a point of departure for exploring how the category of youth has both "gone global" and become an object of transnational governance through which proper dispositions and behaviors are specified not just for individuals but also for organizations and other social actors. Many scholars have noted that at least since the end of the 19th century, across the globe, "the child" has been a target of regulation and social administration (often as a subject of transnational reform initiatives); this essay examines how "youth" has also become a globe-spanning object. I also examine how demarcations between "children" and "youth" are established and enforced—distinctions that are not clear-cut even in U.N. documents. Often in academic scholarship these categories are elided, yet attention to the ways that these concepts are mobilized is called for because of the regulative strategies that are therein implemented and disseminated globally.

Transnational Governance and the U.N.

In receiving the honor of a U.N.-designated year, youth joins the distinguished ranks of Chemistry, Biodiversity, Natural Fibers, and "the Potato," all of which have also been the recent designees of "International Years." In point of fact, 2010–2011 is the second IYY, the first having taken place in 1985. Gili Drori (2005) argued that in the U.N.'s dedication work one gets a glimpse into the actual formation of "world culture." According to Drori (2005) and other globalization scholars identified as neoinstitutionalist sociologists, since World War II we have increasingly seen the spread of global models that work on a cultural plane by specifying normative principles. Over time, through repetition (even if initially at a ritualistic, symbolic level), these global norms actually do come to be embedded in thought and action across multiple societies. In the view of these scholars it thus becomes possible to conceptualize the U.N. and its various agencies as the "organizational carriers of the world educational order" (Ramirez & Meyer, 2002, p. 95). In focusing global attention on youth, the U.N. is overtly and explicitly attempting to present a set of best practices and "correct" policies. As Collette Chabbott (2003) has pointed out in reference to the 1990 Education for All (EFA) initiative, part of what gives these directives their significance is that they are not just directed to national governments but also aimed at local nongovernmental organizations (NGOs). Furthermore, these directives enter the citation webs of academic scholarship and become reference points for research and practice across multiple disciplines and professional fields.

The U.N. is by no means the only organizational site at which "global governmentalities" are consecrated. While it is clearly one of the more significant sites for transnational norm formation and world-level political and social activism, we also need to study other organizational sites of transnational governance (e.g., charitable foundations, scholarly and professional associations, and international NGOs). Research is also warranted into how conceptualizations of youth and best practices surrounding youth are promulgated through other world-level formations (Stichweh, 2008) such as global media, the Internet, global finance, and even "world-level events" such as 9/11 and the Olympics.

Youth as a Surface of Intervention; Youth as a Vehicle of Intervention

Returning to the 2010–2011 IYY, it behooves us to ask what makes youth an issue that all people(s) around the globe are supposed to take an interest in, and what cultural models are being advanced as concerns about youth are global-ized in this manner. The answers to these questions are readily available in the U.N. documents themselves. Additionally, when we compare the principles and recommendations from 1985 with those of 2010–2011, we can draw tentative conclusions about shifts presently under way in how youth is positioned as an object of transnational governance.

The International Youth Year of 1985 bore as its subtitle "Participation, Development and Peace" (U.N., 1979, p. 175). Particularly in the conceptual-ization of youth "participation," U.N. texts echoed one of the most persistent problematizations of youth, which is that they represent both a societal hope and a social danger. The U.N. resolutions that led to the designation of 1985 as the International Youth Year prominently noted "the imperative need to harness the energies, enthusiasms and creative abilities of youth to the tasks of nation building [and] the struggle for national independence and self-determination" (U.N., 1979, p. 175). It is worth remarking that the idea of "harnessing" and the allusion to inner "energies" and "enthusiasms" evoke the long-standing cultural notion (Lesko, 2001) that youthness is located in the body and that youth bodies need to be properly directed—with progress and national development the intended outcome of the proper harnessing. In the 1985 International Youth Year iteration, the youth body was foremost viewed as a nationalized one and here "development" seems only to have been used in reference to the economic and social advancement of nation states. Yet, the cause of international peace did enter through acknowledgment of the "necessity to disseminate among youth the ideals of peace, respect for human rights, fundamental freedoms and human solidarity" (p. 175). As this suggests, in addition to specifying a host of tasks for adults *vis-à-vis* youth (e.g., "harness" as above, but also "increase opportunities for"), the U.N.'s International Year also posed youth themselves as surfaces of intervention. Alongside commitments and dispositions connected with peace, freedom, and human rights, the U.N. called for inculcating among youth "dedication to the objectives of progress and development" (p. 175). In these unabashed proclamations of normative principles, the U.N. can be seen as explicitly attempting to set a globe-spanning agenda for what should be done about/with/for/to that set of human beings considered to be "youth."

Before moving to 2010–2011 we should note that, in addition to taking an interest in youth, the U.N. has, since its founding, made the health, welfare, and education of children one of its major concerns. Much of this culminated in the 1989 Convention on the Rights of the Child (CRC), which defined "children" as anyone under 18 years. In U.N. youth-related action plans and programs, "youth" is anyone in the 15- to 24-year age cohort. A noteworthy overlap. However, these two conceptualizations of human kinds elide into one another in more subtle but equally significant ways. Moving toward a "rights-based approach" to children's issues is an effort to uproot a view of children which views them simply as "victims" in need of perpetual protection (Kjørholt, 2002). This approach, which has also been characterized as treating children as "human beings" and not "human becomings" or imperfect/yet-to-be-perfected adults, corresponds with a shift in academic scholarship that stresses a view of children as active agents whose everyday lives are worth serious study in their own right (Jenkins, 1998). The emphasis that the CRC places on children's participation in decisions that affect their lives echoes the framing of youth participation that we saw above. While there are significant differences, we should not overlook the fact that at the present moment "participation" has become a master concept of Western democratic (and neoliberal) political rationalities. As Tracey Skelton (2009) points out, the notion of the "participating child" is enabled by particular social circumstances and what Foucault would call certain "regimes of truth." This is equally true for the "participating youth," as we will see below.

The U.N. resolution designating 2010–2011 as the IYY recycles some of the language of youth-related U.N. resolutions of three decades earlier. The 2010 U.N. resolution notes, for example, that it is "necessary to disseminate among young people the ideals of peace, respect for human rights and fundamental freedoms, solidarity and dedication to the objectives of progress and development" (U.N., 2010, p. 1). Similarly, there is mention of the "energy, enthusiasm and creativity" of youth. However, rather than stating that there is an "imperative need" to "harness" this "to the tasks of nation building [and] the struggle for national independence and self-determination," the proclamation of 2010 as the IYY remarks that "young people should be encouraged to devote their energy, enthusiasm and creativity to economic, social and cultural development and the promotion of mutual understanding" (U.N., 2010, p. 1). In connection with this shift the adolescent body has been somewhat stabilized: no longer is it a teeming mass of energies and enthusiasms (in the plural, as earlier) but rather is the more docile—and presumably more economically productive—seat of energy, enthusiasm, and creativity (in the singular).

Though the national belonging of youth does not completely fade from the multitude of U.N. texts connected with the 2010–2011 International Year, it is notable that the nation building and national self-determination we saw in the 1985 iteration has disappeared from the 2010–2011 IYY proclamation. Instead, there is a new focus on the global—the youth body becomes resituated in a purportedly borderless world of trade, entrepreneurship, and mobility. In a telling example, the IYY website, under the heading of "Participate," poses the question "are you a young person and a global citizen?" (International Year of the Youth, n.d.). While the theme of global social activism on the part of youth saturates IYY documents, this is eclipsed by the emphasis placed on the inclusion of youth in/preparation of youth for "the global economy." A 2008 General Assembly resolution (A62/126) that was part of the lead-up to the IYY devotes a whole section to the question of globalization and youth. As testament to the scope of its norm-creation agenda, the U.N. recommended supporting "the efforts of Governments, together with civil society, including youth-led organizations, the private sector and other parts of society, to anticipate and offset the negative social and economic consequences of globalization and to maximize its benefits for young people" (U.N., 2008, p. 7).

As we see here, working toward economic justice on a global scale is one of the U.N.'s central concerns—and, to be sure, an extremely laudable one. Of concern, however, are the categorizations and regulative principles that accompany these projections of youth around the globe.

Changing Transnational Governance and Changing Youth

If part of the historical story of youth is the emergence of a lifecycle phase that is seen as transitional to productive adult life, current U.N. initiatives suggest that there are transnational social and cultural projects under way that attenuate the "always-in-betweenness" of the category of youth. Among the normative principles being enacted in the U.N.'s dedication work is a view of youth as intrinsically productive. Current constructions of youth participation, tied as they are to engagement, activity, and responsibility, seem to be closing some of the "preparation-for" gap that has traditionally been inserted into the space between the state of childhood and the state of adulthood.

As "youth" moves transnationally today, a rigid binary that distinguishes in an absolute manner between the normal and the pathological increasingly seems to be giving way to more nuanced and complex systems of inclusion and exclusion. Some of these complexities become visible when we consider the category of "youth development." In contrast to "child development," which is an area of medical and psychological knowledge production whose precepts are also diffused through the activities of organizations like UNICEF, "youth development" is better viewed as an area of social practice that has very little to do with any concept of maturation and even quite tenuous links with notions of transition. Instead, the increasingly globalized impetus to implement "youth development" projects (something the 2010–2011 IYY explicitly discusses) furthers a "human resources" perspective on the productive capacities of youth and the worthiness of youth as a "sector" with which NGOs and governments should be concerned. Marching hand-in-hand with the globalization of a view of youth as human resource are notions of opportunity, access, equality, and flourishing—in other words, the universals of our present to which it is difficult to say no (Spivak, 1999).

However, this does not mean that notions of delinquency and forms of marginalization disappear. Deviance and "exceptions" among kinds of youth persist. And, pace Agamben (2005), the exception—the youth that we "include" by noting their exclusion—may in fact be the ordinary and necessary mechanism that allows the extension of authority and governance in the first place. As youth becomes an increasingly institutionalized global model, it may be that what we face around the globe is less the danger of distinctions among kinds of youth than the danger of distinctions among "human kinds."

References

Agamben, G. (2005). *State of exception*. Chicago: University of Chicago Press.
Chabbott, C. (2003). *Constructing education for development: International organizations and education for all*. New York: RoutledgeFalmer.

Drori, G. S. (2005). United Nations' dedications: A world culture in the making? *International Sociology, 20,* 175–199.

"International Year of the Youth" Website. (n.d.). Retrieved from http://social.un.org/youthyear/

Jenkins, H. (1998). *The children's culture reader.* New York: New York University Press.

Kjørholt, A. T. (2002). Small is powerful: Discourses on children and participation and Norway. *Childhood, 9,* 63–82.

Lesko, N. (2001). *Act your age! A cultural construction of adolescence.* New York: RoutledgeFalmer.

Ramirez, F. O., & Meyer, J. W. (2002). National curricula: World models and national historical legacies. In M. Caruso, & H. E. Tenorth (Eds.), *Internationalisierung/internationalisation* (pp. 91–107). Frankfurt am Main: Peter Lang.

Skelton, T. (2009). Children, young people, UNICEF and participation. In S. Aitken, R. Lund, & A. T. Kjørholt (Eds.), *Global childhoods: Globalization, development and young people* (pp. 165–182). London: Routledge.

Spivak, G. C. (1999). *A critique of postcolonial reason: Toward a history of the vanishing present.* Cambridge, MA: Harvard University Press.

Stichweh, R. (2008). The eigenstructures of world society and the regional cultures of the world. In I. Rossi (Ed.), *Frontiers of globalization research: Theoretical and methodological approaches* (pp. 133–150). New York: Routledge.

U.N. (1979). Res. 34/151, General Assembly.

U.N. (2008). Res. 62/126, General Assembly.

U.N. (2010). Res. 64/134, General Assembly.

SECTION III

Populational Reasoning

Gordon Tait

This section focuses on systems of reasoning that imagine youth as a unified whole, one that can be researched, talked about, planned for, and managed. Even research that focuses on individuals or specific contexts depends on and reproduces ideas of youth as an identifiable population. This section interrogates the rules and scaffolding of discourses that construct the social spaces in which we problematize and study youth in society.

This introduction will set the agenda by addressing four elements of this process: the first addresses the rise of some of the crucial elements of contemporary governance, the instrument and practices through which the notion of the population was able to take shape. The second examines the rise of the personage of "the child," and how new forms of governance not only utilized this new identity for the purposes of ongoing social management, but also organized its differentiation into a growing array of new social and administrative categories. The third specifically addresses "youth," examining its various predecessors as targets for moral concern, as well as some of the recent cultural triggers for its formation. Finally, there is an assessment of the contemporary governance of populations of youth, based as it is around its twin existence as a governmental object, a target for an almost endless array of social, educational, legal, and psychological concerns and interventions, but also as an identity, a set of practices of the self.

The Rise of Governance

It would be tempting to think that the category of youth emerged into our cultural landscape already fully formed, and reliant upon nothing but its own ontological validity for its ongoing existence. However, in spite of this position—one somehow regarding youth as a form of Platonic "ideal type," with fixed and essentially self-evident boundaries—the better evidence suggests that the emergence of youth as a category relied upon a number of significant historical precursors.

The first, and likely the most important for the purposes of the arguments run here, is the rise of the notion of the population. Foucault (1991) has discussed at length important changes that occurred to the mechanisms of rule, most notably the decreasing centrality of the imperatives of the sovereign, and the simple, foundational objective of increasing the sovereign's wealth. This began to be replaced by other forms of political arithmetic from the 18th century onward, most notably that the population was now to become the central raison d'être of government—both in terms of government as an institution, but also as a complex and densely saturated set of disparate interventions. This occurred both directly and indirectly, by not only seeking to improve the conditions and opportunities of the population, but also to manage its aspirations, habits, and interests—what Gordon (1991, p. 2) refers to as "the conduct of conduct." In addition to this foundational change, the blunt instruments of sovereign rule—laws, decrees and regulations—were slowly superseded in importance by new, and more pervasive, methods of social management, and in doing so, the traditional symbolic model of government, that of the benevolent family, slowly came to be abandoned, displaced in time by the increasing focus on "the population." Foucault contends that this switch largely occurred as the increasing use of statistics showed that populations, in all their complexity, had internal configurations and regularities that were irreducible to the simple template of the family. In fact, rather than providing an idealized model for rule, the family was now to become a crucial mechanism through which the population could be governed effectively.

One of the most important side effects of this new technique of governance, largely a product of the massive accumulation of data (what Hacking [1982] called an "avalanche of printed numbers"), was a previously unthinkable augmentation in the possibilities of differentiation. That is, through continual and wide-ranging assessment, measurement, and review, and not just through centralized instruments such as the census, but also within the information-gathering practices of newly formed agencies such as the police, welfare, school, health, child guidance, and so on, it became possible to identify particular characteristics, skills, capacities, or weaknesses of any person, or subcategories within the population. In combination with the effective keeping of records, new identities started to emerge—identities with far greater depth, texture, permanence, and legitimacy than was previously thought possible. For instance, no longer were there just "thieves," to be caught and punished. Sufficient data were gathered to break this category down into a large number of subcategories—"cracksmen," "drummers," "dead-lurkers"—each of which could be addressed and managed in their own way, a process out of which developed the science of criminology. Likewise, the nebulous character of "the pauper" began to be subdivided, giving way to a series of well-delimited categories based upon perceptions of their relative idleness: "good poor," "bad poor," "willfully idle," "involuntarily unemployed" (Foucault, 1984). Modern medicine developed largely as a result of new forms of information gathering, recording, and categorization. New categories of illness were invented, burgeoning throughout the 19th century, and which still continue to burgeon, each more specific and targeted than the last. Importantly, this relatively new imperative of relentless categorization of the social body eventually turned its attention to the young.

The Personage of "The Child"

The second element of the process to be outlined here examines the rise of the personage of "the child." The argument here is not that the child emerged as a product of this new, differentiating form of governance, or that, due to its seeming permanence and popularity as a category, it somehow possessed an epistemological validity other categories of preadulthood lack. Far from it, on both counts. Aries (1960) contends that, in medieval times, the category of the child did not exist, with preadulthood consisting solely of being an infant, a social grouping that lacked any real importance. However, upon reaching the age of 6 or 7 years, infants transitioned directly to the full status, rights, and obligations of adults. It was not until the 16th century that the single status of adult started to fragment, with young people from the upper classes beginning to be represented distinctively in art, not just in the structure of their faces, but also in the way they were clothed. Eventually, in part as a response to social and cultural changes brought about by the invention of the printing press (Postman, 1994), the separate status of child came to be definitively demarcated from the broader status of adult, in that the far broader distribution of literacy resulted in the "natural" delineation of those who could read (adults), from those who could not (children).

This emergence of the persona of "the child" well predated the rise of contemporary forms of rule, and although it continued to evolve and solidify as a "natural" stage of life, it was not taken up as one of the central vehicles for social governance until significantly later. Arguably, it was only with the rise of liberalism, and the concomitant notion "of governing at a distance" via the medium of expertise (Rose & Miller, 1992)—that is, not seeking to rule through direct and immediate intervention, but rather indirectly, through the subtle guidance and steering of those with appropriate "knowledge"—that the full organizational potential of the child began to be more fully utilized, with the child positioned as one of the most crucial and effective sites of ongoing social management of the citizenry. Significantly, the laws and decrees of sovereign rule were clearly going to prove inefficient and inappropriate mechanisms for managing the conduct of this new social entity. Rather, as Donzelot (1979) points out, a far more effective way of governing childhood involves the enlistment of the family in the production of good children, a process overseen by medical, educational, and psychological experts who successfully bridge the gap between the broadest objective of government and the inner workings of the family unit. Furthermore, it was through the piecemeal assemblage of the objects of these various forms of knowledge that the modern child eventually appeared—seemingly fully formed and objectively valid. And so, in the same way that Foucault (1976) imagines "sexuality" to be shaped as the product of innumerable discourses concerning sex, so too "childhood" became a unified and naturalized stage of life through the plethora of governmental programs, policies, and forms of intervention that came to define its boundaries.

Targets for Moral Concern

The third element of contemporary governance relevant here is the focus on the young as a target for moral concern, and out of this concern ultimately the disparate development of the contemporary category of youth, a category that is fashioned by, and within, a multiplicity of diverse knowledges and contexts (Hopkins, 2002). The concern over the moral welfare of the young is hardly new, but within contemporary governance it has been honed and directed with far greater acuity than ever before. After all, as Foucault (1977) notes, in modern society, where power is generally anonymous and functional, there tends to be a strong process of individualization of those upon whom it is exercised, and those who do not conform to expected norms are the subject of the greatest attention. He states that "in a system of discipline, the child is more individuated than the adult, the patient more than the healthy man, the madman and the delinquent more than normal and non-delinquent" (Foucault, 1977, p. 193). It is through the construction and demarcation of pathologies (such as the juvenile delinquent) that social, legal, psychological, and medical norms can be reinforced (Tait, 2010). According to Rose (1990), this process is especially evident when addressing the young:

> It is around pathological children—the troublesome, the recalcitrant, the delinquent—that conceptions of normality have taken shape . . . expert notions of normality are extrapolated from our attention to those children who worry the courts, teachers, doctors and parents. Normality is not an observation but a valuation.
>
> (p. 131)

Indeed, the history of the production of categories of preadulthood can be seen as the history of various groupings that have caused particular types of social concern. McCallum (1993) uses the example of "problem children," arguing that, like the broader concept of the child itself out of which it evolved, this new figure did not have any essential, transhistoric validity as a category. Rather, the "problem child" was an artifact produced during the early decades of the 20th century at the intersection of a number of governmental strategies, shaped by professional knowledges circulating within the discourses generated by social workers, psychologists, psychiatrists, child guidance experts, and family counselors. He also maintains that it was primarily through the burgeoning of various governmental techniques of information gathering and collating that the persona of the "problem child" was first identified and, subsequently, became the object of administration. In addition, legal changes delineating between different types of offenders also began to produce numerous new subcategories of this persona, such as "juvenile criminals," "criminal children," and "neglected children," all of which gained currency at various times as characters requiring intervention and reformation.

It was largely out of the persona of "problem child," and following a differentiating logic of governance, that new categories of young person began to emerge. Initially, the most significant of these was "the adolescent," which, in spite of early concerns during the latter part of the 19th century, did not assume any coherent shape until the publication of G. Stanley Hall's massive study on the subject in 1904. Hall's adolescent was firmly rooted within the realm of biology, with his book *Adolescence* containing numerous chapters on subjects such as physical growth, instincts, and evolution. Furthermore, Hall's emphasis on "storm and stress" came to form one of the central, recurrent foundations of ensuing depictions of the innate temperament of young people.

Following "the adolescent" came the familiar character of "the juvenile delinquent" and "the teenager," both of which acted as the focus for social and moral concern, as well as an effective mechanism of governance. Arguably, then, the latest persona to add to this list is the very subject of this book—"youth"—a category somewhat different to its predecessors in both its scope and the nature of the capacities it has been allocated, but alike in important aspects of its constitution, that is, its status as an artifact of populational reasoning, surveillance, and ongoing regulatory intervention (Pitts, 2004). This final (and continually expanding) category has become carved out of the space between the existing notions of childhood and adulthood—possessing the same apparent ontological status as the paradigms from which it evolved, and likewise being comprised of a complex amalgam of disparate discourses and forms of governance. That is, the category of youth is not constituted in terms of a unitary object. It is instead a plural concept, given shape within a wide range of contexts and, as such, possesses neither a linear history nor a clearly demarcated present (Tait, 2000).

It has been argued here that the category of youth developed as an artifact of differentiating forms of governance. However, this is not the only plausible explanation, as two other, partially related logics can be seen to constitute necessary preconditions for its eventual emergence. The first mirrors Postman's (1994) argument about the importance of the invention of the printing press for the development of childhood—that is, mundane technological changes having unforeseen social and cultural consequences. In this instance, it has been argued that both the widespread postwar phasing out of National Service in a number of industrialized countries, resulting in a new generation of school leavers without the traditional sense of a direct and inevitable transition to the full responsibilities of adulthood, in combination with the introduction of hire purchase, which played a large role in young people becoming a viable and energetic target market, set the conditions wherein a new persona—"youth"—could form and thrive (Cashmore, 1984).

The second logic ties more directly to differentiating forms of governance, but relates to some of the reasons for that differentiation. The argument here is that subcategories are produced, not simply as part of an ever more nuanced and finely meshed web of governmental intelligibility, but due to a continual dissatisfaction with the governmental possibilities afforded by previous incarnations of the same target groupings. Just as "the juvenile delinquent" traversed new terrain to "the problem child," and hence afforded new possibilities of administration and intervention, so too does the notion of "youth" take up where previous personae were deemed to have been unsuccessful as strategies for effective population management. This should not come as a surprise.

Wickham (1993) argues that a perpetual dissatisfaction with government is actually essential to its continued operation; indeed, he suggests that government is necessarily never complete, never totally successful, and it is through the continually disappointed reassessment of governmental outcomes that more effective programs, and personae, are introduced, in time only to be replaced themselves.

Youth and Governance

The final issue here involves an assessment of the contemporary governance of youth, based as it is around its twin existence as a government object, and also as an identity, a set of practices of self-management. That is, it is suggested here that the category of youth is now constituted by two parallel elements: the first is its existence as a target for an almost endless array of social, educational, legal, and psychological concerns and interventions; the second involves its existence as a habitus, a vocabulary of ways of regulating the self.

First, then, youth has been produced as a governmental object at the intersection of certain legal, educational, medical, and psychological problematizations and interventions. These include debates over legal definitions of consent and criminal liability, changes in strategies regarding juvenile delinquency, concerns regarding age-appropriacy of educational programs and practices, arguments over the disciplinary normalization of targeted populations, ongoing panics over media content and popular culture, psychological concerns over increasingly numerous disorders of development and behavior, public health initiatives over alcohol, tobacco, and diet, worries and fears over venereal disease and public morality, and so on. However, despite this fragmented history, youth has repeatedly been regarded as one of the most important contemporary social problems, and social problems in a singular sense. That is, out of this dense and disparate network of governmental intelligibility, youth still manages to be sketched largely as a unified whole.

Importantly, the youth research that adopts and accepts this social category in an unproblematic and uncritical way, pertaining simply to report the social forces that act upon it, the disadvantages to which it is subjected, and the forms of resistance it manifests in response, does not stand outside the shaping of the entity it attempts to objectively report upon. The knowledges such researchers, writers, policy makers, social workers, and concerned citizens deploy, as well as the data they produce and reproduce—for example, see the recent research and writing on the subject of Generation Y (Huntley, 2006)—are every bit as much a part of the piecemeal process by which youth is shaped, as are the documents which demarcate age of consent, criminal liability, or the right to vote.

An additional, related point here is that it would be a mistake to understand youth simply as the target for a diverse series of interventions into the conduct of a given cohort of the population. While this is true to some extent, the situation is significantly more complicated. Youth is not so much a target for intervention, as a vehicle through which a series of interventions occur. Not only is youth an artifact produced through a range of governmental concerns, it is also a logic through which those concerns become operationalized, a rationale which permits ideas to take form and outcomes to be envisaged, and a practical, discursive, and symbolic pivot-point within the broader strategy of creating a docile and productive citizenry. For example, the social inclusion agenda common to many Western democracies during the past decade has ostensibly employed "youth" as the target for concern and intervention, while in practice it is simply the vehicle through which particular types of broader social change are discussed, and alternative futures imagined (Edwards, 2008).

The second governmental issue here involves the fact that governmental programs do not directly and unproblematically translate into a modified and regulated target population. Whether legal, educational, or psychological, those programs targeting various aspects of the conduct of youth do not work simply by establishing a new guideline for policy, or by setting a new benchmark for health. As has been previously discussed, as government is a continually failing operation, often they do not work at all. However, on those occasions when they do, more often than not, it is by enrolling specific groups in their own self-reformation, by the effective translation of government into self-government. In an extension of the logic of the panopticon, the heart of effective contemporary governance lies not in the imposition of rule upon the population, but rather in that moment when acceptable selves are voluntarily shaped and reshaped in accordance with broader social objectives. Youth is not just an artifact of contemporary governance, it is an identity to be fashioned within interrelated sets of practices of the self.

Within this understanding of governance, youth becomes a specific way in which a self is fashioned, still within the logic of a constructed and regulated persona, but organized around the patterning of a kind of habitus, a "youthful" way of making a self. Young people shape themselves as youth, not by inevitably expressing their inner youthfulness, or even in a more contrived way, of having to look inside to somehow find this mysterious essence. Rather, they actively assemble a particular type of persona, one with a correlative collection of habitus. This habitus of youth is constituted in a plurality of ways, some axiomatic to the category—forms of dress and body adornment, practices of physical self-regulation, issues of taste and consumption, styles of self-interrogation and expression—others less so. Likewise, the self is assembled through governmental information and templates, most often cobbled together from an array of different sources. These manuals of self-formation provide a vocabulary of ways in which young people learn appropriate ways of shaping a self. This not only includes some of the formal ways in which acceptable identities are forged, such as through the identity-shaping elements of both the formal and hidden curricula of the mass school, but also through more mundane technologies, such as magazines, cultural activities and pastimes, and the trivia and minutiae of contemporary fashion.

It is, in large part, due to the high cultural profile given to the existence of the authentic, inner "youthful self" that helps cement the erroneous belief that "youth" has a biological and psychological reality as a category, independent of history or culture. If youth were simply a generalized label given to the target of various governmental programs, such as "the poor" or "the disabled," then essentializing arguments would be much more difficult to sustain. However, the successful extension of governance into the regulation of associated subject positions— selves—has helped foster the conviction that such positions have an objective reality, in and of themselves. In fact, far from being an inevitable stage of the human story, youth is best understood as an example of the piecemeal formation of specific types of person, and as the doing of specific types of work on the self.

In conclusion, the approach to youth described above, and in the essays that follow, rejects what is often taken as the dominant, commonsense understanding of the category: youth as a unified whole; youth as an objective facticity; youth as a stage of life through which we all pass. Instead, it is argued here that youth is best located as an artifact of the government of populations, an amalgam of previous personae, forms of knowledge and strategies of intervention, a piecemeal and nebulous focus for moral and administrative concern, and simultaneously both a governmental object, and a set of identities and practices of self-management. Understanding youth in these terms not only avoids an essentializing approach to young people, but also permits the establishment of a research paradigm flexible enough to cope with the complexity and contingent nature of the subject matter.

References

Aries, P. (1960). *Centuries of childhood*. Harmondsworth: Penguin.

Cashmore, E. (1984). *No future: Youth and society*. London: Heinemann.

Donzelot, J. (1979). *The policing of families*. New York: Pantheon Books.

Edwards, K. (2008). Social inclusion and youth participation: A new deal for Australia's young people. *Youth Studies Australia, 27*, 11–17.

Foucault, M. (1976). *The history of sexuality, volume 1: An introduction*. Harmondsworth: Penguin.

Foucault, M. (1977). *Discipline and punish: The birth of the prison*. Harmondsworth: Penguin.

Foucault, M. (1984). The politics of health in the eighteenth century. In P. Rabinow (Ed.), *The Foucault reader* (pp. 273–290). London: Penguin.

Foucault, M. (1991). Governmentality. In G. Burchell, C. Gordon, & P. Miller (Eds.), *The Foucault effect: Studies in governmentality* (pp. 87–104). London: Harvester Wheatsheaf.

Gordon, C. (1991). Governmental rationality: An introduction. In G. Burchell, C. Gordon, & P. Miller (Eds.), *The Foucault effect: Studies in governmentality* (pp. 1–51). London: Harvester Wheatsheaf.

Hacking, I. (1982). Bio-power and the avalanche of printed numbers. *Humanities in Society, 5*, 275–295.

Hall, G. S. (1904). *Adolescence: Its psychology, and its relation to physiology, anthropology, sociology, sex crimes, religion and education* (2 vols.). New York: Appleton.

Hopkins, S. (2002). *Girl heroes: The new force in popular culture*. Annandale: Pluto Press.

Huntley, R. (2006). *The world according to Y: Inside the new adult generation*. Sydney: Allen & Unwin.

McCallum, D. (1993). Problem children and familial relations. In D. Meredyth, & D. Tyler (Eds.), *Child and citizen: Genealogies of Australian childhood* (pp. 129–152). Queensland, Australia: Centre for Cultural Policy Studies, Griffith University.

Pitts, J. (2004). Korrectional karaoke: New Labour and the zombification of youth justice. In R. Hil, & G. Tait (Eds.), *Hard lessons: Reflections on governance and crime control in late modernity* (pp. 73–97). Aldershot: Ashgate.

Postman, N. (1994). *The disappearing child.* New York: Vintage Books.

Rose, N. (1990). *Governing the soul: The shaping of the private self.* London: Routledge.

Rose, N., & Miller, P. (1992). Political power beyond the state: Problematics of government. *British Journal of Sociology, 43,* 173–205.

Tait, G. (2000). *Youth, sex, and government.* New York: Peter Lang.

Tait, G. (2010). *Philosophy, behaviour disorders, and the school.* Rotterdam: Sense.

Wickham, G. (1993, December). *Citizenship, governance and the consumption of sport.* Paper presented at the Australian Sociological Association Conference, Sydney, Australia.

14

AGE

Yen Yen Woo

We use age to judge everything: when one should be walking or talking, allowed to drive, drink alcohol, vote, marry, retire, or watch certain movies. Even when we acknowledge that everyone develops at different paces and that the categories of age are at best a shorthand designed for administrative convenience, we have nevertheless come to assume assessing someone based on age is scientific, natural, and even moral.

"Sexting": An Example

The furor over "sexting" (the sending of racy photographs via cell phones) among teenagers shows how a strict age-based approach can produce many pathologies. Responses in the media and from school authorities betray a particular understanding of adolescence—as a dangerous cocktail of hormones and the influence of peers and the media that adults should worry about, watch over, and correct (see, e.g., Richmond, 2009; Stone, 2009). School authorities are even seizing and searching cell phones and laptops on suspicion of containing nude images (see, e.g., American Civil Liberties Union, 2010; Zahn, 2010), a reaction that seems understandable until we realize it is predicated on the delusion that one should be sexually innocent until the age of majority. This has also created the absurd situation whereby adults may legally send nude photographs of themselves to one another, while teens who do so may be charged with child pornography (Richards & Calvert, 2009).

How did it become so easy for us to assume that teenagers are an undifferentiated group, uniformly hormonal, rebellious, and not wholly responsible, while the mere crossing of some arbitrary temporal line confers upon one individuality, moral authority, and responsibility?

A Brief History of the Language of Age

In his account of the language of age, Joseph Kett (1977) tells of a preindustrial America when terms such as "childhood" and "youth" had very nonspecific parameters. Partially due to inaccurate record-keeping, a young person's specific age was less meaningful as an identifier than characteristics such as physical size (e.g., "large boy") for agricultural communities, or degree of independence from home (e.g., "young man" for someone who has left home for work).

The looseness of age-based categories also meant social and civic spaces were not as age-segregated as they are now. Teenagers were common attendees at political meetings, and, in fact, in the 1800s, most young people's societies "were voluntary, organized and conducted by young people themselves" (Kett, 1977, p. 43). Prior to the 1840s, schools were not the primary institution of education, and if children attended school, they ranged from one-room schoolhouses to "dame schools" conducted in the homes of literate women, or fairly unstructured "writing schools" (Bowles & Gintis, 1976, p. 153). Academies and colleges also enrolled students across a wide range of ages (Kett, 1977).

Industrialization and the fascination with the logic of the machine engendered a belief in the organization of life based on a linear, modern temporality toward a productive purpose (Greenhouse, 1996). As an expression of such a temporality, the precise language of age becomes very useful in the organization of schools, articulation of laws, and prescriptions for "normal" development toward "proper" adulthood.

Just as factories provided efficiencies in production, age-graded schools provided a powerful technology for the surveillance of young people toward their productive purpose. In Lowell, Massachusetts, the School Committee made the analogy between schools and factories explicit, stating that the "principle of the division of labor holds good in schools, as in mechanical industry" (as cited in Bowles & Gintis, 1976, p. 168). In these schools, immigrant children could be trained to be "better workers" through an education that would "instill obedience … [and] promote self-control" (Bowles & Gintis, 1976, pp. 161, 170) and the new middle class could gain "respectability and security" (Bowles & Gintis, 1976, p. 159). It was, in other words, socially efficient to separate the age groups.

The work of G. Stanley Hall (1904) provided the scientific language of "storm and stress" and the assumption that an individual's development recapitulates the development of human society, thereby establishing the separateness and precariousness of adolescence, as well as its inferiority compared to adulthood. Increasingly romantic notions of childhood as a time of innocence also led to the perception of adolescence as a time of risk and corruption.

Meanwhile, the widespread introduction of child labor laws by the late 1800s separated the young from the old in workspaces and, increasingly, schools became the only legitimate spaces for young people. The emergence of the middle class and their "success philosophy" made being successful an increasingly important goal for normally developing adolescents (Kett, 1977, p. 45). The language of science, facilitated by schools and attenuated legal rights, made it easy to see teenagers as a separate group with uniform characteristics, dependent on adults, and deserving of supervision to ensure stage-by-stage development toward "normal," "successful" adulthood.

The Politics of Age

People of different ages are valued differently. Johannes Fabian (1983), writing about the anthropological method, reminds us how colonial reasoning constructs the Other as not existing in the same present, but as stuck in a more savage, primitive, and younger time. Just as native peoples were seen as "simple" children of nature (Baxter, 2008, p. 79) or "savages" (Rist, 1997), or homosexuals as afflicted with "arrested development" (Stockton, 2004, p. 289), adolescents are similarly perceived as hormonal, easily influenced by peers, corruptible, and immature (Lesko, 2001). This discursive strategy of assigning the Other to an inferior time assumes we know everything about them, and that they should be denied "coevalness" (Fabian, 1983, p. 37), deserving surveillance, temporal discipline, and intervention, because they do not share the "advanced stage of civilization" (Rist, 1997, p. 54).

Those deserving of surveillance will have their spaces and times scrutinized, through a "biopower" (Foucault, 2009, p. 1) that infuses every aspect of life. Age-graded schools provide a highly efficient way of surveillance and discipline, while tests that separate students into different tracks provide a language and value system that extends beyond the school to how parents, employers, and society make sense of achievement and failure, and, in turn, individual subjectivities. The "hidden curriculum" of schools (Jackson, 1968/2004, p. 99) constructs hierarchies of achievers and strivers, nerds and jocks, straight and gay, and so on, ensuring the success of the powerful and the failure of the powerless (Deschenes, Cuban, & Tyack, 2001).

Meanwhile, adolescents' times outside school are seen as particularly dangerous, and also deserving of scrutiny. For instance, the report, *A Matter of Time* (Carnegie Council on Adolescent Development, 1992), states that "unsupervised after-school hours represent a period of significant risk; it is a time when adolescents may engage in dangerous and even illegal activities" (p. 33). The solution to the danger of unstructured time is to ensure adolescents make "constructive use of this time" (p. 19), or risk not achieving "productive adult-hood" (p. 28). As schools, workspaces, and entertainment venues are all now regulated based on age (Harris, 2004), fewer and fewer unsupervised, free, and public spaces exist for young people.

Not just external behavior, but internal orientations, attract scrutiny and intervention as well. We now lament "at-risk" students, who display "poor time allocation," and "weak future orientation" (Bruno, 1995, p. 102), and who invariably come from poor and traditionally marginalized groups, while we laud the discipline of future-oriented students (who often have greater access to social and cultural capital) and their willingness to sacrifice their interests, sleep, and physical well-being to ensure the attainment of the necessary credentials (Humes, 2003; Pope, 2001).

Different Times

We now live in very different times from the era of industrialization, when age emerged as a convenient and believable discourse for the management of the population. Now, the technologies of biopower that regulate "normal" development are more intense, sophisticated, and pervasive than ever. In the United States, with education policies such as the No Child Left Behind Act and Race to the Top, students are tested with far greater intensity; they are compared not just to their age peers in school, but even to those in other schools, states, and countries. Increased testing is only one aspect of a massive growth in surveillance over the experience of youth; there are now police in schools, closed circuit cameras, and websites charting exactly what the physical, social, psychological, and moral developmental milestones should be for each period of childhood and adolescence.

At the same time the pressure to conform is intensifying, we are also witnessing an explosion of multiple expressions of different selves—whether blogging, engaging in social networks, crowdsourcing, creating avatars in online role-playing games, or even sexting—that undermine what is regarded as "normal" development.

We need new ways of understanding young people; perhaps we should start by assuming coevalness rather than denying it as we have done for so long. We would do better to research and evaluate based on our lived experience, which means seeing ourselves and youths as occupying the same world, and valuing different ways of growing rather than the linearity that age presupposes. With sexting, for example, we should not dismiss teens' sexual practices as simply deserving of reform and surveillance, but rather, we should seek to understand and discuss the sexual impulses in both adults and youths, as well as the increased commercial marketing of sexuality, and issues of marginality and oppression in cases when images are circulated to embarrass or hurt. We should also remind ourselves that age-graded schools have always been places of success for privileged children and can be punitive spaces for those outside the mainstream, and begin to ask questions such as: Is segregating young people by age in schools really the most educational option? Is it fair to constantly accuse young people of disrespecting the old, when all their lives they have been deliberately separated from them (Hagestad & Uhlenberg, 2005)? How do we expect young adults to participate in the voting process when they are permitted few decision-making powers and little participation in unsupervised activities? How can we claim to be open to the future when, in the context of increasingly uncertain career prospects, we continue to insist the young buy into "a one-to-one link between qualifications and ongoing career attainment" (Dwyer & Wyn, 2001, p. 198)?

Seeing youth from a position of coevalness means looking for different ways of growing, not just a linear and uniform "growing up" (Stockton, 2004, p. 279) into a predetermined notion of normal adulthood. We need to ask not just why some young people are not developing according to the norm, but what possibilities for growth and different versions of adulthood we are eliding when we insist on what we have come to believe is "normal" development.

References

American Civil Liberties Union. (2010, September 15). ACLU settles student-cell-phone-search lawsuit with Northeast Pennsylvania school district. Retrieved from http://www.aclu.org/free-speech/aclu-settles-student-cell-phone-search-lawsuit-northeast-pennsylvania-school-district

Baxter, K. (2008). *The modern age: Turn-of-the-century American culture and the invention of adolescence.* Tuscaloosa: University of Alabama Press.

Bowles, S., & Gintis, H. (1976). *Schooling in capitalist America: Educational reform and the contradictions of economic life.* New York: Basic Books.

Bruno, J. E. (1995). Doing time—Killing time at school: An examination of the perceptions and allocations of time among teacher-defined at-risk students. *The Urban Review, 27,* 101–120.

Carnegie Council on Adolescent Development. (1992). *A matter of time: Risk and opportunity in the nonschool hours.* Washington, DC: Carnegie Council on Adolescent Development.

Deschenes, S., Cuban, L., & Tyack, D. (2001). Mismatch: Historical perspectives on schools and students who don't fit them. *Teachers College Record, 103,* 525–547.

Dwyer, P., & Wyn, J. (2001). *Youth, education and risk: Facing the future.* London: RoutledgeFalmer.

Fabian, J. (1983). *Time and the other: How anthropology makes its object.* New York: Columbia University Press.

Foucault, M. (2009). *Security, territory, population: Lectures at the College de France 1977–1978* (G. Burchell, Trans.). New York: Picador.

Greenhouse, C. J. (1996). *A moment's notice: Time politics across cultures.* Ithaca, NY: Cornell University Press.

Hagestad, G. O., & Uhlenberg, P. (2005). The social separation of old and young: A root of ageism. *Journal of Social Issues, 61,* 343–360.

Hall, G. S. (1904). *Adolescence: Its psychology and its relations to physiology, anthropology, sociology, sex, crime, religion, and education* (2 vols.). New York: Appleton.

Harris, A. (2004). *Future girl: Young women in the twenty-first century.* New York: Routledge.

Humes, E. (2003). *School of dreams: Making the grade at a top American high school.* Orlando, FL: Harcourt.

Jackson, P. (1968/2004). The daily grind. In D. J. Flinders, & S. J. Thornton (Eds.), *The curriculum studies reader* (pp. 93–102). New York: RoutledgeFalmer.

Kett, J. (1977). *Rites of passage: Adolescence in America 1790 to the present.* New York: Basic Books.

Lesko, N. (2001). *Act your age! A cultural construction of adolescence.* New York: RoutledgeFalmer.

Pope, D. (2001). *Doing school: How we are creating a generation of stressed out, materialistic, and miseducated students.* New Haven, CT: Yale University Press.

Richards, R. D., & Calvert, C. (2009). When sex and cell phones collide: Inside the prosecution of teen sexting cases. *Hastings Communication and Entertainment Law Journal, 32,* 1–39.

Richmond, R. (2009, March 26). Sexting may place teens at legal risk. *New York Times.* Retrieved from http://gadgetwise.blogs.nytimes.com/2009/03/26/sexting-may-place-teens-at-legal-risk/

Rist, G. (1997). *The history of development: From Western origins to global faith.* London: Zed.

Stockton, K. B. (2004). Growing sideways, or versions of the queer child: The ghost, the homosexual, the Freudian, the innocent, and the interval of the animal. In S. Bruhm, & N. Hurley (Eds.), *Curiouser: On the queerness of children* (pp. 277–315). Minneapolis: University of Minnesota Press.

Stone, G. (2009, March 13). "Sexting" teens can go too far: Sending provocative images over cell phones is all the rage, but it can all go wrong. *ABC News.* Retrieved from http://abcnews.go.com/Technology/WorldNews/sexting-teens/story?id=6456834

Zahn, D. (2010, November 26). Sorry kids, no privacy for you: State gives teachers free access to student cell phones, laptops. *WorldNetDaily.* Retrieved from http://www.wnd.com/?pageId=233145

15

DISORDERLY

Valerie Harwood

Over the past 30 years the word disorderly has become increasingly linked to discourses of mental disorder. This change points to the effects that the social and cultural has in the production of "scientific" knowledge of youth. Unlike uses in the mid-20th century, the word disorderly is now medicalized, conjuring images of aberrant behavior together with psychopathology. Earlier depictions of disorderliness such as James Dean's famous role as Jim Stark, the drunk and disorderly youth outsider in *Rebel Without a Cause* (Weisbart & Ray, 1955), were not underwritten with medicalized notions. Such representations linked youth with "out of order" behavior, attributing youthfulness with drunkenness and irresponsibility. The somewhat uncomplicated incorporation of mental disorder into the everyday is due to the creep of psychiatric concepts into wider cultural knowledge. From this perspective the production of disorderly meanings can be understood as cultural effects of medicalization and psychopathologization.

The *Diagnostic and Statistical Manual of Mental Disorders*

Current concepts underlying the word disorderly are largely informed by the American Psychiatric Association's (APA) *Diagnostic and Statistical Manual of Mental Disorders (DSM)*. This manual is the dominating system for classifying mental disorder, producing definitions used worldwide. Intriguingly, practices of defining people as disorderly are based upon the idea of mental disorder for which there is not an adequate definition (Bailey, 2010; Harwood, 2006). Over the years different *DSMs* have been produced, with the number of mental disorders increasing with each version (American Psychiatric Association, 1980, 1987,1994,2000; American Psychiatric Association Committee on Nomenclature and Statistics, 1952, 1968). While proponents of the *DSM* maintain changes reflect enhanced scientific knowledge, other viewpoints emphasize the role scientific and cultural processes play in the construction of knowledge (Bailey, 2010; Harwood, 2006, 2010). The first *DSM* (known as *DSM-I*) was published in 1952 and was 132 pages long. Three new editions and two revisions have since been produced: *DSM-II* (1968); *DSM-III* (1980); a revised third edition, *DSM-III-R* (1987); *DSM-IV* (1994); and a text revision, *DSM-IV-TR* (2000). Compared to the first edition, the most recent is 943 pages long. Also, the first *DSM* did not have a distinct section on childhood (or youth) disorders. While more attention was placed on childhood issues in *DSM-II* (1968), the greatest change occurred in *DSM-III* (1980) (Kirk & Kutchins, 1992), and the current edition, *DSM-IV-TR*, has a section titled "Disorders Usually First Diagnosed in Infancy, Childhood or Adolescence" that numbers almost 100 pages. With each *DSM* new disorders are introduced and disorders may be removed or modified. Numerous changes and additions are listed for the forthcoming fifth revision (known as *DSM-V*) to be published in May 2013. This revision may include six new childhood disorders and numerous new adult disorders. One of these adult disorders, Hoarding Disorder, has been represented on the U.S. reality show *Hoarders* (Chan, Severson, Flynn, Berg, & Sharenow, 2010), now in its third season. This show depicts hoarders as obese, lower social class or racialized, which are characterizations that link difference with mental disorder. The show's popularity prompts consideration as to how media representations may positively influence the legitimacy of the new disorders such as the *DSM-V* Hoarding Disorder.

The Effect of Media Portrayals

Media representations that spread knowledge about disorderly youth include forms such as film, song, and television series. These portrayals have what Henry Giroux (1999) calls a public pedagogy role; that is, they have constitutive effects that participate in the construction of disorderly youth subjectivities. This idea can be used to grasp how representations of disorderly youth influence young people's understandings of mental disorder. For instance, words linked with mental disorder such as psychopath or sociopath are used in Macy Gray, Ruzumna, Wilder, and Swann's (2001) "Relating to a Psychopath," a funky tune that includes the lines "You must be real far gone/You're relating to a psychopath/

Noah's elephants are leaving the ark in eights/during the upside of my manic depressive state." Likewise, Andrew Bird's (2009) *Oh No* incorporates an upbeat melody to accompany the chorus line "arm and arm with all the harmless sociopaths." While these lyrics are provocative insofar as they ironically situate sociopathy as harmless, they nevertheless insert specialist psychiatric terminology into fashionable discourse.

Like popular songs, cinematic and television portrayals of disorderly youth distribute knowledge about mental disorders to a wider audience. There are numerous examples of these, such as *Temple Grandin* (Ferguson & Jackson, 2010), starring Clare Danes as a young woman diagnosed with Autism, and the cult classic *Donnie Darko* (Ball and Kelly, 2001), where Jake Gyllenhaal plays a young man who experiences visual and auditory hallucinations (and who is taken by his parents to see a psychiatrist). Researchers in the field of adolescent psychology have suggested film depictions of mental disorder can convey valuable information about treatment (Jamieson, Romer, & Jamieson, 2006). Alternately, emphasis on mental disorders can be critiqued for providing psychopathological interpretations as an explanatory force. This force can be especially problematic when portrayals are misinformed, since mistakes can be difficult to recognize for a nonspecialist audience.

This is the case with *Girl, Interrupted* (Konrad, Wick, & Mangold, 1999), the film adaptation of Susanna Kaysen's (1993) bestselling memoir. Set in an adolescent psychiatric hospital in the 1960s, the film depicts young women with a range of mental disorders including Borderline Personality Disorder, Depression, Antisocial Personality Disorder, Obsessive Compulsive Disorder, Schizophrenia, and disorderly behaviors such as psychopathy. In the film and memoir, Susanna, the main character, is given the *DSM* definition of Borderline Personality Disorder. While Kaysen's records (displayed in the memoir) list "borderline personality" as diagnosed at the hospital in 1967, this is not identical to the mental disorder introduced to the *DSM* in the 1980s. The Borderline Personality Disorder of the lead character, both in the film and the memoir, is the representation of the 1980s *DSM* definitions onto the 1967 event (Marshall, 2006). Prior to the 1980s the term borderline had not been nailed down, as it were, to a psychiatric definition of disorder (Wirth-Cauchon, 2001). This rendition of the 1980s *DSM* Borderline Personality Disorder introduces audiences and readers alike to a specific form of disorderly subjectivity that is effectively written into *DSM* criteria. The film *Girl, Interrupted*, like the memoir, was highly successful, with Angelina Jolie winning an Oscar for best supporting actress. Despite the inaccuracies in the depictions, popular forms influence how disorderly youth subjectivities are to be understood. A film such as *Girl, Interrupted* informs knowledge on young women, depression, and disorderliness, identifies their symptoms, and reinforces the one treatment modality, namely medication (see also the discussion of *House MD* in Harwood, 2010). The film and the memoir, from the perspective of public pedagogy, are consequently much more than entertainment.

Disorderly Producing Disorder

Attention Deficit Hyperactivity Disorder (ADHD) is a well-known and controversial mental disorder that has prompted a great deal of medical and scholarly debate about diagnosis and medications. Unfortunately, this issue is not evenly presented to children and youth or to their parents and caregivers. This is readily apparent in teacher education, where in countries such as Australia and the United States preservice teachers are instructed on the diagnostic characteristics of ADHD, pharmacological treatments, and behavioral interventions (Graham, 2010; McMahon, in press). When this fails to address the vigorous debates, the possibility is lowered for parents, children, and teachers themselves to find alternatives to diagnostic routes or to medication. Research into behavioral issues and young people also tends to be largely medically or psychologically oriented, a bias that is reflective of funding agendas that tend to favor quantitative medicalized perspectives that are in line with the dominant (and largely *DSM*) interpretation of youth behavior. This one-sided presentation results in the snowballing of truths of disorderliness that produces the trend toward "diagnosing disorderly children" (Harwood, 2006).

When the procedure of diagnosing disorderliness is treated as unambiguous, social and cultural considerations can become easily concealed. This is a matter of concern when popular media portrayals such as in *Hoarders* depict classed, gendered, or racialized stereotypes. Obscuring social and cultural considerations has been raised as a problem in relation to gender and sexuality (Harwood, 2004), in terms of the racialization of disorders and disability (Ferri & Connor, 2005; Fitzgerald, 2009), and in respect to social class and disadvantage (Harwood, 2010). Given that a diagnosis of mental disorder conveys the sense that the problem resides in the individual, veiling social and cultural considerations carries considerable implications. One important dilemma that arises is that issues such as poverty, racism, heterosexism, homophobia, and classism are elided. Another is that, by virtue of being diagnosed as disorderly, a young person is introduced to the numerous *risks of diagnosis*. For example, there is the assumption conveyed via the *DSM* that through having a mental disorder one is more likely to have future health problems and, in some instances, at greater risk of engaging in criminality, practices which subjectify and produce disorderly youth subjects (Harwood, 2006).

Even though the process of creating a new disorder reveals the relationship between psychiatric knowledge and mental disorders, this relationship is seldom made explicit. It remains to be seen whether, with the advent of *DSM-V*, the growth in the disorderly problems of youth can be recognized as a product of a particular knowledge generation and the ensuing formation of disorderly subjectivities.

References

American Psychiatric Association. (1980). *Diagnostic and statistical manual of mental disorders (DSM-III)* (3rd ed.). Washington, DC: APA.

American Psychiatric Association. (1987). *Diagnostic and statistical manual of mental disorders, third edition, revised (DSM-III-R)* (3rd Rev. ed.). Washington, DC: APA.

American Psychiatric Association. (1994). *Diagnostic and statistical manual of mental disorders, fourth edition (DSM-IV)* (4th ed.). Washington, DC: APA.

American Psychiatric Association. (2000). *Diagnostic and statistical manual of mental disorders, fourth edition, text revision (DSM-IV-TR)* (4th ed.). Washington, DC: APA.

American Psychiatric Association Committee on Nomenclature and Statistics. (1952). *Diagnostic and statistical manual of mental disorders (DSM-I)* (1st ed.). Washington, DC: APA Committee on Nomenclature and Statistics.

American Psychiatric Association Committee on Nomenclature and Statistics. (1968). *Diagnostic and statistical manual of mental disorders (DSM-II)* (2nd ed.). Washington, DC: APA Committee on Nomenclature and Statistics.

Bailey, S. (2010). The DSM and the dangerous school child. *International Journal of Inclusive Education, 14*, 581–592.

Ball, C. (Producer), & Kelly, R. (Director). (2001). *Donnie Darko* [Motion picture]. United States: Newmarket Films.

Bird, A. (2009). *Oh no. On noble beast* [Album]. Chicago: Fat Possum.

Chan, M., Severson, D., Flynn, J., Berg, A., & Sharenow, R. (Executive Producers). (2010). *Hoarders Complete Season 1* [Television series]. Manhattan: Arts & Entertainment Network (A&E).

Ferguson, S. (Producer), & Jackson, M. (Director). (2010). *Temple Grandin* [Motion picture]. United States: HBO.

Ferri, B. A., & Connor, D. J. (2005). In the shadow of brown. *Remedial and Special Education, 26*, 93–100.

Fitzgerald, T. D. (2009). Controlling the black school-age male. *Urban Education, 44*, 225–247.

Giroux, H. (1999). Cultural studies as public pedagogy: Making the pedagogical more political. *Encyclopaedia of Philosophy of Education*. Retrieved February 15, 2005, from http://www.ffst.hr/ENCYCLOPAEDIA/doku.php?id=cultural_studies_and_public_pedagogy&s=cultural&]=studies&s=public&s=pedagogy

Graham, L. J. (Ed.) (2010). *(De)Constructing ADHD: Critical guidance for teachers and teacher educators*. New York: Peter Lang.

Gray, M., Ruzumna, J., Wilder, D., & Swann, D. (2001). Relating to a psychopath. In M. Gray, *On id* [Album]. USA: Epic Records.

Harwood, V. (2004). Subject to scrutiny: Taking Foucauldian genealogies to narratives of youth oppression. In M. L. Rasmussen, E. Rofes, & S. Talburt (Eds.), *Youth and sexualities: Pleasure, subversion and insubordination in and out of schools* (pp. 85–107). New York: Palgrave.

Harwood, V. (2006). *Diagnosing "disorderly" children: A critique of behaviour disorder discourses.* Oxford: Routledge.

Harwood, V. (2010). Mobile asylums: Psychopathologisation as a personal portable psychiatric prison. *Discourse: Studies in the Cultural Politics of Education, 31*, 437–451.

Jamieson, P. E., Romer, D., & Jamieson, K. H. (2006). Do films about mentally disturbed characters promote ineffective coping in vulnerable youth? *Journal of Adolescence, 29*, 749–760.

Kaysen, S. (1993). *Girl, interrupted.* New York: Vintage.

Kirk, S. A., & Kutchins, H. (1992). *The selling of the DSM: The rhetoric of science in psychiatry.* New York: Aldine De Gruyter.

Konrad, C., Wick, D. (Producers), & Mangold, J. (Director). (1999). *Girl, interrupted* [Motion picture]. United States: Columbia.

Marshall, E. (2006). Borderline girlhoods: Mental illness, adolescence, and femininity in Girl, Interrupted. *Lion and the Unicorn, 30*, 117–133.

McMahon, S. (in press). Doctors diagnose, teachers label: The unexpected in pre-service teachers' talk about labelling children with ADHD. *International Journal of Inclusive Education.*

Weisbart, D. (Producer), & Ray, N. (Director). (1955). *Rebel without a cause* [Motion picture]. United States: Warner Brothers.

Wirth-Cauchon, J. (2001). *Women and borderline personality disorder: Symptoms and stories.* New Brunswick, NJ: Rutgers University Press.

16

GENERATION

Cindy Patton

A full genealogy of the Western concept of generation might trace the idea to Greco-Roman theories of heredity, in which social reproduction was dependent on the quality of biological matter transmitted by successive parents through time, something like a character gene in our contemporary imaginary. In *On the Generation of Animals*, Aristotle (2004/350BCE) characterized and typologized different modes of reproduction (sexual, asexual, and spontaneous). He supposed that females contributed only undifferentiated mass to their offspring, while males contributed the specific characteristics that defined an individual. Although seemingly archaic, this idea that male input is responsible for character, generational continuity, and historical change persisted through a range of scientific regimes, continued, by analogy through the Enlightenment, and reared its head in 1960s research on "youth culture."

Aristotle's ideas were highly influential in premodern science, but with the emergence and 1,200-year dominance of Christianity in the West, ideas of generation held little explanatory utility in a theocentric universe that cast Time as the march toward God's Kingdom. The Enlightenment reignited questions about social and political legitimation, and by its end, the natural and human sciences, once close cousins, took up the concept of generation for quite different explanatory tasks. Nineteenth-century historians began to speculate about the role of generations as a mechanism of history and the emergent, empirical field of sociology took up the idea of generations as a way of understanding social time. German historians dominated the debates about the meaning and motor of history, and generations seemed to provide an explanation for the smaller changes that were embedded in larger epochs (King, 1972; Marias, 1970). One side of the debate saw generations as a process of perfection, with occasional spates of degeneration; this "pulse-rate" theory of generations viewed historical change and continuity as the outcome of the successive generations, defined reproductively as about 30 years apart.

The reality that generations often overlap particular sets of years, and that different nations and civilizations exhibited peaks and valleys out of synch with one another, required a new understanding of generations. Instead of seeing history as the unified expression of regular human succession, other historians, but especially sociologists (many initially trained in philosophy), argued that early experiences of the world formed common impressions in the mind of persons born in a common milieu; a generation saw the world through a particular framework, but did not generate it (Jaeger, 1985). This individualistic model—a generation is the sum of the individuals who were imprinted in a particular way—collapsed in the face of obvious differences in experience among those in a generation who were of different social classes (gender was ignored as an important ground for experiential differences). Debate about generations expanded outside the historical and philosophical domain. German sociologists of the late 1800s inaugurated an empirical challenge to the speculative histories used to justify totalitarian and fascist political regimes. Treading a fine line between an idealist understanding of the spirit of an era as the outcome of moral-historical forces, and a social relativism that might have little purchase against fascisms, art historian Wilhelm Pinder (1878–1947; an enthusiastic supporter of cultural National Socialism) and sociologist Karl Mannheim (1893–1947; a Hungarian Jew teaching in Germany until he fled to England in 1933) developed Aristotle's concept of entelechy (a force being actualized) into ideas of generation that differently weight social and temporal structures.

Pinder (1926) wrote extensively about the relationship between art forms (architecture, painting, sculpture) and national or regional character. From his chair at Berlin University, his interpretations of German art heritage as the realization of a national artistic spirit were widely influential in national socialist political circles. Pinder's method of analyzing artistic development as generational collisions between established and new artists laid the groundwork for one strand of contemporary thinking about cultural generation.

Mannheim (1928) grapples with generational tensions embedded in a theory of social reproduction embedded in a sociology of knowledge. Rejecting strict models that derive ideology and social location from class structure, Mannheim assigns equal weight to class formation and generational formation—or what he calls "generational stratum," a hypothetical confluence of historical and social features that are the reference point for persons coming of age in a specific place and time. He distinguishes this "stratum" from generational context, which he describes as actual social and intellectual content actively shared among actual people. Eschewing the tendency of idealist histories to weight continuity over difference, he suggests a third concept—generational unit—to describe subgroups of individuals who share a context, but have different interpretations of it (Kettler & Loader, 2004; Pilcher, 1994).

Commentators have pointed out that, while the wars of the early 20th century were significant (generation forming) events, Americans as a group were not as dramatically shaped by the rapid sequence of political and economic upheavals that mark European—and especially German—theorizations of history and society. American post-World War II works like *The Lonely Crowd* (Reisman, Glazer, & Denney, 1950) did not take major political events as the principle for generational demarcation. Instead, Reisman identified American cultural types that he argued had evolved generations defined by tradition-directedness to inner-directedness and finally to other-directedness. In the postindustrial era, he argued, the middle class (in the apotheosis of the suburb) moved away from attending to tradition and a sense of worth grounded in traditional structures (like church or family) and toward a concern with building a visible model life defined by what others owned or did for work or leisure. Reisman broke completely with the idea that generations last a set period of time (indeed, generations seem to become shorter and shorter in and after his work) and replaced the idea that a generation is the aggregate of individuals who share an historical context, with the idea that a generation is defined by its mode of finding meaning.

Reisman's book popularized the idea of a developmental American character that was conceptually unlike the entelechial national character that had been popularly valorized in Nazism. But academic research in Reisman's wake flattened out what was most interesting about his relationship model of national character. Instead, the impulse to quantify and parse the potentially alarming rise of the "other-directed" national character was abetted by the rise of new statistical methods and, soon, computational power that made it possible for Americans to imagine themselves as the subjects of population-scale research. Soon, newspapers were filled with statistics that explored generational differences in religion, political opinion, and family structures. Insidiously working hand in glove with the very capitalism that Reisman argued had provided the material demarcators that "other-directed" persons required, the new demography of generations enabled marketers to target goods by generational group, actually helping create a "generation."

Identifying with alienation novels and films of the 1950s and 1960s (William Golding's sentinel *Lord of the Flies* [2004/1954], the earlier and more philosophical *L'Etranger* [1942/1992] [sometimes translated in English as *The Stranger*, sometimes as *The Outsider*] by Albert Camus, Nicholas Ray's James Dean vehicle, *Rebel Without a Cause* [1955], and message-film producer Stanley Kramer and director Laslo Benedek's *The Wild One* [1953], which solidified Marlon Brando's hair as a protest symbol), young people began "dropping out" and contesting the stunting of self-knowledge that Reisman's work had warned of. By the 1960s, this ennui turned into more direct protests of specific government policies and practices (the Vietnam War, the draft, drinking and voting age, age of consent in sexual matters), creating two youth protest cultures that were frequently conflated in the media (Feuer, 1969). The "hippy" counterculture popularized in the media was focused on sexual experimentation and use of drugs to expand consciousness, manifest as alternative family structures, music festivals, health food, and the Westernization of Eastern spiritual practices, including Buddhism and yoga. Youth International Party members—yippies— who directed their activities toward political rather than cultural change, used theatrical protest of the kind later revived by ACT UP and were among those who went on trial in 1968 for disrupting the Republican National Convention in Chicago. The Black Civil Rights movement also spawned a youthful and more confrontational wing in the Black Power movement, who were uneasily aligned with White-dominated youth movements and, by the late 1960s, with the gay movement, which though not defined publicly by generation saw itself as breaking from a quietist "generation" of homosexuals who were afraid to "come out of the closet."

These many forms of lifestyle counterculture politics and the increasingly violent protests of the student left and Black Power movements made the idea of a generational divide intuitively plausible (e.g., Esler, 1974; Mead, 1970). Liberal and progressive writers in the mainstream media and pop sociology presented the values and actions of youth and of "adults" as profoundly at odds. The Port Huron Statement—"an agenda for a generation"—that was the founding document of the Students for a Democratic Society was heavily influenced by "older generation" radical sociologist, C. Wright Mills (1951, 1956). The high availability of mass media communication technologies— television, radio, and the still-vital newspapers—simultaneously documented and created what was soon described as a "generation gap" so extreme that those on the two sides were strangers to each other. (Few shoppers today know that The Gap started in San Francisco in 1969 selling Levi jeans and long-play records.) Liberals like Edward Kennedy, who took up the mantle of youthful politician of the new era after the assassination of his brothers, argued that the youth movements possessed a superior moral sensibility in their vision of a less capital-driven society. Using survey data that made the difference in opinions less clear, conservatives argued that the 60s generation was no different than any other, and chided liberals for pandering to what it viewed as over-privileged youth (Fairlie, 1967). Socialists argued against both liberals and conservatives, suggesting instead that a cultural definition of generation obscured the economic system that exploited youth, who worked at low-paid jobs or were conscripted into the military that enabled American imperialist-capitalist ambitions (Burgess & Hofstetter, 1971).

While researchers and commentators continued to debate the extent and meaning of a "gap," there was no longer any debate about whether "generation" was a natural or invented phenomenon. In a parallel process of social constitution, youth had become an essentialized category, and it required an age-structured other for its definition. Age became a standard variable to collect in demographic studies, rhetoricians analyzed youth culture speech (including folk and rock songs), sociologists analyzed youth subcultures and styles (especially in the work of the Birmingham Centre for Cultural Studies), and marketing research continued to bore down into details of what the young might be persuaded to buy (or, what older persons might buy to signify their "hip"ness).

There remains little debate about the concept of generations, although some researchers prefer the more objectivist concept of cohort. In descriptive and analytical work on the generations after the baby boom, time is speeding up. By the 1990s, generations were marked not in terms of cryptic biological turn- over of families, of world wars, or even in terms of conflict between younger and older persons, but (possibly echoing Reisman) in terms of social relation- ship to information technologies, itself described in terms of generations (1.0, 2.0, 2.2, etc.). Rapid advances in the technology that now coevolves with social relationship has produced myriad generational names: for example, the self- named Yuppies, Twinkies, and GenX, and the externally described Gen Y, Gen Why?, and Gen Z (or Gen I) (Wagner, 2007). Most research on the proliferating generations (or minigenerations—"2.2") no longer debates the value of thinking in terms of generations, nor is it very critical about the differences that certainly exist between generations on paper (Mannheim's "stratum") versus affective generations (Mannheim's context) (Samuelson, 2010). Instead, much research deploying the idea of generations seems content to draw hazy lines based on dates relevant within its particular research domain (immigration, cultural attributes, work and leisure habits, and purchasing power and product desires) without worrying too much if the concept of generation can stand the strain of so many uses. Although it seems doubtful that researchers will be willing to try to live without generations, it might be useful to turn back to the beginning of 20th-century debates about the idea. Bloch (1977/1932) starts his 1932 work on social forms and times with these very postmodern-sounding words: "Not all people exist in the same Now . . . different years resound in the one that has just been recorded and prevails" (p. 22).

References

Aristotle. (2004/350BCE). *On the generation of animals* (A. Platt, Trans.). Whitefish, MT: Kessinger Publishing.

Bloch, E. (1977/1932). Nonsynchronism and the obligation to its dialectics. *New German Critique, 11,* 22–38.

Burgess, P. M., & Hofstetter, C. R. (1971). The "student movement": Ideology and reality. *Midwest Journal of Political Science, 15,* 687–702.

Camus, A. (1942/1992). *L'Etranger.* Paris: Gallimard.

Esler, A. (Ed.). (1974). *The youth revolution.* Toronto: D. C. Heath and Company.

Fairlie, H. (1967). How is youth to be served? *New Republic, 156,* 12–14.

Feuer, L. S. (1969). *The conflict of generations: The character and significance of student movements.* New York: Basic Books.

Golding, W. (2004/1954). *Lord of the flies.* London: Faber and Faber.

Jaeger, H. (1985). Generations in history: Reflections on a controversial concept. *History and Theory, 24,* 273–292.

Kettler, D., & Loader, C. (2004). Temporizing with time wars: Karl Mannheim and problems of historical time. *Time and Society, 13,* 155–172.

King, J. K. (1972). The generational theory in German literary criticism. *German Life and Letters, 25,* 334–343.

Kramer, S. (Producer), & Benedek, L. (Director). (1953). *The wild one* [Motion picture]. USA: A Stanley Kramer Company Production.

Mannheim, K. (1928). Das Problem der Generationen. *Kölner Vierteljahrshefte für Soziologie, 7,* 157–185, 309–330.

Marias, J. (1970). *Generations: A historical method* (H. C. Raley, Trans.). Tuscaloosa: University of Alabama Press.

Mead, M. (1970). *Culture and commitment: A study of the generation gap.* Garden City, NY: Natural History Press.

Mills, C. W. (1951). *White collar: The American middle classes.* New York: Oxford University Press.

Mills, C. W. (1956). *The power elite.* New York: Oxford University Press.

Pilcher, J. (1994). Mannheim's sociology of generations: An undervalued legacy. *British Journal of Sociology, 45,* 481–494.

Pinder, W. (1926). Die "Ungleichzeitigkeit" des Gleichzeitigen. In W. Pinder (Ed.), *Das Problem der Generation in der Kunstgeschichte Europas* (pp. 11–22). Berlin: Frankfurter Verlags-Anstalt.

Ray, N. (Director). (1955). *Rebel without a cause* [Motion picture]. USA: Warner Brothers.

Reisman, D., Glazer, C., & Denney, R. (1950). *The lonely crowd: A study of the changing American character*. New Haven, CT: Yale University Press.

Samuelson, R. J. (2010). The real generation gap: Young adults are getting slammed. *Newsweek, 155*, 11.

Wagner, T. (2007, December 1). *Dealing with generation why: Workers 18 to 34 grew up in a different world than their older counterparts, so understanding them can sometimes be challenging. South Central Construction*. Madison, MS: McGraw-Hill.

17

RESISTANCE

Elisabeth Soep

Resistance Has Its Moments

Though rooted in histories, intentions, and effects that endure, resistance comes in moments. The moment a teenage White boy in Paul Willis's (1977) canonical *Learning to Labour* empties his pockets of ID, pulls on gloves, and sets off with fellow lads to break into the school building after hours. Willis says that, by carrying out this kind of "thievery," the boys challenge authority through well-calculated risk. The moment a South Asian Muslim high-school student in Boston a week after September 11 chooses to write the words "INDIA + MUSLIM" on her bag. It's a gesture that reinforces the girl's analysis linking domestic and imperial warfare and tells us something important about "the nature of dissent at a time of political repression," according to Sunaina Maira's (2009, p. 208) study of youth, citizenship, and empire. The moment a young woman at a subway station in Oakland, California, uses a digital camera to capture the commotion she hears out on the platform after transit police officers detain a group of young men in the early morning hours of New Year's Day 2009. Despite her own fear and orders to stay back, the passenger keeps rolling as one of the officers, a 27-year-old White man named Johannes Mehserle, shoots and kills a 22-year-old Black man, Oscar Grant, while Grant lies chest-down and unarmed on the platform, hands restrained behind his back.

What mileage do we get out of framing these disparate moments as acts of resistance? The researchers documenting these events don't necessarily even use that terminology. Willis speaks of "counterculture" and "partial penetration." Maira offers the concept of "dissenting citizenship." I have written about the Oscar Grant shooting and young reporters' coverage of the event to reveal how young people can strategically embed on-the-fly digital recordings inside sustained, collective calls for truth and public accountability (Soep, 2011). But regardless of whether we call it resistance, each of these accounts undeniably draws on a fraught tradition of analyzing how young people's everyday actions, popular culture expressions, and joint efforts can transform the social structures and policies that govern lives including but not limited to their own.

What Counts

Part of what makes this work fraught has to do with the history of resistance studies itself, especially as applied to youth, a population that is served, surveilled, managed, celebrated, trained, and targeted in particular ways. The Birmingham School has been faulted for finding resistance at every turn in youth activities, especially among White working-class males like the lads in Willis's game-changing ethnography. Though crucial in drawing attention to young people's agency in the face of inequality—and in revealing *how* their "partial penetrations" ultimately help reproduce the very conditions they rail against—these early resistance studies missed political subtleties and contradictions especially as related to nuances of race, gender, and sexuality (Maira & Soep, 2005). Followers of the Birmingham tradition—especially those eager to counter stereotypes of youth delinquency and moral panic—sometimes leave readers with the impression that all oppositionality can be interpreted as a form of resistance. That's an error Pedro Noguera and Chiara Cannella (2006) say ultimately offers a rationale for antisocial or self-destructive behavior (and subsequent discipline and punishment), and thus does little to reframe the conditions bearing down on young people in the first place.

Perhaps in response to these well-established critiques of the tendency to overinterpret resistance in cultural studies research, there are those, like Henry Giroux (2001), who want to see evidence of young people's conscious and intentional critique of social conditions in order for behavior to count as resistance and not mere opposition. This line of thinking would hold that analysts overstep their bounds when they see resistance inside young people's activities and expressions if the actors themselves don't frame what they're doing as such. That criterion certainly simplifies matters, and it usefully restrains researchers from indulging our own desire to align ourselves without reflexivity alongside youth in struggle, and to graft our hopes onto their actions. But ultimately a hard-line standard that resistance only resides where young people are deliberately and collectively acting to transform their communities is also unsatisfying. It leaves us without a framework to understand the gray areas between action, intention, and social implications and no way to account for the possibility that young people, like everyone, can find meanings in retrospect that may not have been available to them ahead of time or in the midst of an unfolding event. It also ignores the ways in which even apparently individual actions are formed out of sometimes-invisible social interactions and institutional histories; not only when young people are explicitly banding together are they not working alone. Moreover, if we always defer to young people's reflections on their own activities as the single analysis that trumps everything else, we can miss the ways in which their self-reports are themselves performances crafted for audiences (including researchers). We run the risk of reifying the "authenticity" of their voices (Fleetwood, 2005) while ignoring other forces and incentives that structure what they do and say out loud, to whom, when, and what it means.

A Scene

Let me return, for a moment, to that scene on the subway platform in Oakland when Oscar Grant was killed. While approaching the station for the first time since the incident, the teenage passenger who recorded the shooting acknowledged, "I feel a little nervous and I don't know why." "This is where I peeked my head out," she said once she'd stepped inside the station, remembering that the young men who'd been pulled from the train were lining up "against that wall over there." At one point that night, she said there were so many people and so much going on, she got scared, hopped back on the train, and turned off her camera. But when it started getting loud again, she turned the camera back on and stepped onto the platform, walking closer and closer to the scene. "I'm standing 10 feet away," she said, using the present tense to describe what happened that night as she approached. She remembered Grant's words to the officers: he told them please not to shoot him, please go easy on him. "I keep recording and they throw him on his belly," the passenger continued. "Another officer puts his knee on his neck, and another officer stands directly on top of him . . . and he's laying flat on his belly." And the gun went off.

This passenger did not narrate these events to me. She was talking to a 19-year-old reporter, Denise Tejada, who was covering the shooting and its aftermath for Youth Radio, a national youth-driven media education program and production company headquartered in Oakland, California, where both Denise and I work. Recruited primarily from local public schools, Youth Radio participants collaborate with professional journalists to produce content that is distributed through broadcast and digital outlets including National Public Radio (NPR), *The Huffington Post*, and iTunes. Seeking various youth angles on the Oscar Grant story, Denise had seen a local TV spot featuring the girl who'd recorded the shooting and tracked her down via MySpace. Denise sent a message requesting an interview. The video she produced out of that interview inter-cut with footage of the shooting became part of more than a year's worth of coverage by Youth Radio reporters, producers, photographers, and commentators.[1] The body of work included online reports on the community's response to the killing, talk shows with artists and musicians, breaking news dispatches from the courtroom where the transit officer was eventually tried for murder, a digital photo magazine called Grant Station, and radio features bringing the local story to NPR's more than 30 million listeners.

When Is Resistance?

I share this description of a killing, a witness recording, and a sustained period of collaborative media coverage, all with young people at the center of events, as a way to run these ruminations on resistance through a concrete example. I'm not so much interested in "what" is resistance from within this account, but "when" is resistance useful to think with.[2] If we focus too tightly on what the passenger did in that moment, her insistence on staying close and continuing to roll, we run the risk of projecting our own wishes onto her intentions and celebrating a lone girl's actions without recognizing the various conditions that supported her behavior—not least availability of low-cost mobile digital recording devices and sites through which to share uploads. If we say resistance resides in that in-the-moment act of recording and stop there, we lose sight of the resources—money, other forms of capital, access to education and equipment as well as networked publics—required for concerned youth citizens to come together in a collective effort to draw critical attention to this one event embedded within a history of tensions and brutalities between and within law enforcement and youth communities. And if we don't critically examine the body of youth-generated media that has been produced about Grant's killing and its aftermath, we fall into the trap of assuming young people always "get it right" because of who they, essentially, are. We fail to engage with them as serious cocreators of public narratives that are, like Willis's lads' shenanigans, and like resistance itself, always partial, never complete.

Asking the resistance question in terms of when, and not what, acknowledges how very much context matters. Any given act can mean something completely different depending on the discourses, histories, and collective efforts in which it is embedded—by actors on the scene, and by researchers after-the-fact. For example, writing the words INDIA + MUSLIM on a book bag will have very different implications depending on whether it's done in the immediate wake of 9/11 or, say, during the more recent panic surrounding the proposed building of a Muslim community center at Ground Zero. Its relationship to resistance will vary based on the larger context of the school the writer attends, the networks she's a part of, and what kind of public gaze falls on her action. And the meaning will evolve over time, as it already has, being presented as part of a book about 9/11 published nearly 10 years later. Orienting ourselves around the "when" of resistance in this way saves us from locating the unit of analysis inside the psychologies of individual minds and turns our attention to the shifting dynamics of social worlds.

There is another theme across resistance studies with relevance here. For critical researchers, there can be a tendency not to romanticize resistance, but to do the opposite. We can flex our analytical muscles to reveal how, inevitably, even progressive efforts to challenge dominant structures and unsettle inequalities in one way or another are always complicit in those systems and fall short of realizing lasting change. One could certainly make that case regarding the Oscar Grant story. The officer who shot him, after all, received an involuntary murder conviction that many in Oakland and beyond saw as falling well short of justice. What good, then, were acts of resistance along the way?

One way to answer that question is to recognize how resistance unfolds and transforms over time, that we can never freeze it in an ethnographic present. This is especially the case among young people, as more and more of them deploy digital technologies to record, report, and critique their social worlds, sending transmissions via social media into networks the original authors can never control. In this sense, resistance is always also an act of surrender—knowing one's efforts are likely to be remixed and spit back in forms that might be unrecognizable or even abhorrent. Laced inside acts of resistance and studies of resistance, then, is always this hovering possibility of disappointment, a product of the gap between what young people set out to do, or thought they were doing, and what happens. And yet it seems to me a move in the right direction to recognize that youth resistance is defined not by its fixed properties, but by its contingent uses. The meanings of resistance may not be immediately evident nor fully known by participants, and can change over time, and researchers participate in shaping how those meanings move.

Notes

1 A record of Youth Radio's coverage of Oscar Grant's shooting can be found at: http://www.youthradio.org/topic/oscar-grant.
2 For this framing I am indebted to Nelson Goodman's (1991) influential essay, "When Is Art?", in which he argues that the endless effort to determine what is art is ultimately futile because it asks the wrong question.

References

Fleetwood, N. (2005). Mediating youth: Community-based video production and the politics of race and authenticity. *Social Text, 23*, 83–109.

Giroux, H. (2001). *Theory and resistance in education: Towards a theory for the opposition, revised and expanded edition.* Westport, CT: Bergin & Garvey.

Goodman, N. (1991). When is art? In R. Smith, & A. Simpson (Eds.), *Aesthetics and arts education* (pp. 108–118). Champaign: University of Illinois Press.

Maira, S. (2009). *Missing: Youth, citizenship, and empire after 9/11.* Durham, NC: Duke University Press.

Maira, S., & Soep, E. (Eds.). (2005). *Youthscapes: The popular, the national, the global.* Philadelphia: University of Pennsylvania Press.

Noguera, P., & Cannella, C. (2006). Youth agency, resistance, and civic activism: The public commitment to social justice. In S. Ginwright, P. Noguera, & J. Cammarota (Eds.), *Beyond resistance! Youth activism and community change* (pp. 333–348). New York: Routledge.

Soep, E. (2011). All the world's an album: Youth media as strategic embedding. In J. Fisherkeller (Ed.), *International perspectives on youth media: Cultures of production & education.* New York: Peter Lang.

Willis, P. (1977). *Learning to labour: How working class kids get working class jobs.* New York: Columbia University Press.

18

SUBCULTURE

Martha Marín Caicedo

Although the term "youth subculture" coined at the Birmingham Centre for Contemporary Cultural Studies refers to cultures born after World War II and is mostly associated with teds, mods, skinheads, rockers, punks, and rude-boys, in the 1930s it was already possible to find the Mexican American youth culture of pachucos in the border area between the United States and Mexico. Like the first teds in Great Britain, as well as youth subcultures in different times and places, pachuco culture was criminalized in 1942 in Los Angeles and connected to the 1943 "zoot-suit riots." Juvenile criminalization in the first half of the 20th century used representations of youth forged in the 19th century that were nurtured by adultism and constructions of pathology articulated to racism and the imposition of middle-class values on the poor (Finn, 2001; Mintz, 2004). In this framework underprivileged youngsters were (and still are) supposed to exhibit innate moral flaws and their symbols became targets of widespread hostile crowd behavior.

The pachuco metamorphized into the cholo in the 1950s, drawing on cultural symbols from Mexico, some of which ended up "giving voice to cultural resistance in the Chicano movement and among Mexican-born youths throughout the United States" (Valenzuela, n.d.). By the late 1970s, the cholo youth phenomenon traversed borders, and cholos in Mexico began to "integrate and redefine [the symbolic legacy] into their own speech, graphic arts and symbolism"(Valenzuela, n.d.; see also Valenzuela, 1997). These youth expressions have been positioned, since the 1940s, through the practices of the police, welfare agencies, schools, the juvenile justice system, and the mass media as sites for social management of immigrant and Latin American youth in the United States.

Uses of the Idea of Youth Subcultures in Latin American Contexts

Such a complex network of phenomena displayed by youth cultures in Latin America could not be easily perceived in the late 1970s or 1980s when youth cultures from countries such as England, Germany, Spain, and the United States "became visible": punk (1978), skinhead (1980), heavy metal (1981), and hip hop (1984).[1] Academic contexts mainly interpreted youth (sub)cultures as a "response to crisis," framing their attitudes, behaviors, and musical, visual, or stylistic expressions as reflections of the socioeconomic and historical moment many Latin American nations were going through. Neoliberal policies imposed during the 1980s simultaneously resulted in strengthened concentration of wealth and acute economic recessions, socioeconomic exclusion, the growth of unemployment and underemployment, the aggravation of social and political conflicts, the onset of dictatorships, civil wars, the weakening of civil society, and the degradation of ecosystems. The landscape of youth cultures' constitution in Latin America was highly convoluted and very different than that of the Birmingham School's conceptualization of youth subculture.

During those years, awareness of the critical situation of young populations in the region began, as youth unemployment, judicial/criminal concerns, and moral panics about youth arose in many countries:

> Young women or young popular urban men [were] seen as experiencing great difficulties. We could say that the renewed interest in youth population was the result of [an incitement to understand] young people as social danger, as "damaged social agents."
>
> (Szulik & Kuasñosky, 1994, p. 229; my translation)

Shifts to late capitalism in Latin America were accompanied by cultural dynamics and adult reconfigurations of adolescence that constructed young people through contradictory discourses as "victims," "problems," "potential consumers," "assets," "social agents," and as "people to be blamed for a host of social ills," among other representations. Understanding youth cultures as "responses to crisis" enabled researchers to clean up the public image of an entire youth population and make it "presentable" and "useful," thus questioning an entire apparatus of social classification and regulation.

Problems with "Subculture"

Feixa (1995) has criticized the Birmingham Centre for Contemporary Cultural Studies' conceptualization of "subculture":

> Subculture studies have focused mainly on deviant and not on conventional young people; on working class adolescents rather than on their contemporary middle class peers; [they] have favored young men over young women, and the little world of "youth leisure" over the "broader world" of adult institutions.
>
> (p. 73; my translation)

Feixa proposes the term "youth cultures" in an attempt at "integrating not only the deviant but the conventional, the marginal and the normal, [the youth's] relative autonomy and their steady link to family, education, commerce, State and labor structures" (p. 73). By youth cultures, he refers to "the collection of life styles and values expressed by generational collectives in response to their social and material conditions" (p. 73).

The concept of "youth culture" began to appear in scholarly and mass media discourses along with terms like "gangs," "youth tribes," or "urban tribes." These interwoven discursive practices created specific conditions for visibility, resulting in a deepening knowledge of the socioeconomic, cultural, and political realities in which many youngsters of the region lived (Reguillo, 1995); the "discovery" of different ways of being young (Arroyo & Salinas, 1999; Margulis & Marcelo, 1994; Marín & Muñoz, 1995); and growing attention to urban youth identities, communication styles, circuits, tastes, and cultural consumption practices (Di Marco, 2005; Reguillo, 1994).

Some continuing problems were indiscriminate use of the terms "gangs" and "youth cultures" as synonyms that erased specificities, differences, and interconnections between the two phenomena and indirectly contributed to the stigmatization of punks, metal heads, skinheads, rappers, and their derivations. Moreover, it was difficult to conceptualize these groups beyond the Birmingham School's relationship between infrastructure and superstructure, thus reducing subcultures to "spectacular styles" or attempts to "express and resolve, albeit magically, the contradictions which remain hidden or unresolved in the parent culture" (Cohen, as cited in Hall & Jefferson, 1980, p. 32).

Latin American sociological studies followed the Birmingham School's class-based analysis, constructing a logic that assimilated youth cultural activity to *bricolage*. These studies used the binary identity/consumption to reduce cultural activity to precise coordinates of identities and differences where youth were always linked to a "parent culture" and recycled symbols and objects of consumption, performed rituals, and marked territories in order to express their identities. However, these concepts could not reflect personal and cultural mutations found in ethnographic studies, *in situ* wanderers' experiences, changing ways to construct subjectivities, or the multiple paradoxes faced by youth cultures in their journey through a globalized world. Elements such as the trance-like togetherness and emotional community experienced by 1980s youth cultures—so dominated by electronic music—became understandable only through microconcepts like those proposed by Maffesoli (1990): "processes of de-individualization" (p. 34), the "fluidity" and variety of "tribal formations" (p. 29), multiplicity of the self, nomadism, and an empathic sociality expressed in a succession of communal atmospheres and emotions.

The Aesthetic Dimension: Expanding Conceptualizations of Subculture

Marín and Muñoz's (2002) *Secretos de mutantes: Música y creación en las culturas juveniles* moved beyond concepts like identity and difference to understand youth cultures as "heterogenetic subjectivities," as processes of singularization that favor the creation of what is unique and unrepeatable (Guattari, 1995, p. 5), to make an esthetic dimension of youth cultures visible. The aesthetic dimension transcends stylistic expressions and comprises a creative order related to the artistic process, which propels the search for and creation of other modes of existence and of "something else."[2] From the practice of self-styling and the aesthetics of existence conceptualized by Foucault (1994), cultures might be seen as huge experimental laboratories where participants take themselves as the very object of a complex elaboration, where young people transform themselves to accede to a certain way of being and work for the creation, transformation, and development of new modes of existence, ethical frameworks, art forms, and unique types of knowledge converted into praxis (for an example in youth studies, see Amaya & Marín, 2000). These processes occur in the midst of the characteristic libertarian gestures and microfascisms, between lucidity and the ghetto attitudes of youth cultures, and the struggle to escape from them.

The heterogenesis[3] of youth cultures evidences the precariousness of causal approaches to explain the emergence of these cultures, or existential territories, on the basis of sociohistorical or economic factors. Microhistories of youth cultures show that many other factors contribute rhizomatically to their creation: the sensibilities and legacies passed on by inspiring outsiders and mentors; the existential coordinates present in music; the unique circumstances surrounding these cultures' foundational acts; some singular translations of "carpe diem"; the composition and attitude of the groups that "started it all"; and the meanings attached to inviting/irresistible gestures and interactions with the mass media industry, among many others.

To make visible the aesthetic dimension necessitates transcending representations of youth as "incomplete human beings who know less," or are "passive," "at risk," or "in transition," giving prominence to youths' active engagement in the production of meanings and other ways of existing. From the aesthetic dimension, the study of youth cultures has begun to establish that every youth culture has its own nonlinear history and ways of creating multiplicity inside itself, similar to the logics of the ongoing diversification of music. Punk, hip hop, metal, skinhead, and their ramifications advance in diverse times and geographies, organizing themselves around specific musical cores. They are neither closed systems, always identical to themselves everywhere, nor subject to central command (Marín & Muñoz, 2006). Youth cultures have motor forces of creation such as the punks' "do it yourself" (DIY) and hip hoppers' "create your own style." DIY has remained in punk culture—in different moments and geographies—as a spirit to return to when this culture (or its descendants, such as hardcore and straight edge) reaches a dead end. When hip hop demands that its participants "create their own style," it lays the basis for hip hoppers throughout the world to develop local forms of expression and to use the raw materials of sound, images, rhythm, and movement in processes of self-creation. Each youth culture contains within itself a set of impulses that tend to carry out all of their potential. This is the reason for the constant defining of branches, subbranches, and fusions within and among these cultures. The development or suppression of these impulses or "seeds" rules not only the interaction of these cultures but also their possibilities of ramification and multiplicity.

Mutation is a facet of the creative impulse present in youth cultures that cannot be confined into the well-known linear and predictable boxes that developmental psychology attributes to this age. Mutation is linked to the quest for new possibilities of being and allows for the unfolding of totally new configurations of what is possible: good skinhead students becoming night warriors and functioning surreptitiously in the underground world. "Alternative" boys—besieged by who they are and by the heinous borders that contain their being—dye their hair and eventually practice cross-dressing to "change . . . not to progress in the sense of becoming better, but in the sense of alternating" (Marín & Muñoz, 2002, p. 274). Young women and men "travel" among youth cultures and are called to let go of blind points of perception and "ways of being" promoted by the culture they belonged to. They either subvert their youth culture codes or move to new existential coordinates, encounters, and territories.

Since the concept of the aesthetic dimension of youth cultures was born at the intersection of theory and detailed field work, it opens up new challenges, possibilities, and questions regarding diverse contemporary youth culture's functioning:

- The need to deepen knowledge of contemporary processes of creating one's self, other frameworks of reference, and new collective subjectivities. These processes are characterized by young people's oscillations between belonging and becoming, mutations, singularization, and the creation of multiplicities within cultures.
- Consideration of how theories of profound social, economic, and political changes and categories like "populational reasoning," "biopower," and "immaterial labor" can offer valuable and alternative visions of youth, social justice, and collective and personal autonomy that youth cultural practices suggest.
- Reflection on how young people actively constitute their subjectivities through mediums of music and other forms of creation, dealing not only with the complex entwining between cultural industries and youth cultures but also (and surprisingly) with the socioeconomic transformations according to which technologies of domination do not target specific productive activities but subjects' very capacity of producing and creating in itself.

Although many participants simply enjoy, cherish, or bemoan their cultures, others ask themselves relevant, Foucauldian (1994) questions: What is it that we don't need anymore? What wouldn't be indispensable to constitute ourselves as autonomous beings?

Notes

1   Feixa (2008, p. 253) documents the presence of punk in Mexico since 1978. According to young skinheads on the web and in diverse fanzines, skinhead culture entered Latin America from 1981 to 1985. Foundational films like *Wild Style*, *Beat Street*, and *Break Dance* were featured in many Latin American countries around this time, and are considered by young hoppers as the beginning of b-boying.

2 In Guattari's (1994) aesthetic paradigm, art has no monopoly on creation but takes to an extreme the capacity of inventing mutant coordinates, of engendering unknown qualities, never seen or thought of before.

3 Heterogenesis refers to the reinforcement of heterogeneity and singularization of youth cultures' components (see Guattari, 1995, p. 5). As a facet of creative processes, heterogenesis works on "what already exists and always on what could be" and constitutes a focal point of resistance in the face of homogenesis (universes of unidimensional reference) (Guattari, 1994, p. 193).

References

Amaya, A., & Marín, M. (2000). Nacidos para la batalla. *Revista Nómadas, 13*, 64–73.

Arroyo, B., & Salinas, F. (1999). Jóvenes, cultura juvenil y subjetividad en el Chile de los 90. *Estudios del INJUV, 1.* Retrieved from http://intranet.injuv.gob

Di Marco, A. (2005). Rock: Universo simbólico y fenómeno social. In M. Margulis (Ed.), *La cultura de la noche: La vida nocturna de los jóvenes en Buenos Aires* (pp. 31–49). Buenos Aires: Biblos.

Feixa, C. (1995). Tribus urbanas, chavos banda y culturas juveniles en Cataluña y México. *Revista Nueva Antropología, XIV*, 71–93.

Feixa, C. (2008). *De jóvenes, bandas y tribus* (4th ed.). Barcelona: Ariel.

Finn, J. (2001). Text and turbulence: Representing adolescence as pathology in the human services. *Childhood, 8*, 167–179.

Foucault, M. (1994). *La ética del cuidado de uno mismo como práctica de la libertad: Hermenéutica del sujeto.* Madrid: La Piqueta.

Guattari, F. (1994). El nuevo paradigma estético. In D. F. Schnitman (Ed.), *Nuevos paradigmas, cultura y subjetividad* (pp. 185–204). Buenos Aires: Paidós.

Guattari, F. (1995). *Chaosmosis: An ethico-aeshtetic paradigm.* Bloomington: Indiana University Press.

Hall, S., & Jefferson, T. (Eds.). (1980). *Resistance through rituals: Youth subcultures in post-war Britain.* London: Hutchinson.

Maffesoli, M. (1990). *El tiempo de las tribus: El declive del individualismo en la sociedad de masas.* Barcelona: Icaria.

Margulis, M., & Marcelo, U. (1994). *Juventud más que una palabra: Ensayos sobre cultura y juventud.* Buenos Aires: Biblos.

Marín, M., & Muñoz, G. (1995). *Qué significa tener 15 años en Bogotá.* Bogotá: Caja de Compensación Familiar Compensar.

Marín, M., & Muñoz, G. (2002). *Secretos de mutantes: Música y creación en las culturas juveniles.* Bogotá: Siglo del Hombre Editores-Universidad Central-DIUC.

Marín, M., & Muñoz, G. (2006). Music is the connection: Youth cultures in Colombia. In P. Nylan, & C. Feixa (Eds.), *Global youth? Hybrid identities, plural worlds* (pp. 130–148). New York: Routledge.

Mintz, S. (2004). The social and cultural construction of American childhood. In M. Conegan, & L. Ganon (Eds.), *Handbook of contemporary families: Considering the past, contemplating the future* (pp. 36–53). Thousand Oaks, CA: Sage.

Reguillo, R. (1994). Las tribus juveniles en tiempos de la modernidad. *Estudios sobre las culturas contemporáneas, V*, 171–184.

Reguillo, R. (1995). *En la calle otra vez: Las bandas, identidad urbana y usos de la comunicación* (2nd ed.). Jalisco: Instituto Tecnológico y de Estudios Superiores de Occidente (ITESO).

Szulik, D., & Kuasñosky, S. (1994). Jóvenes en la mira. In M. Margulis (Ed.), *La juventud es más que una palabra: Ensayos sobre cultura y juventud* (pp. 222–229). Buenos Aires: Biblos.

Valenzuela, J. (1997). Mexican cultural identity in the U.S. city: The roots of collective action in Los Angeles. In J. Rodriguez, & K. Vincent (Eds.), *Common borders, uncommon paths: Race,*

culture and national identity in US–Mexican relationships (pp. 79–98). Wilmington: University of California-Institute for Mexico and the United States.
Valenzuela, J. (n.d.). Cultural identities on the Mexico–United States border. Retrieved from http://www.smithsonianeducation.org

19

TRANS

Alejondro Venegas-Steele

What is the *trans* of trans youth? Many books, dissertations, and Internet forum threads have been devoted to parsing out the histories and implications of the ways that the terms "trans," "transgender," and "transsexual" are used with and against each other, and it would be impossible to do these things justice in the space I have here.[1] Briefly and unjustly, then: transgender has come in many institutional and activist spaces to signify as an umbrella term covering a variety of genderings (and sometimes sexings) deemed atypical or inauthentic or wrong in a given social context.[2] Transsexual often comes to signify something imagined as more corporeal and more likely to involve medical intervention.[3] Many times both endings are dropped and trans is used a capella as a compact reference to both words.

It makes some sense, then, that the words "trans" and "transgender" are utilized at far higher rates in reference to youth than is "transsexual": a 2010 Google search for the exact phrases brings up more than 47,000 hits for "transgender youth" (mostly in the context of the phrase "gay, lesbian, bisexual, and transgender [GLBT] youth" and its variants), more than 16,000 hits for "trans youth" (many in a similar context), and less than 8,000 hits for "transsexual youth" (often in the context of "transgender and transsexual youth" and much less frequently in the GLBT style). The extent to which "transgender" and "trans" have come to be more proper associates with "youth" while "transsexual" and "youth" conduct a relation of much less certain propriety, though, may also point to other dynamics at work.

The attachments of transgender and trans to youth should be read in the context of their association with ostensibly all-inclusive GLBT-style constructions. This trans youth that exists in explicit connection to gay, lesbian, and bisexual youth can be seen to offer an important site for coalition building, and to some extent a useful description of the social organization patterns of some youth communities. But the GLBT construction can also function to obscure youthful needs and desires that might go outside of those teleological and tolerant narratives that are the norm of much of GLBT youth discourse, with their focus on achieving and managing an outness that should eventually grow into an integrated, adult gay lifestyle (Talburt, 2004). It seems to me that the term "transsexual" in particular rarely ends up in the "GLBT" context when it ends up with youth at all in part because of the specificity of corporeal desire that the term "transsexual youth" implies. Because of the popularized idea equating "sex" with the (really) biological and "gender" with the (merely) social, the terms trans and transgender carry less implication that youth may be capable of knowing their own bodily wants and needs, or that a desire to access medical transition can be a knowable want or need at all. Youth with identities or even sexualities may be easier to accept than youth with specific types of knowledge about and desires or needs for their bodies and sexes—not least because they may suggest a responsibility on the part of advocates for GLBT youth to strive to foster access to trans-specific medical care that may fall well outside of neoliberal acceptance narratives.

Knowing Trans Youth

"Youth" and "adolescence" have a fuzzy relationship to one another, but the connection is at least as intimate as it is ambiguous: youth evokes to a large extent narratives of raging hormones and of moodily confused sexual becoming that ends in finished, coherent adult bodiness. Certain youth who access or wish to access certain medicalized practices of gender- or sex-management can upset or complicate such stories—first by disrupting the association of puberty with both nature and trauma, and second by decoupling adultish modes of bodily "completion" from the ability to know or act on one's own body. Youths' desires for and use of exogenous hormones can strongly disrupt images of puberty as a wholly ordinary but out-of-control thing, a natural and unstoppable biological process inherently confusing and generally traumatic. Trans youth *do* often utilize such trauma narratives in relation to their endogenous puberty (if they experienced one)—often with even more vehemently negative emotion than has been normalized for puberty narratives in general. However, many trans youth also access exogenous hormones, and often take great pleasure in the experience of a wanted puberty. A desire for or pleasure in the bodily conditions and changes culturally associated with puberty is certainly not exclusive to trans youth, but expressions of happiness with and a sense of knowingness about puberty is very much contrary to narratives that deem it torrential.[4]

Additionally, the ability to know and to really take pleasure in one's own body is often constructed as the prerogative of adults, necessarily developed in postpubescent, well-cortexed brains—and such knowing pleasure is deemed a prerequisite for being *ready* for a good or right transition. Youthful experiences of bodily knowing are deemed nonknowing, and adulthood is set up as the only or best space from which to know one's bodies and desires, and from which to make decisions on the basis of that knowing.[5] The transsexual youth is rendered almost unthinkable. While much anxiety over the idea of the youthful transsexual gets coded in terms of concern about the "permanency" and "irrevocability" of medical transition, such objections miss that endogenous puberties have biological-social effects no less and no more long-lasting than do exogenous hormones or surgeries. In ascribing permanency and irrevocability only or particularly to trans-specific medical practices, an imagined potential non-trans body that goes through an endogenous puberty is renaturalized as the way the body *should be* or *would be* if not for an interloping transness— despite the fact that many trans people who medically transition at a young age benefit greatly from being able to prevent some effects of an unwanted endogenous puberty.

Youthful Movements of Sex and Gender

At the same time, while some youthful movements through various gender and sex technologies are marked as movements that trans, other movements are obscured as being movements at all. Based on the prefix "cis" (meaning "on the same side as" or "near to"—contrasting with trans' denotations of crossing and beyondness), "cisgender" and "cissexual" are terms in common use in some trans communities that have developed to designate nontransgender and nontranssexual people and practices.[6] I said before that the language of trans is intensely spatial; it is also crucially geographical, if we regard borders and zone delineations as implicit parts of geography. The meanings of trans and cis, then, are very much about staking out and highlighting different heres and theres, and reckoning which movements keep on the same side and which cross over. Not all gender and sex movements by youth get named as trans: movements from (female-assigned) girlhood to womanhood are naturalized, as are movements from (male-assigned) boyhood to manhood. The motion and making here are obscured.

It is also not only along this particular latitude that this sort of map can announce a crossing or deny that one has happened. For example, a recent article in prominent hip hop magazine *VIBE* (Martinez, 2010) interviews a group of feminine-gendered, male-assigned-at-birth young people who are or had been students at a largely middle-class and historically Black men's college in Atlanta, asking the youth about their experiences with the school. Several of the young people interviewed wear clothing conspicuously gendered as female, and one youth utilizes exogenous hormones for gendering purposes. However, the words "transition" and "crossdressing" each appear only once in the article, and "transgender," "transsexual," and "trans" appear not at all—and several of the interviewed youth refer to themselves as "men" and as "gay" in ways that confound many understandings of those categories. Emerging from this particular story about youth are heres and theres much different from more normative GLBT geographies which outline a linear developmental process for youth with the end-goal of declaring publicly the existence of a real and eternal inner self, and which ask for a clear break between experiences of gender identity and sexual orientation (Valentine, 2007). It is not the case, though, that these geographies develop only or cleanly along racial or locational lines. For example, there is also a trans activist organization in Atlanta to which many Black youth and adults have ties called Transgender Individuals Living Their Truth (TILTT) which deploys transgender rhetoric in its generalizing and coalition-building modes as a way of negotiating the fact that many marginalized genders are illegible to (or totally unseen by) more mainstream and whiter accounts of transness. Gender and sex geographies emerge and disappear in racialized and local contexts without being reducible to a preexisting racial or area-based system of knowledge.

On this note, I conclude with Deleuze and Guattari (1987). In *A Thousand Plateaus*, they ask their reader to make maps and not tracings: in other words, to engage in analysis that is boldly artificial—in the best sense of the word— instead of believing that one can simply replicate on paper a system of power or knowledge or meaning. If you believe it appropriate and useful to approach the subject of "trans youth" at all (and it might or might not be), then it is in that spirit that I would ask you to do so: with a firm belief that both terms in the phrase are at least as contested and contingent as any other, and with a dedication to self-critical theorizing that does not try to pass off its own power and debts with claims of blank descriptivity.

Notes

1   Much of the most important thinking on trans issues that I have read has come from academic and nonacademic Internet communities, and I owe great debts to those communities for conversations which I do not cite directly here because many are intentionally or effectively inaccessible to noncommunity members. As of 2010, the blog at QuestioningTransphobia.com is a useful and intentionally public space that can give some idea of the conversations going on. Relatedly, a great deal of the theoretical and activist work coming from these and other contemporary trans communities is being done by trans women and by otherwise male-assigned-at-birth people who get read as female or as conspicuously feminine-gendered. The importance and value of such people's analysis—indeed, the importance and value of such people—have been marginalized in many feminist and queer spaces. Such marginalization has been the source and product of much violence and foolishness, and should be a matter of concern for people wanting to work with or think on transness, youth, queerness, or feminism.

2   Valentine (2007) offers an overview of both the "traditional story" of how the term transgender emerged—that it was invented in the 1970s by Virginia Prince, a gender activist who coined it to describe her position as a full-time crossdresser not seeking surgical transition—as well as evidence suggesting a more complicated beginning. Valentine also explores how the term has always had multiple and contested uses despite (and because of) its huge popularity in contemporary institutional and progressive settings.

3   Stryker (2008) gives useful background and analysis on the developments of the terms transgender and transsexual, where transgender was first popularized as a word to talk about trans people who did not seek surgical transition and has since been a wildly contested term favored by identitarian institutional policies and radical queers alike.

4   Relatedly, the expectation or demand that trans people experience exogenous puberty as *only* pleasurable or empowering or congruent and nothing else can serve to limit and discipline the ways that trans people talk about their selves and their bodies and their relationships to puberties of any type.

5 For example, see many of the adult engagements with the idea of young people medically transitioning in the 2006 documentary *Boy I Am* (Feder & Hollar, 2006), which features several older queers and trans people expressing disbelief at the idea of young people "being ready" or "knowing themselves" enough to medically transition—as well as an excellent rebuttal by legal activist Dean Spade.

6 It is difficult to give an accurate history of the terms cisgender and cissexual, and to my knowledge there has so far been no academic study of their development. They seem to have surfaced on a few trans email lists in the 1990s, then were further popularized through the popular book *Whipping Girl* (Serano, 2007), and then came into more common usage through the web.

References

Deleuze, G., & Guattari, F. (1987). *A thousand plateaus: Capitalism and schizophrenia* (B. Massumi, Trans.). Minneapolis: University of Minnesota Press. (Original work published 1980.)

Feder, S., & Hollar, J. (Co-Directors/Producers). (2006). *Boy I am* [Motion picture]. USA: Women Make Movies.

Martinez, A. (2010, October 11). The mean girls of Morehouse. *VIBE*. Retrieved from http://www.vibe.com/content/mean-girls-morehouse

Serano, J. (2007). *Whipping girl: A transsexual woman on sexism and the scapegoating of femininity.* Emeryville, CA: Seal Press.

Stryker, S. (2008). *Transgender history.* Emeryville, CA: Seal Press.

Talburt, S. (2004). Intelligibility and narrating queer youth. In M. Rasmussen, E. Rofes, & S. Talburt (Eds.), *Youth and sexualities: Pleasure, subversion, and insubordination in and out of schools* (pp. 17–40). New York: Palgrave Macmillan.

Valentine, D. (2007). *Imagining transgender: An ethnography of a category.* Durham, NC: Duke University Press.

SECTION IV

Citizenship Stories

Anita Harris

Citizenship is a concept with a troubled and contested history and yet has a taken for granted status within youth policy and research: it is routinely regarded as a good thing for young people to have citizenship education and to achieve citizenship rights and responsibilities. Debates within fields such as feminism, queer studies, and ethnic and racial studies have highlighted the normative assumptions of the notion of citizenship and there are long-standing disputes over the capacity of such a loaded concept to be redeemed or utilized for groups who have been intrinsic to hegemonic imaginings of citizenship as everything they are not. Formal and informal exclusions around race, gender, sexuality, and ability are at the heart of the ways we think about entitlement to participate, rights, recognition, and power. However, youth studies has been slow to consider these critical analyses of citizenship, especially the fundamentally raced, classed, and gendered nature of citizenship and its entanglement with dominant assumptions about responsible adulthood. Such a lack of critical curiosity reveals the usefulness of this notion as a disciplining technology: one which both constrains and enables what we can say about and do with young people as a population; one that above all else conjures this very population into being.

Citizenship is perhaps then such a charged concept within youth research and policy because it contains so many fantasies, expectations, and disappointments about the proper place of young people in the community and the nation, and offers so many ways for adult experts to define, monitor, manage, and discipline youth for the purpose of shaping them into the right kinds of adults. Youth citizenship studies say less about young people than they do about the kinds of communities, societies, nations, and civic subjects that such knowledges attempt to produce. The construction of the achievement of citizenship for youth as a risky business and the formal status of youth as precitizens is alluring because this makes permissible and necessary the adult crafting of appropriate trajectories, identities, and hierarchical statuses that make up good ways of being participants in the nation. Even well-intentioned efforts to enhance and defend young people's entitlement to legitimately inhabit the category of citizen ought be interrogated as part of the circuitry of citizenship technology, equally drawing upon wishes for and investments in youth as particular kinds of models for nation, civic engagement, and political status.

From Apprentice-Citizens to Self-Actualizers

The period of youth has been imagined above all as a time of citizenship training (during which young people are taught about participation if not facilitated to engage in it). As Rob White and Johanna Wyn (2007) note, citizenship education is part of a tradition of policies designed to control rather than empower young people (p. 112). Citizenship is linked to adult status, and youth studies as well as social policy that address youth citizenship have tended to tell a story about young people as passive recipients of civic education that will prepare them for their future adult role. One of the most prominent and long-standing discourses to circulate about youth citizenship is that young people are not yet citizens, and need guidance and training to become the right kinds of active participants in their civic and political worlds. This conceptualization of youth as citizens in the making had considerable purchase around the turn of the 19th century. Nancy Lesko (2001) argues that, in this context of the shift toward modernity,

> adolescence became a social space in which to talk about the characteristics of people in modernity, to worry about the possibilities of [. . .] social changes, and to establish policies and programs that would help create the modern social order and citizenry.
>
> (pp. 5–6)

At this time a new modern political and civic order was being established in the West; one preoccupied with nationalism, "civilization," and racial progress. As I have written elsewhere:

> The behavior, attitudes and development of adolescents were all monitored closely in the interests of producing rational, patriotic and productive citizens for a modern nation-state. The state, scientists and the community paid considerable attention to young people's social and moral development because they embodied the ideals of national progress. Young people were expected to personify modern civic values, such as responsibility, strength and sacrifice, and model the new style of nation-defending citizenship.
>
> (Harris, 2004, p. 2)

Modern concerns with both massive social change and progress thus became tightly tied to the civic education of the next generation. If educators "got it right" with youth, then nations themselves would have their futures secured. The establishment of the juvenile justice system, mass secondary schooling, youth organizations, movements such as the Boy Scouts, borstals and homes for wayward youth, and the public identification of youth gangs and subcultures were all late 19th- and early 20th-century mechanisms by which youth as a social category, as well as the bodies of individual young people, were managed into appropriate forms of citizenship. Young people were trained through such programs and institutions to be law-abiding, educated for employment, healthy and clean, morally sound, and patriotic. Whiteness, masculinity, heterosexuality, and able-bodiedness were both produced by and made intrinsic to such notions of good citizenship.

These practices may appear both quaint and obvious today, but their purpose—to shape appropriate and successful ways of being adult participants in modern life—endures in many other forms. In recent times, government youth policies as well as youth studies agendas have focused anew on citizenship as rapid social change in the shift to late modernity has again generated debate about the role of young people in social cohesion and national identity. Children and young people have been prominent in citizenship debates about responsibilities and rights in postwelfare states, often newly figured as a potential resource or worthy of strategic kinds of state investment for what they might represent in future returns as responsible adults-to-be (see, e.g., Dobrowolsky, 2002). From the 1990s onward there has been an explosion of interest and concern regarding young people's participatory citizenship in particular; their civic and political knowledge and the extent of their take up of the responsibilities of citizenship. International comparative studies and other large-scale research projects out of political science, sociology, and education have frequently identified a "civics deficit" and many national governments have developed policies, programs, and school curricula to address this problem. There have also been supranational policy recommendations such as the European Commission's 2001 White Paper on youth (*A New Impetus for European Youth*). At the same time, a strong interest in youth civic engagement has emerged, with debates particularly influenced by Robert Putnam's work on social capital and civic engagement in the United States (see *Bowling Alone*, 2000) and the concerns it raises about young people's commitment to civil society, including volunteering and other kinds of community service and involvement. Citizenship in its most literal form, meaning membership in the nation-state, has also come into question in regard to youth since the intensification of migration and other forms of transnational population flows in globalized times. Much contemporary debate about multiculturalism constructs youth as a space for "worrying about the nation" (Hage, 2003, p. 2). For example, there are rising concerns about migrant background youth who are failing to "integrate": a view that has spotlit Muslim youth in the West in particular, and has ushered in policies regarding religious dress, "mainstream" values education in schools, and minority-youth-oriented policing practices. As Anne-Marie Fortier (2008) writes, the form of multicultural youth "is taken up repeatedly as the reflection, expression or promise (utopian or dystopian) of the changing nation" (p. 41).

This renewed interest in youth citizenship has emerged at a time when fresh anxieties have arisen about both the legitimacy and authority of the nation-state and the effects of socioeconomic changes, in this case individualization, globalization, and deindustrialization, on social order. Current times, sometimes characterized as "late modernity," are marked by dislocation, flux, and rapid global flows of peoples, and demand citizens who are flexible and self-realizing. We are all subject to a greater array of information about how to present and identify ourselves. Global economic and political changes have also meant we receive less direct guidance from authorities about how to be or economic security in the form of state-administered social services. As I have written elsewhere (Harris, 2004), direct intervention by institutions has been replaced by self-governance, or the devolution of power onto individuals to regulate themselves through the "right" choices (p. 2). The social and economic logic of late modernity compels people to become self-inventing and responsible citizens who can manage their own development and adapt to change without relying on the state.

As a result of these changes, older stories about the slow, systematic accrual of adult experiences and civic knowledge that would earn youth some of the more formal aspects of citizenship have become harder to tell, with conventionally imagined pathways to adult status and rights disrupted by these conditions of deindustrialization, a restructured economy and labor market, and the retreat of the welfare state. For example, compared to earlier generations, young people today stay in education longer, reside in the family home for extended periods, and move in and out of the job market rather than find a job for life (see White & Wyn, 2007). The absence of clear milestones along a linear trajectory toward adult status has coalesced with new requirements to shape one's own future without relying on the state or traditional forms of security and predictability. As a result of extended and/or scrambled pathways to what is conventionally perceived as adulthood, and increased uncertainty about the signifiers for this status, children and young people are more visible as "youth" and there is considerable public anxiety about their capacity to follow the appropriate trajectory to responsible adult citizenship. What was once perceived as a solid brick path has become crazy paving on quicksand. It is no wonder then, to paraphrase Anne-Marie Fortier (2008), that we see today the evocation of the youth figure in regard to wider anxieties, concerns, desires, and imaginings that haunt the project of national self-transformation and citizenship (p. 41). In times of immense change, young people have again emerged as the sign and site of concern about civic bonds, legitimacy, and the social order. In the process, some categories of youth are both constructed and overdetermined as worthy of special scrutiny, for example Muslim youth in the West or young mothers. These young people become the protagonists in a tale about citizenship that is insufficiently progressive because they remain cleaved to old identifications, make demands on the state, or in other ways resist new requirements to self-actualize. Those who fail to adapt to flexibility and self-invention are cast as the at-risk and often undeserving because they are insufficiently responsible, and require surveillance and intervention.

Contemporary civics education programs, policies, research, and public debates thus reflect anxieties about containing the youthful subject and constructing the responsible adult evident in the apprentice-citizen model of the *fin de siècle*, but also reveal a new focus on self-actualizing citizenship rather than youth as passive recipients of civic education. It is important to understand that older, more didactic technologies of youth citizenship have not been simply replaced or erased, but may morph and persist even while new forms of management of youth into responsible adulthood emerge that respond to contemporary socioeconomic conditions. How then does the field of youth studies imagine young people as citizens today in ways that both extend and break with the past, and what forms of responsible participation in civic and political life are encouraged?

The Production of Self-Actualizing Citizenship

Even while anxieties abound about the failure of some youth to prevail under these circumstances, others are imagined as a valuable resource for reshaping citizenship for the 21st century. These youth are seen as exemplifying the new, flexible, and entrepreneurial forms of self-making required in these new socio-economic conditions. Their voices are increasingly sought in roundtables, consultancies, and advisory groups and both youth policy and research are newly focused on active participation. Some young people are celebrated for their "can-do" citizenship; that is, for their commitment to personal effort as the best path to success, legitimacy, and power, and some emergent forms of civic capacity, in particular consumption, are seen to be best accomplished by young people. Middle-class, White young women, for instance, have become the exemplars of new self-crafted individualist citizens who use spending power and self-belief to make a successful place for themselves in the new economy and social order (see Harris, 2004). Heteronormative and gendered expectations as well as anxieties about the maintenance of hierarchies of class, race, and ability continue to drive the identification of suitable paths to successful citizenship, but these have become complicated by the prevailing emphasis on meritocracy and individual self-making. The politics of identity and disadvantage that shape citizenship possibilities are today reinvented as lifestyle choices alone, such that ethnicity or sexual preference, for example, become accessories or identity flavors unhinged from structural conditions and collective analysis. The story goes that those who overcome adversity through personal effort, who do not imagine themselves to be victims of structural disadvantage but inventors of their own futures, are those best placed to make it.

Some young people are increasingly positioned as important participants in debates and activities regarding the common good. Policies, programs, and research about contemporary youth citizenship have been fundamentally shaped by a rights-based discourse but one that primarily defines participatory rights as young people's entitlement to speak up and be heard. There now exist many more opportunities for youth to be involved in decision-making processes through bodies such as student councils, youth reference groups for government, and community-based advisory groups and programs. Young people are encouraged to speak up, speak out, have their voices heard, make a noise, and so on. Indeed this kind of so-called active citizenship is the cornerstone of policies and programs throughout the West. However, these forms of participation are often tokenistic and require young people to adhere to conventionally recognized styles of engagement and representation that can be easily understood by traditional institutions of power. What can we make of a participatory framework that is only designed to listen to those who can easily shape themselves into articulate "youth leaders" (see, e.g., Bo'sher, 2006), and what are they constructed to hear? A common narrative can be identified: young people's stories of self-made success and the overcoming of adversity through personal effort are solicited in the roundtables and consultations designed to listen to youth. For example, Australia's recent Muslim Youth Summit involved hand-picked Muslim youth leaders sharing stories of personal success in order to advise government about improving volunteering, role modeling, and mainstream engagement on the part of Muslim youth.

This notion of citizenship as speaking up, leading by example, and exhibiting successful self-invention has ironically emerged at the same time that most young people have fewer means to enact their social rights because of socio-economic marginalization from institutions and processes of power. As Judith Bessant (2004) writes, "the failure to recognise the very noticeable and real obstacles that most young people face in their bid to engage in democratic practices raises questions about the efficacy of the official youth participation agenda" (p. 397). This new focus on self-actualizing citizenship serves to both conceal the material circumstances that constrain young people's real capacity to shape their social worlds and to reimagine participation primarily as speaking about one's own journey to success, and even then only in ways that can be easily depoliticized and/or converted to background static. Ultimately, the story of self-actualization only "responsibilizes" youth, such that personal choice and individual effort are constructed as the sole drivers of good citizenship.

Self-actualizing citizenship for youth is also increasingly constructed around consumption. As I have written elsewhere,

> the domains of community and the polity, where civic belonging and identity, as well as rights and responsibilities were traditionally enacted, have become fragmented. In their place are individualized relationships to the market as sources of youth agency and expression.
>
> (2004, p. 69)

Young people are encouraged to take charge of their lives and articulate their rights and needs through practices of consumption as the state and especially the welfare system diminish in their capacity to provide economic security and a space for democratic expression. Privatization of state services, as well as tenuous connections to the new, unpredictable labor market, force youth to position themselves as civic agents and effective participants in consumer society, where they are imagined to have a voice and shape (market) decisions. Civic rights are reinvented as consumer choices, and young people are encouraged to see themselves as powerful players in the global economy as trendsetters and savvy choice-makers. Young women are especially targeted as a new breed of economic agents, driven by female economic independence reinvented as girl-power and ready to utilize this pseudo-feminist form of female "political" empowerment as a market force. Young women's apparent girl-powered capacity to be confident and in charge, and make autonomous decisions, is an image drawn upon by marketing companies, government programs, and not-for-profits alike as this construction of citizenship as individual empowerment through personal choices and spending power takes hold.

The Production of Failed Citizenship

If active participation in self-invention, consumption, and engagement in mainstream political and civic activities are at the core of self-actualizing citizenship for young people today, then it is youth incapable of flexible self-making and disengaged from both politics and the market who are figured as most problematic for citizenship projects. Youth studies has a long history of the construction of "problem youth," and has become a field of study primarily by creating this very category of young people, who can then be researched, analyzed, categorized, and assisted or punished. Within youth citizenship studies, programs, and policies, it is young people at risk of social and market exclusion or those who make insufficient effort who have become the problem youth for the dominant model of active citizenship.

Just as young people are exhorted to take personal responsibility for active participation and for the tackling of social issues within the community, processes of responsibilization are also at play with the production of the failed youth citizen. Efforts to improve youth engagement and enhance civic knowledge focus on the individual risk factors that might limit young people's capacity for self-actualizing citizenship. Kathy Edwards (2010) notes that newly crafted social inclusion initiatives to enhance youth participation, prominent in the United Kingdom and Australia, focus on the deficits of individual young people which see them as "in some way responsible for their own exclusion" (p. 20). She suggests that such initiatives have much in common with youth at-risk programs, which have tended to increase surveillance of young people and induce stigma. Some groups of young people are frequently identified as those most at risk of failing to engage in active citizenship, including Indigenous youth, minority youth, young mothers, and youth with disabilities. Efforts to enhance their participation have tended to focus on individual empowerment, self-esteem, entrepreneurialism, leadership, and creating pathways to engagement in mainstream cultural activities. Less attention is given to the alternative or unconventional participatory practices they may already be engaged in (many of which exclude adults and thereby bypass adult surveillance), the structural barriers to participation that they may face, or their own capacity to critically disengage from debates and programs that persist in positioning them as a problem to be understood and then managed by adult experts.

In current times, particular forms of self-actualizing citizenship are demanded of some young people more than others. Those of minority background are increasingly targeted for programs that encourage youth leadership and participation. They are often perceived as "caught between two cultures" and this is a common explanation for their marginalization from mainstream institutions of integration and conventional forms of associational life. Civil unrest involving young people, such as the so-called youth race riots that occurred in several U.K. cities in 2001, Paris in 2005, Sydney in 2005, and Copenhagen in 2008, led to increased calls for better mechanisms for community cohesion to ensure the integration and active participation of youth (see, e.g., the United Kingdom's Cantle Report, Home Office, 2001). The terrorist attack in London in 2005 spotlit the problem of disaffected youth becoming vulnerable to recruitment by extremist groups. Many youth policy and youth studies responses to these attacks focused on issues of integration and the importance of encouraging the participation of minority young people, especially Muslims, in "mainstream" activities (see Gifford, 2004). Leadership programs for minority and especially Muslim youth became one of the most popular approaches to enhancing youth citizenship. These tend to focus on personal responsibility and individual behavior rather than the institutional barriers, socioeconomic disadvantage, or discrimination in broader society that constitute considerable limits to active citizenship.

Such strategies reveal a profound discomfort with the kinds of citizenship belongings that are being forged by some minority youth, especially second-generation migrants and those of Muslim backgrounds. Citing the U.K. experience, Ash Amin (2002) argues that notions of failed citizenship that problematize minority youth for split loyalties and unwillingness to participate in a national community of shared values indicate a deep fear of the ways some youth are fundamentally reshaping national belonging. He describes "a new generation of British Asians claiming in full the right to belong to Oldham or Burnley *and* the nation, but whose Britishness includes Islam, halal meat, family honour, and cultural resources located in diasporic networks" (p. 965). Calls for integration and civic engagement forged through participation in an imagined mainstream community are a disavowal of the ways these youth may be refiguring both citizenship and the nation without White ethnicity or shared dominant values at its center. They do not sit easily with some young people's own contingent and multiple constructions of national identity, participatory practice, and civic belonging; instead recasting these as indications of failure to correctly engage.

Young people's disengagement from conventional forms of participation can itself be a political act that refuses the "failed citizen" position. Adreanne Ormond (2004) notes that reluctance to participate can be interpreted as an effort to elude power, to retain knowledge within youth cultures and communities, and, importantly, to resist the colonial capacity of the youth at-risk industry. She quotes a young Maori (Indigenous New Zealand) woman in a research focus group as follows:

> Well, they'll read what we say and they'll think they understand us . . . you know, they'll think that they know what it's like for us, they will imagine that they know the solution to us, the problem, but they won't know 'cause they don't understand. They'll just think "oh, poor losties"; they'll feel sorry for us, but they're all talk 'cause they like us the way we are so they can keep on feeling sorry for us, gives them something to do in their offices. Nah, they won't understand, and we're poor in their eyes, poor dumb brownies.
>
> (p. 249)

At the same time, there are enabling ways to work with the "bad citizen" paradigm that positions some youth as at-risk, disengaged, or having failed to successfully self-actualize. For example, Dave Palmer (2003) notes that youth work with Aboriginal youth in Australia is characterized by narratives of cultural impoverishment, crime, violence, marginalization, and disadvantage. However, while the management of Aboriginal youth through such "at-risk" discourses, practices, and policies serves to legitimize the regulation of Aboriginal people, it also creates possibilities for empowerment and intervention. He writes (2003) that the construction of Aboriginal youth as a disadvantaged "problem group" allows Aboriginal people and their advocates to point out the contradiction this represents for a society "politically administered according to principles of fairness and equity" (p. 14). Citing unpublished research by Mickler, he demonstrates how Aboriginal activists draw strategically upon ideas such as victimhood and pauperism to argue for increased expenditure and involvement in governance. In other words, "talk about Aboriginal problems opens up conditions that allow Aboriginal people to exert influence on governmental work" (p. 14). In some contexts, it has been talk about the intransigence of Aboriginal young people's problems on the part of non-Aboriginal youth workers that has forced a review of governmental youth work and a substantial increase in Aboriginal influence over their practice. Palmer (2003) quotes a youth worker documenting a series of failed strategies, concluding "none of these things have worked, so finally we have had to go back to Aboriginal people and ask them what we should do" (p. 15). As a result of the construction of Aboriginal youth as a problem group who fail to respond to youth work, the reviewed youth work itself has become highly dependent on Aboriginal guidance and participation.

Youth service providers and young people themselves are well used to drawing on the prevailing and contradictory discourses of youth citizenship to attract funding and service programs. For example, in Australia, programs for young Muslim women to have a space to themselves for socializing and learning about sexual health as well as undertaking fun activities like beauty practices and fashion design are pitched as "leadership programs" in order to gain government funding. Programs for "at-risk" youth frequently gain financial support for offering suicide prevention, mental health improvement, enhanced social cohesion, and pathways to mainstream participation. While this is not to say that many young people do experience significant social, psychological, and health problems, the work that such programs do under the umbrella of service provision for the "at-risk" often links such issues to structural inequities and offers young people space to shape political responses to these constructions of youth. In other words, practitioners, service providers, young people, and youth studies scholars find enabling ways to work with citizenship stories that break open and make unpredictable these methods of containing and disciplining youth.

Recent times have seen renewed focus on youth citizenship as a key issue for policy, education, and research. Youth studies and youth policy no longer simply construct youth as citizens-in-the-making, although this does remain an important aspect of the youth citizenship project. Recent socioeconomic changes have also led to new ways to imagine and craft young people's participation and belonging through tropes of self-actualization, and through practices of soliciting youth voice, enhancing youth leadership, and encouraging entrepreneurialism and consumerism. In the process, young people are encouraged to take personal responsibility for their capacity to succeed within their civic and political worlds and are rewarded for conventional participation in mainstream institutions and practices. Discourses about the "at-risk," who suffer from "social exclusion" or "integration challenges," serve to construct some youth as requiring extra scrutiny and expert assistance to improve their attempts at self-actualizing citizenship. As always, however, efforts to manage young people into the right kinds of adults via citizenship projects have unpredictable consequences. Youth studies scholars, youth workers, and young people themselves find that the current youth citizenship agenda has not only made possible new modes of regulating youth but also unexpected ways for young people to contest this regulation through refusals, denials, disengagements, mimicry, and performance. It has provided openings for youth researchers to reflect on the politics of efforts to engage young people in civic projects and to advocate for their entitlement to be heard as legitimate players in their social worlds, still so fundamentally shaped by adult agendas. It has also given us pause for thought about the ways contemporary youth studies has remained so deeply complicit with the disciplining of youthful subjects, not least through the elicitation of voice and the call to self-actualization.

References

Amin, A. (2002). Ethnicity and the multicultural city: Living with diversity. *Environment and Planning A, 34*, 959–980.

Bessant, J. (2004). Mixed messages: Youth participation and democratic practices. *Australian Journal of Political Science, 39*, 387–404.

Bo'sher, L. (2006). Where are the priorities? Where is the action? *Children, Youth and Environments, 16*, 338–347.

Cantle, T. (2001). *Community cohesion: A report of the independent review*. London: Home Office.

Dobrowolsky, A. (2002). Rhetoric versus reality: The figure of the child and New Labour's strategic "social investment state." *Studies in Political Economy, 69*, 43–73.

Edwards, K. (2010). Social inclusion: Is this a way forward for young people, and should we go there? *Youth Studies Australia, 29*, 16–24.

Fortier, A. (2008). *Multicultural horizons: Diversity and the limits of the civil nation*. London: Routledge.

Gifford, C. (2004). National and post-national dimensions of citizenship education in the UK. *Citizenship Studies, 8*, 145–158.

Hage, G. (2003). *Against paranoid nationalism: Searching for hope in a shrinking society*. Annandale: Pluto Press.

Harris, A. (2004). *Future girl: Young women in the 21st century*. New York: Routledge.

Lesko, N. (2001). *Act your age! A cultural construction of adolescence*. New York: Routledge.

Ormond, A. (2004). Beneath the surface of voice and silence: Researching the home front. In A. Harris (Ed.), *All about the girl: Power, culture and identity* (pp. 243–252). New York: Routledge.

Palmer, D. (2003). Youth work, Aboriginal young people and ambivalence. *Youth Studies Australia, 22*, 11–18.

Putnam, R. (2000). *Bowling alone: The collapse and revival of American community*. New York: Simon & Schuster.

White, R., & Wyn, J. (2007). *Youth and society: The social dynamics of youth* (2nd ed.). London: Oxford University Press.

20

DEMOCRACY

Benjamin Baez

Curious word, democracy. It has been claimed by almost everyone, in liberal as well as in totalitarian societies, in capitalist and in socialist ones, as both supporting individualism and communitarianism, and as a synonym for singularity as well as typicality (Ruttenburg, 1998, p. 10). "Democracy" thus represents an imagined present but also a dream for the future. It is a mystical idea because it is everywhere, hovering, always ready to justify any action, or always ready to express itself in "reality," even if it never actually does. It is the horizon of much that we imagine as political. And so no one can argue against it. To argue against democracy is like saying one is against freedom. And in many societies that is akin to advocating for slavery or despotism—it is crazy, if not (also) treasonous; it is misanthropic, if not (also) evil.

When ideas about democracy are linked up with those about youth, one can see how, following Edelman (2004), the *democratic youth* becomes the "perpetual horizon of every acknowledged politics" (p. 3); the democratic youth becomes emblematic of society's fantasy—its "future's unquestioned [and unquestionable] value and purpose" (p. 4). The democratic youth is our investment in the present; our returns come in the future. Such a youth represents a fantasy, a promise we make to the future, and for which we must regulate ourselves. The youth is the target of democracy because she will later be its steward. Yet, what kind of fantasy is this?

What Is Democracy?

Can we say for certain what democracy is? Democracy as a word has a long history in Western thought, calling upon vague ideas about who we are and why we form formal governments (Williams, 1983). According to Williams (1983), the word "democracy" connotes people and rule, and thus people who rule themselves, but only more recently has this idea had positive connotations (pp. 93–94). Democracy gained its positive connotations when it was tied to republicanism, that is, when democracy became "representative democracy." So for political scientists and philosophers, democracy is necessary because formal government is necessary. To the extent that democracy connotes rule by the people, it is a rule that can enact itself only through informed representatives. Yet, even then democracy has been constantly criticized, probably because republicanism never really achieves the hopes we have for it, being always, as it were, in perpetual crisis (e.g., structurally vulnerable to mob rule, elitism, uninformed electorates, unscrupulous representatives). But while existing realities are criticized, democracy as a dream remains. Much like our dreams about youth, its materiality might be nightmarish, yet the dream itself is unassailable.

The critiques of democracy, however, do require a reimagination of it, and so ideas about democracy change from "representative democracy" to "participatory democracy." So that now "true" democracy is a mode of participation with one's fellow citizens that is animated by a sense of responsibility for one's society (Elshtain, 2000, p. 117). Here we can think of democracy as not necessarily, or perhaps not even fundamentally, tied to political government; we now have civil (democratic) society. As de Tocqueville (1945) argued, only when democracy is "slowly and peaceably introduced into institutions and customs" (p. 9) will effective government take place. Only when democracy voluntarily touches on all of society will true government happen.

Participation in society's institutions must become, then, concerns of governmental rationalities, for at stake is our future. Dewey (1986) argued that it is a fallacy to believe that democracy happens automatically; "it is a personal way of life, signifying possession and continual use of certain attitudes, forming personal character and determining desire and purpose in all relations of life" (p. 148). In liberal forms of government, however, democracy cannot appear to be authoritarian; it must inhere in the voluntary actions of individuals. Voluntary associations of all kinds now become the objects of governmental rationalities, for social life becomes the stage for and in which democracy takes place. Democracy as republicanism, according to Cruikshank (1996), was a part-time activity taking place in established public spheres; democracy as participation, however, is detemporalized and despacialized and inheres in the voluntary associations of all kinds and in the capacities and actions of individuals (p. 244). Thus, she argues, the ties that must be cultivated are not political, but social; "democracy entails the transformation of politics from activity dependent on a conception of the public life to a matter of social life and the life of society" (p. 244).

Participatory democracy does seem to make less salient the traditionally political field and the activities associated with it. That is, engagement with formal government (e.g., voting, contacting legislators, formal protests) seems to become less and less important as evidence of our democratic personalities. But perhaps also what is happening is that the traditional political field has been opened up, recouched in terms of the social, and as such opened up to all kinds of individuals, identities, claims, and activities. Youth, for example, become political actors by the mere fact of their sociality. Just as second wave feminism disrupted the distinction between the public and the private, participatory democracy disrupts the distinction between the political and the social, requiring an investment of one in the other, requiring a rethinking of one because of the other. And while this change exposes us to new kinds of controls, it also gives us new avenues for rejecting them. The point here, however, is that the fields in which, and the subjects for which, we stage our fantasies about our future have changed.

In liberalism, individuals must become politically active and capable of self-government. For de Tocqueville (1945), "subjects" act only upon the will of external forces, but "citizens" govern themselves. The task of democratic rationalities is to change subjects into citizens. This logic makes thinkable, then, the notion that, while democracy requires formal government, it also requires, as Elshtain (2000) argues, democratic "dispositions," such as preparedness to work on shared ends with others different from oneself, strong convictions with a readiness to compromise, and a sense of individuality and commitment to civic goods (p. 101). Society, then, becomes a stage for governmental rationalities in the name of democracy; it must be invented and produced where it is not, and maintained and policed where it is. And this can be done rather easily, by having us reimagine our associations as participation in the political decisions that affect our lives; our associations become democratic; our participation in them becomes democracy. For, as Dewey (1944) argued, democracy is more than a form of government; it is primarily a mode of associated living.

So all kinds of associations—families, religious organizations, work, schools, philanthropic activities—are reinvented as ways in which we participate in a democracy. Such reinventions then make interventions into our "associated living," previously seen as inappropriate interventions into our private lives, more or less rational, for our associations now hold the future of democracy itself. This future must be assured, and we have to get this right for our youth. De Tocqueville (1945) argued that problems in democracy happen when it is abandoned to its wild instincts, allowed to "[grow] up like those children who have no parental guidance, who receive their education in the public streets, and who are acquainted only with the vices and wretchedness of society" (p. 8). And here, then, we may consider how the fantasies of democracy are linked up with those of youth.

The "Democratic Youth" and Education

Susan Talburt and Nancy Lesko argue in the introduction to this volume that the "youth" is imagined as a transitional subject, neither child nor adult, but in the making. In Erikson's (1993) imagination, the youth comes with an "ideological mind," that is, one always looking to develop an identity approved by society. So it is the ideological outlook of a society that speaks most clearly and forcefully to youth, who wants to be affirmed by their peers and who are ready to be confirmed by the rituals, creeds, and programs of a society, which also work to define for youth what is acceptable and what is evil, uncanny, and inimical (p. 356). Yet American society, in particular, for Erikson, is full of contradictions, creating role confusion for youth. Given the power that society exerts on its youth, and thus on its future, it must be governed for youth, and youth must be governed for society.

If democracy is a fantasy directed toward the future, and if youth are also this future's possibility, then how might we imagine the "democratic youth"? In a truly participatory democracy, Leistyna (2003) argues, the voices of youth must be recognized, heard, and critically engaged, no matter how theoretically insightful or weak (p. 122). This emerging democratic voice is most effectively cultivated by the school, for that is the most effective institution we invent for governing youth. Schools now become crucial technologies for the invention of the democratic youth, an invention made most saliently by Dewey (1944), for whom democracy, which can never be subject to external authority, can only be created by education (p. 87). The school, then, becomes the avenue for a certain dream of what society should look like. As such, it entails attempts, albeit only marginally successful, to actualize certain underlying principles, such as equality, liberty, and rationality, making the school the democratic means to forming a society of free, self-governing individuals (Hunter, 1996, p. 231).

The democratic youth is one who must acquire the knowledge, skills, and dispositions that will enable him to function in a society imagined as democratic. Yet, to rationalize the intervention necessary for producing democratic youth, a number of other inventions must also be ensured. First, democracy must be reinvented to mean associations and associated living (see Elshtain, 2000), for in the name of democracy one can rationalize interventions into such activities. Our associations must be reimagined as acts of citizenship, and so interventions to ensure effective citizenship are rational. Youth must be reinvented as our future, and we must ensure a good future. The school must be reinvented to ensure that education cannot simply be an academic affair; it must educate for citizenship; it must educate for democracy; it must educate for the future.

With regard to the former ideas about democracy as formal political action, our fantasies about youth required very little for and of them, simply a passive education that was "future-oriented," that is, one that explained to them why democracy was important but also one that did not, because it could not give them first-hand knowledge of this: youth could not form an electorate. All youth could do in such a fantasy was to study formal governmental processes, to take social studies classes, perhaps even to "play" at voting via mock election exercises and the like. But "participatory democracy" requires for youth a drastically different kind of education and of them drastically different kinds of things: they must construct their own education as a stage for democracy (e.g., they must support their schools via bake sales; they must engage in school government; they must debate the political issues of the day; they must support the environment). Education, then, can now be reimagined on the basis of "experience," for only via direct experience in democracy can youth really *know* democracy. Only by truly knowing it can they become its stewards; only then can they achieve the future we hope for them.

Youth and the democracy for which such a youth is imagined are inventions, but as Walkerdine (1990) argued about the child, they entail sites for the creation of realities that cannot actually exist but which are terrifyingly powerful in their implications (p. 116). Similarly, following Edelman (2004), we are no more able to imagine a democracy without a fantasy about the future than we are able to imagine a future without fantasies about the youth. None of this, however, is by definition oppressive or authoritarian, for participatory democracy might also give youth a political claim in the fantasy that inheres directly from their sociality, one that could not have been possible under a different understanding of democracy. For youth studies, therefore, we may want to consider how and why democratic youths are invented by others, and by themselves, as fantasies of, and tactics for, democracy—or perhaps it is the other way around.

References

Cruikshank, B. (1996). Revolutions within: Self-government and self-esteem. In A. Barry, T. Osborne, & N. Rose (Eds.), *Foucault and political reason: Liberalism, neo-liberalism and rationalities of government* (pp. 231–251). Chicago: University of Chicago Press.

de Tocqueville, A. (1945). *Democracy in America, Volume 1*. New York: Vintage Books.

Dewey, J. (1944). *Democracy and education*. New York: The Free Press.

Dewey, J. (1986). Democracy as a way of life. In J. Gouinlock (Ed.), *Excellence in public discourse: John Stuart Mill, John Dewey, and social intelligence* (pp. 146–151). New York: Teachers College Press.

Edelman, L. (2004). *No future: Queer theory and the death drive*. Durham, NC: Duke University Press.

Elshtain, J. B. (2000). Democracy on trial: The role of civil society in sustaining democratic values. In D. E. Eberly (Ed.), *The essential civil society reader: The classic essays* (pp. 101–122). Lanham, MD: Rowman & Littlefield.

Erikson, E. (1993). Youth and American identity. In C. Lemert (Ed.), *Social theory: The multicultural & classic readings* (pp. 355–358). Boulder, CO: Westview Press.

Hunter, I. (1996). Assembling the school. In A. Barry, T. Osborne, & N. Rose (Eds.), *Foucault and political reason: Liberalism, neo-liberalism, and rationalities of government* (pp. 143–166). Chicago: University of Chicago Press.

Leistyna, P. (2003). Facing oppression: Youth voices from the front. In K. J. Saltman, & D. A. Gabbard (Eds.), *Education as enforcement: The militarization and corporatization of schools* (pp. 103–125). New York: RoutledgeFalmer.

Ruttenburg, N. (1998). *Democratic personality: Popular voice and the trial of American authorship*. Stanford: Stanford University Press.

Walkerdine, V. (1990). *Schoolgirl fictions*. New York: Verso.

Williams, R. (1983). *Keywords: A vocabulary of culture and society*. New York: Oxford University Press.

21

HIJAB

Amira Jarmakani

The metaphorical force of the hijab, the Arabic word for what is more commonly called a veil in English, belies its quite mundane, quotidian uses. One of the most salient examples of this, particularly in relation to girls, is the French headscarf debate, which is hardly a debate but rather a complex discursive formation that demonstrates the ways in which contested meanings of nationalism, secularism, liberalism, and piety become animated in and against the highly constructed symbol of the hijab. Bordering on a caricature of the way that adolescence can "become a very useful public problem," the hijab has certainly served (somewhat ironically) as a "handy and promiscuous social space" (Lesko, 2001, p. 6). The seeming contradiction between perceptions of the hijab as an oppressive, stifling custom and the promiscuous fascination with it in the Western European, U.S., and Canadian contexts is all the more reified by the multitude of scholarly works, documentaries, and trade publications that seek to get "behind" the veil, or that play with the metaphors of concealing and revealing, and covering and uncovering, those who wear it. For this reason, various meanings of the hijab often seem to be constrained—warehoused, even—within the stark framework of binary oppositions. There seems to always be much to say about the hijab and little to say that is meaningful, perhaps due to the way various meanings tend to sediment onto the garment, rendering it unintelligible by virtue of its hypervisibility.

The headscarf debates, as they are commonly called in English, or the headscarf affairs (*affaires des foulards*), as they are named in French, can be concretized in three distinct moments—in 1989, 1994, and 2003—all of which provoked public debates about a tiny fraction of girls who chose to wear the hijab to school. On the surface, these debates considered whether Muslim girls would be allowed to wear the hijab in public schools. However, they culminated in a law passed on March 15, 2004, by the French government, which codified the notion of the hijab as a highly legible symbol of religiosity, and therefore as a clear, provocative refusal of the secular, universalist ideals of the French state. The law, which prohibits public school students from wearing "conspicuous" or ostentatious religious symbols, therefore reifies the hijab as a quintessential symbol of opposition to "things Western." It is further linked to popular anxieties about terrorism and the notion that religiosity (particularly Islam) is antithetical to modernity. Since the number of French girls and women wearing the hijab comprises a small percentage of France's Muslim population

(Scott, 2007, p. 5), a deep interpretation of the controversies suggests that they actually represent shifting national anxieties about immigration and citizenship (Bowen, 2007; Scott, 2007; Winter, 2008). That the debates have centered around the dress habits of a few girls in public schools points to the liberal-democratic notion that education is the way in which a "citizen is forged" (Winter, 2008, p. 8), thereby implying that youth practices stimulate discourses and anxieties about futurity, and, in this case, about the future of the liberal nation-state.

Citizenship is therefore the key problematic that animates discussions about hijab, and, simultaneously, the convenient receptacle into which broader, often unnamed concerns are housed. In other words, the headscarf debates have certainly highlighted popular anxieties about Muslim immigration and assim-ilation patterns in France (and in Europe more broadly). In doing so, however, they have demonstrated that the overdetermined obsession with the hijab situ-ates it as a multivalent symbol around which various meanings endlessly accumulate. Though any attempt to neatly categorize these meanings would be necessarily partial, I explore the hijab in relation to four interrelated con-ceptual nodes: sexuality, secularism, freedom, and racialization.

Before proceeding, however, it is worth saying a few words about the term itself. Hijab is the transliteration of the Arabic word most commonly used to refer to the general practice of covering oneself (usually one's hair) for reasons of modesty and piety within the framework of the Islamic religion. It comes from the root Arabic verb meaning "to veil, cover, screen, shelter, seclude; to hide, obscure (e.g., from sight); to prevent (the view of some-thing)" (Cowan, 1994, p. 184), and, in its noun form, has the two basic meanings of functioning as a cover and as a partition. Therefore, in the word's Arabic meaning, two complementary meanings coexist; one focuses inwardly, so to speak, gesturing toward the person to be covered, and the other focuses outwardly, on the people prevented from looking. It is not just a garment that conceals, then, it is also a garment that provides a form of "portable seclusion" (Abu-Lughod, 2002). The most commonly used English translation of hijab is veil (voile in French), which elides the latter meaning of hijab. Another problem with the term veil is that it cannot account for the diversity of cultural forms of dress to which it is applied (el Guindi, 1999, p. 7). While hijab can function as a general term for a range of types of covering, it also commonly refers to the specific style of covering with a headscarf (foulard in French), which typically covers one's hair, ears, and neck. Other forms of cover include the niqab, a piece of cloth that covers the face, excluding the eyes, which is usually accompanied by an abaya, jilbab, or other form of long dress that covers the rest of the body; the khimar, a term used in the Qur'an, which can also mean a type of dress that covers the hair, neck, and shoulders; and chador, a term used in Iran which actually refers to the long form of dress covering the body rather than the hijab itself (as the term hijab is also used in Iran).

As indicated by the range of forms it takes, the hijab is both a culturally and religiously specific form of dress. While it existed in the Middle East prior to the advent of Islam (Ahmed, 1992), in the contemporary context it is generally worn as an article of religious belonging, signifying both modesty and piety. The ayah, or verse, that specifically calls upon Muslims to express bodily modesty, as several Islamic feminist scholars have pointed out, does not specify that women should cover their heads (or faces, for that matter), and it does not single women out for the practice of modesty, but requires modesty in dress from both women and men. Nevertheless, these literal meanings in the Qur'an have been interpreted in a range of religious and social contexts, many of which reflect the patriarchal cultural milieu in which they were rendered rather than the meaning given in the Qur'an (al-Hibri, 2000; Barlas, 2002; Wadud, 1999).

Sexuality

As Joan Wallach Scott argues, from the perspective of the French headscarf debates, "There was something sexually amiss about girls in headscarves; it was as if both too little and too much were being revealed" (2007, p. 152). In other words, the "conspicuous" visibility of the hijab highlights the power of female sexuality to disrupt the social order by requiring that female bodies be removed from the scopic order of the public realm. In some ways, then, it seems to be the fact that the hijab both clearly acknowledges and responds to the social fact of patriarchy that makes it so offensive to a Western liberal sensibility, particularly in view of the popular liberal formulation that understands women's ability to reveal their bodies as an indication of female liberation. Insofar as this claim of liberation glosses over the persistent presence of patriarchal constructions that objectify women's revealed bodies, it functions to reinforce the idea that hijab signifies an absolute patriarchy that is unimaginable in a liberal-democratic nation.

Echoing frameworks that characterize youth as "at-risk" or needing protection, publications ranging from young adult novels to Muslim teenagers' and parents' handbooks combat U.S., Canadian, and Western European characterizations of the hijab as oppressive by insisting on its protective function. In the young adult novel *Does My Head Look Big in This?* by Randa Abdel-Fattah, for example, the main character explains that wearing the hijab makes her feel "free and sure of who [she is]" as it protects her from "all the crap about beauty and image" (2005, p. 29). A girl interviewed for *The American Muslim Teenager's Handbook* comes to a similar conclusion, asserting that the purpose of hijab is "to cover your beauty" (Hafiz, Hafiz, & Hafiz, 2009, p. 112). Both examples emphasize the benefits of hijab as a form of protection for girls navigating a patriarchal society focused on consuming women's bodies. As these examples also imply, the hijab has often functioned as a lynchpin in patriarchal contestations over female sexuality. Much of the rhetoric around the French headscarf affairs, for example, invoked the figure of the oppressed Muslim girl needing to be rescued from the imposed patriarchal custom of wearing the hijab (despite the fact that most of the cases around which the debates centered involved girls who had chosen to wear hijab in spite of their parents' disapproval). This rhetoric echoes the multiple historical contexts (e.g., British colonization of Egypt, French colonization of Algeria, and U.S. occupation of Afghanistan) in which the justification for colonization and/or imperialism has been the notion that Muslim women and girls need to be saved from their culture, where the hijab functions as a quintessential example of that culture.

Secularism

As an expression of piety, the hijab also animates discourses of secularism and modernity in Western European, U.S., and Canadian contexts. Not just in France, but also in Belgium, Holland, Australia, Bulgaria, and Turkey, laws banning wearing hijab in public have been either instituted or considered, demonstrating the perceived threat of Islam to the secular order (Scott, 2007, p. 2). Like the 1936 law banning hijab passed by the shah in Iran, and cultural and political shifts away from veiling in Turkey and Egypt during the early 20th century, the hijab has long been associated with a form of traditionalism that is antithetical to modernity. In this respect, it clashes with the secular narrative of liberal-democratic nation-states, whereby Islamic religiosity is seen as incompatible with, and even threatening to, the state. Insofar as it connotes a traditional, atavistic form of religious devotion, the hijab is imbricated in development discourses that have problematic parallels in youth studies (Maira & Soep, 2005, p. xxii). The logic of such a framework constructs secularism as a more advanced developmental stage through which Muslim societies must pass in order to achieve modernity.

Freedom

Public conversations about the hijab often circulate around the idea of personal freedom. The liberal-democratic framework privileges the notion of individual rights, and assumes that the hijab is a cultural-patriarchal imposition that violates the individual rights of Muslim girls and women. Not surprisingly, then, *muhajabaat* (women who wear hijab) are often cast into one of two dichotomous positions: that of the subjugated female needing to be rescued and/or pitied and that of the suspicious and threatening figure. In her study about Muslims in the United States after September 11, 2001, for example, Louise Cainkar notes that the hijab came to symbolize "the choice of American Muslim women to *reject American freedom*" (2009, p. 6). Perhaps due to this perception, while Arab and Muslim men were seen as a security threat to be dealt with by the government, Arab and Muslim women were seen largely as a "cultural threat [to be] dealt with by the public" (p. 5). Here, the hijab simultaneously thrusts Muslim girls and women into public contestations over citizenship and belonging while reifying their association with the cultural realm.

Even in narratives that reject Islamophobic constructions of the hijab as a threatening symbol, the main forms of citizenship available to Muslim girls seem to be cultural and consumerist citizenship. With regard to the latter, it is perhaps not a surprise that the main character in *Does My Head Look Big in This?* experiences her first "feeling of empowerment and freedom" (Abdel-Fattah, 2005, p. 29) while walking around the mall. *Muhajabaat* Muslim girls have been interpellated by the fashion industry as an increasingly recognized consumer demographic (Gökariksel & McLarney, 2010; Moors & Tarlo, 2007), to which an array of products are marketed, including stylish hijabs advertised in niche magazines like *Muslim Girl* and even a Muslim "lifestyle doll" (Yaqin, 2007, p. 174).

Racialization

In *The Souls of Black Folk*, W. E. B. DuBois describes his first understanding of himself as racialized in terms of the metaphor of the veil; he recognizes himself as "different from the others . . . shut out from their world by a vast veil" (1989, p. 2). Tied in literal and metaphorical ways to the concept of the veil, the hijab situates Muslim girls in a distinct, but linked, process of racialization. Though the hijab is usually interpreted as shutting Muslim girls and women out from a vast world, it has also functioned for them as a means of critiquing imperialism. While it has persisted as an overdetermined symbol, some Muslim women and girls who wear hijab have found creative ways to negotiate the persistent desire to get behind their veils (Bartkowski & Read, 2000). Just as DuBois's early experience leads him to theorize the notion of "double consciousness," a creative and necessary response to oppression, the hijab has (in some cases) fostered a form of "dissenting citizenship" (Maira, 2009) among Muslim girls living in the United States, Canada, and Western Europe. In this respect, despite the tired dichotomies that seem to endlessly flutter around the hijab, it has functioned for some as a means of negotiating a "third space" (Khan, 1998) that works to dislodge the metaphorical binaries (i.e., reveal/cover, veil/unveil, submissive/threatening) that seek to discipline Muslim women and girls.

References

Abdel-Fattah, R. (2005). *Does my head look big in this?* New York: Orchard Books.

Abu-Lughod, L. (2002). Do Muslim women really need saving? Anthropological reflections on cultural relativism and its others. *American Anthropologist, 104,* 783–790.

Ahmed, L. (1992). *Women and gender in Islam: Historical roots of a modern debate.* New Haven, CT: Yale University Press.

al-Hibri, A. (2000). An introduction to Muslim women's rights. In G. Webb (Ed.), *Windows of faith: Muslim women scholar-activists in North America* (pp. 51–71). New York: Syracuse University Press.

Barlas, A. (2002). *"Believing women" in Islam: Unreading patriarchal interpretations of the Qur'an.* Austin: University of Texas Press.

Bartkowski, J. P., & Read, J. (2000). To veil or not to veil? A case study of identity negotiation among Muslim women in Austin, Texas. *Gender and Society, 14*, 395–417.

Bowen, J. R. (2007). *Why the French don't like headscarves: Islam, the state, and public space.* Princeton, NJ: Princeton University Press.

Cainkar, L. (2009). *Homeland insecurity: The Arab American and Muslim American experience after 9/11.* New York: Russell Sage Foundation.

Cowan, J. M. (Ed.). (1994). *Arabic-English dictionary: The Hans-Wehr dictionary of modern written Arabic* (4th ed.). Ithaca, NY: Spoken Language Services.

DuBois, W. E. B. (1989). *The souls of black folk.* New York: Bantam Books.

el Guindi, F. (1999). *Veil: Modesty, privacy, and resistance.* New York: Oxford University Press.

Gökariksel, B., & McLarney, E. (2010). Muslim women, consumer capitalism, and the Islamic culture industry. *Journal of Middle East Women's Studies, 6*, 1–18.

Hafiz, D., Hafiz, I., & Hafiz, Y. (2009). *The American Muslim teenager's handbook.* New York: Atheneum Books.

Khan, S. (1998). Muslim women: Negotiations in the third space. *Signs: Journal of Women in Culture and Society, 23*, 463–494.

Lesko, N. (2001). *Act your age! A cultural construction of adolescence.* New York: Routledge.

Maira, S. (2009). *Missing: Youth, citizenship, and empire after 9/11.* Durham, NC: Duke University Press.

Maira, S., & Soep, E. (Eds.). (2005). *Youthscapes: The popular, the national, the global.* Philadelphia: University of Pennsylvania Press.

Moors, A., & Tarlo, E. (2007). Introduction. *Fashion Theory, 11*, 133–142.

Scott, J. W. (2007). *The politics of the veil.* Princeton, NJ: Princeton University Press.

Wadud, A. (1999). *Qur'an and woman: Rereading the sacred text from a woman's perspective.* New York: Oxford University Press.

Winter, B. (2008). *Hijab and the republic: Uncovering the French headscarf debate.* New York: Syracuse University Press.

Yaqin, A. (2007). Islamic Barbie: The politics of gender and performativity. *Fashion Theory, 11*, 173–188.

22

HUMAN RIGHTS

Julie Kubala

Images of youth and children from the "global south"—the starving "third-world" child, the mutilated African girl, the terrorist Muslim youth, the promiscuous (Latina) teenage mother, the victim of sexual trafficking—comprise the iconography used to invoke and solidify human rights rhetoric, through mobilizing apparently contradictory scenarios of affective investment. These stories veer back and forth between moral panics and rescue narratives, sometimes within the very same image. Susan Shepler (2005), for instance, points to the ways in which the image of the child soldier invokes both the fear of the superpredator as well as the innocence of the child. These images also leak into the discourse surrounding youth within the United States to maintain racist and xenophobic narratives of victimization; the aptly titled "Superpredator Meets Teenage Mom" (Hendrixson, 2002) demonstrates how images of transnational youth become saturated with danger through a whole host of associations, such as violent or reproductive takeover, which would deprive "our" future generations of their rightful entitlements. While the discourses of youth as endangered and/or dangerous are apparently opposite, they are equally imperialist and work to solidify notions of adult (White) Western citizens as the ones in charge of (having) rights. These images, and their corresponding narratives, mobilize the necessary affect to support the dominance of human rights as a utopian framework that, despite, or perhaps because of, its claim to universality, upholds notions of humanness that depend on infantilized and pathologized less-than-human others.

One Story of Human Rights

These images accumulate power in part through reinforcing the protectionist impulse of "human rights." While the language of human rights has become so widely accepted and broadly defined that it can be used to support virtually any political position, from the "populism" of the Tea Party to calls for prison abolition, it is most effective when discussing individual bodily harm as the result of state violence (Miller, 2004, p. 23). Popular understandings trace the dominance of the discourse to the 1948 Universal Declaration of Human Rights (UDHR), which constructed a universal framework to "protect" individuals, arguably in response to the atrocities of the Holocaust. During the Cold War, these rights were further divided between "civil and political" rights, primarily associated with the West, emphasizing protection of individuals from the state, and "economic, social and cultural" rights, associated with communist and "developing" countries, that stress state entitlements. In his reconceptualization of human rights history, however, Samuel Moyn (2010) argues that, while popular opinion enshrines human rights as a progressive response to atrocities, both the adoption of the UDHR and the 1970s popularity of international human rights frameworks represent countermoves to claims for self-determination that characterize post-World War II independence movements in Africa and Asia. In other words, the emphasis on protection is partially a conservative response to the transformative claims of sovereignty that were endemic in earlier (1940s) rights notions. The enshrining of human rights as focusing on negative freedoms (freedom from) rather than freedom to parallels the emphasis on protection; not surprisingly, then, two recent treaties cover women and children, two categories of people for whom the rhetoric of protection has particular salience.[1]

Given the steady shift toward protection, visual evidence of violence has become prominent in calls for human rights. In the context of youth, then, human rights language is frequently invoked through a discourse of abjection and the mobilization of shame. Desolate images of impoverished brown children provoke us to moral indignity and toward "helping" the underprivileged through acts of charity which function to deny the coimplication of the West in economic processes that create the very problems we attempt to ameliorate.[2] Images of youth as predatory and overly sexual contribute to this narrative through further positioning the Western benefactor as charitable hero who can "civilize" the primitive. These images merge two distinctions: the endangered/dangerous child and the first/third-world adult. Inderpal Grewal (1998) argues,

> The visual evidence of human rights violations . . . universalize[s] the Third World as a region of aberrant violence . . . in relation to . . . the First World, imperialistic, militaristic, violent, and exploitative, [which] is rarely present in this visual evidence of human rights violations. Its absence constructs the authoritative and objective viewer and rescuer, always outside of history.
>
> (p. 502)

These images then condense two binaries—adult/youth and first world/third world—which reinscribes both of them; as Sara Ahmed suggests, "Signs increase in affective value as an effect of the movement between signs: the more signs circulate, the more affective they become" (2004, p. 45). Similarly, through drawing on both binary oppositions, the affective impact of these images intensifies.

Recapitulation Narratives

The images mentioned above both rely on and reinforce developmental narratives in order to maintain faith in utopian fantasies, both on the ontogenic and phylogenic levels.[3] As the editors, Susan Talburt and Nancy Lesko, argue in the introduction to this volume, developmental narratives of youth universalize and stabilize it as a particular category. This process becomes naturalized through scientific discourses of "stages" through which the biological similarities of youth trump structural inequalities of racism, sexism, or colonialism. The use of rights discourse similarly presumes an equality of subject positions which denies structural inequality through the use of economic development language (Burman, 1995, p. 33). In *Act Your Age!*, Nancy Lesko (2001) powerfully connects the intensified focus on youth as a stage in the late 1800s to primitive/modern dichotomies that structure colonialist understandings of Western nation-states as adults and primitive "others"—colonies rather than nations—as children. The investment in progress narratives also characterizes the utopian fantasy of human rights; the teleological goal is for all nations to live in peace through unified understandings of rational autonomous citizens who will no longer have conflict. Moyn (2010) notes, however, that the utopianness of human rights is projected back through history; he dates it to the late 1970s: "Westerners left the dream of revolution behind, both for themselves and for the third world they had once ruled, and adopted other tactics, envisioning an interntional law of human rights as the steward of utopian norms" (p. 36). The conflation, then, of the rational, autonomous, self-regulating adult/citizen with the rational, peaceful, self-regulating civilized nation provides the fantastical impetus for our continuing investment in these utopian goals, an investment that requires heightened regulation of the child to ensure the flourishing of civilization.

The intensification of surveillance endemic to these fantasies can be traced to the links between "the rights of man," the predecessor of human rights, and modern notions of subjectivity so well described by Michel Foucault (1978). He argues that biopower operates through the twin poles of the individual and social body, providing the theoretical connection between individual and social development; these poles are connected through the family. Here, the family becomes metonymically connected to the nation, so that the productive regulation of the child (as of yet there is little child/youth distinction) becomes supersaturated with cultural fantasies of the health of the nation. Foucault's connection between proper childraising and civilized nations persists in current developmental narratives; Erica Burman (1995) comments, "Colonial legacies blend into humanitarian concerns, where in order to qualify for 'help', parents are either invisible or infantilised as incapable" (p. 23). Part of this infantilization involves the implication that, if these nations understood human rights properly, they would be able to properly provide for "their" children; protectionist rhetoric allows for slippages between human rights and humanitarian aid. Calls for humanitarian aid/human rights that feature images of children, then, displace both the actual adults and the cultural values and norms they "should" embody, creating a landscape of "orphaned" children in need of adult intervention. Given the way the West is imagined in human rights discourse as culturally neutral and impartial, these images work to doubly displace the colonial legacy as contributing to poverty in "developing" nations.

Civilization without Grown-Ups

The landscape of missing or dysfunctional adults from, say, Africa functions not only as a rhetorical device to manipulate potential donors, it also sediments the ongoing construction of Africa as child-like, as incompatible with notions of citizen–adults as possessive individuals, individuals who "have" or "deserve" rights. The ubiquity of these images renders such notions of self-determination impossible; they provide the basis for the claim that "Africa will never improve" or move from a developing to developed set of nations. These images, then, represent colonized lives as what Judith Butler (2004), in a different context, refers to as "unlivable" where legal and political status is in a state of infinite suspension; they provide the basis for a Western civilization that "defines itself over and against a population understood as by definition illegitimate, if not dubiously human" (pp. xv, 91). Moreover, the move to foreclosing "developing" nations as rights-bearing works to secure these countries as sources of resource extraction by the West. Despite human rights activists' best intentions, then, the attribution of "human rights abuses" to "other" countries relies on a developmental narrative that in fact produces that which it claims to redress.[4] Lesko describes how developmental narratives constructed colonized others as primitive at the turn of the last century; here, we see how contemporary discourses of human rights conceptualize the not-yet (who will never be) fully adult as impossible citizen, as incapable of rights, through a conflation of exclusionary notions of the "civilized" with those who have rights.

The emergence of an international framework of human rights and children's rights in the recent past suggests a connection to the concurrent rise of neoliberalism, an intensification of the liberal subject that highlights self-regulation and "personal responsibility." Neoliberalism has taken hold of the public imagination in large part through narratives of family values which shift the responsibility of individual and collective needs from the state to the family. Through this "focus on the family," neoliberalism has triumphed through utopian fantasies that privilege "future" generations as rhetoric over the realities of current inhabitants. As Lauren Berlant (1997) argues, "A nation made for adult citizens has been replaced by one imagined for fetuses and children" (p. 3). The triumph of the imaginary role of future citizens, then, depends on current adults' ability to maintain their innocence, their freedom from the corrupting influence of the non- or inhuman. Civilization as we know it depends on nothing less.

While I have discussed the role of various images that connect innocent American (White) children and pathologized "foreign" youth, I have primarily focused on how images of "third-world" young people function. Here, I switch to a popular culture example to show how these images work in reverse. The movie *Harold and Kumar Escape from Guantanamo Bay* (Hurwitz & Schlossberg, 2008) features a rabid "associate director" of Homeland Security whose paranoid fantasy about terrorism trumps the NASA scientist's "reasonable" attempts to intervene in his pursuit of the title characters. In one brief scene, for instance, in response to the scientist's insistence that these are basically good American kids, the man from Homeland Security whirls around, snatches up a random picture of a secretary's daughter, and yells, "Do you see this cute little White girl? Do you want her to be raped and murdered? This is America. Do you want to rape America?" These questions, obviously rhetorical, achieve their desired impact: he is allowed to continue his quest with no concern for legal rights (later, in fact, he ceremoniously wipes his ass with a page from a law book meant to represent their "rights"). This scene demonstrates the intensity of the affective investment in the nameless, and therefore iconic, "cute little White girl"; her representative status as utopian future illustrates the further sedimentation of the citizen as victim narrative which can, in the extreme circumstances that are our new normal, triumph over the notion of citizen as one who bears rights.

Notes

1 The Convention on the Rights of the Child, for instance, was adopted by the U.N. General Assembly in 1989; interestingly, it has not been ratified by the United States, due in part to conservative fears of being deprived of control over property, that is, children.

2 Sara Ahmed (2004) notes, "The investment in the figure of the suffering other gives the Western subject the pleasures of being charitable" (p. 162).

3 See Maira and Soep (2005).

4 I am not suggesting that all those who use human rights discourse are unaware of these dangers; many argue that the popular appeal of human rights allows for its usage strategically, rather than in an idealized, universalized view.

References

Ahmed, S. (2004). *The cultural politics of emotion*. New York: Routledge.

Berlant, L. (1997). *The queen of America goes to Washington City*. Durham, NC: Duke University Press.

Burman, E. (1995). The abnormal distribution of development: Policies for southern women and children. *Gender, Place, and Culture, 2*, 21–36.

Butler, J. (2004). *Precarious life*. London: Verso.

Foucault, M. (1978). *The history of sexuality: An introduction*. New York: Vintage Books.

Grewal, I. (1998). On the new global feminism and the family of nations. In E. Shohat (Ed.), *Talking visions: Multicultural feminism in a transnational age* (pp. 501–530). Cambridge, MA: MIT Press.

Hendrixson, A. (2002). Superpredator meets teenage mom: Exploding the myth of the out-of-control youth. In A. Bhattacharjee, & J. Silliman (Eds.), *Policing the national body* (pp. 231–258). Cambridge, MA: South End Press.

Hurwitz, J., & Schlossberg, H. (Producers & Directors). (2008). *Harold and Kumar escape from Guantanamo Bay* [Motion picture]. USA: New Line Cinema.

Lesko, N. (2001). *Act your age! A cultural construction of adolescence*. New York: Routledge.

Maira, S., & Soep, E. (Eds.). (2005). *Youthscapes: The popular, the national, the global*. Philadelphia: University of Pennsylvania Press.

Miller, A. (2004). Sexuality, violence against women, and human rights: Women make demands and ladies get protection. *Health and Human Rights, 7*, 16–47.

Moyn, S. (2010, August 30/September 6). Human rights in history. *The Nation*, 31–38.

Shepler, S. (2005). Globalizing child soldiers in Sierra Leone. In S. Maira, & E. Soep (Eds.), *Youthscapes: The popular, the national, the global* (pp. 119–133). Philadelphia: University of Pennsylvania Press.

23

MALLS

Carolyn Vander Schee

Exploring the ways in which youth use and occupy geographical spaces is an important strand of research for the field of youth studies. Work in this area raises important social, cultural, and political questions and suggests that access to space both reflects and produces social arrangements (see, e.g., Goss, 1993; Hil & Bessant, 1999, p. 44; Shildrick, Blackman, & MacDonald, 2009; Vanderbeck & Johnson, 2000). For many youth, the suburban shopping mall has become an important material and symbolic space where they learn to negotiate relationships, participate in the workforce, discover citizenship rights, engage in creative expression, and perform acts of resistance (see, e.g., Anthony, 1985; Flint, 2006; Gray, 2007; Vanderbeck & Johnson, 2000; Voyce, 2006). Malls are also places where youth experience independence and explore the limits of this. Within this context, the suburban shopping mall has become an important point of departure to understand how youth engage with various spaces and how adults challenge this utilization by governing their autonomy. Research in this area, then, highlights critical issues and tensions around citizenship, consumption, spatiality, access, exclusion, and regulation (Valentine, 1996b).

Boundary Disputes

Certainly, young people's use (and misuse) of space has long engendered feelings of apprehension among adults; their presence is often deemed a potential threat to social order (Flint, 2006; Hall, Coffey, & Williamson, 1999, p. 506). For youth inhabiting malls, however, there is perhaps a particular cultural destabilization at stake. In malls, young people are greeted dubiously and censured for loitering, gathering together, and aimlessly wandering the halls. Youth are said to linger, hang out, and congregate "menacingly in areas reserved mainly for 'purposeful' commercial or social activity" (Hil & Bessant, 1999, p. 42). Perhaps it is their "lack of productive activity as much as anything specific which infuriates and prompts allegations of deviance" (Hall et al., 1999, pp. 506–507). Thus despite their potential consumer power, young visitors are more often portrayed as "mall rats" than patrons—"trespassers whose purchases are utterly insufficient to make up for their annoyance and disruption" (Amsden, 2008, p. 409).

In response to this irritation, a growing number of malls across the United States have implemented "curfews" and "parental escort policies." While the logistical details of these policies differ from mall to mall, the general "arguments made in support of mall curfews have been remarkably consistent" (Amsden, 2008, p. 410). Mall curfews and the justifications on which they are founded provide an interesting assemblage of beliefs, rationalities, and practices from which to explore notions of youth/adulthood, public/private, protecting/being protected, freedom/governance, and access/exclusion.

Governing Mall Rats

Popularized in 1996 by Minnesota's Mall of America, now more than 60 malls across the United States enforce some form of curfew or parental escort policy. Like many similar policies Minnesota's regulations required all youth under the age of 16 years to be accompanied by a parent or guardian over 21 years of age on Friday nights and weekends. According to media reports, Minnesota's policies were created in response to frustrated mall owners and annoyed patrons complaining about young people's lack of supervision as well as the disruption they caused: blocking walkways, jostling strollers, frightening the elderly, using foul language, and starting fights (Rawe, 2007).

While the mall is not a public space in the truest sense, it is what many refer to as a "quasi-public space"; that is, a location that holds the allure of the public sphere but is regulated and controlled by the private sector. In reality, however, as Voyce (2006, p. 273) points out, malls are anything but public. Instead they are designed as a "predictable controlled environment which acts like a prison in reverse: to keep deviant behavior on the outside and to form a consumerist form of citizenship inside." Despite this, however, many youth "take seriously the illusion that shopping centers are genuinely public spaces" and utilize them as such (Amsden, 2008, p. 412). If this is indeed the case, the mall is an interesting setting to examine how young people mitigate a global consumer culture where access to public space is diminishing (and, correspondingly, opportunities for civic participation) and increasingly governed by adults as well as privatized commercial sectors (Mansvelt, 2008; O'Dougherty, 2006).

These boundary disputes enable us to better understand how spaces and places are related to the development or derailment of citizenship; more specifically, how our ideas about citizenship, access, and consumption are constructed, defined, and experienced in relation to each other (Hall et al., 1999). For Flint (2006, p. 53), these exclusionary policies are implicitly connected to young people's citizenship rights and further help us explore the ways in which technologies of surveillance and prohibition are "located within wider conflicts about the legitimate use of public space by different sections of the community and the role of consumption as a manifestation of citizenship."

Protected or Protecting?

As pointed out in earlier sections of this book, the construction of youth continues to be a "contested and slippery concept" (Valentine, Skelton, & Chambers, 1998, p. 4). Youth have often been said to lie in an awkward middle space, residing somewhere between adulthood and childhood, a citizen of neither realm. In some instances, youth are "represented as 'innocent children' in need of protection from adult sexuality, violence, and commercial exploitation." On other occasions, they are "represented as articulating adult vices of drink, drugs and violence" (Valentine, 1996a, p. 587). Young people's liminal positionality is, in many ways, reflected in mall curfew and escort policies. On the one hand, malls become extensions of middle-class domestic spaces idealized for their security, controllability, and predictability. Here, youth are constructed as in need of privatized, parental-like protection from the unregulated dangers of society. "From this perspective the panopticon of the adult gaze provides a safety net that enables young people to develop their identity [or] individuality . . . without any real danger" (Matthews, Taylor, Percy-Smith, & Limb, 2000, p. 290). On the other hand, and more consistent with the ways in which curfew and escort policies are discursively produced in the media, it is the shoppers (the "good" capitalist others) who are in need of protection from youth (and not the other way around). From this vantage point, it is young people who need containment (outside the boundaries of malls). At the same time that young people's "becomingness" is highlighted in these policies, the mall itself becomes a kind of geographical middle space. As Matthews et al. (2000, p. 292) write, in malls

> young people are no longer children, living within the safe haven of home, nor quite adult with powers to move freely and unassailably within the public domain. By locating themselves in settings that transgress and so question the spatial hegemony of adulthood, young people journey into the interstitial territory of thirdspace.

Interestingly, escort policies commonly rely on actual or manufactured parental authority as a means of enforcement. In Minnesota, for example, mall owners hired unofficial security personnel, individuals they designated as "Mighty Moms" and "Dedicated Dads," to oversee the policy's implementation. The names of escort policies also often carry a familial flavor. The policy at the Metrocenter Mall in Jackson, MI, is dubbed "The Family First Guardian Policy" while the Abilene Mall in Alibene, Texas, refers to its policy as "The Family First Program." Many policies also rely on normative familial relations as a method of enforcement. At the Frontier Mall in Cheyenne, Wyoming, the escort policy states that "one parent . . . can supervise all of his or her children. Or one escort can supervise up to three youths, at least one of which must be his or her own child" (Evans, 2009). Importantly, and as Amsden (2008, p. 421) points out, here power is "so carefully clothed or stylized to resemble the care of 'private' relations that it ceases to appear as power at all." To ensure that escorts take the policy seriously, authorities have sanctioned a penalty for them as well. According to regulations at the Frontier Mall, if a youth is banned from the mall while under the watch of their guardian, the escort will also be barred from the mall. Thus, at the same time that mall curfews regulate youth's access to space, they also govern parental authority by penalizing those who have not properly monitored their child.

In many ways, policies such as this represent new and somewhat question-able ways of governing youth. They have the effect of targeting spaces, not persons. This, Voyce (2006, p. 280) claims, is one reason why these policies remain relatively uncontested. They are not predicated on disciplining particular individuals per se but, rather, become about governing geographical locations in order to ensure that the spaces are used appropriately and consistent with their designed purpose. And, for the mall, this means creating an environment that will stimulate one thing: a compliant and deliberate form of consumer citizenship.

Clearly, malls and exclusion practices that are enforced within them hold important material ramifications for youth, their citizenship rights, their access to space, and the politics of embodiment. While this essay primarily focuses on the ways in which youth are subject to oppressive tactics, there is a growing scholarship on the ways in which youth have reclaimed aspects of their citizenship that have been appropriated by adults. Therefore, at the same time that the mall is a location where citizenship rights have been abridged, it has also been used by youth as a resource for them to engage in expanding their independence and, at the same time, participation in the public sphere. For, if we are interested in understanding how young people's citizenship rights are derailed, it is also "important that we acknowledge the complex ways in which young people oppose impositions of power and control" (Hil & Bessant, 1999, p. 48).

Lesko (2001, p. 3) writes that it is necessary to take notice of the "cultural weights that are placed on a particular way of understanding." In this context there are various "cultural weights" that influence young people's use of space at the same time that these weights frame reactions to these uses. While research in this area is developing, there are certainly lines of inquiry that necessitate further theorizing. First, scholarship could extend knowledge on how youth engage and disengage (by choice or force) from particular geo-graphical places. This kind of work might specifically reveal those settings where youth are deemed "out of place." This could raise critical questions about youth and adults, their relationships, their (presumed) inclinations, as well as the spaces themselves. Questions could be raised, for example, concerning the beliefs and assumptions about youth that are predicated and make policies like this "reasonable." Correspondingly, questions could surround how geo-graphical form or function influences policies and practices such as surveil-lance or exclusion. By highlighting the rationalities caught up in this kind of governance, scholarship can make more visible those freedoms which are crafted—actively or unwittingly—by particular agents, regimes of truth, and/or discourses. Another line of inquiry involves attending to the ways that young people's consumption habits have become interconnected with the materialization or dematerialization of their citizenship. Finally, future work could explore notions of citizenship as these are interconnected with particular places and spaces. Are there other places, for example like the mall, where young people's citizenship rights have been abridged? And, if so, what effect do these demarcations have? Inquiries like this challenge us to attend to the meanings, contexts, and constructions that influence individual subjectivities as well as broader conceptions of youthfulness.

References

Amsden, B. (2008). Negotiating liberalism and biopolitics: Stylizing power in defense of the mall curfew. *Quarterly Journal of Speech, 94*, 407–429.

Anthony, K. H. (1985). The shopping mall: A teenage hangout. *Adolescence, 20*, 307–312.

Evans, B. (2009, April 4). Teens banned from mall on weekends . . . Unless they have an adult escort. *Wyoming News*. Retrieved from http://www.WyomingNews.com/articles/2009/04/04/featured_story/01top_04-04-09.txt

Flint, J. (2006). Surveillance and exclusion practices in the governance of access to shopping centres on periphery estates in the UK. *Surveillance & Society, 4*, 52–68.

Goss, J. (1993). The "magic of the mall": An analysis of form function, and meaning in the contemporary retail built environment. *Annals of the Association of American Geographers, 83*, 18–47.

Gray, M. L. (2007). From websites to Walmart: Youth identity work, and the queering of the boundary publics in small town USA. *American Studies, 48*, 49–59.

Hall, T., Coffey, A., & Williamson, H. (1999). Self, space and place: Youth identities and citizenship. *British Journal of Sociology of Education, 20*, 501–513.

Hil, R., & Bessant, J. (1999). Spaced-out? Young people's agency, resistance and public space. *Urban Policy and Research, 17*, 41–49.

Lesko, N. (2001). *Act your age! A cultural construction of adolescence*. New York: RoutledgeFalmer.

Mansvelt, J. (2008). Geographies of consumption: Citizenship, space and practice. *Progress in Human Geography, 32*, 105–117.

Matthews, H., Taylor, M., Percy-Smith, B., & Limb, M. (2000). The unacceptable *flaneur*: The shopping mall as a teenage hangout. *Childhood, 7*, 279–294.

O'Dougherty, M. (2006). Public relations, private security: Managing youth and race at the Mall of America. *Environment and Planning D: Society and Space, 24*, 131–154.

Rawe, J. (2007). Bye-bye mall rats. *Time Magazine*. Retrieved from http://www.time.com/time/magazine/article/0, 9171,1638449,00.html

Shildrick, T., Blackman, S., & MacDonald, R. (2009). Young people, class and place. *Journal of Youth Studies, 12*, 457–465.

Valentine, G. (1996a). Angels and devils: Moral landscapes of childhood. *Environment and Planning D: Society and Space, 14*, 581–599.

Valentine, G. (1996b). Children should be seen and not heard: The production and transgression of adults' public space. *Urban Geography, 17*, 205–220.

Valentine, G., Skelton, T., & Chambers, D. (1998). Cool places: An introduction to youth and youth cultures. In T. Skelton, & G. Valentine (Eds.), *Cool Places: Geographies of Youth Cultures* (pp. 1–32). New York: Routledge.

Vanderbeck, R. M., & Johnson, J. H. (2000). "That's the only place where you can hang out": Urban young people and the space of the mall. *Urban Geography, 21*, 5–25.

Voyce, M. (2006). Shopping malls in Australia: The end of public space and the rise of "consumerist citizenship." *Journal of Sociology, 42*, 269–286.

24

NATION

Rupa Huq

Along with "citizenship," another keyword in this volume regularly and explicitly linked to youth, the idea of the "nation" is not new. This is in sharp contrast to other topics we associate with contemporary youth culture such as "downloading" or "social networking." From "nation" stems the more politically defined "nation-state" and consequent sense of "nationhood." The standard sociological undergraduate text, Fulcher and Scott (2003, p. 872), explains nation as "[a] people with a sense of identity, a common language and a distinct culture." This definition is wider, then, than simply topographical but, at the same time, given the increasing ethnic diversity within the territorial borders of modern countries in the era of globalization, it seems strangely narrow to presume cultural and linguistic uniformity. This essay will use two case studies, Britpop in the United Kingdom in the late 1990s and French hip hop, to look at how the "nation" has been almost rewritten by these twin musically based youth cultural forms through performativity at the turn of the century. These are powerful examples of how difference underscores the modern nation.

Lingua Franca: French Hip Hop

France and the United Kingdom share the same 21st-century fate that has seen them forcibly have to come to terms with losing an empire and gaining a multicultural population. French imperial possessions once spanned the globe. A legacy of associated cultural export can be seen in the concept of *Francophonie*, which on one level means the global community of French-speaking people and on another the International Organization of the Francophonie, which ostensibly promotes French national culture, an outfit that could be described as a collection of former French colonies. Crucially, youth with origins in French former colonies in West and North Africa are among the most vocal in its contemporary youth culture. The much-quoted fact that France is the world's second biggest hip hop market after America can in part be explained by France's own indigenous French-language hip hop market. The social commentary and angst articulated in French hip hop's lyrical themes tell us at least as much about youth in France as any decent sociological or anthropological ethnography ever could. French hip hop's unfolding since the 1980s also presents an alternative youthful model of nationhood to that proposed by the French state with its tricolor flag and official tripartite ideal of liberty, equality, fraternity.

Ambiguous attitudes to American cultural influences have been enduring in France, as in the United Kingdom (Bazin, 1995; Hebdige, 1988), revolving around repulsion at a perceived antiintellectual inability to compete cerebrally with established civilizations and a simultaneous fascination for its hedonistic codes of youth cultural liberation. French hip hop has also been an unintended beneficiary of central government policies to preserve and protect the French language, seen as under threat from English. Reflecting its circumstances of production, rap in France accordingly both uses U.S. musical influences while resisting cultural domination. French cultural policy has protectionist tendencies: the French film industry is hugely subsidized and government-imposed quotas of French language output on national and local radio instituted in 1994 have unwittingly ushered in a new generation of hip hop heroes of youth originating from former French colonies including second-generation French-Arab "beurs"[1] and African youth, such as Senegal-born Paris literature graduate MC Solaar.

For Poulet (1993, p. 312) the multiple youthful ethnic communities of urban France are giving rise to musical hybrids reflecting both their ancestral musical heritage and their quotidian French setting. Youth culture is littered with the formerly dispossessed "made good," in the style of the Beatles, who began in Liverpool but bought country mansions on acquiring wealth and status. Yet, rather than "making good," remaining in touch with the roots is promoted outwardly by French rappers. Lapassade (1996, p. 93) observes that their role is primarily to document bad in the world and tell of desolation of the ghetto or "banlieue."[2] The 1990s band NTM made much of humble origins in the north Parisien banlieue; a location where the band's Joey Starr was proud to claim he still lived in a major television interview in 2002 (Joey Starr, n.d.). The group Ministère A.M.E.R. produced the album 95 200 after the postal code of Sarcelles, another tough north Parisien banlieue in the same way as NWA proudly proclaimed that they were "Straight Outta Compton." As well as rap music, hip hop provides multiple avenues for youthful lived urban expression spanning physical dance and visual art/graffiti practiced on urban canvas, such as public transport. The term "street credibility" has always been central to youth culture. Here we see an overt visiblization of dispossession that contradicts official versions of the statist French nation where the government is all-providing.

French rap's political dimension has extended from documenting localized struggles of youth to broader geopolitical statements. The live performance of Paris-based Senegalese-born rappers Djoloff combines French and Woloff language lyrics, traditional African costumes, instruments, and various anticolonial political pronouncements, critiquing corrupt African dictators and third-world debt. Their Manchester concert of 2000 saw a set with songs tackling colonialization, African unhappiness, and dictatorship. In an interview, lead-rapper Mbegane N'Dour (personal communication, June 16, 2000) rejected the project of integrating youth into a French ideal:

It's all about making you into a French citizen to alienate your spirit, to wipe it out so you forget all your differences. France risks exploding because it's two-faced integration. They're all for us integrating to do low-level cheap labor but they don't want us to be lawyers, doctors, engineers, television presenters, parliamentarians, or executives. Integration is the new colonialization.

It is almost a given that youth complain of officialdom's condescending regard for them. Here African politics is critiqued for its corruption as well as "tolerant" French multiculturalism for being patronizing. No solutions are proposed, underlining the fact that it is easier to critique than suggest alternatives. Homegrown rap in France is more than a wholesale importing of U.S. hip hop culture in French and more a reworking which also reinterprets nation in the process.

Early U.S. rap theorists (e.g., Gilroy, 1993; Rose, 1994) influentially positioned Afrocentrism within the Black Atlantic, which is a sophisticated model of transnational Afrodiasporic Black cultures in Western modernity that transgresses different national paradigms for thinking about history. Blackness in rap has been seen in Public Enemy's album entitled "Fear of a Black Planet" or NWA's use of the word "Nigger," which they see as a positive reclaiming of the word. Africa has been a historic seedbed for rap on both sides of the Atlantic (Calio, 1998; Toop, 1990). Afrika Bambaataa's Zulu nation collective, named after an 18th-century South African tribe who fought White colonization (Toop, 1990, pp. 56–59), for example, idealize the continent as a model of peace, harmony, and rights. Perhaps more useful is Lapassade's (1996, pp. 52–65) notion of "noirceur'(blackness) as critical to rap which can be seen as crossing nations and continents.

Britpop

The notion of nation was also playfully reinterpreted in the United Kingdom by a contrastingly White-faced music, Britpop, which detractors critiqued for the lack of attention paid to blackness/noirceur. Like France, Britain too has ex-colonial hang ups and hangovers (the Commonwealth is the U.K. equivalent of La Francophonie). Mercer (1994, p. 251) has stated, "The terrain of postimperial Britain is the site of many, overlapping diasporas, including the Indian, Pakistani, Bangladeshi and broader South Asian diasporas, as well as the diaspora of Islam." Onto this cultural landscape appeared Britpop, which entered common usage in the mid-1990s, but, like many contested categories of music and youth culture, has multiple origins. Unlike other genre disputes, for example over garage (alternatively seen as a 1960s U.S. guitar sound or a 1990s U.K. electronic dance music one) or punk (seen variously as from CBGBs in New York or Bromley, a far flung suburb of London), Britpop's geographical location is clearly in the United Kingdom, or more accurately in England, even though its name suggests the wider "British Isles" encompassing England, Scotland, Wales, and Northern Ireland. The band Blur saw its stated aim as to "get rid of grunge," "declare war on America," and make music that was identifiably English (Youngs, 2005).

The essays in part one of Bennett and Stratton's (2010) edited volume trace Britpop's origins back to music-hall and skiffle among precursors, but Britpop's 1990s became strongly associated with the post-1997 Labour government. Labour's accompanying vision of "cool Britannia" was used to explain attempts to rebrand the United Kingdom as less stuffy, more forward looking, and culturally diverse, prioritizing the knowledge economy and projecting a youthful multicultural national image (Oakley, 2004), in sharp contrast to predecessor John Major's much-maligned retrograde monocultural narrow version of English nationhood based on nostalgia for an imagined past of an olde England, yet to be corrupted by technology, modernity, and multiculturalism.[3] The victorious Tony Blair (as cited in Dowd, 1997), youngest premier since Lord Liverpool in 1812, declared "New" Britain to be a "young country" emphasizing his youthfulness and leisure background: "I am . . . from the rock and roll generation, the Beatles, colour TV, all the rest of it, that's where I come from." The "New" Labour desire for updating old stereotypes began in its own renaming and was exemplified in its modernization of political institutions, such as devolved parliaments in Scotland and Wales. The Union Jack appeared to be more in favor than the trade unions: campaign imagery saw a center-left reclaiming of the flag that had long been co-opted as an emblem of the far-right.

Britpop is now itself viewed nostalgically and sometimes seen as something of an embarrassment, recently called "a dirty word" by one journalist (Beaumont, 2009), but at its height in 1996, it was co-opted by "New" Labour to suit their own ideas of nationhood constructed in deliberate opposition to those of the preceding Conservative administration. Blair thanked Noel Gallagher, guitarist/songwriter of leading Britpop band Oasis, for the band's support in his Brit Awards speech that year and was photographed carrying a guitar into number 10 on becoming prime minister, then having Gallagher over to a Downing Street reception soon after (see Harris, 2002). Chris Rojek (2007) writes:

> The aim was to identify with figures in British youth culture that carried international and multi-ethnic prestige, in keeping with the domestic realties of transnationalism and multiculturalism, and the opportunities presented by globalisation. This was an exercise in political location and cultural recognition that sought to exploit trends in British pop culture, music, art, music, fashion and comedy and film and present them as evidence that Britannia was reinventing itself from the crabby dowager of the recent Conservative era.
>
> (pp. 23–24)

The picture of when-Tony-met-Noel evoked memories of when Harold Wilson nominated the Beatles Member of the British Empire (MBE) medals awarded by the Queen. New Labour was a rebranding of the party that was originally a creature of the trade union movement into a less identifiably socialist outfit that accepted market forces and was an election-winning machine. A 1960s template and imagery whereby the once taboo Union Jack flag was reclaimed from being symbolic territory was common to both New Labour and Britpop.

Conclusion: Back to the Future?

It can be something of an oversimplification to draw nonexistent parallels between these two musical styles and their roles in the history of their respective nations. For one, Britpop was a somewhat transitory style or "fad" (largely dead by the advent of the second millennium and now viewed as historical) whereas French hip hop is a constantly evolving genre still on the record rack classifications today as "rap Francaise." Many original fans of both styles are now entering middle age with new ones created by archival sources such as YouTube and LastFM. However, when looking further at what these musics share, many of their defining forces (against America) have much in common with the early U.K. cultural studies theorists such as Richard Hoggart, who feared creeping U.S. influences eroding British culture. In the months following the 2010 general election that finally saw New Labour dethroned, newly elected Conservative Prime Minister David Cameron (2010) attacked Labour's attempts to rebrand Britain while in power, claiming: "They just didn't get our heritage. They raided the national lottery taking money from heritage because it didn't go with their image of 'cool Britannia.' At one point they even referred to Britain as a young country." Time will tell whether in a decade things have gone full circle. What is clear, however, is that French rap and Britpop each present refined versions of their two nations redefined away from popular stereotypes. Both are located in countries now grappling with the search for a postimperial role on the world stage while managing complexity at home. Multicultural communities that have now made France and Britain their home and have a younger age profile than the "indigenous majority" make it imperative that we reframe interpretations of the word "nation" already replete with difference, be it gender, class, or generation.

Notes

1 The word "beur," used in self-appellation, describes second-generation youth of the Mahgrebian countries of Tunisia, Morocco, and Algeria.
2 The word "banlieue" means literally "suburb," although many British commentors, such as Hargreaves and McKinney (1997) and Thoday (1995), leave it untranslated as it has negative ghetto-type associations that the word "suburb" is devoid of.
3 The words "Fifty years on from now, Britain will still be the country of long shadows on cricket grounds, warm beer, invincible green suburbs, dog lovers and pools fillers" (John Major, n.d.) uttered in 1995 had many critics.

References

Bazin, H. (1995). *La culture hip hop*. Paris: Desclee de Brouwer.

Beaumont, M. (2009). It's time to let Britpop die with dignity. Retrieved from http://www. nme.com/blog/index.php?blog=58&title=it_s_time_to_let_britpop_die_with_ dignit&more=1&c=1&tb=1&pb=1

Bennett, A., & Stratton, J. (Eds.). (2010). *Britpop and the English music tradition*. Aldershot: Ashgate.

Calio, J. (1998). *Le rap: Une réponse des banlieues?* Lyon: Collection pour Mémoire Entpe Aléas.

Cameron, D. (2010). PM's speech on tourism. Retrieved from http://www.number10.gov. uk/news/speeches-and-transcripts/2010/08/pms-speech-on-tourism-54479

Dowd, M. (1997, April 23). Labour's love lost. *New York Times*. Retrieved from http://query. nytimes.com/gst/fullpage.html?res=9804E7DE133EF930A15757C0A961958260&;sec= &spon=&pagewanted=all

Fulcher, J., & Scott, J. (2003). *Sociology* (2nd ed.). Oxford: Oxford University Press.

Gilroy, P. (1993). *The black Atlantic: Modernity and double consciousness*. London: Verso.

Hargreaves, A., & McKinney, M. (Eds.). (1997). *Post colonial cultures in France*. London: Routledge.

Harris, J. (2002). *The last party: Britpop, Blair and the demise of English rock*. London: Fourth Estate.

Hebdige, D. (1988). *Hiding in the light: On images and things*. London: Routledge.

Joey Starr. (n.d.). Tout le Monde en Parle 1/3. Retrieved from http://www.youtube.com/ watch?v=1Qql-f-yKts

John Major. (n.d.). Retrieved from http://www.number10.gov.uk/output/Page125.asp

Lapassade, G. (1996). *Le rap ou la fureur de dire*. Paris: Loris Talmart.

Mercer, K. (1994). *Welcome to the jungle: New positions in black cultural studies*. London: Routledge.

Oakley, K. (2004). Not so cool Britannia: The role of the creative industries in economic development. *International Journal of Cultural Studies, 7,* 67–77.

Poulet, G. (1993). Popular music. In M. Cook (Ed.), *French culture since 1945* (pp. 192–214). Harlow, Essex: Longman.

Rojek, C. (2007). *Brit-myth*. London: Reaktion.

Rose, T. (1994). *Black noise: Rap music and black culture in contemporary America*. Hanover: Wesleyan University Press.

Thoday, P. (1995). *Le Franglais*. London: Athlone.

Toop, D. (1990). *Rap attack*. London: Pluto Press.

Youngs, I. (2005). Looking back at the birth of Britpop. Retrieved from http://news.bbc. co.uk/1/hi/entertainment/4144458.stm

25

POSTCOLONIAL

Aaron Koh and Allan Luke

The term "postcolonial" refers to the historical period of statehood and governance, and the cultural and political life, after colonization by an external imperial state. Postcolonial writing in the social sciences and cultural and literary studies documents and theorizes human experience in the cultural and political contexts during and after colonialism. This corpus of work arose from communities that gained autonomous rule through dissent and revolution against European, American, and Asian empires in the mid and late 20th century, and from diasporic communities created through migration and partition. Postcolonial studies also describe economic and cultural domination by transnational corporations and imperial powers after the colonies had achieved political self-determination (Hardt & Negri, 2000). As a result, postcolonial studies of youth and education have expanded from the study of ex-colonies to include the experiences of those communities living under conditions of neocolonial economic control and cultural hegemony (Smith, 1999).

Key literary and political works from Africa, Asia, the Pacific, the Caribbean, and the Americas documenting the human experience of colonial ideologies and institutions, militarism, and social control captured the attention of the postwar Western academy. One such work was Edward Said's *Orientalism* (1979), which explained how Western science, art, and literature defined and positioned colonial human subjects in relation to dominant normative categories. This and other works embody some of the major themes in the field of postcolonial studies: the cultural, spiritual, and psychological impacts of colonialism; new models of political and cultural analysis and action; and hybrid, intercultural identities, texts, and cultural practices (e.g., Ashcroft, Griffiths, & Tiffin, 2005; Spivak, 2006). This essay outlines general educational issues raised by colonialism and its aftermath. Because of the broad international purview of postcolonial studies, we have focused our discussion on the local knowledge of youth and education in East Asia. Our aim is to flag emergent issues of political engagement and dissent *after* postcolonialism.

Postcolonial Education and Youth Studies

The establishment of schools and universities has been a central colonial strategy, with curriculum purpose-built for the transmission of colonial ideologies and values (Pennycook, 1998). In many sites, colonial education entailed symbolic violence—an active displacement of local knowledge, languages, traditions, and beliefs and the introduction of Eurocentric discipline and practice as a normative benchmark for value. Thus, a key move in colonial education was the suppression of indigenous local voice and identity, vernacular language, and cultural practice (Fanon, 1967; Vera, 2002). The genocidal effects of reservation and missionary education upon indigenous peoples are well documented. In this regard, there are parallels between postcolonial educational studies and current indigenous educational theory. Both have raised questions about the educational significance and place of local knowledges and epistemologies that were historically repressed (Grande, 2004; Martin, 2008). In the social sciences, there is an emergent debate among postcolonial, indigenous, and Islamic scholars about the place of non-Anglo/European theory and knowledge in the Western academy (Alatas, 2006).

The process of decolonization generated "nationalist and 'nativist' pedagogies that set up the relation of Third World and First World as a binary structure of opposition" (Bhabha, 1994, p. 173). Former colonies typically engaged in significant curriculum revision, alteration of canonical histories and literatures, and changes in educational *lingua franca*. In instances, this led to the replacement of a colonial language by a vernacular language (e.g., Indonesia, Malaysia). At the same time many national educational systems retained the selective traditions of examination systems and school structures. Former French colonies in Africa, for example, retain the structures and disciplines of the *lycee*. Cambridge-style O and A level examination cultures are still intact across former British colonies worldwide. Moreover, despite decolonization, certain knowledge systems continue to be marginalized.

In the last decade, Western cultural and youth studies has extended its purview to youth in non-North American and European societies (e.g., Chen, 1998). Studying Cantonese-speaking youth in Hong Kong, Lam (2006) documented the use of mobile and online technology in building new forms of cultural identity and exchange. In East Asia, youth studies have focused on emergent issues of cultural and subcultural identity and *voice* via the appropriation of Western popular cultural forms. Prototypical studies describe the transnational impact of Pokémon, Manga, and other *comic* cultures in the 1990s (Iwabuchi, 2002), Hip-hop and other African American cultural forms in Asia, and domestic soap culture among Korean and Chinese youth (Lin & Tong, 2007). This work examines issues of psychosexual identity and the local appropriation of popular cultural texts. Western genres and media become means for cultural politics, and, in some cases, overt political and social critique (Pennycook & Alim, 2007). In her analysis of Japanese anime, Napier (2008) discusses the use of popular culture and mass media for critique of the infantilization of Japanese youth.

In contrast, Western educational research has discovered that Other cultural/geographic spaces may have distinctive local and regional educational cultures (Alexander, 2001). The result is a broad description of teacher-centered, autocratic culture and learning style (Watkins & Biggs, 2002), with various bids to apply Western progressivism as a corrective to what is perceived as East Asian educational traditionalism (Mok, 2006). Indeed, empirical differences in pedagogy and curriculum between East and West, North and South reflect profoundly different cultural genealogies and pedagogical traditions.

The resultant picture of East Asian youth is, in part, an artifact of the uneven extension of Anglo/American youth studies and educational research to postcolonial settings: emergent transnational youth culture juxtaposed to autocratic educational systems. In what follows, we describe one neglected subject in East Asian youth studies: the underground political analyst, critic, and activist.

Youth and Political Activism: A Singaporean Case

In the postcolonial states of East Asia, digital cultural exchange has flourished among urban, *global*, and interconnected youth. Singaporean youth are turning to alternative platforms in cyber-space to participate in cyber-citizenship and counterpolitics. Singapore began from a position of a weak national identity (Gandhi, 1998). The People's Action Party (PAP) government, in power since independence in 1959, has anchored national identity in a narrative of economic rationalism, technical efficiency, and racial harmony (Venn, 2006). The threat of global financial crisis and volatility has provided the government with an even stronger case for central management and control. Singapore's postcolonial challenge has been scripted into an official narrative about a relentless and flexible capitalist project: nation building requires a technocratic elite, highly educated, pragmatic, and theoretically adept, and capable of offering technical solutions to all matters cultural and social.

There is an external perception that Singaporeans live in an "air-conditioned" nation (George, 2000)—a metaphoric social contract where individual freedom is exchanged for material comfort. Youth aim for what locals call "the 5Cs" (cash, car, credit card, condominium, country club). Lee (2010) documents an entrenched culture of fear and repercussions for critiquing the government, based on self- and auto-censorship. He argues that the panopticism is dependent upon key regulatory strategies for the monitoring and administration of traditional print and broadcast media. This is expanding into a fuller government creative industries strategy.

Yet new media technologies provide avenues for political activism. The *Temasek Review* (http://www.temasekreview.com) is a popular platform for young Singaporeans to participate in cyber-citizenship and oppositional politics. What follows is from a themed reflective blog, "This National Day is not mine, it's the PAP's," posted by a netizen "Tony L" on the eve of Singapore's National Day. This blog garnered 115 responses, an indicator of the controversial issues that were raised by Tony L. In the context of surveillance described by Lee (2010), this is a remarkable response.

In the blog, Tony L reminisces how Singapore has changed over the years and that he no longer feels he belongs to Singapore. He asserts that Singapore "belongs to the Lee family and the PAP" and that foreigners continue to come to Singapore "to keep the PAP in power." A main theme that runs across a number of the blogs is the push for authentically representative politics:

> August 9, 2010 at 12:10 am
>
> Let's hope voters will all work together to claim our country back from the PAP!
>
> August 9, 2010 at 12:40 am
>
> Year after year the cheats get voted in agains and again.
>
> Hope that S'poreans are braver and smater this time round. Tell your mother, father, wife, husband, brothers, sisters, uncles, aunts, cousins, neighbours to vote the opposition for a better future for the ordinary Singaporean.

A more vehement blog proclaims the following:

> August 9, 2010 at 3:00 am
>
> Here is the most meaningful national pledge since our independence:
>
> Vote Out The PAP.
>
> Vote Out The PAP.
>
> Vote Out The PAP.

These blogs are counterscripts to the Singapore story—incidents of talking back to the official narrative of economic success and nation building. They critique a political order in an environment where opposition political activity, public political gatherings, and media are closely monitored. Comparable spaces have opened (and, periodically, are closed through censorship and surveillance) in China, Malaysia, Indonesia, and other East Asian states where the overt political dissent is risky.

After Postcolonialism

Asia—like Africa, Latin America, and the Middle East—is an imaginary geographic and cultural entity produced in academic studies, mass media, and popular culture, geopolitical strategy, and national and regional ideology (Wilson & Dirlik, 1996). Our brief comments have focused on the definition and positioning of East Asian youth in postcolonial contexts. How have youth and cultural studies defined and positioned youth from China, Japan, Korea, Singapore, and other East Asia states? The representation of East Asian youth has been strongly influenced by American critiques of the transnational corporate order as a pervasive global neocolonialism (Spring, 2008).

One effect has been to underplay local bids for social agency and cultural self-determination among the current generation of youth in postcolonial societies, many of which remain autocratic and authoritarian well after decolonization. Our aim is to challenge the stereotypical construction of East Asian youth as voiceless, politically disengaged, and disempowered. In the scapes of the new digital undergrounds that we have briefly visited here, we find the texts of a new generation. These voices are increasingly adept at repositioning themselves and reinterpreting their worlds: material and virtual, social and political—albeit in very different semiotic and cultural forms than those used by their parents and grandparents against a colonial order.

References

Alatas, S. (2006). *Alternative discourses in Asian social sciences*. London: Sage.

Alexander, R. (2001). *Culture and pedagogy*. Oxford: Blackwell.

Ashcroft, B., Griffiths, G., & Tiffin, H. (Eds.). (2005). *The postcolonial studies reader* (2nd ed.). New York: Routledge.

Bhabha, H. (1994). *The location of culture*. New York: Routledge.

Chen, K. H. (Ed.). (1998). *Trajectories*. New York: Routledge.

Fanon, F. (1967). *Black skin, white masks* (C. Farrington, Trans.). New York: Grove Press.

Gandhi, L. (1998). *Postcolonial theory: A critical introduction*. Australia: Allen & Unwin.

George, C. (2000). *Singapore: The air-conditioned nation*. Singapore: Landmark.

Grande, S. (2004). *Red pedagogy*. New York: Roman and Littlefield.

Hardt, M., & Negri, A. (2000). *Empire*. Cambridge, MA: Harvard University Press.

Iwabuchi, K. (2002). *Recentering globalization: Popular culture and Asian transnationalism*. Durham, NC: Duke University Press.

Lam, E. (2006). Culture and learning in the context of globalization: Research directions. *Review of Research in Education, 30*, 213–237.

Lee, T. (2010). *The media, cultural control, and government in Singapore*. London: Routledge.

Lin, A. M. Y., & Tong, A. (2007). Crossing boundaries: Male consumption of Korean TV dramas and negotiation of gender relations in modern day Hong Kong. *Journal of Gender Studies, 16*, 217–232.

Martin, K. L. (2008). *Please knock before you enter*. Brisbane: Post-Pressed.

Mok, I. H. (2006). Shedding light on the East Asian learner paradox: Reconstructing student-centeredness in a Shanghai classroom. *Asia Pacific Journal of Education, 26*, 131–142.

Napier, S. J. (2008). *Anime from Akire to Howl's moving castle*. London: Palgrave Macmillan.

Pennycook, A. (1998). *English and the discourses of colonialism*. London: Routledge.

Pennycook, A., & Alim, S. (2007). Glocal linguistic flows: Hip hop culture(s), identities, and the politics of language education. *Journal of Language, Identity and Education, 6*, 89–100.

Said, E. (1979). *Orientalism*. New York: Vintage.

Smith, L. T. (1999). *Decolonising methodologies*. London: Zed.

Spivak, G. (2006). *In other worlds* (2nd ed.). New York: Routledge.

Spring, J. (2008). *Globalization of education*. New York: Routledge.

Venn, C. (2006). *The postcolonial challenge: Towards alternative worlds*. London: Sage.

Vera, Y. (2002). *Without a name and under the tongue*. New York: Farrar, Straus and Giroux.

Watkins, D., & Biggs, J. (2002). *Teaching the Chinese learner*. Seattle: University of Washington Press.

Wilson, R., & Dirlik, A. (Eds.). (1996). *Asia/Pacific as a space for cultural production*. Durham, NC: Duke University Press.

26

SEX EDUCATION

Mary Louise Rasmussen

In a study of Sex Education in the United Kingdom in the 20th century Hall (2004) portrays the state as failing to provide adequate Sex Education insofar as it has been unable or unwilling to resolve fundamental epistemological questions, such as: Who should be teaching whom about sex? When should they be teaching it? What content should they cover? If Sex Education frames youth-as-future-citizens-in-the-making, what sort of citizens should the state produce? Like Hall, I believe that the state response to this question is incoherent. This is not surprising, as clearly there is no community or professional consensus about the role of the state in Sex Education. This keyword essay considers some historical imaginings of Sex Education. These imaginings are significant because the future of Sex Education depends on the traditions that influence contemporary thought. I then turn to some imaginings of "queer futurity" (Edelman, 2004) and their influence on contemporary conceptualizations of Sex Education.

Crafting Young People through Sex Education

Nationalist and eugenic discourses have influenced Sex Education, seeking to use it as a vehicle in the production of young people as citizens who are religiously or racially pure, as indicated in studies of the history of Sex Education in 20th-century Australia and the United States (Curthoys, 1989; Moran, 2000). This tradition continues in contemporary Sex Education, where debates about issues such as abstinence and teen sex play out differently according to young people's identifications relating to class, gender, sexuality, religiosity, race, and ethnicity (Fields & Hirschman, 2007; Fine & McClelland, 2006). Sex Educators in the past and present have also foregrounded philosophical and moral issues (Hall, 2004; Robinson & Davies, 2008) assuming that Sex Education relates to ethical and religious choices and that these should be considered in the process of teaching young people about sex. In this frame young people may be called upon to become the masters of their sexual destiny. Contemporary comprehensive Sex Education with its focus on the production of young people as agentic sexual subjects is informed by these traditions. Regardless of the moral or philosophical approach one adopts, there is recognition of young people's capacity to participate in sexual life and that the style of that participation is not preordained but is open to persuasion and instruction.

Probably the most prominent theme in Sex Education is its strong relationship with health. For some, this relationship is axiomatic; an axiom explicit in titles such as *Talking Sexual Health* (Australian National Council for AIDS, Hepatitis C and Related Diseases [ANCAHRD], 2001), the name given to a prominent Australian Sex Education curriculum document. This relationship extends to the early 19th century (Curthoys, 1989; Moran, 2000). Within this paradigm the purpose of Sex Education is clear. It "is to improve health outcomes in a population—typically, young people" (Kippax & Stephenson, 2005, p. 359). Related to this focus on health is the conceptualization of Sex Education as a response to a problem, namely young people's sexuality (Hall, 2004; Moran, 2000). Here Sex Education is foremost a prophylactic against disease and unwanted pregnancy, a counterpoint to popular discussions of the connections between sexuality pleasure and desire (Fine, 1988). In this tradition young people are often constituted as incapable of sufficient reason or knowledge to make good decisions. Consequently they are often construed as "at risk" and in need of adult advice and support to set them on the "right path," a style of thought that also continues to be pervasive in contemporary Sex Education. Debates about sexuality and age of consent also often highlight young people's sexuality as problematic (Waites, 2005). The effects of this framing of Sex Education as related to disease and pregnancy prevention have been powerful. In school curricula Sex Education continues to be strongly associated with Health and Physical Education.

In the United States Sex Education has also been the subject of much religious and political debate, underscoring how different approaches to Sex Education are seen to influence the production of youth as future citizens in the making. Janice Irvine locates debates about Abstinence Only (AO) and Comprehensive Sexuality Education (CSE) in the context of the "culture wars"—"a bruising set of conflicts" in which political organizing focuses explicitly on values and lifestyles rather than economics and foreign policy (2004, p. 9). Irvine emphasizes the religious and political differences in these approaches to youth, sex, and citizenship, while Nancy Lesko focuses on what she perceives as the similarities in the two approaches, arguing both emphasize how "knowledge can solve all problems smoothly and happily. Mistakes, negativism and confusion are excluded from both sets of sexual knowledge" (2010, p. 281). There is a politics of affect operating within many political, religious, scientific, and rationalist imaginaries of Sex Education that all relate to "a form of simpler sexual relations that are obtainable through active implementation of stable knowledge and rationality" (Lesko, 2010, p. 282). So Sex Education has embraced stable forms of knowledge that can be conveyed to young people in a mode that reinforces the liminality of adolescence. This is based on the belief that Sex Education, if properly administered and adhered to, may produce certain types of sexual subjects (McLeod, 1999) and, consequently, certain types of ideal sexual citizens.

Researchers have also critiqued the tendency to construct Sex Education in narrowly medicalized terms because they believe such a focus can result in a curriculum primarily concerned with issues of safety/risk, disease, and biology (Halstead & Reiss, 2003). Attention on medicalized issues may also result in the marginalization and erasure of other issues related to sexuality that are more pressing in the minds of young people (Allen, 2005). For instance, Sex Education curriculum often assumes students are heterosexual except when focusing on issues explicitly related to disease transmission (Ellis & High, 2004; Rasmussen, 2006). A health focus, when narrowly applied, can leave out important issues in terms of citizenship such as how to develop and practice sexual ethics (Carmody, 2008). Debates about Sex Education and citizenship are also influenced by debates about sex and gender roles (Hillier, Harrison, & Warr, 1998), the role of the state in providing information about sex and sexuality to children (Moran, 2000), issues of ethical consent (Carmody, 2008), competing community values about morality and sexual pleasure (Halstead & Reiss, 2003), and the boundaries of age—who can have sex with whom, when, where, and with whose permission (Angelides, 2004)?

Youth-as-Future-Sexual-Citizens-in-the-Making

To this point my discussion of the key term Sex Education has focused primarily on the intellectual history of this field and how this relates to different conceptualizations of youth as future citizens in the making. This brief history demonstrates that the type of citizens Sex Education has in mind is the continuing subject of debate. Foucault uses the process of inquiry into histories of thought to see the "limits imposed on us and an experiment with the possibility of going beyond them" (1997, p. 117). This brief inquiry into Sex Education is a way of acknowledging its limitations, and imagining possibilities for innovation.

In *The Empire of Love* Elizabeth Povinelli (2006) focuses on Australian Aboriginal people and radical faeries in the United States to consider how normative love is framed and how commonsense understandings about sex and sexuality might be dislodged. This work is valuable to conceptualizing Sex Education and youth-as-future-sexual-citizens-in-the-making because of its capacity to capture how physiological and psychological, economic, and social processes are distributed, felt, and embodied in the production of what she terms the "intimate event." For Povinelli, the "intimate event" is located at the intersection of autological and genealogical understandings of the subject. The former describe "fantasies about self-making, self-sovereignty, and the value of individual freedom" while the latter focus on "social constraints placed on the autological subject by various kinds of inheritances" (Povinelli, 2006, p. 4). Sex Education, whether configured by the autological subject or the genealogical society, presupposes certain desires and capacities to make choices, to act as individuals (with or against kin and community)—"as if all other actual and potential positions and practices were impractical, politically perverse, socially aberrant" (Povinelli, 2006, p. 6).

So Povinelli inspires a turning away from a questioning of what sorts of citizens might be produced by discourses and practices related to Sex Education; recognition that Sex Education, of the Left and the Right, always already presupposes who we are, what we want, and what is best for us. By refraining from the impulse to resolve Sex Education's fundamental epistemological questions we can turn our attention to how Sex Education is distributed, felt, and embodied in different spaces and places. This is a process that many people, young and old, are already engaged in, but its influence on youth-as-future-sexual-citizens-in-the-making is little understood because "intimate events" are often overshadowed by autological and genealogical fantasies embedded in Sex Education.

In conjunction with Povinelli, Judith Halberstam's work is also instructive in imagining youth-as-future-sexual-citizens-in-the-making. In an article titled "The Anti-Social Turn in Queer Studies," Halberstam situates her own project as to work on "'alternative political imaginaries,' [which] embod[y] the suite of 'other choices' that attend every political, economic and aesthetic crisis and their resolutions" (2008, p. 153). In this frame Sex Education might be reenvisaged as a project that focuses on "other choices" people make, negotiate, perform, and reject. It is a movement away from Sex Education as the provision of stable and rational knowledge that will help young people to one day become better sexual subjects, and toward the production of an archive of "intimate events" and alternative imaginaries of Sex Education.

References

Allen, L. (2005). "Say everything": Exploring young people's suggestions for improving sexuality education. *Sex, 5*, 391–406.

Angelides, S. (2004). Sex and the child. *Meanjin, 63*, 28–36.

Australian National Council for AIDS, Hepatitis C and Related Diseases (ANCAHRD). (2001). *Talking sexual health: A teaching and learning resource for secondary schools.* Canberra: Commonwealth of Australia.

Carmody, M. (2008). *Sex and ethics: Young people and ethical sex.* London: Palgrave Macmillan.

Curthoys, A. (1989). Eugenics, feminism, and birth control: The case of Marion Piddington. *Hecate, 15*, 73–89.

Edelman, L. (2004). *No future: Queer theory and the death drive.* Durham, NC: Duke University Press.

Ellis, V., & High, S. (2004). Something more to tell you: Gay, lesbian or bisexual young people's experiences of secondary schooling. *British Educational Research Journal, 30*, 213–225.

Fields, J., & Hirschman, C. (2007). Citizenship lessons in abstinence-only sexuality education. *American Journal of Sexuality Education, 2*, 3–25.

Fine, M. (1988). Sexuality, schooling, and adolescent females: The missing discourse of desire. *Harvard Educational Review, 58*, 29–53.

Fine, M., & McClelland, D. (2006). Sexuality education and desire: Still missing after all these years. *Harvard Educational Review, 76*, 297–338.

Foucault, M. (1997). What is enlightenment? In P. Rabinow (Ed.), *Ethics: Subjectivity and truth* (pp. 114–120). New York: The New Press.

Halberstam, J. (2008). The anti-social turn in queer studies. *Graduate Journal of Social Science, 5*, 140–156.

Hall, L. (2004). Birds, bees and sexual embarrassment: Sex education in Britain from social purity to section 28. In R. Aldrich (Ed.), *Public or private education? Lessons from history* (pp. 98–115). London: Woburn Press.

Halstead, J. M., & Reiss, M. J. (2003). *Values in sex education.* London: RoutledgeFalmer.

Hillier, L., Harrison, L., & Warr, D. (1998). When you carry condoms all the boys think you want it: Negotiating competing discourses about safe sex. *Journal of Adolescence, 21*, 15–29.

Irvine, J. (2004). *Talk about sex: The battles over sex education in the United States*. Berkeley: University of California Press.

Kippax, S., & Stephenson, N. (2005). Meaningful evaluation of sex and relationship education. *Sex Education, 5*, 359–373.

Lesko, N. (2010). Feeling abstinent? Feeling comprehensive? Touching the affects of sexuality curricula. *Sex Education, 10*, 281–297.

McLeod, J. (1999). Incitement or education? Contesting sex, curriculum and identity in schools. *Melbourne Studies in Education, 40*, 7–40.

Moran, J. P. (2000). *Teaching sex: The shaping of adolescence in the 20th century*. Cambridge, MA: Harvard University Press.

Povinelli, E. A. (2006). *The empire of love: Toward a theory of intimacy, genealogy and carnality*. Durham, NC: Duke University Press.

Rasmussen, M. (2006). *Becoming subjects: Sexualities and secondary schooling*. New York: Routledge.

Robinson, K., & Davies, C. (2008). Docile bodies and heteronormative moral subjects: Constructing the child and sexual knowledge in schooling. *Sexuality & Culture, 12*, 221–239.

Waites, M. (2005). *The age of consent: Young people, sexuality and citizenship*. New York: Palgrave Macmillan.

SECTION V

Mobilities and the Transnationalization of Youth Cultures

Fazal Rizvi

More people are now moving across national boundaries than at any time in the history of humankind. People move for a variety of reasons: for migration; for trade and business; for employment opportunities; for education; as tourists; and to attend international conventions and conferences. There are more international migrants—both documented and undocumented—than ever before, even more than after World War II, when a large number of displaced people sought residence and safer havens around the world (Cohen & Kennedy, 2007). People migrate now for reasons not only of economic prosperity but also of life style. Despite declining instances of major wars, political conflict, and famines, more refugees are now registered with the United Nations than at any time in that organization's history, more than 18 million (Marfleet, 2005). Refugees today are more aware of the possibilities of relocation, and have better sources of information, advice, and support from government and nongovernment organizations, on the one hand, and are subjected to criminal exploitative practices of the "people smugglers," on the other.

With the globalization of economic activity and trade, business executives are constantly on the move, as indeed are workers recruited and employed by transnational corporations. Many people, both professionally educated and those who are not, no longer hesitate, as they once did, to take employment opportunities abroad, creating a large global remittances economy, now estimated to be over 800 billion dollars (Guarnizo, 2003). According to the World Tourism Organization (2010), international tourism, measured in terms of the number of arrivals to another country, expanded 17-fold between 1950 and 1990, and has more than doubled in numbers since then, through the availability of cheap flights and the shifting cultural attitudes toward international travel and cosmopolitan experiences. International conferences and conventions have now become commonplace, despite the enhanced possibilities of online communication. And the number of international students is now more than 2.2 million, up from just 300,000 in 1970, and is expected to more than double by 2020 (Guruz, 2008), with the creation of an international education industry.

This unprecedented increase in people mobility is, of course, linked to the ways in which the contemporary global economic and political systems have developed over the past few decades. But, in a manner that is equally significant, the movement of people is driven by consumerist desire and subjective aware-ness of global opportunities, mediated by ubiquitous global media. In turn, this awareness has the potential to transform social institutions, cultural practices, and even people's sense of identity and belongingness. Shifting patterns of migration have certainly changed the nature of cities, creating urban conglom-erates at the intersection of global flows of finance and capital (Sassen, 1991). It is in these "global cities" that most migrants settle, creating new economic and social spaces, but also raising major issues of security, environmental sustain-ability, and adaptation, as well as a highly contentious politics of cultural diver-sity. With the abundant possibilities of communication created by the new social media, not only the immigrants but others as well are now able to live across multiple time horizons, shifting the nature of their relationship to the location where they might physically reside.

The mobility of people cannot hence be understood within its own terms, but is linked to many other forms of mobility. As the sociologist, John Urry (2000, p. 1), has suggested, multiple new cross-national, cross-cultural flows and networks of people define the global world of the 21st century; but, he insists, only in relation to the diverse mobilities of capital, images, information, and technologies, and "the complex interdependencies between, and social consequences of, these diverse mobilities." Appadurai (1996) has similarly noted the emergence of com-plex articulations across global flows of people, finance, media, ideologies, and ethnicities, which, he has noted, can sometimes be "disjunctural." What this means is that the relationships across various flows are not consistent, uniform, and pre-dictable, but contingent and context-specific. Nikos Papastergiadis (2000) has shown how these complexities demand new ways of thinking about the mobility of people. In relation to migration, for example, the traditional push–pull and structural theories, theories invoking distinctions between economic and forced migration, and representations based on classic South–North flows, are no longer adequate. What this implies is the need to understand how spaces in which people now move and in which the various effects of mobility are experienced are now "transnationalized." This space is constituted by the complex relationships across diverse mobilities, but refers also to a place that is neither "here" nor "there" in the traditional sense, but represents various relations of connectivity.

In this essay, I want to discuss the ways in which global mobilities are trans-forming youth cultures everywhere; how youth identities are now performed in spaces that are increasingly transnationalized; and how the cultural practices of young people are forged at the global intersection of these social, economic, political, and cultural flows. Global mobility of people, I want to suggest, has not only transformed the demographic composition of communities, but is also creating new challenges and opportunities for young people, within a framework of possibilities created by the historically unprecedented levels of cultural interactions. It is now possible, for example, for youth identities and cultural practices to be forged out of long-distance cross-border connections, and for these connections to deeply affect the social constitution of local relations. However, it is equally the case that while global mobility is transforming social spaces, making them transnational, the engagement of young people with the processes of transnationalization, as well as the impact these processes have on their experiences and life chances, are uneven and reflect new patterns of inequality.

Theorizing Youth Cultures

The idea of youth is a relatively recent historical construction, which, in developmental psychology, represents a stage in between childhood and adulthood. In sociology, on the other hand, it is viewed as a variable for an analysis of the processes of socialization into the norms of a society. According to Nayak and Kehily (2008), recent theoretical work on youth cultures has largely rejected both of these approaches, focusing instead on the agency of the young people and the structural locations within which their life experiences and chances are located. Recent studies of young people have been dominated by two contrasting approaches: youth cultural studies and studies of youth transitions. Following the pioneering work of Birmingham University's Centre for Contemporary Cultural Studies (CCCS) in the 1970s, youth cultural studies have highlighted a collective sense of style, attitudes, and self-expression of young people as various forms of *resistance through rituals*. Inspired by Gramsci, these studies have suggested that young people's subcultures reflect their attempts to "talk back" to their parents and teachers within the broader socio-political contexts of their lives. The subcultures thus articulated express purposeful political agency through which young people seek to negotiate new ways of living and relating to the broader community.

Since the 1990s, the Gramscian influence on the cultural studies of young people has waned, replaced by an interest in the theories of postmodernism, which have focused on the significance of various patterns of consumption and cultural affiliations. These studies have shown cultural practices to be more fragmented and ephemeral than was suggested by the idea of coherent subcultures. Youth cultures are thus viewed as fluid, based on fashions and fads that are often driven by the global corporate media. Redhead (1997) refers to these as "clubcultures," which express both an escape and a riposte to contemporary political realities. According to Nayak and Kehily (2008, p. 13), a key feature of the postmodern approach to youth cultures is its emphasis on stylized tastes and consumption patterns and practices that enable individuals to create moments of sociality. The problem with this approach, however, is that it focuses almost exclusively on matters of life styles, overlooking the importance of class, economic context, and social change. It offers little in the way of an analysis of how cultures of consumption have created new social divisions within the global cultural economy; and how, while youth cultures are no longer locally bound, but are globally connected, the opportunities to participate in them are at best uneven.

In contrast to these culturally oriented accounts of youth cultures, Nayak and Kehily (2008) observe, the youth transitions approach focuses on the structural arrangements that define young people's lives, experiences, and opportunities. Since the 1980s, the notion of transitions has been used to understand how young people manage their shift from school to work, from dependent to independent citizens. Unlike the postmodernist approach, transition studies examine the ways in which structural inequalities affect young people's experiences of school, work, family, and the community. While recognizing that youth transitions are inherently complex and unpredictable, McDonald (2001) insists that the strength of this approach lies in its potential to understand the complex relationship between personal agency and structural constraints as they play out in young people's lives and the manner in which these constraints shape their aspirations and life chances. A major limitation of this approach, however, is its assumption that youth cultures are shaped mostly by considerations of work and employment and that they are largely future oriented. Overlooked is a fact highlighted by postmodernist theories that the cultural context of young people is increasingly influenced by matters of style, taste, and consumption promoted by the global media, especially within the context of the uncertainties surrounding the nature and availability of employment.

While they recognize many of the strengths of both the cultural studies and youth transitions approaches, Nayak and Kehily (2008) argue that neither is capable of accounting for the complexities of youth cultures in the "new times," characterized by major economic, social, cultural, and political shifts shaped in particular by the revolutionary developments in communication technologies and the new social media. They find helpful instead the sociological notions of risk, individualization, and globalization. A move from an industrial to post-industrial society, they suggest, has not only changed the nature of work and labor relations but has also transformed the ways in which young people think about work and its relationship to various other interests and aspirations they have. Young people realize that the "new times" are governed by greater levels of risk, and strategize their identities and cultural practices accordingly. For them, a risk society demands, as Nayak and Kehily (2008, p. 21), following Beck (1992), note, the need "to become more reflexive and develop individualized biographies comprised of enterprising skills, technical expertise and entrepreneurial behaviour, adapted to the changing world that surrounds them." This involves a process in which agency is set free from structures.

What this suggests is that youth cultures can no longer be inferred from a grid of structural processes, articulated in terms of such categories as nation, class, gender, or race, through which common experiences are described. In a world that is increasingly insecure and fragmented, young people now need to negotiate on a daily basis the changing landscape of challenges and opportunities within the context of global flows. The conditions in which they forge their identities can no longer be interpreted through a pre-determined cultural script concerning relations of locality, traditions, family, class, and community. This is so because the emergence of various global flows and networks has undermined endogenous social structures, creating social spaces that are more contingent and dynamic. These spaces are effectively transnationalized, and require young people to develop, however tentatively and implicitly, a sense of the relative importance of various mobilities. It is in these emergent spaces that they now create and perform their identities, develop social relations, navigate transitions, and consider and enact life options.

Recent studies of young Americans of various different cultural backgrounds serve to illustrate this point. For example, Jun Sun Park (2004) has shown how the ways in which Korean American youth engage with transnational flows are not set by any pre-determined script, but involve not only global imagination but also engagement with local conditions in the United States, shaped by the dynamics of race, class, and gender. Park argues, moreover, that Korean American youth are subjected to a form of "racial globalization," with the processes of their racialization deeply affected by the transnational flows of information and cultural products, especially as these are mediated through media, both American and Korean. This racialization does not only, however, affect the young located in the United States, but also the youth in Korea itself, as images of race found in the media in the United States, for example, are readily consumed in Korea. What this suggests is that, in the formation of youth cultures, the locational differences are not as significant as is often assumed, as the binary between "here" and "there" begins to collapse in the face of spatial reconfigurations.

Transnationalization of Space

Recent theoretical work on space is important to my arguments. This work has abandoned an understanding of space as an objective phenomenon (Massey, 2005), and replaced it with a notion that suggests that space is constituted by a socially constructed grid within which people are located and move, events occur, and relations articulated. In this sense, space is no longer assumed to be natural, describable solely in terms of preexisting geographical laws. Indeed, recent critical geographers, such as Nigel Thrift (2007), contend that the search for general spatial laws is futile, because such laws explain very little about the interrelationship between people and place. They do not reveal anything meaningful about patterns of human settlement and relationships. As Thrift argues, absolute and essentialized conceptions of space run the risk, paradoxically, to reduce the world into "spaceless abstractions." In contrast, Thrift suggests a more relational view of space, which seeks to provide an account of how space is constructed and given meaning through the various dynamics of social relations and affectivity. In this way, space no longer represents a passive geometry, but a complex formation that is continuously produced through shifting socio-cultural relations. It is something that is socially experienced and represented and is forged through an interaction between social relations and material objects and processes (Massey, 2005).

This complex relational view of space is a useful theoretical resource with which to understand how contemporary drivers, forms, and consequences of global mobilities steer the development of youth cultures—the ways in which mobilities shape the spaces in which youth identities are now performed. Spatial analysis of mobility is useful not least because mobility is primarily a spatial notion, but also because it underscores the importance of collective human agency, and because it points to the connections between macroeconomic and geopolitical transformations, as well as the various trajectories in the politics of identification. It promises an account of the ways in which young people interpret various generalized processes associated with global mobilities, on the one hand, and forge their own distinctive constructions, everyday practices, social relationships, and collective action, on the other. It suggests that global mobilities are best represented as both expressions of transnationality as well as key drivers of the processes through which young people interpret the space in which they perform their identities. These processes, however, are not entirely transparent and coherent, but describe the messiness of living and acting in the mediated world of today.

The idea of transnationalization thus implies a set of processes through which youth cultures are now constituted through cross-border relationships, patterns of economic, political, and cultural relations, and complex affiliations and social formations. It names the multiple and messy proximities through which human societies have now become globally interconnected and interdependent. According to Vertovec (2009, p. 3), transnationalism describes "a condition in which, despite great distances and notwithstanding the presence of international borders (and all the laws, regulations and national narratives they represent), certain kind of relationships have been globally intensified and now take place paradoxically in a planet-spanning yet common—however virtual—arena of activity." In this sense, the processes of transnationalization name systems of ties, interactions, and exchanges that spread across and span the world.

Vertovec (2009) discusses various aspects of these processes. First, he suggests, transnational processes involve social formations that cut across national borders. "Dense and highly complex networks spanning vast spaces are transforming," he suggests, "many kinds of social, cultural, economic and political relationships" (p. 5), producing transnational spaces that have rendered a strictly bounded sense of community obsolete. Second, he argues, transnational networks have produced a type of consciousness, marked by multiple senses of identification, consisting of ever-changing representations. Third, transnational processes involve a mode of cultural production, associated with "a fluidity of constructed styles, social institutions and everyday practices" (p. 7). Fourth, transnational processes are linked to new practices of capital formations that arguably involve globe-spanning structures or networks that are now largely disconnected from their national origins. Thus, new global systems of supply, production, marketing, investment, and information management have become major drivers for transnational mobility and practices. And finally, transnational processes have created new sites for political engagement where cosmopolitan anti-nationalists often exist alongside reactionary ethno-nationalists within various diasporas, representing the dynamism of the relationships between different sites of political activity.

Significantly, Vertovec (2009) argues, various combinations or indeed all of these processes together have reconstituted communities. Largely as a result of the diverse mobility of people, communities have become entangled with the flows of ideas, capital, and technologies, with cultural practices and meanings derived from multiple geographical and historical points of origin. This has transformed people's relations to space in ways that connect and position some actors in more than one community or country (Vertovec, 2009, p. 12). Among young people in particular, these transformations have created a new sense of possibilities, aspirations, and desires. This does not, of course, imply an entirely positive set of experiences. Indeed, the sense young people have of the new possibilities is deeply shaped by existing conditions of asymmetries of power. As Massey (2005) has argued, time–space compression associated with transnational mobilities affects people differently. To overlook this fact is to ignore the workings of what Massey has called "geometries of power": it is to fail to recognize that in their specificities the drivers of mobilities are gendered, raced, and classed.

Their analysis suggests that there are close connections between youth identity and brand culture and that this is indicative of a larger cultural connection between consumption habits and citizenship. These connections are complex and ambiguous. Banet-Weiser (2007) has argued, for example, that current brand strategies often invoke "empowerment" as a key theme in selling products. The branding strategies of contemporary youth culture also co-opt the language of empowerment and youth rebellion in a way so that corporate media culture ironically adopts a kind of counter-hegemonic identity. This has consequences in terms of racial and gender identity, because the contemporary economic and political context has made it profitable to include particular representations of people of color and women within popular culture in ways different from other eras. However, not just any representation of race or gender will do in the contemporary media context; rather, the kind of ethnicity and the particular gender identity need to be produced in ways that are ironically nonspecific and ambiguous.

In the next section, I discuss a number of illustrative cases of how youth cultures are now forged and performed in transnational spaces created by a range of intersecting mobilities. I argue that it is not only the young people who are mobile who are affected, but also implicated are those who are not, as the mobility of just a few has the potential to transform entire communities through the creation of transnational desires, dispositions, and practices, involving a complex web of multidirectional relationships. These desires, dispositions, and practices do not emerge, however, in a cultural vacuum, but are linked to various geometries of power that are deeply shaped by transnational flows and contemporary discourses of what Kenway and Bullen (2001) refer to as "consuming culture." This culture, they suggest, resides at the intersection between education, entertainment, and advertising in an increasingly market-driven society, in ways that are at times alarming and frightening, but also empowering.

Formation of Youth Cultures

In her much-cited study, Aihwa Ong (1999, p. 37) illustrates how Hong Kong immigrants in the United States live and work in transnational spaces, taking advantage of the emerging patterns of global trade, which are shaped not only by neoliberal markets but also by ethnic solidarities across the Chinese diaspora. Hong Kong immigrants are constantly "on the move" between their homes in Hong Kong and in the United States, and are happy to live their lives in what Beck (2000) calls "place polygamy," developing multiple senses of belonging and citizenship. Their mobility generates a range of transnational practices, resulting in a realignment of political, ethnic, and personal identities that strategically negotiate disjunctures of shifting political landscapes. This is not to suggest that they are totally without roots, but rather that they engage in more creative articulations between subject positions and specific requirements of localities, the extended family, the nation-state, and global capital. Ong's work places their strategic transnational calculations at the center of the ways in which young Hong Kongites in particular develop skills of navigating cultural meaning within the normative framework of late capitalism. It needs to be noted, however, that this negotiation of meaning is never straightforward, and is often accompanied by various dilemmas that young people face, which pulls them in the direction of "flexible citizenship," on the one hand, and a desire for a clearer and more rooted form of identity, on the other.

Poorer immigrants face similar dilemmas, within the transnational space created by mobilities. At the core of this space are the regular remittances that working-class immigrants and refugees send back to their countries of origin. These remittances are often used to provide educational opportunities to the young people in the communities from where the immigrants come. This inserts the youth of that community into the processes relating to the global flows of both money and consumption. In her book, *The Transnational Villagers*, Peggy Levitt (2001) argues that, contrary to the popular perception, an increasing number of immigrants in the United States continue to participate in the political, social, and cultural lives of their countries of origin. With a great deal of evidence from her ethnographic work in a village in the Dominican Republic and in Boston, she shows how this regular contact between those who move and those who have not changes most aspects of everyday life in the village, as well as the Dominican community in the United States. This contact endures, she maintains, not only because of the possibilities of regular communication created by the new media but also through social remittances. The idea of social remittance does not refer to the money that is sent back to the village, but to the ideas, behavior, and social capital that flow across the transnational space. For young people, the immaterial aspects of the flows are perhaps even more important than the movement of money, as these create in them a general sense of desire for travel and for those global consumer products that they often assume everyone living in the United States to possess.

In my own studies of international students in Australia (Rizvi, 2000, 2005), I have found that these students often communicate to the young people at home a most exaggerated set of narratives—mostly the positive aspects of living abroad. This gives rise among young people at home for a strong desire to have similar experiences of global mobility and international education. As for the international students themselves, the experiences of mobility require them to do a great deal of identity work. This is so because identities are always rooted in part in actual experiences and in part in ideals and aspirations that cannot be fully realized. The processes of identity formation are saturated with the legacies of personal histories, local and global political dynamics, media representations, and the complexities of contemporary life. It is in the complex assemblage of these factors that transnational spaces are created and are best defined, and in which youth cultures are forged. The ways in which this occurs cannot, however, be adequately understood without also paying attention to the diverse mobilities of money, information, ideas, and images, as well as of desires and aspirations. These mobilities contribute to the formation of a "global imaginary" among international students, and often also their friends at home, though admittedly in ways that are different. As Appadurai (1996) has pointed out, an imaginary is not merely a personal attribute but denotes a collective sense a group of people have of "being in the world." While located within a particular community, this imaginary now increasingly transcends national borders in a variety of ways, and operates within the transnational spaces in which young people are able to develop new cultural practices, in ways that are decidedly discerning and creative.

In another study conducted around the turn of the century, Pilkington, Omel'chenko, Flynn, Bliudina, and Starkova (2002) provide a rich illustration of the discerning and critically aware ways in which Russian young people engage with the western media. Not afraid to embrace and experiment with many of the cultural practices emanating from Europe and the United States, young people in Russia nonetheless remain proud of their national traditions. In general terms, Russian youth express a strong desire for global mobility, not necessarily to emigrate but to facilitate cross-fertilization of cultural practices and values. So, for example, while they admire western traditions of citizenship rights, they are also critical of the west for its selfishness, and life styles driven by a culture of consumption. In this way, a sense of Russian identity represents for them a significant mediating force in their practices of engagement with the cultural flows of globalization. Their engagement with western music, styles, and outlooks produces a diverse range of narratives shaped by global cultural formations and locally produced meanings alike. Pilkington and his colleagues' study thus points to the inadequacy of the core–periphery model of global mobilities, highlighting instead a more complex pattern of interactivity, shaped both by global processes but also a reaction to them.

In a recent book, *Being Young and Muslim*, Linda Herrera and Asef Bayat (2011) provide a very rich account of these complexities. They bring together a number of essays which show how young Muslims negotiate the conflicting pressures of political and moral authorities who regard it as their role to manage and control youth cultures, on the one hand, and of the global market and media that young Muslims are happy to consume and produce, on the other. Herrera and Bayat argue that, since September 11, the global media constructions of Muslim youth, and of young men in particular, have deeply affected the formation of youth cultures in various communities where Muslims live. However, this has happened in ways that are not uniform but are deeply contested among the young people themselves, as they seek to negotiate different ways of performing their identities. In countries where they are regarded as immigrants, such as the United States, their religious activity and appearance often place them in a position where they have to struggle for equality and recognition for citizenship. When they are shunned in countries where they have long been legal citizens, but are now treated as "outsiders," Muslim youth feel more comfortable in transnational spaces that they view as more hospitable. The new social media provides them with such a space. However, their participation in this media has the divergent consequences of either steering them toward radicalism or toward practices that are viewed by some as compliant, and by others as creative and strategic. What this analysis shows is that, while Islam plays a different role in the lives of young people in different locations, a global event like September 11 now appears to play a symbolic role in every Muslim community. Yet, among young Muslims, it has generated higher differentiated responses, demonstrating the complex articulations of their political agency, affected by diverse mobilities.

Global Mobilities and Youth Cultures

There is, of course, nothing new about global mobilities and the ways in which they ignite and affect the exercise of political agency among young people, but what the illustrative cases in the previous section demonstrate is that the contemporary dynamics of mobility are much more complex. Not only has the number of mobile people increased significantly in recent years, so have the ways people think about and approach mobility. In the past, mobility was relatively permanent, now it is more contingent and flexible, with new information and communication technologies enabling people to keep their options open and retain links with their countries of origin. As Aihwa Ong (1999) argues, in the era of globalization, mobile individuals develop a flexible notion of citizenship often designed to accumulate capital and power. The logic of capital accumulation is to "induce subjects to respond fluidly and opportunistically to changing political-economic conditions" (p. 33). In the global era, powerful incentives exist for individuals to emphasize practices that favor "flexibility, mobility and repositioning in relation to markets, governments and cultural regimes" (p. 33).

However, economic motivations are not the only drivers of mobility, especially among the young. Nor are they the only aspect of mobility that defines the shifting nature of the transnational spaces in which youth cultures are increasingly forged and performed. A wide variety of political and cultural factors are involved in the processes associated with the transnationalization of youth cultures. What is clear is that while traditionally discussions of mobility were largely couched in terms of a range of realist distinctions, such as between home and abroad, and between emigration and immigration, such distinctions have become overwhelmed by cultural and technological innovations, as people are able not only to travel with greater regularity and ease than ever before but also to remain in touch with each other on a daily basis, using new media and communication technologies such as e-mail and Skype. These changes have swept across frontiers, contributing to the declining capacity of the nation-states and ethnic and religious leaders to maintain and police borders. It has given young people in particular a greater opportunity to experiment with different cultural forms. Youth cultures have become a site of struggle to define what is authentic and what needs to be overhauled.

Even as nation-states seek to tighten physical borders with heightened security regimes, cultural borders are becoming increasingly porous. James Clifford's (1997) idea of "travelling cultures" captures some of the fuzzy logic of interpenetration of cultural mobility, to which many young people are particularly attracted. Even if they do not physically move, they are attracted to virtual mobility, and to the mobilities of ideas, images, and information, as well as tastes and styles. This has led to the emergence of new cultural practices, competences, and performances, especially among the young, that link together places that would otherwise be widely separated. Clifford uses the term "travel" to underscore contingency and dynamism and suggests a two-way relation, an interactive creative process in the formation of new cultural practices. This indicates that the contemporary cultures associated with mobilities cannot be viewed as being bound by exclusionary national, ethnic, religious, or gender regimes. Imagined constructions of nation-states tie "locals" to a *single* place, gathering people and integrating ethnic minorities. Global mobilities, in contrast, disrupt this logic of national "belonging," as people are able to imagine the possibility of belonging to several places at once. Clifford (1997, p. 137) uses the phrase "dwelling in travel" to refer to "the experiences of mobility and movement, through which people develop a range of new material, spatial practices, that produce knowledges, stories, traditions, comportments, musics, books, diaries and other cultural expressions." In this way, mobilities do not only have the potential to reshape cultural expressions and practices among the young, but also their association with particular territories.

The transnational spaces forged out of diverse mobilities thus represent spaces of exchange and communication, not necessarily based on a one-way determinism, but involving rather a set of multifaceted and multidirectional cultural practices. However, the illustrative cases discussed in the previous section should also lead us to be cautious about generalizing from this valorization, for mobilities are not available equally to everyone, and are certainly inflected by gender, class, and race considerations. As bell hooks (1992) has remarked, mobility can often be unsafe and insecure for women. It is experienced differently by different racial groups, and its social consequences are unevenly distributed. Under the conditions of globalization, according to Bauman (1998), voluntary mobility is available largely to elites, a new global cosmopolitan class of people. He euphemistically calls them "tourists," the mobile people who contribute in one way or another to the rapid development of the consumer economy. In a globalized era, for the mobile tourists—the global businessmen, culture managers, and knowledge workers—the "state borders are levelled down, as they are dismantled for the world's commodities, capital and finances" (p. 89). In contrast, global mobilities, Bauman has argued, have created a class of "vagabonds," people who live on the social margins of the societies, permitted to look on to the world of consumerism without the economic means to participate in it.

What this shows, however, is that even those without the means to benefit from diverse mobilities are nonetheless implicated in the formations of transnational spaces. The global flows of capital across borders have, for example, reconstituted the nature of work and labor relations everywhere, with the potential to reshape entire communities, even in the poorest parts of the world. Communities in Africa, for example, live in the shadows of global capitalism, as Ferguson (2006) points out. Global capital flows have resulted in changes in the mode of production and consumption, affecting the structures of opportunity, and the life chances of people, both mobile and immobile. In a period of economic globalization, rapid technological shifts, post-Fordism, and the hegemonic dominance of neoliberal policies, not only have labor conditions been transformed, but so have the aspirations and desires of young people, and the calculations they now make about their sense of identities and strategic location (Rizvi & Lingard, 2009). The new media has become an important source in the development of these aspirations and desires, as people have been able to access information and develop a new perspective on career and even citizenship possibilities. It has enabled youth cultures to be increasingly elaborated and negotiated within and against a transnational spatial awareness, constructed out of material and symbolic resources that reach beyond local boundaries, and are forged in spaces that are mediated and mitigated by cultural turbulence of globalizing forces, connections, and desires.

References

Appadurai, A. (1996). *Modernity at large*. Minneapolis: Minnesota University Press.

Banet-Weiser, S. (2007). *Kids rule! Nickelodeon and consumer citizenship*. London: Duke University Press.

Bauman, Z. (1998). *Globalization: The human consequences*. Cambridge: Polity Press.

Beck, U. (1992). *Risk society: Towards a new modernity*. Translated by M. Ritter. London: Sage.

Beck, U. (2000). *What is globalization?* Cambridge: Polity Press.

Clifford, J. (1997). *Routes: Travel and translation in the late twentieth century*. Cambridge, MA: Harvard University Press.

Cohen, R., & Kennedy, P. (2007). *Global sociology* (2nd ed.). New York: New York University Press.

Ferguson, J. (2006). *Global shadows: Africa in the neo-liberal world order*. Durham, NC: Duke University Press.

Guarnizo, L. E. (2003). Economics of transnational living. *International Migration Review, 37*, 666–699.

Guruz, K. (2008). *Higher education and international student mobility in the global knowledge economy*. Albany, NY: SUNY Press.

Herrera, L., & Bayat, A. (Eds.). (2011). *Being young and Muslim*. Oxford: Oxford University Press.

hooks, b. (1992). Black looks: race and representation. Boston, MA: South End Press.

Kenway, J., & Bullen, E. (2001). *Consuming children: Education, entertainment, advertising.* Buckingham, UK: Open University Press.

Levitt, P. (2001). *The transnational villagers.* Berkeley: University of California Press.

Marfleet, P. (2005). *Refugees in a global era.* Basingstoke, UK: Palgrave.

Massey, D. (2005). *For space.* London: Sage.

McDonald, R. (2001). Disconnected youth. *Journal of Youth Studies, 4,* 373–391.

Nayak, A., & Kehily, M. J. (2008). *Gender, youth and culture: Young masculinities and femininities.* London: Palgrave.

Ong, A. (1999). *Flexible citizenships: The cultural logics of transnationality.* Durham, NC: Duke University Press.

Papastergiadis, N. (2000). *The turbulence of migration: Globalization, deterritorialization and hybridity.* Cambridge: Polity Press.

Park, J.-S. (2004). Korean American youth and transnational flows of popular culture across the Pacific. *Amerasia Journal, 30,* 147–169.

Pilkington, D., Omel'chenko, E., Flynn, N., Bliudina, U., & Starkova, E. (2002). *Cultural globalization and the Russian youth cultures.* College Park: Pennsylvania State University Press.

Redhead, S. (1997). *Subcultures to clubcultures.* Oxford: Blackwell.

Rizvi, F. (2000). International education and the production of global imagination. In N. Burbules, & C. Torres (Eds.), *Globalization and education: Critical perspectives* (pp. 205–226). New York: Routledge.

Rizvi, F. (2005). International education and the production of cosmopolitan identities. In A. Arimoto, F. Huang, & K. Yokoyama (Eds.), *Globalization and higher education* (pp. 77–92). Hiroshima University, Japan: Research Institute for Higher Education.

Rizvi, F., & Lingard, R. (2009). *Globalizing education policy.* London: Routledge.

Sassen, S. (1991). *The global city: New York, London, Tokyo.* Oxford: Blackwell.

Thrift, N. (2007). *Non-representation theory: Place, politics and affect.* London: Routledge.

Urry, J. (2000). *Sociology beyond societies.* London: Routledge.

Vertovec, S. (2009). *Transnationalism.* London: Routledge.

World Tourism Organization. (2010). UNWTO world tourism barometer. Retrieved from http://www.unwto.org/facts/eng/barometer.htm

27

HEALTH

Emma Rich

This keyword essay considers the term "health" and how its various uses and meanings over time have come to frame not only medical issues, but our understandings of youth, morality, citizenship, and responsibility. Concerns about young people's health have long been the subject of health campaigns, government interest, and school curricula. Consequently, discussion concerning health has occurred across multiple disciplines and subdisciplines either as a central theme within youth studies (e.g., health, well-being, vulnerabilities) or within other related disciplines (e.g., critical weight studies, pedagogy, sociology of education, sociology of health and illness, and more recently children's geographies [Colls & Horschelmann, 2009] and new social studies of childhood [Holloway & Valentine, 2000], and surveillance studies). Given the contentious nature of some of the emerging and continued issues surrounding young people's health (weight, sexuality, drinking, etc.), many of these themes are subject to discursive and policy contestations among diverse constituencies. In examining the formation of "health" as a keyword within the field of youth studies, the essay concludes with suggested alternatives for future approaches toward reimagining health.

Contemporary Health Crises and Young People

Historically young people have long been subject to health interventions, which serve to discipline bodies to address what are conceived as social ills and risks. However, partly due to an increasing emphasis on embodiment in the constitution of subjectivity in postmodern society, the shifting focus toward health rather than just illness marked a key transition in the focus of work in fields such as sociology of health and illness (see Bury & Gabe, 2004). Following the rise of medicalization (Conrad, 1992) and medical surveillance (Armstrong, 1995), increasingly, everyday activities are placed under scrutiny and regarded as medical issues, thus playing an instrumental role in the broader constitution of deviance and sickness. Scholarly work on medicalization, for example, has highlighted how such surveillance of the everyday can be manifest as a lived experience of heightened health risks evoking imperatives for one to protect oneself against future ill-health (see Armstrong, 1995). Thus, certain behaviors are constituted as risky, leading to the classification of otherwise everyday behaviors as "unhealthy" and of healthy individuals as ill. The resultant focus on the "health" of populations rather than just illness, and its accompanying investment in early prevention, has meant children and young people have occupied a more central position in health policy, debates, and interventions.

   This scholarship has begun to make explicit that the ways in which health has been understood cannot be separated from the wider social and moral understandings of particular health conditions and understandings of childhood and youth. This means examining the moral, cultural, and political situatedness of images and policies associated with young people and health. This point is made evident by the intensification of moral panics associated with health and illness (e.g., obesity, HIV) in recent years, which tap into broader "vulnerabilities" and "fear" (Furedi, 2005). Specifically, Katz (2008) points toward the broader political, economic, and geopolitical anxieties that underpin attempts to shape the future through the control of children and young people (see also Steeves & Jones, 2010). The combination of these broader anxieties about the nature of youth, alongside the shifting focus toward health rather than just illness, has had significant implications for the way in which imaginings of youth have been critical to contemporary understandings of health.

The status of youth health has been problematized, imagined, and endowed with meaning through the construction of moral crises, which in postmodern times tap into broader fears about social ills. Health issues such as those concerned with weight, drug use, binge drinking, sexuality, and mental health have at various moments been worked up into "crisis," formed through an assemblage of media, meanings and beliefs, official policy, mediating agents, and medical knowledge.

Surveillance, Young People, and "Future Health"

Young people are central to the construction of moral panic through what Katz (2008) observes as the constitution of childhood as an investment for the future. As Evans and Colls (2011) suggest, through this logic, children's bodies are imbued with a capacity to reveal the state of future adult bodies. The moral panic over the childhood obesity epidemic (perceived or otherwise) underscores how threats to young people's health not only comment upon a health problem but also participate in the construction of young people as vulnerable or at future risk. Distinctions are often invoked between good and bad parents, good and bad bodies, such that the obese young person (or in the case of the young child, the parent) is held culpable and positioned as irresponsible. These health crises are also tied to broader social fears; for example, childhood obesity is perceived to threaten the national economy with its future costs and unsustainable demands placed on national health care. Similarly, moral panics around "binge drinking" tap into broader mass-mediated panics over disaffected youth engaging in antisocial behavior.

Health concerns are, in this sense, rooted in particular understandings of the body, childhood, youth, and responsibility. Within these health crises, young people are constituted as "symbols of the future" rather than read as complex embodied beings in the now. Thus, contemporary health crises rely upon a "preemptive and anticipatory logic" (Evans & Colls, 2011; drawing on Ruddick, 2006) in which childhood is constructed through its focus on future problems. Such conceptions of young people thus align neatly with "surveillance medicine" (Armstrong, 1995) where it is argued that entire populations need to protect themselves from the risk of assumed future disease.

Health strategies within contemporary schooling cultures (Rich & Perhamus, 2010) are employed and mobilized in ways that often regulate students' physical activity, weight, sexual activity, and health identities. There has been a con-comitant proliferation of information-gathering techniques, state/government policy, and more local (e.g., school-based) interventions which discipline the body and seek to "make up the child" (Vander Schee & Baez, 2009).

Surveillance of young people's health is taking place at an increasing younger age, for example through initiatives focused on preschool diets and activity schemes and weighing of primary school children in the United Kingdom. Questioning the surveillance of children and young people, Steeves and Jones (2010, p. 189) ask, "Is it a means of reproducing adult society in perpetuity at the expense of the alterity that might flourish in young life and which might challenge dominant ideologies and orders of society?"

Underpinning the series of contemporary youth health crises (whether this be drinking, weight, sex, etc.) is the recurring construction of youth as already or potentially "at risk" or in crisis and the need to govern the future adult. Moreover, these discourses may come to constitute particular bodies and subjects as problematic and deviant; through which fatness is constructed as abnormal and grotesque and a sign of irresponsibility and lack of control; or the sexually active youth as "problematic" and a sign of broader moral decline. As the subject of such moralizing debates, *particular* young people may thus be seen as flawed subjects and unable to make the right decisions.

In this way, contemporary understandings of young people and health draw upon a curious mix of risk and responsibility. On the one hand young people are seen as always "at risk" and in need of the correct health education. At the same time, contemporary discourses of health continue to explicitly draw upon forms of liberal individualism which emphasize decontextualized readings of health and which locate accountability and responsibility for health with the individual. By way of example, through such frameworks, youth binge drinkers are often individualized, rather than understood in their social and cultural situatedness of what Szmigin, Hackley, Bengry-Howell, Griffin, and Mistral (2011) refer to as a "culture of intoxication" which has become a normalized and all but compulsory aspect of many young people's social lives. Decontextualized conceptualizations of health fail to take into account the way an individual's capacity to enact health is influenced by class, disability, ethnicity, gender, sociocultural, and sociopolitical contexts.

Reimagining Health

In reimagining how we might think about young people and health this essay concludes by pointing toward some recent key analytical turns which focus our attention on children as agents and embodiment as an ongoing and complex process. Crucial to this has been the recognition that we need to better understand the rights and experiences of young people in contemporary visions of health and their accompanying forms of surveillance, which, as Evans and Colls (2011) suggest, far from a concern for the well-being of children and young people, are focused more on guarding the "health of the future nation." A concern for what young people might become as some inevitability of what they do now constitutes them in ways which may restrict not only their agency and well-being but also the terms of their personhood. Challenging the notions of a progressive trajectory and causal relationship between youth health and adult health is important, not only for enriching our understandings of health, but such imaginings may revitalize other imaginings about childhood, responsibility, and the future.

Other research is building on our understandings of the social, cultural, and moral contexts of health. Theorizations of assemblage and affect may help us look differently at how health knowledge and practices flow across, through, and within different sites. How, for example, are young people variously negotiating, managing, and experiencing "health" within different sites and cultures? A growing body of work draws on theoretical analyses and empirical evidence about how young people experience health promotion messages across sites of learning (Rich & Perhamus, 2010). The limitations of conceptualizations of childhood and youth place restrictions on how young people's voices are heard in broader debates about health; for example, how are young people experiencing health discourses? Some scholars are embracing notions of affect (Blackman & Venn, 2010), emotion, and kinesthetic experience to reexamine recontextualization (Perhamus, 2010). If we are to understand how competing views about health and illness are manifested in and through the uptake or resistance to particular forms of surveillance over young people's health, we also need to look more closely at how those deemed responsible engage with notions of the child, authoritative knowledge, citizenship, and morality in affective ways. Such questions are pertinent given that the political economy of embodiment is increasingly significant in contemporary society and in the neo-liberal backdrop against which parents are encouraged to seek out opportunities for the child to enact health (e.g., undertaking particular forms of physical activity). Such questions may be particularly important for understanding those in more vulnerable situations facing issues of exploitation, welfare concerns, mental health, and disability.

References

Armstrong, D. (1995). The rise of surveillance medicine. *Sociology of Health and Illness, 17,* 393–404.

Blackman, L., & Venn, C. (2010). Affect. *Body and Society, 16,* 7–28.

Bury, M., & Gabe, J. (Eds.). (2004). *The sociology of health and illness.* London: Routledge.

Colls, R., & Horschelmann, K. (2009). Editorial: Geographies of children's and young people's bodies. *Children's Geographies, 7,* 1–6.

Conrad, P. (1992). Medicalization and social control. *Annual Review of Sociology, 18,* 209–232.

Evans, B., & Colls, R. (2011). Doing more good than harm? The absent presence of children's bodies in (anti) obesity policy. In E. Rich, L. F. Monaghan, & L. Aphramor (Eds.), *Debating obesity: Critical perspectives* (pp. 115–138). London: Palgrave Macmillan.

Furedi, F. (2005). *Politics of fear: Beyond left and right.* London: Continuum.

Holloway, S. L., & Valentine, G. (2000). Spatiality and the new social studies of childhood. *Sociology, 34,* 763–783.

Katz, C. (2008). Childhood as spectacle: Relays of anxiety and the reconfiguration of the child. *Cultural Geographies, 15,* 5–17.

Perhamus, L. (2010). "But your body would rather have this": Conceptualizing health through kinaesthetic experience. *International Journal of Qualitative Studies in Education, 23*(7), 845–868.

Rich, E., & Perhamus, L. (2010). Editorial: Health surveillance, the body and schooling. *International Journal of Qualitative Studies in Education, 23,* 759–764.

Ruddick, S. (2006). Abnormal, the "new normal" and destabilizing discourses of rights. *Public Culture, 18,* 53–78.

Steeves, V., & Jones, O. (2010). Editorial: Surveillance and children. *Surveillance & Society, 7*, 187–191.

Szmigin, I., Hackley, C., Bengry-Howell, A., Griffin, C., & Mistral, W. (2011). Social marketing in a culture of intoxication. *European Journal of Marketing, 45*(5).

Vander Schee, C., & Baez, B. (2009). HIV/AIDS education in schools: The "unassembled" youth as a curricular project. *Discourse: Studies in the Cultural Politics of Education, 30*, 33–46.

28

IMMIGRANT

Claudia Matus

This work takes up the figure of the "young immigrant" as a concept produced and put to work in particular times and places. The construction of the young immigrant emphasizes forms of temporalities such as developmental or generational trajectories and concerns with spatiality such as the relations between young people's identities and "the street," "the school," "the mall," and so on (Skelton & Valentine, 1998; Vanderbeck, 2000). Therefore, the dominant way to understand the figure of the young immigrant uses metaphors such as the one who crosses borders, the one who does not belong, and the one who is included and excluded in different ways. These prevailing understandings legitimate institutions producing statuses for the immigrant, stimulate claims of nation, and affirm identities as real and natural (Luibhéid, 2007). As a consequence, the young immigrant, as a body that is never independent of the representations of space and the effects of time, is constructed as the object of regulation, reparation, and risk discourses.

In the neoliberal present, youth is constituted as a new socialized subjectivity where the imperatives of consumerism and the self-responsible citizen guide much of educational, labor, and immigration policies. When official documents describe the reasons why young people migrate, policies present them as people seeking to achieve goals related particularly to education and labor. For instance, the United Nations Economic Commission for Latin America and the Caribbean (CEPAL) produced a report on the International Migration of Latin American and Caribbean Youth (Martínez, 2000) that provides information on youth, population, and development. The document imagines young immigrants as "a group of people whose stage in the cycle of life and exposure to changes in their individual and social environment (such as the incomplete acquisition of sexual rights, family, economic, and political privileges) makes them potentially vulnerable" (Martínez, 2000, p. 10 [my translation]). The report also stresses the idea that young people are always "close" but not quite "there" yet. For instance, it states,

> [Young people's] integration to the work force, . . . decisions about family constitution, the completion of school or university degrees, among other aspects involved in the process of moving to a foreign country, represent a group of reasons to make young immigration important.
>
> (Martínez, 2000, p. 10 [my translation])

The report recirculates at least three common ideas that put to work the figures of the youth and the immigrant. Together, these transitional positionalities become exponential in the production of the figure of the young immigrant as a visible deviant. First, young people's identities are constituted through the logics of trajectories that they have not completed yet. The construction of youth that stresses temporality as development signals static points in the constitution of subjectivity where only hegemonic notions of space and nation are recognized. As a consequence, youth countercultural expressions are read as "nontraditional" and as "reactions" to the dominant culture. Youth as constructed in deficit or in the state of arriving to adultness (Besley, 2009) allows the proliferation of discourses of youth "at-risk" that emphasize problems of drugs, crime, violence, gangs, teen pregnancy, dropping out, and so on.

Second, the report emphasizes the concept of the immigrant as the material expression of the meanings of *entering* an already defined place, such as the idea of the "host country" that represents a community with recognized boundaries of belonging in which outsider groups are thought as needing either to "preserve" or "adapt" their cultural practices to the dominant culture. Taken-for-granted understandings of place as a container ready to be filled (Massey, 2005) act on subjects to normalize and anticipate positions for selves and others, such as the culturally disabled, the one in need of acculturation activities, the one "at risk" because of language competence, and so on. These ideas constitute static positions waiting for these young people to occupy. This understanding of place confines the self as someone we already know; as a consequence, the one that we do not know can be constructed as a stranger.

Third, such policy representations connect the idea of the young immigrant to specific goals related to education and labor. Young people become "engines" or renewed forces to regenerate societies, particularly when young immigrants are constructed as a "contribution to enhance the human capital of areas of origin and destiny" (Martínez, 2000, p. 11 [my translation]). Technologies of innovation, development, and social change are put to work to make sense of young people's migration practices as supportive of the market economy.

Such commonly named positions for young immigrants as those expressed in the United Nations CEPAL report reinforce traditional relations of nation, space, and time. In other words, these dominant circulations of ideas of the young immigrant animate instrumental associations of territories, belongings, and cross-border practices. Thus, it is common to refer to young immigrants' experiences using static concepts such as "arriving," "returning," "home country," "host country," and so on. These concepts portray the spatial and temporal structures through which young immigrants are told to make sense of their experiences of movement. To imagine young immigrants' movement in this context is to reproduce their experiences as linear narratives of travel. As these terms stress the starting and ending points in the young immigrant's experience of travel, bodies are territorialized by stopping movement (Manning, 2009, p. 23). The territorialization of bodies positions them as occupying a space regulated by laws through which they can be named and monitored via categories, such as the culturally disabled, the model minority, and the second class citizen, among many others.

Surfaces and Movement

What might it mean to move from dominant imaginings and policy talk to a different view of the cultural practices of movement in order to open alternative understandings of the figure of the young immigrant? Today, the concept of style emerges as an important marker in the constitution of young identities through the combination of local and contemporary global consumer cultures (Besley, 2009). Young people are positioned in cultures of consumption as they produce their identities in the global marketplace "where style and identity become inextricably mixed" (Besley, 2009, p. 192). Contemporary practices of virtual migration of identities allow the questioning of taken-for-granted territorial positions for the subject to occupy. Virtual migration allows the interruption of the production of space in relation to specific identities and boundaries and can interrogate the ways nations are ideologically produced through political and cultural practices (Abu El-Haj, 2007). In fact, "the flow of cultural images and objects which play with 'otherness' and 'difference'" (Ahmed, 2000, p. 116) threatens conventional understandings of gender, class, sexuality, and nation, among other hierarchies.

As an example of how virtual migration constitutes different representations of the young immigrant, Yumiko Iida (2005) describes the emergent Japanese cultural trend in which young men employ feminine aesthetic practices to explore new masculinities. These young men challenge "the phallocentric economy . . . to open up a space for the subjective feminine gaze to rise, to which young men are now responding with efforts to redefine masculinity" (Iida, 2005, p. 57). In the construction of alternative gender identities, Japanese young people not only resist dominant ideas of masculinities but also add a critique of nationalist affects. As Iida (2005) states,

Any practice that claims [that] non-hegemonic gender identities disturb cultural norms and pose a challenge to the patriarchal economy would point to the fact that the existing order is not natural nor consented to, but open to contestations and possible negotiations.

(p. 61)

As an example of how these images circulate, in Chile there are a number of groups of young males who adopt images of Japanese youth as a cultural expression with critical representational effects of the figure of the immigrant, such as questioning traditional associations of territorial positions. These groups, placed under the umbrella term *the visuals*, appropriate images "imported" from Japan, hyperemphasizing female features, with a strong emphasis on aesthetics, and use these representations of femininity to challenge gendered, sexualized, and nationalized orders.[1] Young males' expressions of a sense of community through fashion choices has been studied by Rubin and Melnick (2007), who note that zoot suits in 1943 in the United States represented "a signal of desire for, an achievement of, cultural mobility" on Mexican immigrants' part. But most importantly they ask "But what happens when a suit of clothes gets named as deviant?" (p. 50).

What the Chilean males represent not only contradicts essentialized, natural, and transparent relations between nation and identities but also interrupts gender-dominant correspondences; moreover, their embodied representations are also constructed as nonuseful to the state and to the project of social and cultural conformity. As they refer to themselves, they do not position themselves as either male or female, Chilean or Japanese, nor gay or straight. Furthermore, their "migration" practices are oriented to using their bodies as visible representational surfaces to become the undecidable (Sarup, 1996). The creation of "deviant" images of youth through the production of global youth identities interrupts understandings of the local ideal youth culture that is presented as fully self-recognized and intelligible (Besley, 2003).

Static and rigid representations of migration as the displacement of bodies between bounded territories produces, and at the same time confirms, already known positions of distance and difference among people. These traditional encounters allow the distancing of oneself from the figure of the *stranger* through specific relations of difference (Ahmed, 2000). In the case of visual migration practices, different ways to think of proximity are possible. Young people using global identities create a particular mode of relation in which the commodity object is the "image and [the] material thing, [that] enables subjects to have a closer encounter with a distant other (the one already recognized as 'the stranger')" (Ahmed, 2000, p. 114). This "mode of proximity" (Ahmed, 2000, p. 13) is put to work through the relational experience between the "imagined" and the "real" self depending on particular modes that constrain and open possibilities to new relations and constructions of nation, gender, and sexuality. These exploratory representations of difference by Chilean young males stress the lack of attachment to traditional ideas about either national or cultural singularities involved in thinking themselves. For instance, they express no commitment to "knowing Japan."

In conclusion, the dominant figure of the young immigrant, which focuses on the displacement of bodies between territorial units, reiterates the "happening" of static boundaries, attachments, and belongings. This thinking obscures possibilities to question what counts as movement and its political uses, and how this movement affects the recomposition of the body in relation to space and time. In contrast, the virtual migration of images, signs, and practices opens up possibilities to think about the politics of movement where questions about subjectivities in motion are defined by emergent forms of composition, affected and being affected by trajectories, connections, and disjunctures. These configurations and relations represent the always-evolving processes of the constitution of subjectivities in relation to space and time, in which the figure of the young immigrant is thought as an effect of the relations through which spaces are constituted and temporalities are imagined. Here, one's imagination of space and the uses of time become political forces.

Note

1 Special thanks to Toshi who provided me with information about the group *the visuals*. For more information visit http://www.myspace.com/kheybanda.

References

Abu El-Haj, T. R. (2007). "I was born here, but my home, it's not here": Educating for democratic citizenship in an era of transnational migration and global conflict. *Harvard Educational Review, 77*, 285–316.

Ahmed, S. (2000). *Strange encounters: Embodied others in post-coloniality*. London: Routledge.

Besley, A. C. (2003). Hybridized and globalized: Youth cultures in the postmodern era. *The Review of Education, Pedagogy, and Cultural Studies, 25*, 153–177.

Besley, A. C. T. (2009). Governmentality of youth: Beyond cultural studies. In M. A. Peters, A. C. Besley, M. Olssen, S. Maurer, & S. Weber (Eds.), *Governmentality studies in education* (pp. 165–199). Rotterdam: Sense.

Iida, Y. (2005). Beyond the "feminization of masculinity": Transforming patriarchy with the "feminine" in contemporary Japanese youth culture. *Inter-Asia Cultural Studies, 6*, 56–74.

Luibhéid, E. (2007). Immigration. In B. Burgett, & G. Hendler (Eds.), *Keywords for American cultural studies* (pp. 127–131). New York: New York University Press.

Manning, E. (2009). *Relationscapes: Movement, art, philosophy*. London: MIT Press.

Martínez, J. (2000). Migración internacional de jóvenes latinoamericanos y caribeños: protagonismo y vulnerabilidad [Report on international migration of Latin American and Caribbean youth]. CELADE-FNUAP (Population Fund of the United Nations). Retrieved from http://www.eclac.org/publicaciones/xml/6/4916/lcl1407e.pdf

Massey, D. (2005). *For space*. London: Sage.

Rubin, R., & Melnick, J. (2007). *Immigration and American popular culture: An introduction*. New York: New York University Press.

Sarup, M. (1996). *Identity, culture, and the postmodern world*. Edinburgh: Edinburgh University Press.

Skelton, T., & Valentine, G. (1998). *Cool places: Geographies of youth cultures*. London: Routledge.

Vanderbeck, R. (2000). "That is the only place where you can hang out": Urban young people and the space of the mall. *Urban Geography, 21*, 5–25.

29

INTERNET

Lori B. MacIntosh, Stuart Poyntz, and Mary K. Bryson

Focusing on specific elements within the shifting terrain of networked media, this essay engages with the more salient components that characterize youth Internet engagement. Youths' production, consumption, play, and emergent political positioning are part of a critical media witnessing (Coleman & Ross, 2010) central to youths' sociocultural production.

The Internet could be characterized as a primary public—an interstitial space—wherein youth engage with, share, and construct identificatory, socio-cultural, political, informational, and other frameworks, observing, exchanging, and creating knowledge about each other and various social cultural interpretations of the world. Warner's (2002) notion of *a public* as the "social space created by the reflexive circulation of discourse" (p. 62) is useful in framing youths' relationship to the Internet writ large. For Warner, a public is not merely the collection of people or an audience addressed but, rather, it must recognize and organize itself as such. A public exists "*by virtue of being addressed*" (p. 50). In 2006, *Time* magazine's person of the year was, quite simply, "you." The "you" in this case was a celebratory acknowledgment of a mediated network of individuals, the Web 2.0 generation, "ordinary people . . . adding their voice to the Web's great evolving conversation" (Johnson, 2006, ¶1).

Definitions of "media literacy" frequently include the "ability to access" information, knowledge, and social networks as (1) a foundational 21st century competency (Buckingham, 2005) and (2) a cluster of sociotechnical practices that manifests significant age-related and generational cohort differences. Internet researchers (Pew Research Center, 2010) have reported that for "millennials"—the first generation of youth for whom the Internet is not a "new technology"—access is qualitatively distinctive and that this technological exceptionalism includes near ubiquitous Internet access via mobile hand-held devices, very high levels of participation in online social networks and gaming locations, and a much higher likelihood than any other age cohort to be a competent and active producer and distributor (as well as consumer) of digital content online. As a space of self-making and place-making, new media often serve as public platforms through which youth trace the intimate patterns of who they are as part of the larger exploratory terrain of youthful becoming and quest for belonging. Gray (2009) aptly refers to these generative spaces as "boundary publics . . . metaphorical landscapes of social interaction" (p. 105).

Jenkins (2006) has argued that today's youth represent the first generation for whom there is a participatory divide in place of the access divide that characterized differences in Internet usage across the primary digital divide factors such as social class, race and ethnicity, and gender (see also boyd, 2007).

Recent PEW Internet research notes that 73% of youth who access the Internet use social networking sites (Lenhart, Purcell, Smith, & Zickuhr, 2010). These networked communities produce affective attachments among users that grow exponentially in a circulatory cycle that Jodi Dean (2010) has dubbed "communicative capitalism." As youth facebook, blog, and text message their way into multiple publics, forming a knowledge exchange that is constantly circulated and reconstituted through a networked sociality of "consequential strangers" (Fingerman, 2009), the relational and participatory multidimensionality of new media practices becomes increasingly complex.

The idea of participation, or taking part, operates in complicated ways in relation to contemporary cultural and political life. For youth, the affective and temporal spaces facilitated by the Internet offer a way to negotiate the various, overlapping, and paradoxical publics that constitute contemporary socialities. Where participation is often associated with notions of citizenship (Macpherson, 1977), in the age of the Internet, the relationship between participation and democracy is not always evident. Youth are often understood through the key social organizations with which they interact such as family, government, education, church, and so on. These relationships in turn are undergirded by institutionally specific notions of democracy, civic engagement, empowerment, agency, rights, and responsibility, and are complicated by contradictory definitions, institutional barriers, and, increasingly, access to technology. Youth are often constructed as citizens-of-the-future or citizens in training, with a desire to make "good citizens," rather than recognize them as already formed. This is especially true for youth for whom full citizenship does not avail itself. Significant to this, as Dahlgren (2009) notes, is the fact that "[h]ow we define citizenship is inseparable from how we define democracy and the good society" (p. 63). While "disengaged" is an adjective too often used in conjunction with communities of youth, it is essential to note that "young people cannot simply be divided into those who participate more and those who participate less" (Livingstone, Bober, & Helsper, 2004, p. 14). Youth participation and engagement cannot be homogenously packaged without taking into account the complexities of so-called passive engagement and the social and political mechanisms that structure patterns of Internet usage.

On this, access is the primary trope that has organized discourses concerning the democratizing efficacy of the Internet, with a preponderance of arguments focused on "access to knowledge" (A2K) in particular. In the "information society" (Castells & Himanen, 2002), proponents of the ameliorative impact of A2K argue that the Internet provides people (on a scale that is qualitatively distinct from anything prior) with the socially networked means to locate, share, and avail themselves of the world's informational and social capital (Willinsky, 2009). Of course, these kinds of opportunities are unevenly realized around the world

(Poyntz & Hoechsmann, 2011). The World Internet Project (2010) notes that the percentage of Internet users is relatively low across a range of nations including: Portugal (37%), Cyprus and Colombia (45%), Czech Republic (51%), and Chile (55%).

Youth populate the age cohort most likely to be online. In particular, it is commonly argued that the Internet provides youth subcultures with access to differentiated social networks that are affiliative and communitarian in nature so that folks can locate and congregate with others "like them," and in so doing, obviate the apparent distancing effects of geographical separation or other affiliative obstacles. Critical Internet Studies researchers (e.g., Bryson & MacIntosh, 2010; Dean, 2002; Gray, 2009) have emphasized, however, that arguments for the ameliorative impact of the Internet tend to exhibit manifold and robust forms of political quietism regarding the norms that structure both participation in these locations and engagement with information lodged therein. Legal theorist Amy Kapczynski (2008) has argued convincingly that the "new politics of intellectual property" suggest that, in place of an emphasis on A2K per se as the primary mediator of encouraging free and open models of innovation, knowledge, and culture, it is, critically, access to knowledge *mobilization* that matters today for any social movements organized in relation to socially and geopolitically significant disparities.

In addition, we also know that astute media conglomerates are "co-conspirators in the emergence of a participatory media culture" (Deuze, 2006, p. 67). Across most of the world's youth cultures, giant media companies provide wholly integrated, technologically imbued environments through various platforms, products, and resources that enable young people's interactivity, but in such a way as to shape youthful identities and social futures. In practice this means that any number of young people's online play spaces and practices (i.e., the guerilla marketing network, Girl's Intelligence Agency; web spaces such as Lego's Factory, Club Penguin, Webkinz, and NeoPets; and the Canadian Broadcasting Corporation's children's site, *The Outlet*) now nurture children's creative expression and/or sense of responsibility through a sociality knit to the development of new products and dynamic data maps that track kids' everyday lives. Together, these strategies produce interactive and sustained relationships between media conglomerates and young Internet users, but in such a way that media participation comes to be intimately tied to the accumulation of capital. What results is a participation paradox. On the one hand, Internet-mediated communication creates new opportunities for the expression of "youth voice"; yet, Internet-based platforms are now the focal point for developing new corporate strategies and marketing practices that leverage youths' online participation in ways that have less to do with democracy than with the accumulation of profit.

The integration of the Internet into youths' daily life and the pervasiveness of digital knowledge production have meant that, while the threat of technology itself has lessoned, the focus on its users has increased (boyd, 2007). One result is that like many public spaces before it—think, for instance, of the role of the "street" in various youth cultures—the Internet has become the focus of a particular form of moral panic that categorizes new media space as a site of imminent danger and risk to young people (Finkelhor & Ybarra, 2008). This panic, driven by both popular media (Schrobsdorff, 2006) and research, constructs the Internet as a space where there is a heightened possibility of negative outcome for youth who engage in public forms of Internet usage, with social networking platforms in particular singled out for their seemingly inherent predatory potential (Livingstone & Helsper, 2010). The always already assumed and therefore ominous presence of pedophiles, online bullying, human-trafficking, and personal indiscretions are ubiquitously linked to social media and social networking platforms, while filters, numerous state-sanctioned attempts at regulation, and various monitoring services offer up apparent "solutions" to the "problem" of youth Internet engagement.

While there is ample research acknowledging the educative potential within digital literacies (Burgess & Green, 2009; de Castell, 2010; Poyntz & Hoechsmann, 2011), new media are also often problematically framed as a distraction from, and deterrent to, literacy and social development. The proliferation of social networking platforms and seemingly mindless acquisition of "common" knowledge are framed as numbing young minds to standard forms of literacy and restricting more meaningful social interaction. However, these constructions are dependent upon the ongoing bifurcation of on and offline worlds, the same binary logic that fueled widely critiqued celebratory and utopian accounts of new media possibilities.

For youth, part of the social and cultural affordance (Wellman et al., 2003) of being online is the possibility of connecting with multiple publics simultaneously. While extending the notion of public participation, civic engagement, and sociality, we are not advancing a celebratory account of democratized media spaces. Indeed, youths' online social networking has made increasingly transparent historically rigid distinctions between public and private and the often furtive regulatory codes of publicness. While contemporary media cultures may engage young people's "collective imagination and [afford] new 'genres of participation'" (Livingstone, 2009, p. 25), many of the familiar inequities remain. Moreover, a culture of choice and personalized consumer goods that dominates young people's online lives tends to encourage children and youth to "behave in an individualized way" when it comes to acts and practices of identity formation and personal development (p. 11). This in turn makes the work of nurturing young people as civic actors more challenging because, significantly, young people's media lives can privilege personalized acts of decision making, rather than collective acts of political commitment and community engagement. These are the challenges of youths' digitally mediated lives, and while not divorced from the tensions and problematics produced in a mass-mediated culture, they suggest new dilemmas and possibilities worthy of the critical attention of youth studies researchers, educators, service providers, and others.

References

boyd, d. (2007). Why youth (heart) social network sites: The role of networked publics in teenage social life. In D. Buckingham (Ed.), *Youth, identity, and digital media* (pp. 119–142). Cambridge, MA: MIT Press.

Bryson, M., & MacIntosh, L. (2010). Can we play Fun Gay? Disjuncture and difference, and the precarious mobilities of millennial queer youth narratives. *International Journal of Qualitative Studies in Education, 23,* 101–124.

Buckingham, D. (2005). *The media literacy of children and young people: A review of the research literature.* London: OFCOM.

Burgess, J., & Green, J. (2009). *YouTube: Online video and participatory culture.* Cambridge: Polity.

Castells, M., & Himanen, P. (2002). *The information society and the welfare state.* Oxford: Oxford University Press.

Coleman, S., & Ross, K. (2010). *The media and the public: "Them" and "us" in media discourse.* New York: Wiley-Blackwell.

Dahlgren, P. (2009). *Media and political engagement: Citizens, communication and democracy.* Cambridge: Cambridge University Press.

Dean, J. (2002). *Publicity's secret: How technoculture capitalizes on democracy.* Ithaca, NY: Cornell University Press.

Dean, J. (2010). Affective networks. *MediaTropes, II,* 19–44.

de Castell, S. (2010). Exquisite attention: From compliance to production. *Language and Literacy, 12,* 4–17.

Deuze, M. (2006). Participation, remediation, bricolage: Considering principal components of a digital culture. *The Information Society, 22,* 63–75.

Fingerman, K. (2009). Consequential strangers and peripheral partners: The importance of unimportant relationships. *Journal of Family Theory and Review, 1,* 69–82.

Finkelhor, W., & Ybarra, M. L. (2008). Online "predators" and their victims. *American Psychologist, 63,* 111–126.

Gray, M. L. (2009). *Youth, media, and queer visibility in rural America.* New York: New York University Press.

Jenkins, H. (2006). *Confronting the challenges of participatory culture: Media education for the 21st century.* Chicago: MacArthur Foundation.

Johnson, S. (2006). It's all about us. *Time.* Retrieved from http://www.time.com/time/magazine/article/0,9171,1570717,00.html

Kapczynski, A. (2008). The access to knowledge mobilization and the new politics of intellectual property. *The Yale Law Journal, 117,* 806–883.

Lenhart, A., Purcell, K., Smith, A., & Zickuhr, K. (2010). *Social media & mobile Internet use among teens and young adults.* Philadelphia: Pew Internet & Life Project.

Livingstone, S. (2009). *Children and the Internet: Great expectations, challenging realities.* Cambridge: Polity Press.

Livingstone, S., Bober, M., & Helsper, E. (2004). *Active participation or just more information? Young people's take up of opportunities to act and interact on the Internet.* London: Department of Media and Communications, London School of Economics and Political Science.

Livingstone, S., & Helsper, E. (2010). Balancing opportunities and risks in teenagers' use of the Internet: The role of online skills and Internet self-efficacy. *New Media Society, 12,* 309–329.

Macpherson, C. B. (1977). *The life and times of liberal democracy.* Oxford: Oxford University Press.

Pew Research Center. (2010). Millennials: A portrait of generation next. Retrieved from http://pewresearch.org/millennials/

Poyntz, S. R., & Hoechsmann, M. (2011). *Media literacies: Between past and future.* Malden: Wiley-Blackwell.

Schrobsdorff, S. (2006). Predator's playground. *Newsweek.* Retrieved from http://www.newsweek.com/2006/01/26/predator-s-playground.html

Warner, M. (2002). Publics and counterpublics. *Public Culture, 14*, 49–90.

Wellman, B., Quan-Haase, A., Boase, J., Chen, W., Hampton, K., Díaz, I., & Miyata, K. (2003). The social affordances of the Internet for networked individualism. *Journal of Computer-Mediated Communication, 8.* Retrieved from http://jcmc.indiana.edu/vol8/issue3/wellman.html

Willinsky, J. (2009). Derrida's right to philosophy, then and now. *Educational Theory, 59,* 279–296.

World Internet Project. (2010). Retrieved from http://www.worldInternetproject.net

30

MUSICKING

Julian Henriques

Music is vital to youth culture, and it is difficult to imagine many popular cultural contexts without it. Music often defines a scene, even an era, from the earliest Blues and Jazz through Folk and Rock and Roll, to Hip Hop and Grime (Adorno & Horkheimer, 1944/1972; Hebdige, 1979). One reason for its centrality is that music makes connections with feeling, emotions, affect, intensities, moods, and "vibes." In *The Republic*, Plato famously had musicians and poets banned on the grounds of their dangerous power to evoke an emotional rather than rational response from the populace. Music often defines identity, friendships, interests, memories, and moods; in short, who you are. Your music taste "says something about you." This kind of musical meaning has most often very little to do with linguistic or graphic representation or what is conventionally understood as signification; Anahid Kassabian states the failure to interpret music in this way: "Somehow, 'representation' and 'meaning' come to be synonymous, and arguments that music is 'nonrepresentable' are (implicitly, at least) understood as proving that music does not 'mean' in any recognisable sense of the term" (2001, p. 6). The importance of music for youth cultures—and youth studies—is its power to open up a corridor of communication outside image and text.

A second reason why music is particularly important for youth culture is its comparatively modest means of production. Almost any object can be purposed for musical expression, such as the oil drums on which Trinidadians steel pan music, and most laptops have preinstalled garage band software. Indeed, the body itself is endowed with possibly the most remarkable of musical instruments with the human voice, as heard with barbershop quartets and a cappella groups. This makes music accessible as a form of communication and expression for those with the least resources—in many societies, young people.

A third ground for music's importance for young people is how its minimal means of production and ephemeral time-based nature make it difficult for the authorities to control. Again, Plato was aware of music's social role: "any musical innovation is full of danger to the whole State, and ought to be prohibited ... when modes of music change, the State always changes with them" (*The Republic*, trans. 1881). This belief that music and musical change can encourage social and political change is not new, with Woody Guthrie and Bob Dylan's protest songs in 1950s and 1960s America, Victor Jara's in Chile, or Bob Marley's in Jamaica in the 1970s as examples. Though the lyrical content of such singer-songwriters' songs is obviously important, the music itself has its own message, more difficult to censor than words. In 1944 Duke Ellington put it this way: "You can say anything you want on the trombone, but you gotta be careful with words" (Cohen, 2004, p. 1003).

Making connections between individual and society, music also opens up an entire avenue for research that is distinct and different from the conventional "reading" of social "texts." As Jacques Attali puts it, "For twenty-five centuries, Western knowledge has tried to look upon the world. It has failed to understand that the world is not for the beholding. It is for hearing. It is not legible, but audible" (1985, p. 3). Youth cultures are likely to require listening as much as reading. This gives music an important methodological role in youth studies.

Musicking: Relations, Actions, and Processes

But while music is central to many youth cultures, it has its strongest effects when combined with style, fashion, and attitude. Again, Punk is a good example of this, with its D.I.Y. antiprofessional approach influential long after its origin with the Sex Pistols in Britain in the late 1970s. Similarly, a music video combines music with image. This takes us to the idea of *musicking*, coined by music theorist and educationalist Christopher Small (1998). The activity of *musicking* opens up the research phenomenon to include all these activities and people involved in the event. *Musicking* is comprehensive. Small makes the point as follows: "The act of musicking establishes ... a set of relationships, and it is in those relationships that the meaning of the act lies ... between the people who are taking part, in whatever capacity, in the performance" (1998, p. 13). The international success of the Simon Bolivar Youth Orchestra of Venezuela, both in terms of musicianship and in transforming the lives of the young players, serves as an excellent example of the power of the social relationships that the concept *musicking* recognizes.

This comprehensive approach immediately indicates the second of the defining qualities of *musicking*: it is a practice, not an object. As Small states:

"The fundamental nature and meaning of music lie not in an object, not in musical works at all, but in action, in what people do" (1998, p. 8). *Musicking* is a verb:

> To music is to take part, in any capacity, in a musical performance, whether by performing, by listening, by rehearsing or practising, by providing material for performance (what is called composing), or by dancing. We might at times even extend its meaning to what the person is doing who takes the tickets at the door or the hefty men who shifts the piano and the drums or the roadies.
>
> (Small, 1998, pp. 8–9)

This shift from noun to verb also expresses the political shift to political activism that was part of the American civil rights movement, as described in terms of music by Amari Baraka (a.k.a. LeRoi Jones) in his 1963 essay "Swing—from verb to noun" (Jones, 1999). This idea of music as an integrated part of life is at the heart of the concept of *musicking* as exemplified in John Chernoff's (1979) account of the traditions of musicking-making in contemporary West African countries—on which Small draws in his *Music of the Common Tongue* (1987). It could also be said that a similar shared social experience of music in the developed Western world is achieved through the digital technologies that allow recorded music to be ubiquitous—in cafes, elevators, lobbies, retail spaces, and more or less everywhere else, not to mention the media of Internet, film, and television, as well, of course, as our iPods. It is as if the long march of technological progress has simply returned us to where we began. Silicon-integrated circuits mimic socially integrated ones.

The shift from the noun of music to the verb of *musicking* is also a shift in cultural traditions. The idea of music as an object is comfortable in the world classical or high culture that often privileges the romantic ideal of the individual artist as the creative genius, archetypically suffering to work in poverty and isolation. Here the musical "work" is often considered to be the score, awaiting interpretation from the musicians' performance. *Musicking*, by contrast, can also be particularly useful for understanding popular traditions. In the past these have often been oral rather than scriptural, handed down from generation to generation, rather than written down for posterity.

The emphasis of *musicking* on activity contrasts with approaches where music is considered only as an object, either as defined by its internal form and structure and expressed in musical notation, or as a commodity, such as a CD, that it becomes when recorded, reproduced, and exchanged. The ubiquity of music as a digital file to be copied and shared at will—even though the files themselves are intangible—has only tended to increase this impression of music as an object:

> Considered as a product, reproduced sound might appear mobile, decontextualised, disembodied. Considered as a technology, sound reproduction might appear mobile, dehumanized, and mechanical. But considered as a *process*, sound reproduction has an irreducible humanity, sociality, and spatiality.
>
> (Sterne, 2003, p. 236; emphasis added)

Musicking, thus, places music in a cultural and social context.

What Musicking Does

There is no limit to the range of musicking activities that can be considered, particularly in popular and youth culture. In my own research I have found it useful to describe the *musicking* that goes on as part of the reggae sound system dancehall sessions on the streets of Kingston, Jamaica (Henriques, 2011). This includes not only the sound system crew of selectors, MCs, engineers, owners, promoters, maintenance crew, and so on, but also the crowd, dancers, video crews, food and drink vendors, and bar owners, as well as the truck drivers, fashion designers, poster and hand bill printers, the fly-posters, and mix CD sellers. The list of *musicking* participants is almost endless. The inclusive concept of musicking is particularly useful, compared to conventional ideas of music, because, like Hip Hop and many popular musical cultures, the sound system scene is phonographic. This is to say the music itself—as distinct from the vocals of the rapper, DJ, or MC—is provided by already recorded music tracks, rather than live musical performance. These tracks, like computer composed and performed electronic music, are just as much a part of musicking as traditionally composed and performed pieces of "music."

The value of any concept comes from how useful it might be for understanding the phenomenon at hand and the questions it raises. With *musicking*, Small argues, "Who is doing it? where? and who is listening? then become the primary questions. By looking at music this way, we begin to understand the relationship between music, people, history and the larger culture" (Small, n.d.). In youth studies the *musicking* question becomes: How does it—the scene, club, event—actually work? Or, what do we need to know in order to understand how and why things have come to be the way they are? In this way, *musicking* suggests a research methodology that starts with a detailed description of what is actually going on. From this it might bring in further theoretical concepts to yield a deeper understanding of the patterns or forces that could be shaping what is seen and heard. As Small puts it: "It is only by understanding what people do as they take part in a musical act that we can hope to understand its nature and the function it fulfils in human life" (1998, p. 8).

Musicking helps to dissolve the traditionally hard and fast division between transmission and reception, or performing and listening, or, most importantly, production and consumption. It refuses to allow a fissure between the activities of performing, playing, and making music, on the one hand, and participating, clapping, dancing, paying attention, listening, and otherwise appreciating and enjoying, on the other. This is particularly relevant to contemporary traditions of scratching and turntablism:

> DJ culture denies the binary opposition between the proposal of the *transmitter* and the participation of the *receiver* . . . The work of the DJ consists in conceiving linkages through which the works flow into each other, representing at once a product, a tool and a medium. The producer is only a *transmitter* for the following producer, and each artist from now on evolves in a network of contiguous forms that dovetail endlessly.
> (Bourriaud, 2002, p. 34)

Musicking as embodied practices draws on the philosophical tradition of phenomenology that, according to Maurice Merleau-Ponty (1962), emphasizes *being-in-the-world*, rather than the kind of withdrawal from it associated with analytical philosophy. *Musicking* is thus consistent with British cultural theorist Raymond Williams when he says: "We have to break from the common procedure of isolating an object and then discovering its components." Williams continues, "On the contrary, we have to discover the nature of a practice and then its conditions" (Sterne, 2003, p. 219). This emphasis on activity, practice, and doing was also critical for the linguistic philosophers, as with philosopher Ludwig Wittgenstein's assertion that "the meaning of a word is its use in the language" (1953, p. 43), or more emphatically, "Don't think but look!" (1953, p. 66). It is part of what he would call a *form of life*, or what sociologist Pierre Bourdieu describes as a *habitus*.

To conclude, it can be said that, by emphasizing music as social practice and process, the concept of *musicking* helps to capture something of the depth, texture, and tone of music itself. This is especially valuable for youth studies when the MP3 file has made music continually available and endlessly reproducible and disposable. The upside is that a young person's back catalog can be more extensive now than ever before. The downside is a flattening, dehistoricing effect that makes all music commensurable—original sample and current remix alike, no matter when or where each was created. Similarly, the MP3 file itself reduces dynamic and frequency range to optimize the sound for iPod listening. In this way the concept of *musicking* helps remind us of the particular history and unique social context of every piece of music—qualities of musical enjoyment that often tend to be sacrificed for the sake of convenience.

References

Adorno, T. W., & Horkheimer, M. (1944/1972). The culture industry: Enlightenment as mass deception. In *Dialectic of enlightenment* (pp. 120–167). London: Verso.

Attali, J. (1985). *Noise: The political economy of music*. Manchester: Manchester University Press.

Bourriaud, N. (2002). *Postproduction, culture as screenplay: How art reprograms the world*. New York: Lukas & Sternberg.

Chernoff, J. M. (1979). *African rhythm and African sensibility: Aesthetics and social action in African musical idioms*. Chicago: University of Chicago Press.

Cohen, H. G. (2004). Duke Ellington and *Black, Brown and Beige*: The composer as historian at Carnegie Hall. *American Quarterly, 56*, 1003–1034.

Hebdige, D. (1979). *Subculture: The meaning of style*. London: Methuen.

Henriques, J. (2011). *Sonic bodies: Reggae sound systems, performance techniques and ways of knowing*. New York: Continuum.

Jones, L. (1999). Swing—from verb to noun. In *Blues people: Negro music in white America* (pp. 142–165). New York: HarperCollins. Retrieved from http://xroads.virginia.edu/~asi/musi212/emily/jonestext.html

Kassabian, A. (2001). *Hearing film: Tracking identifications in contemporary Hollywood film music*. London: Routledge.

Merleau-Ponty, M. (1962). *The phenomenology of perception*. London: Routledge and Kegan Paul.

Small, C. (1987). *Music of the common tongue: Survival and celebration in Afro-American music*. London: Calder.

Small, C. (1998). *Musicking: The meaning of performing and listening.* Hanover: Wesleyan University Press.

Small, C. (n.d.). Musicking. Retrieved from http://sunsite.queensu.ca/memorypalace/parlour/Small02/

Sterne, J. (2003). *The audible past: Cultural origins of sound reproduction.* Durham, NC: Duke University Press.

Wittgenstein, L. (1953). *Philosophical investigations* (G. E. M. Anscombe, Trans.). Oxford: Blackwell.

31

SEXUALITY

Mary Jane Kehily

Jeffrey Weeks (1986) highlights the difficulties of understanding sexuality in contemporary culture as a "transmission belt for a wide variety of needs and desire: love and anger, tenderness and aggression, intimacy and adventure, romance and predatoriness, pleasure and pain, empathy and power" (p. 11).

Such powerful feelings locate the sexual domain as a vehicle for strong emotions, deeply embedded in Western culture. The range and scope of these feelings convey notions of sexuality as a natural force, occurring between members of the opposite sex and through sex we are "expected to find ourselves and our place in the world" (Weeks, 1986, p. 12). These cultural assumptions invoke the term "sex" as both an act and a category of person. The approach to sexuality as natural and naturalized has, according to Weeks, been endorsed by modern sexologists who have codified and thereby regulated how sexualities are lived and organized. For Weeks, the sexual tradition of the West offers two ways of looking: sex as dangerous, needing to be channeled by society into appropriate forms; and sex as healthy and good but repressed and distorted by society. Weeks poses an alternative to the binary of regulatory versus libertarian positions:

> that sex only attains meaning in social relations . . . we can only make appropriate choices around sexuality by understanding its social and political context. This involves a decisive move away from the morality of "acts" which has dominated sexual theorising for hundreds of years and in the direction of a new relational perspective which takes into account context and meanings.
>
> (1986, p. 81)

In this formulation sexual practices can be understood in relation to, and as part of, wider social relations through the contexts in which acts become meaningful. Weeks' influential body of work has applied this framework productively to sexuality and particularly the study of homosexuality. In tracing the socio-historical specificities which define the "act" and thereby the identity, the "sodomite" *becomes* the "homosexual" and, more recently, "gay" or "queer."

Changing Sexual Cultures

Considering the shaping of contemporary sexualities in the West, the importance of context emerges as a scaffold for the ways sexuality is experienced and understood. The sexual sphere has been framed by the postwar period of intense social change. The loosening up of traditional structures and the emergence of "permissiveness" and countercultural forms in the 1960s (Green, 1999) signaled a changing sexual climate. At the level of popular discourse, the new sexual order *belonged* to the young. Commenting on the shift to a more open era, Philip Larkin (1974) famously noted:

> Sexual intercourse began
>
> In nineteen sixty-three
>
> (Which was rather late for me)—
>
> Between the end of the Chatterley ban
>
> And the Beatles' first LP.

(p. 25)

The date may be speculative but Larkin's poem imaginatively, if a little miserably, captures the zeitgeist of the 1960s and 1970s as a period of sexual liberation that changed the lives of young people forever. The period was marked by significant social and scientific advance: the advent of the pill, gay liberation, second wave feminism, abortion rights, and a proliferation of ways to talk about and practice sex—in Foucauldian terms an "incitement to discourse" in which self-regulation replaces the authority of church and state.

Sexuality in "New" Times

Giddens (1992) describes sexuality as "a terrain of fundamental political struggle and also a medium of emancipation" (p. 181). Late modernity sees the emergence of new practices of intimacy in which egalitarian and emotionally contingent couple relationships take priority over ties that bind individuals to the social obligations of the past.

Brian McNair (2002) expands upon Giddens' comments by adding that, despite the intimate nature of sexuality, these struggles have taken place in public and are increasingly part of the public domain. McNair's analysis of contemporary culture suggests that the postwar period in the West has been characterized by the commodification of desire, witnessed in the increased sexualization of culture across a range of local and global media. Central to McNair's argument is the role of the media and particularly new media technologies. McNair suggests that new media technologies have aided the growth of a more commercialized, less regulated, and more pluralistic sexual culture, promoting, in his terms, "a democratisation of desire" (2002, p. 11). For McNair, the "democratisation of desire" describes the present period of popular and widespread access to diverse forms of sexual expression, such as the availability of pornography through the internet, simultaneously offering more ways of being a sexual subject within Western cultures. Illustrating his argument, McNair considers the ways in which pornography and homosexuality no longer have subterranean or subordinate status; they now exist as part of mainstream media culture. Gay bars and clubs flourish in city centers, to be enjoyed by a gay and straight clientele, while "porno chic," as McNair terms it, is ubiquitous in popular culture.

Considering these themes in relation to young people's lives, it may be possible to suggest that young people are the newly emergent sexual citizens of a democratized and richly diverse sexual culture. But are they? Drawing upon Weeks and Foucault, the following discussion contours some of the ways in which concepts of "youth" and "sexuality" become conjoined and acquire meaning in social relations. Recognizing the importance of context, youth researchers produce versions of youthful sexuality anchored in time and place. Accounts of young people and sexuality remain marked by pendulum swings in the struggle for meaning, prompting questions: What work does sexuality do for young people and what investments do youth researchers have in young people as sexual subjects?

Researching Youth and Sexuality

The sexuality of youth has long been a cause for concern for adults in the West. Youth in popular discourse commonly encode G. Stanley Hall's (1904) idea of adolescence as a time of "storm and stress." Hormonal change and peer pressure become familiar motifs in adult perceptions of a burgeoning sexual subjectivity. Sociological studies of youthful sexuality aim to question the biologism of popular accounts, paying attention to the ways in which young people's sexuality is shaped by adult and societal norms. In the shadow of adults, young people rehearse, act out, and elaborate upon normative sex-gender relations as documented by generations of youth scholars (Aapola, Gonick, & Harris, 2005; Kehily, 2002; Lees, 1986; Mac an Ghaill, 1994; McRobbie & Garber, 1982; Nayak & Kehily, 2008; Skeggs, 2004).

Influential parallel studies highlight the asymmetrical gender relations that characterize young people's sexual cultures (Thomson & Scott, 1990, 1991). Focusing on the disjuncture between young people's sexual practices and health promotion, the Women, Risk and Aids Project (WRAP) provides an up-close account of the conservatism inherent in young people's practices of intimacy.

Young women, for example, did not ask their partners to use condoms as, in keeping with local mores, this indicated a sexual looseness open to the charge of "slag." To avert the moral pincer movement of entrapment and censorship, young women tended to characterize all sexual encounters as a pursuit for love, trust, and companionship.

Considering what sexuality means to young people sees the emergence of two themes: sexuality as *risk*; and sexuality as *resistance*. Formulations of sexuality as risk highlight the hierarchies that position some young people as in need of protection. The dominance of young men and the routine harassment of girls and sexual minorities remain strong features of these accounts. Studies of sexuality as resistance, by contrast, focus upon the ways young people use sexuality within a repertoire of self-expression that responds to the normative and, in many cases, reacts against the pervasive sex-gender order. Classic studies of youth subcultures in the postwar period (see Hall & Jefferson, 1976) document the collective stylizations that symbolically resisted the authority of parents and state. A sexual history of youth subcultures could explore expressive sexuality as protests in search of solutions (Cohen, 1955). The hippie ideal of free love can be seen as a quest for sex-without-shame, self-consciously eschewing the morality of the 1950s. Following postwar migration and changing notions of community, skinhead subculture embraced the nihilism of working-class youth as sex and violence became markers of a good night out (Healy, 1996). Punk subculture, in an inversion of all things hippy, fashioned a display of sexual excess through wearing bondage gear and rapists' masks—disgust and shock-ability being an integral and long-standing feature of the subcultural landscape (Hebdige, 1979).

Pursuing themes of risk and resistance in a school-based study, I explored the way sexuality weaves into young people's lives and considered why the sexual arena is so combustible (Kehily, 2002). I concluded that, in the context of the increased regulation of school life through processes of individualization, student sexual cultures achieve significance as autonomous, peer-generated sites providing "adult-free and education-free zones in which students can collectively negotiate what is acceptable, desirable and what is 'too much'" (2002, p. 207). Inspired by each other, young people use sexuality to challenge adults, generate humor, flout middle-class norms, and define their own rules (Kehily & Nayak, 1997). Creative, multiply invoked expressions of an ever-present sexuality remain a recognizable part of young people's social worlds (Nayak & Kehily, 2008).

Overall, youth researchers appear invested in characterizations of youthful sexuality as shape-shifting figurations in which young people can simultaneously be positioned as in need of protection and agentic critics of societal norms and adult sensibilities. Becoming sexual in late modernity involves the elaboration of a sexual biography that reworks expressions of youthful sexuality. Through the simultaneous embodiment of risk and resistance, telling sexual stories can be seen as a way of living the contradictions of late modern selfhood, as the final section demonstrates.

Creating a Sexual Biography

A final portrayal of youthful sexuality is provided by modern artist Tracey Emin's (2004) autobiographical account of sexual initiation in Margate, United Kingdom. As a working-class girl growing up in the faded splendor of an English seaside resort in the 1970s, Emin recalls a local practice in which teenage girls were "broken in" for sex by local boys. First sex could involve the less than romantic experience of penetration, and possibly coercion, in the public pleasure zone of the sea front. Emin herself was "broken in" at the age of 13 years. Characteristically, she turns personal experience into art in the feature film *Top Spot* (2004). Emin provides the establishing narrative:

> *Top Spot* was here somewhere. Giant ballroom with chandeliers and red velvet curtains. We'd snog and kiss, be fingered, titted up, a place to experiment. You know what top spot is don't you? Top spot is when a man has sex with a woman or a girl, when the penis hits the neck of the womb. That's when it hits top spot. I mean who would ever call a teenage disco *Top Spot?*

Top Spot creatively reveals the messiness of adolescent girls' life-worlds as they seek pleasure in the real-life seaside postcard of snatched moments and erotic opportunity. Emin's work and the WRAP research serve as powerful reminders that the sexual liberation heralded by the 1960s and 1970s remains patchy, haphazard, and contextually specific. Working-class young women, for example, remain subject to structures of constraint. Amidst the trauma of showing and telling, Emin insists the message is an empowering one:

> When you're growing up things can look really totally bleak. And I'm here to tell you it doesn't have to be like that . . . You can turn your experiences into something positive and that's what I hope the film gives to people, a positive outlook in the end.

References

Aapola, S., Gonick, M., & Harris, A. (2005). *Young femininity, girlhood, power and social change.* Basingstoke: Palgrave Macmillan.

Cohen, A. K. (1955). *Delinquent boys: The culture of the gang.* New York: The Free Press.

Emin, T. (Producer). (2004). *Top spot* [Television broadcast]. London: BBC3.

Giddens, A. (1992). *The transformation of intimacy: Sexuality, love and eroticism in modern societies.* Cambridge: Polity Press.

Green, J. (1999). *All dressed up: The sixties and the countercultural.* London: Pimlico.

Hall, G. S. (1904). *Adolescence: Its psychology and its relations to physiology, anthropology, sociology, sex, crime and education* (2 vols.). New York: Appleton.

Hall, S., & Jefferson, T. (Eds.). (1976). *Resistance through rituals: Youth subcultures in postwar Britain.* London: Hutchinson.

Healy, M. (1996). *Gay skins: Class, masculinity and queer appropriation.* London: Cassell.

Hebdige, D. (1979). *Subculture: The meaning of style.* London: Methuen.

Kehily, M. J. (2002). *Sexuality, gender and schooling: Shifting agendas in social learning.* London: Routledge.

Kehily, M. J., & Nayak, A. (1997). Lads and laughter: Humour and the production of heterosexual hierarchies. *Gender and Education, 9,* 69–87.

Larkin, P. (1974). Annus Mirabilis. In *High windows* (p. 25). London: Faber.

Lees, S. (1986). *Losing out: Sexuality and adolescent girls*. London: Hutchinson.

Mac an Ghaill, M. (1994). *The making of men*. Buckingham: Open University Press.

McNair, B. (2002). *Striptease culture: Sex, media and the democracy of desire*. London: Routledge.

McRobbie, A., & Garber, G. (1982). Girls and subculture. In S. Hall, & T. Jefferson (Eds.), *Resistance through rituals: Youth subcultures in postwar Britain* (pp. 209–222). London: Hutchinson.

Nayak, A., & Kehily, M. J. (2008). *Gender, youth and culture: Young masculinities and femininities*. Basingstoke: Palgrave Macmillan.

Skeggs, B. (2004). *Class, self, culture*. London: Routledge.

Thomson, R., & Scott, S. (1990). *Researching sexuality in the light of AIDS: Historical and methodological issues*. London: Tufnell Press.

Thomson, R., & Scott, S. (1991). *Learning about sex: Young women and the social construction of sexual identity*. London: Tufnell Press.

Weeks, J. (1986). *Sexuality*. London: Tavistock.

32

TV AND FILM

Bill Osgerby

The media are a pervasive presence in the lives of contemporary youth. The television shows they watch, the music they listen to, the video games they play, and the websites they visit all play a considerable part in young people's lives, offering them a constant stream of different experiences, ideas, and knowledge. Developments in communications technology, moreover, have brought the media into young people's reach as never before. With the rise of digital media platforms and the growth of the Internet, the amount of time young people spend engaging with the media has risen dramatically. According to research undertaken by the Kaiser Family Foundation in 2009, the amount of time American 8- to 18-year-olds devoted to using entertainment media increased by 1 hour and 17 minutes a day over the previous 5 years, rising from 6:21 hours in 2004 to 7:38 hours. And, because young people spend so much of that time "media multitasking" (using more than one medium at a time), the total amount of media content they consumed during that period had increased from 8:33 hours in 2004 to 10:45 hours (Rideout, Foehr, & Roberts, 2010, p. 2). Mobile and online media, the study showed, had made significant inroads in young people's lives, but the "older" media of TV and film remained hugely important. Indeed, TV represented the dominant media young people consumed, youngsters viewing an average of nearly 4.5 hours daily, while on any given day about 12% of 8- to 18-year-olds watched a movie in a cinema (Rideout et al., 2010, p. 15). Elsewhere, particularly in developing societies, media access for many young people is inhibited by economic privation and limited communications infrastructures. Nevertheless, across the world, the media are a significant aspect of young people's lives. Surveying global statistics, for example, Susan Gigli (2004) concluded that average daily use of TV among school-aged children ranged from between 1.5 hours to more than 4 hours, and the prominence of TV in young people's daily lives made it one of their major information sources about the world around them. Radio, too, still plays an important role in many young people's lives, Gigli noting a particularly high number of listeners in regions such as Africa and the former Soviet Union. In analyzing the part played by such media in the lives of young people, researchers have given particular attention to both the historical development of media texts aimed at a youth audience and the possible impact of texts on young people's attitudes and behavior.

The Development of Youth-Oriented TV and Film

Young people first emerged as a significant media audience during the late 19th century as the cities of Europe and North America grew into bustling centers of entertainment and consumption. Kathy Peiss (1987), for example, shows how young, working women were pivotal to the development of commercial leisure—dancehalls, amusement parks, and movie houses—in *fin de siècle* America. With economic prosperity and the expansion of education, the early 20th century saw young people develop into a more distinctive consumer market. Sarah Smith (2005), for instance, demonstrates how youth represented one of the largest audiences for the early film industry in both the United States and Europe, young people colonizing movie theaters and establishing their own, distinctive cinema culture.

After 1945 the youth market and its associated media underwent a period of spectacular expansion. The growth was partly a consequence of demographic trends. In the United States, for example, wartime increases in the birth rate and a postwar "baby boom" rocketed the U.S. teen population from 10 million to 15 million during the 1950s, eventually hitting a peak of 20 million by 1970. A postwar expansion of education, meanwhile, further accentuated the profile of youth as a distinct generational cohort (Modell, 1989, pp. 225–226). However, the vital stimulus to the youth market was economic. Although full-time youth employment declined after World War II, a significant rise in youth spending was sustained by a combination of part-time work and parental allowances, with some estimating that young Americans' average weekly income rose from just over $2 in 1944 to around $10 by 1958 (Macdonald, 1958, p. 60).

Along with other entertainment industries, the cinema scrambled to cash in on the burgeoning youth market. A decline in adult audiences intensified

Hollywood's growing focus on teenage cinemagoers and, as Thomas Doherty (2002) shows, an extensive "teenpic" business took shape during the 1950s and 1960s. Melodramas such as *The Wild One* (1953), *Rebel Without a Cause* (1955), and *Blackboard Jungle* (1955) featured young characters and adolescent themes, but were only partially aimed at a youth audience. Movies geared more explicitly to the burgeoning youth market began with a wave of releases that capitalized on the 1950s rock 'n' roll boom. Columbia Pictures, for example, backed singer Bill Haley in *Rock Around the Clock* (1956), while Universal-International and 20th Century-Fox released *Rock Pretty Baby* (1956) and *The Girl Can't Help It* (1956), respectively. Also in 1956, MGM contracted Elvis Presley to a lucrative movie deal, and the singer went on to deliver 31 pictures for the studio. There were numerous other subgenres in the "teenpic" pantheon. Juvenile delinquent (or "JD") movies such as Warner's *Untamed Youth* (1957) and MGM's *High School Confidential* (1958), for example, focused on antisocial tearaways. "Clean teenpics," in contrast, were syrupy romances such as Pat Boone's movies for 20th Century-Fox, *Bernardine* and *April Love* (both 1957).

Young audiences were also addressed by the budding medium of television. During the 1950s teenage life was a firm feature in many American TV soap operas and family-based sitcoms. Shows such as *The Adventures of Ozzie and Harriet* (1952–1966), *Father Knows Best* (1954–1962), and *Leave It to Beaver* (1957–1963) all featured teenage characters, who became increasingly central to storylines over the course of the 1950s. The launch of the situation comedy *The Many Loves of Dobie Gillis* (1959–1963), meanwhile, saw the arrival of the first prime-time TV show focused on teenage characters. The ABC network was particularly known for its appeal to young audiences. Since its bigger, more established rivals (CBS and NBC) were best placed to exploit the mass TV audience, the younger and smaller ABC network courted more specialized markets such as youth and young families. For example, in 1957 the Philadelphia-based music show *American Bandstand* transferred to the ABC network, where its audience figures touched 20 million.

During the 1970s TV networks began giving more attention to Black youth culture and audiences. In 1970, for example, the Chicago TV station, WCIU, launched *Soul Train* as a Black counterpart to *American Bandstand*, the show's success leading to its syndication the following year, while youth-oriented TV dramas such as *Room 222* (1969–1974) and situation comedies such as *What's Happening!!* (1976–1979) focused on the experiences of young African Americans.

In Europe the development of the youth market was slower and more partial than in the United States. Nevertheless, by the late 1950s, the rise in young people's spending power was also galvanizing the growth of youth-oriented film and TV. In Britain, for example, TV music shows such as *Six-Five Special* (1957–1958) and *Ready, Steady, Go!* (1963–1966) proved popular. And, while Britain had nothing to match the American "teenpic" phenomenon, British filmmakers pitched movies featuring popular singers such as Tommy Steele and Cliff Richard. The Beatles, meanwhile, featured in film successes *A Hard Day's Night* (1964) and *Help!* (1965).

Despite economic downturns and a decline in the youth populations of most Western countries, the market for youth-oriented film and TV remained buoyant throughout the 1980s and 1990s. The box office success of the horror movies *Halloween* (1977) and *Friday the 13th* (1978), for example, was followed by a cycle of teen "slasher" films, while *The Breakfast Club* (1985) and *St. Elmo's Fire* (1985) heralded a succession of "coming-of-age" movies. The success of the *Porky's* movie series (1981, 1983, 1985), meanwhile, signposted the arrival of the teen sex comedy, a genre sustained in films such as the *American Pie* series (1999–2009). For the TV industry, too, youth remained a crucial audience. Indeed, from the moment it began broadcasting in 1986, the Fox network candidly pursued the youth market; and, across American TV, the 1980s and 1990s witnessed a legion of new "teen-oriented" dramas and soap operas, such as *21 Jump Street* (1987–1990), *Beverly Hills 90210* (1990–2000), and *Dawson's Creek* (1998–2003).

The Impact of TV and Film on Young Audiences

There exists a long history of concern about the potentially adverse impact of TV and film on young people, especially the possible links between violent media content and aggression. In the United States during the 1960s, a set of influential, laboratory-based psychological studies by Leonard Berkowitz (1962) and Albert Bandura (1973) seemed to point unequivocally to a causal link between media depictions of violence and aggressive behavior. Subsequently, however, media and cultural studies theorists have been critical of the approach taken by such research. Laboratory-based studies, critics argue, are far removed from "real-life" social conditions and consequently their findings are unreliable. Moreover, such research gives little attention to the social meanings that surround both media texts and social behavior. Most obviously, scant regard is given to the meaning of TV and film "violence." Little attention is given to the way different *kinds* of violence set in different contexts (e.g., "violence" depicted in a cartoon, presented in a news report, or featured in a horror movie) might be interpreted by audiences. As David Buckingham has explained, such approaches have invariably ignored the way young people make sense of media texts and give meaning to their social behavior:

> Meaning is seen to be inherent in the "message," and to be transmitted directly into the mind and thence the behaviour of the viewer. As a result, it becomes unnecessary to investigate what viewers themselves define as violent, or the different ways in which they make sense of what they watch.
>
> (1993a, p. 7)

Rather than employing experiments and quantitative methodologies to "discover" laws of media "cause and effect," the disciplines of media and cultural studies have preferred the use of qualitative research methods (e.g., ethnography, interviews, and focus groups) to explore the various meanings and interpretations viewers give to TV and films. Adopting such strategies, researchers such as

Buckingham (1993b, 1996) and Bob Hodge and David Tripp (1986) found that even very young audiences were proficient, discriminating media consumers. Similarly, Andrea Millwood Hargreave's research based on interviews and focus groups concluded that young children (aged between 9 and 13 years) were very "literate" TV viewers, and were "able to distinguish between fictional violence and violence that is 'real'" (2003, p. 5).

This is not to say that TV and films have no impact whatsoever on young audiences. Evidence regarding the media's negative "effects" on young people, however, remains (at best) inconclusive, while the relationships between youth and the media are much more complex and multifaceted than simple "cause-and-effect" models suggest. Rather than being passive recipients of media messages, young people are better understood as actively constructing meanings around TV and films, making informed judgments about genre and representation. Indeed, during the 1980s and 1990s, cultural theorists such as Paul Willis (1990) highlighted the way young audiences activate their own values and meanings through their patterns of media consumption, creatively using TV and films to engineer their own cultural spaces and identities. More recently, the advent of new, affordable media technologies—digital video and photography, websites, and mobile phones—has allowed for an outpouring of cultural creativity by young people themselves. Mary Celeste Kearney (2006), for instance, charts a proliferating universe of young women's media production where girls "express themselves, explore their identities, and connect with others" (p. 3). From this perspective, young people's engagement with media, such as TV and film, can be seen as not simply a setting for self-exploration and expression, but as a site of powerful self-representation that has the capacity to diversify and democratize the wider world of contemporary popular culture. The analysis of young people's engagement with TV and film, therefore, must take account not only of the media's potential power, but also of the agency of youth as an active and discriminating audience.

References

Bandura, A. (1973). *Aggression: A social learning analysis*. London: Prentice-Hall.

Berkowitz, L. (1962). *Aggression: A social psychological analysis*. New York: McGraw-Hill.

Buckingham, D. (1993a). Introduction: Reading audiences—Young people and the media. In D. Buckingham (Ed.), *Reading audiences: Young people and the media* (pp. 1–23). Manchester: Manchester University Press.

Buckingham, D. (1993b). *Children talking television: The making of television literacy*. London: Falmer Press.

Buckingham, D. (1996). *Moving images: Understanding children's emotional responses to television*. Manchester: Manchester University Press.

Doherty, T. (2002). *Teenagers and teenpics: The juvenilization of American movies in the 1950s* (2nd ed.). Philadelphia: Temple University Press.

Gigli, S. (2004). *Children, youth and media around the world: An overview of trends and issues*. Paper delivered at the 4th World Summit on Media for Children and Adolescents, Rio de Janeiro, Brazil. Retrieved from http://www.unicef.org/videoaudio/intermedia_revised.pdf

Hodge, B., & Tripp, D. (1986). *Children and television: A semiotic approach*. Cambridge: Polity.

Kearney, M. C. (2006). *Girls make media*. New York: Routledge.

Macdonald, D. (1958, November 22). A caste, a culture, a market. *New Yorker*, pp. 57–94.

Millwood Hargreave, A. (2003). *How children interpret screen violence*. London: BBC/BBFC/BSC/ITC.

Modell, J. (1989). *Into one's own: From youth to adulthood in the United States, 1920–1975*. Berkeley: University of California Press.

Peiss, K. (1987). *Cheap amusements: Working women and leisure in turn-of-the-century New York*. Philadelphia: Temple University Press.

Rideout, V., Foehr, U., & Roberts, D. (2010). *Generation M2: Media in the lives of 8- to 18-year-olds*. Menlo Park, CA: Kaiser Family Foundation.

Smith, S. (2005). *Children, cinema and censorship: From Dracula to the dead end kids*. London: I. B. Tauris.

Willis, P. (1990). *Common culture: Symbolic work at play in the everyday cultures of the young*. Milton Keynes: Open University Press.

Videography

Extensive filmographies of "teenpics" and youth-oriented movies can be found in the following:

Doherty, T. (2002). *Teenagers and teenpics: The juvenilization of American movies in the 1950s* (2nd ed.). Philadelphia: Temple University Press.

SECTION VI

Everyday Exceptions: Geographies of Social Imaginaries

Sunaina Maira

This essay addresses the ways in which youth studies can address the exceptions created for certain categories of young people who are imagined as "other" by the U.S. state, and are part of geographies of managing, disciplining, and disappearing people in the post-9/11 era. The pairing of "geography" and "imaginary" suggests the paradox and also potential of imagined geographies of youth—social, cultural, and political. On the one hand, the notion of a cultural "imaginary" can evoke a unified set of governing values, rules, and conventions, as suggested by Susan Talburt and Nancy Lesko (Introduction, this volume). On the other hand, social imaginaries can also include the envisioning of alternative possibilities—of lives, identities, struggles—by other people and in other places. Imaginaries of "otherness" are often intertwined with imaginaries of youth and youthfulness, who generally represent the edge of "difference" and symbolize new temporalities, the next generation, or "the future."

States of Exception: Youth and the War on Terror

In this essay, I will dwell on social imaginaries of, and also by, youth in relation to the geography of empire in the post-9/11 era and the spaces and states of exception in which certain groups of young people find themselves. I argue that youth studies has not sufficiently grappled with the question of imperialism, nor has empire studies adequately addressed the experiences of youth. The field of youth studies in the United States has generally been imbued with some of the same blind spots that have characterized other fields and disciplines in the United States that have long exhibited a denial of the nature of American empire (Kaplan, 1993). This absence or evasion has meant that the notion of empire is not always understood as being relevant to "youth studies," which has tended to focus on issues pertaining to youth within a national, if not nationalist, frame. It is important to note that empire always works on two fronts, the domestic and the global; the War on Terror is an extension of earlier processes of disciplining and subjugating marginalized and dissenting groups at home while consolidating hegemony overseas (Román, 2002). The national consensus for U.S. foreign policies is strengthened through historical processes of scapegoating "outsiders" and conflating internal and external enemies, as is only too apparent with the surveillance and profiling of Muslim and Arab Americans and crackdown on Muslim and Arab political movements overseas (Stoler, 2006, p. 12). It is important to note that the backlash against Muslim and Arab Americans after 9/11 was not exceptional, but part of a longer history of state regulation and repression of groups defined as "enemy aliens" or "anti-American." Focusing on the experiences of Muslim and Arab American youth in the post-9/11 moment, as I do in this essay, necessitates grappling with technologies of empire that have also shaped the realities of other groups of young people, with the notion of "youth" itself, and also with the boundaries of youth studies.

In my previous work, Elisabeth Soep and I developed the notion of youthscapes, "an analytic and methodological link between youth culture and nationalizing or globalizing processes," that conceptualizes a "site that is not just geographic or temporal, but social and political as well, a 'place' that is bound up with questions of power and materiality" (Maira & Soep, 2004, p. 262; see also p. xviii). One of the interventions suggested by this approach is a shift away from a U.S.-centric approach and a more rigorous critique of the unexamined nationalisms that permeate some work in youth studies, which is smart, creative, and even innovative, but still evades the geography of empire. This geography is central to understanding the experiences of young people whose lives have been deeply shaped or transformed in the War on Terror.

While there is a growing body of research on Muslim and Arab American youth after 9/11, the problem is that much of the social imagining *of* who these young people are in the field of youth studies—whether based in anthropology, sociology, psychology, education, or other disciplines—tends to be driven by a liberal impulse that challenges Islamophobia without also critiquing U.S. imperialism. Young people from Muslim communities tend to be read primarily or solely as "Muslim," and there is a particular preoccupation with issues of cultural conflict, a clash between "Western" cultures and Islam, which presumably underlies the oppression of young women and the "radicalization" of young men. A focus on religion, narrowly defined, reinscribes an Orientalist approach that sidesteps more difficult questions of nationalism and U.S. hegemony, including U.S. foreign policy in the Middle East and South Asia, that shape the lives of Muslim and Arab youth and underlie the suspicion and scrutiny directed against them. Liberal responses to the post-9/11 backlash were evident in many campus programs that framed the problem as one of only domestic racism to be addressed by multicultural inclusion of Muslim students. A liberal critique of "racial profiling" or "hate crimes" generally leaves unexamined the imperial structures that undergird these acts of violence or of racialization, evading more difficult questions of state terror and overseas occupation and invasion, not to mention the longer history of home-grown settler colonialism, that underlie the War on Terror. This is not surprising, for there is a long history of the conjuncture between liberalism and imperialism that is manifest in the current project of humanitarian imperialism or invasion for "human rights" and "women's rights" (Brown, 2006; Mehta, 1999), legitimized by expert knowledges about other regions and other cultures. Youth studies, thus, has the potential to be complicit in producing authoritative knowledge that can be used to justify, if not facilitate, the regulation and repression of target populations. However, if it can integrate a more critical and self-reflexive framework that accounts for imperial power, it may help to expose the role of knowledge production, at the least, if not challenge state policies and the national consensus.

In the current moment, the image of immigrant or minority youth and the specter of "militant" or "fundamentalist" Muslims and Arabs threatening "the American way of life" or European and "Western values" reveal a particular global and racial imaginary about youth. This imaginary, I will argue, is embedded in technologies of nation and empire that use a colonialist logic of projection to invert the threat of imperial intervention that have destroyed other peoples' ways of life and means of livelihood. This devastation of other societies is masked by a discourse of "democracy" and "freedom" and by neoliberalist notions of individual autonomy and "choice" embedded in free market rationalities (Ong, 2006). Young people, it is assumed, must choose between the "American way of life" (self-realization through capitalism/consumption) and "anti-Americanism" (self-annihilation through militancy/resistance to "the West"). This essay focuses on how a particular geography, that of U.S. imperialism, is connected to a technology of nation-making that produces youth as subjects that must be preserved and protected, as well as monitored, contained, repressed, or removed, if necessary through violence. Youth studies offers us the analytic tools to challenge rationalities of imperial nationalism, but it is also sometimes complicit with them through technologies of expertise and objectivity.

Imaginaries of youth as a site that is simultaneously threatening and hopeful, or deviant and liberating, are fundamentally tied to the conceptualization of youth as a transition between "childhood" and "adulthood." American and European notions of adolescence and psychological theories of stage-based development have produced an association of youth with liminality (Erikson, 1994). This notion of in-betweenness is at the heart of the ambivalence with which youth are often viewed and also the exceptionalism that sometimes overdetermines this category. Youth are assumed to fall between the cracks of "innocent" childhood and "stable" adulthood, to be dangerously outside of normative social structures and teetering on the brink of revolt. The romanticization of young people as agents of social change is the other side of the fear of that very change (Lesko, 2001; Shepard & Hayduk, 2002). This duality underlies what scholars of youth studies have critiqued as moral panics about youth, underlying which is an anxiety about threats to the status quo that young people are perceived to embody (Cohen, 1997).

The notion of "youth-as-transition" is not only culturally constructed but also necessary to the division of labor and the hierarchy of material relationships specific to various forms of the capitalist state. The categorization of youth as a population with distinct rights and limitations is necessary for the broader age-graded social relations that underpin systems of labor, education, criminal justice, taxation, property, marriage, and family (Mizen, 2002). Foucauldian analysis has helped demonstrate how "age provides a precise method of calibration for state administrative practices as the means to define subordinate populations in order to effect their control" (p. 12). While the state imagines "youth," young people also imagine the state—as powerful, disruptive, duplicitous, irrelevant, or necessary—in various arenas of their everyday life, such as schooling, immigration, policing, social services, popular culture, or the prison-industrial complex.

In my own research on South Asian Muslim immigrant youth in the United States and the War on Terror (Maira, 2009), I have tried to explore what anthropologists of the state describe as the "everyday and localized forms" of the state for young people who grapple with the intimacy of state power in their everyday lives (Hansen & Steputat, 2001, p. 5). Regimes of surveillance, detention, and deportation as well as everyday instances of profiling, suspicion, and harassment have created a climate of fear for Muslim and "Muslim-looking" individuals cast as the "enemy" population after 9/11. Muslim and Arab youth, particularly young males, have been viewed as objects of suspicion in the War on Terror due to a particular Orientalist conflation of Muslim and Arab masculinities with violence and irrationality (Said, 1981). The presumed liminality of youth makes young Muslim and Arab men even more suspect as they are considered vulnerable to "radicalization" by militant or fundamentalist groups. Muslim and Arab women, as well as girls, are viewed as objects of rescue to be saved by the West from oppressive and patriarchal traditions considered specific to Islam and the Middle East (Abu-Lughod, 2002; Nader, 1989; Razack, 2008). So, for example, the rhetoric justifying the U.S. invasion of Afghanistan and also the current proxy war and drone attacks on the Taliban in northwest Pakistan have been framed through a discourse of women's rights and "liberation" of Muslim women. While the Taliban are clearly misogynist and fanatical, this discourse obscures the work of indigenous feminisms that have challenged fundamentalisms and patriarchy and also evades the role of the United States in funding and arming Islamist groups, such as the mujahideen who formed the Taliban (Cooke, 2002; Lazreg, 2008; Mohanty, 1988).

While increasing attention has been paid to the exclusion of Muslims from national belonging after 9/11, it is important to note that the current "state of emergency" affecting Muslims and Arabs in the United States, the suspension of civil rights, and targeting of certain groups by sovereign violence have also affected other immigrant and minority communities. In other words, this exclusion of certain categories of people—defined according to race, religion, or citizenship—is not exceptional but the norm. This "state of exception" is constitutive of an imperial governmentality which rests on the exclusion of certain groups from citizenship at different historical moments (Agamben, 2005;

Ganguly, 2001). Thus, the post-9/11 moment is not a radical historical rupture but builds on forms of power already in place that target different groups to varying degrees and in specific ways, particularly in moments of national crisis—this is a state of everyday life in empire. This everyday "state of exception" is particularly acute for groups of young people who are labeled as culturally anti-thetical to Western modernity, for youth are also seen as potentially deviant and threatening to the social order. This dual exceptionalism (predicated on race/religion and on generation) makes the predicament of Muslim and Arab youth in the post-9/11 era an important one for youth studies scholars to theorize. The analytic tools developed by youth studies can be used to interrogate the categorizations of populations in relation to disciplinary regimes and cultural discourses of normativity.

Situating the exceptionalisms that frame social imaginaries of Muslim or Arab youth in a larger historical and political context is important for understanding the exclusion of Arab and Muslim Americans. These two labels, Arab and Muslim, are often conflated in dominant cultural imaginaries but their disentanglement has important implications for framing Arab and Muslim American youth in relation to empire. Anti-Arab racism in the United States has been given less attention in scholarly and public discourse than Islamophobia and has been difficult to name as such in the United States, even within a discourse of liberal multiculturalism in which Arab Americans are generally invisible (Salaita, 2006). A point to note is that, while anti-Arab racism overlaps with Islamophobia, it targets Muslim as well as Christian (not to mention secular) Arabs, but imaginaries of "Arab-ness" and "Muslim-ness" are often distinct in the United States.

Furthermore, young Arab and Muslim activists and Arab American student organizations have historically encountered repression in the United States due to their mobilization around the Palestine issue, an unpopular and controversial issue in a state that has unequivocally supported and funded the state of Israel and occupation of Palestine (Abraham, 1994; Orfalea, 2006). The targeting of Muslim and Arab communities, including Muslim and Arab youth, after 9/11 is thus part of a much longer history of containment of groups that have challenged U.S. policies in the Middle East and official mythologies of the beacon of the "free world." In my research on Arab and Muslim American college students in northern California, for example, I found that their political subjectivity was deeply shaped by the recognition that the historical experiences of their communities troubled dominant narratives about the Middle East that obfuscate political realities through Orientalist imaginaries of "terrorists" and "Islamic militants." Critiquing social imaginaries of Muslim and Arab youth thus involves challenging frameworks of racialization both within and beyond the United States, which would be productive for youth studies because it would encourage work that situates the historical conditions of youth in the United States within a larger political context than that prescribed by nation-centered approaches. Thus while challenging the exceptionalism associated with the category "youth," it could also challenge the exceptionalism of U.S.

empire and the everyday states of exception experienced by particular groups of young people.

Technologies of Empire and Imperial Feelings

I argue here that youth studies needs to engage more rigorously with the notion of empire as a dominant technology that shapes the lives of youth, within and beyond the United States. While I will not delve here into theories of U.S. imperialism and empire, and the genealogies of these two distinct terms, I want to note that U.S. imperialism has historically been marked by nebulous, nonterritorial forms of domination (Magdoff, 2003; Smith, 2005); these do not resemble traditional forms of territorial "colonialism" but they coexist with the "formal" colonialism evident in the occupation of Iraq, not to mention in Hawaii, Puerto Rico, and Guam. Unlike earlier European empires that relied on direct colonization, the United States has a history of using secret interventions in other sovereign nation-states, proxy wars, and client states (Kaplan & Pease, 1993). U.S. imperial power also cloaks itself in the discourse of human rights, so "freedom" and "democracy" becomes, paradoxically, the justification for dominance and neocolonial occupation. U.S. policies of military, political, and economic domination have re-emerged as the focus of public debate since September 11, 2001 and in the War on Terror, but they are rooted in a larger history of U.S. imperial power that has long illustrated the "state of exception" (see Dawson & Schueller, 2007; Gregory, 2004; Razack, 2008).

The flexibility, ambiguity, and secrecy of U.S. imperialism have helped sustain a discourse of exception and collective amnesia. Amy Kaplan (2005) points out that the U.S. brand of imperialism has been obscured by the creation of new designations of overseas territories, under varying degrees of U.S. control, and new categories of persons and citizens serving imperial interests. Ambiguous or secret sites of incarceration and disappearance such as Guantánamo, Abu Ghraib in Iraq, and lesser known sites such as Bagram prison in Afghanistan, as well as secret planes used by the CIA to ship "ghost detainees" to prisons in Europe and other countries, represent the "spaces of exception" that make the empire's violations of international law the norm (Hansen & Steputat, 2001, p. 1; see, e.g., Meyer, 2001). This geography of exceptionalism has violent consequences; to take just one example, the United States has rewritten the definition of what constitutes "torture" by internationally accepted minimum standards in order to subject the men, women, youth, and children it has captured to cruel, inhumane, and degrading punishment (Puar, 2007; see also Khan, 2008). Young people have been included in the category of "enemy combatants," a new designation created to evade the rights afforded to prisoners of war, let alone political prisoners, incarcerated in Guantánamo, Bagram, and secret prisons ("black sites") that the public knows nothing about. The hidden geography of empire entails a murky world of gulags, ghost planes, and disappeared men, women, youth, and children (Grey, 2006).

The "removal" of youth caught up in the War on Terror includes detention in and deportation from the United States, but it also includes abduction or "extraordinary rendition," another euphemism from the imperial vocabulary masking extraordinary violence and violations of human rights. In many cases, countries other than the United States have assisted in the kidnapping, detention, and abuse of innocent individuals who were later imprisoned in Bagram or Guantánamo, such as youth and men who were sold for bounty to the U.S. military by Pakistani military or intelligence agents (see Khan, 2008). For example, the youngest prisoner held in Guantánamo is Omar Khadr, a Canadian citizen of Egyptian origin, who was captured by the United States in Afghanistan at the age of 15 and imprisoned in Bagram and later Guantánamo ("Edging Toward the Right Thing," 2010). His story is little known to most people in the United States but reveals the horrific implications of imaginaries of youth that are too easily ignored in the rhetoric infusing the U.S. War on Terror. It was alleged that Khadr threw a grenade at U.S. soldiers, contrary to the Pentagon's later report (Shephard, 2009). Khadr was found crippled and trapped in a demolished house and tortured in U.S. prisons; in Bagram, he reported that he was threatened with dogs, forced to do hard labor, and to urinate on himself. In Guantánamo, he has been subjected to solitary confinement, shackling, tied in stress positions, and dragged in his urine ("Omar Khadr," n.d.). No doubt such treatment would lead to feelings of rage against the United States. What, then, are the sentiments that one can associate with the torture and incarceration of youth, with spaces of violence and confinement?

I argue that it is important to consider the affective dimensions of technologies of empire because U.S. imperialism is an assemblage of political, historical, and economic structures but it is also a pyschic apparatus. Cultural critics and historians have pointed to the ways in which empire in the United States has long been a "way of life" (Williams, 1980, p. ix), a structure of feeling that underlies the relationship of the individual to society. This is what I call the imperial feeling, the complex of psychological and political belonging to empire that is often unspoken, but always present in daily life. The notion of "imperial feelings" follows in the genealogy of Edward Said's (1993) seminal work on "structures of attitude and reference" that are part of the "cultural topography" of empire. There are a range of feelings associated with the United States' imperial role that have been intensified after 9/11 and that are experienced by young people as well: anger, loathing, fear, uncertainty, ambivalence, apathy, and denial. Notions of national belonging and responses to the War on Terror by Arab and Muslim youth need to be linked to the collective denial and repression of knowledge of U.S. empire that underlies everyday imperial culture.

It is apparent that young people are part of the affective and cultural life of empire, and that they respond with a range of imperial feelings, depending on their relationship to the U.S. state and nationalism. Not all immigrant or minority youth, or even Muslim and Arab youth, automatically oppose or abhor U.S. empire; there are complex responses to the imperial state, which include "mixed feelings" such as (partial) identification or deep ambivalence, and desires for belonging and acceptance (Maira, 2009). Furthermore, it is clear that the production of new identities by the imperial state includes the redefinition of "youth" itself so that certain groups of young people are seen as outside of the rights legally guaranteed to youth, by a state that variously classifies youth as in need of its protection or an inherent threat to the status quo, by virtue of their race, religion, or ideology. For example, the United States has violated the Optional Protocol of the Convention on the Rights of the Child (UNICEF, n.d.) in refusing to acknowledge that Khadr was a child at the time of his capture and is entitled, at the least, to the rights afforded to a child soldier ("UNICEF Defends . . .," 2008).[1] Khadr was incarcerated with adults, he was not allowed educational opportunities, and he was denied access to a lawyer for two years; the two other juveniles imprisoned with him at Guantánamo both attempted suicide ("Why Was a Child . . .," 2008). The incarceration and torture of youth in Guantánamo, as well as in less publicized prisons such as Bagram, shatter the mythologies of democracy and liberation that the U.S. state invokes in legitimizing its imperial interventions and its domestic as well as global regime of prisons (Rodríguez, 2006). However, a cultural discourse about Islamic "terrorism" and a civilizational battle between "the West" and "Islam" is still used to justify the encampment of particular groups of people, including young people, as it did for Japanese Americans who were viewed as enemy aliens during World War II.

The War on Terror sediments domestic discourses that have historically criminalized youth of color, for ongoing panics about deviant gangsters and drug dealers—Black, Latino(a), or Asian American—sometimes blur into the fears of militant Muslim and Arab youth. These racialized panics are collapsed in cases such as that of Jose Padilla, a Latino convert to Islam whose grueling imprisonment in a navy brig left him mentally disturbed (Liptak, 2007). Yet the threat to White American (masculinized) nationalism is not always easily compartmentalized in a racial framework; young White, middle- to upper-middle class male converts to Islam, such as John Walker Lindh, who was captured in Afghanistan, or Adam Gadan, a spokesperson for Al Qaeda charged with treason, are perhaps even more threatening to the consolidation of a racialized and gendered nationalism. Furthermore, technologies of incarceration that have targeted young males of color within the U.S. prison–industrial complex have been extended into the global gulag of prisons which have used some of the same techniques, and personnel, deployed in domestic prison warehouses and super max facilities (Davis, 2005; Gilmore, 2007). Yet the linkage between domestic and global fronts of empire is generally obscured, effectively preventing marginalized groups in the United States from understanding how their subjugation within the nation is connected to dominance overseas and, in many cases, dividing minoritized youth who variously absorb or contest U.S. nationalisms (Maira, 2009; Pease, 1993).

Producing the "Terrorist"

One of the fundamental paradoxes at the heart of the War on Terror is that terrorists must, in fact, exist, in order to justify waging war on them. So the presence of "radicalized" or "extremist" young Muslim men, angry at the United States and willing to attack it, is necessary for the War on Terror and for a public consensus around U.S. invasions and occupations of sovereign nations. As Gayatri Spivak (2004, p. 91) observes: "Something called terror is needed in order to declare a war on it—a war that extends from the curtailment of civil liberties to indefinite augmentation of military self-permission." There have been several instances of the state fostering or inciting statements of radical dissent and plans to attack U.S. targets that it has then used to prosecute and arrest young Muslims on the grounds of pre-emptive detention and counter-terrorism. There is a pattern of FBI informants infiltrating Muslim communities in the United States and befriending young men, in particular, who are outraged about U.S. atrocities in the Middle East, and in some cases even providing these men with the plans and arms for proposed attacks. This was illustrated by the case of the Fort Dix Five, five young Muslim men arrested in New Jersey in 2007 (Mulvihill, 2001), and the four men arrested in 2009 for supposedly plotting to attack a synagogue in New York ("US Men Charged . . .," 2009).

In the case of Hamid Hayat, a 22-year-old Pakistani American arrested in Lodi, California, in 2005, a Pakistani informant was paid $250,000 for spying on Lodi residents and recording conversations with Hayat about militant Islamic groups (Holstege, Marcucci, & Drucker, 2005; Maira, 2009). The informant insisted that the young man attend a jihadi training camp, which Hayat refused (Cockburn, 2006). Yet the young man was found guilty of making false statements and providing "material support" for terrorism, though no evidence was found that Hayat was involved in a sleeper cell as initially alleged (Dubal & Maira, 2005; Hood, 2006). What is also interesting about the Hayat case, as well as other cases involving undercover agents, is that young Muslim men are targeted through the use of "native informants" in conjunction with a quasi-ethnographic mapping of Muslim mosques, communities, and social networks by the FBI and local law enforcement (Elliott, 2006; Rashbaum, 2006; Winton, 2007).

The use of cultural knowledge and "insider" access raises the question of expertise, and its implications for intelligence gathering as well as academic research about Muslim and Arab youth. Authoritative knowledge about Islam, and Muslim and Arab cultures, is required to identify, infiltrate, or incite "terrorist" networks and "anti-American" ideologies, relying on experts who provide presumably "objective," but in reality deeply Orientalist, schema for predicting the political attitudes and religious orientations of Muslim youth.

A dominant theme in the existing literature is that Muslim American youth, generally immigrant and second-generation, are struggling with a "clash of cultures," echoing the neoconservative and Orientalist discourse of a "clash of civilizations" (Huntington, 1996). It is assumed that this essentialized conflict— framed as a binary between "the West" and a combination of "Islam," "other cultures," and static "traditions"—will detach youth from allegiance to liberal democratic values of "secular" and imperial governmentalities and lead them to "extremist" ideologies. The key question underlying the agenda of much research that the state currently seeks, directly or indirectly, through foundations, public policy programs, or research initiatives, is: are Muslim youth being "radicalized"? Radicalization is presumed to mean only politicization by Islamist movements, not secular or otherwise "radical" groups. Implicitly, the interest in "alienated" Muslim youth is driven by a need for data on "home-grown" terrorists from communities or subcultures assumed to be "breeding grounds" for terrorism. This is not to say that desperation, disillusionment, or disenchantment with the United States does not exist among Muslim or Arab American youth, or Muslim and Arab youth outside the United States (how could it not?), but rather that this is understood only as delusion, not despair or dissent.

Contemporary social imaginaries *of* Muslim youth in the post-9/11 moment are co-produced by the state, scholarly research, think tanks, and popular culture, but there is often little room for the social imaginaries produced *by* Muslim youth themselves. Nor is there sufficient interrogation of the label, "Muslim," which tends to subsume all other aspects of the lived experiences of young people included in this category, including issues of labor, education, cultural consumption, sociality, and political or cultural activism (particularly that not easily labeled as "Muslim"). Complex and nuanced issues of youth culture, gender, sexuality, nationalism, migration, and regional and ethnic identities tend to fall out of the reductive portrait that represents much of the existing research on Muslim and Arab American youth.

Conclusion

The exceptionalism of U.S. empire is layered in the current moment with the "state of exception" of Muslim and Arab youth, and of other young people considered a threat to the U.S. state and the values of neoliberal capitalism. The exceptionalization of youth is thus hinged to the current exceptionalism of the U.S. imperial project through geographies of surveillance, detention, deportation, and disappearance. The implications of my argument are that youth studies must not itself indulge in an exceptionalization of youth, by treating young people as if they are a category outside of the technologies of violence and discipline that affect populations at large. The focus of youth studies, in my view, should not be to examine only practices that somehow make youth unique, corralling them off from larger national or global processes, particularly those that trouble the taken for granted boundaries of what defines "youth studies." Youth studies can help us understand that the production of the notion of "youth," not just as a collection of bodies defined by age but as an ideological apparatus, is precisely what can be used to blind us to the naturalization of what is appropriate to turn our lens on when we look at what we call "youth." Torture and rendition are subjects of youth studies as much as cyberculture or punk music; *all* of these are issues that affect Muslim and Arab American youth, whose lives extend beyond the areas mapped out by the interests of the security state. Youth studies is a site where youthscapes of empire could be productively interrogated, challenging imagined geographies and exceptional spaces into which young people have disappeared or in which they have been remade as empire's other.

Note

1 The United States has not ratified the Convention on the Rights of the Child but it has ratified the Optional Protocol to the Convention on the rights of children in armed conflict.

References

Abraham, N. (1994). Anti-Arab racism and violence in the United States. In E. McCarus (Ed.), *The development of Arab-American identity* (pp. 155–214). Ann Arbor, MI: University of Michigan Press.

Abu-Lughod, L. (2002). Do Muslim women really need saving? Anthropological reflections on cultural relativism and its others. *American Anthropologist, 104*(3), 783–790.

Agamben, G. (2005). *State of exception* (K. Attell, Trans.). Chicago and London: University of Chicago Press. (Original work published 2003.)

Brown, W. (2006). *Regulating aversion: Tolerance in the age of identity and empire*. Princeton: Princeton, NJ: University Press.

Cockburn, A. (2006). The war on terror on the Lodi front. Retrieved from http://www.counterpunch.org

Cohen, S. (1997). Symbols of trouble. In K. Gelder & S. Thornton (Eds.), *The subcultures reader* (pp. 149–162). London: Routledge.

Cooke, M. (2002). Islamic feminism before and after September 11. *Duke Journal of Gender Law and Policy, 9*, 227–235.

Davis, A. Y. (2005). *Abolition democracy: Beyond empire, prisons, and torture*. New York: Seven Stories Press.

Dawson, A., & Schueller, M. J. (2007). Introduction: Rethinking imperialism today. In A. Dawson & M. J. Schueller (Eds.), *Exceptional state: Contemporary U.S. culture and the new imperialism* (pp. 1–33). Durham, NC: Duke University Press.

Dubal, V., & Maira, S. (2005, April 2). The FBI "witch-hunt" in Lodi. Retrieved from http://indiacurrents.com/news/

Edging toward the right thing. (2010, February 17). *Globe and Mail*. Retrieved from http://www.theglobeandmail.com/news/opinions/editorials/edging-toward-the-right-thing/article1472060/

Elliott, A. (2006, May 27). As police watch for terrorists, Brooklyn Muslims feel the eyes. *The New York Times*, p. A1.

Erikson, E. H. (1994). *Identity: Youth and crisis*. New York: W. W. Norton.

Ganguly, K. (2001). *States of exception: Everyday life and postcolonial identity*. Minneapolis: University of Minnesota Press.

Gilmore, R. W. (2007). *Golden gulag: Prisons, surplus, crisis, and opposition in globalizing California*. Berkeley: University of California Press.

Gregory, D. (2004). *The colonial present*. Malden, MA: Blackwell.

Grey, S. (2006). *Ghost plane: The true story of the CIA torture program*. New York: St. Martin's Press.

Hansen, T. B., & Steputat, F. (2001). Introduction: States of imagination. In T. B. Hansen, & F. Steputat (Eds.), *States of imagination: Ethnographic explorations of the postcolonial state* (pp. 1–38). Durham, NC: Duke University Press.

Holstege, S., Marcucci, M., & Drucker, D. (2005, June 9). Three more arrests in Lodi terrorism case. *Oakland Tribune*. Retrieved from http://www.oaklandtribune.com

Hood, J. (2006, February 25). Links to terrorism still vague: Observer says FBI needs a "Perry Mason" moment. Retrieved from http://www.recordnet.com

Huntington, S. P. (1996). *The clash of civilizations and the remaking of world order*. New York: Simon and Schuster.

Kaplan, A. (1993). "Left alone with America": The absence of empire in the study of American culture. In A. Kaplan, & D. Pease (Eds.), *Cultures of United States Imperialism* (pp. 3–21). Durham, NC: Duke University Press.

Kaplan, A. (2005). Where is Guantánamo? *American Quarterly, 57*, 831–858.

Kaplan, A., & Pease, D. (Eds.). (1993). *Cultures of United States imperialism*. Durham, NC: Duke University Press.

Khan, M. R. (2008). *My Guantánamo diary: The detainees and the stories they told me*. New York: Public Affairs.

Lazreg, M. (2008). *Torture and the twilight of empire: From Algiers to Baghdad*. Princeton, NJ: Princeton University Press.

Lesko, N. (2001). *Act your age! A cultural construction of adolescence*. New York: Routledge.

Liptak, A. (2007, January 5). In war of vague borders, detainee longs for court. *The New York Times*. Retrieved from http://www.nytimes.com/2007/01/05/washington/05terror.html?_r=1&ref=us&pagewanted

Magdoff, H. (2003). *Imperialism without colonies*. New York: Monthly Review Press.

Maira, S. (2009). *Missing: Youth, citizenship, and empire after 9/11*. Durham, NC: Duke University Press.

Maira, S., & Soep, E. (Eds.). (2004). *Youthscapes: The popular, the national, the global*. Philadelphia: University of Pennsylvania Press.

Mehta, U. S. (1999). *Liberalism and empire: A study in nineteenth-century British liberal thought*. Chicago: University of Chicago Press.

Meyer, J. (2001, 28 February). Human Rights Watch lists 39 secret CIA detainees. *Los Angeles Times*. Retrieved from http://articles.latimes.com/2007/feb/28/world/fg-detainees28

Mizen, P. (2002). Putting the politics back into youth studies: Keynesianism, monetarism, and the changing state of youth. *Journal of Youth Studies, 5*, 5–20.

Mohanty, C. T. (1988). Under Western eyes: Feminist scholarship and colonial discourse. *Feminist Review, 3*, 61–88.

Mulvihill, G. (2001, April 29). 4 life terms, 1 33-year sentence in Fort Dix case. *Associated Press*. Retrieved from http://nl.newsbank.com/nl-search/we/Archives?p_product=APAB&p_theme=apab&p_action=search&p_maxdocs=200&s_dispstring=4%20Life%20terms,%20 1%2033-Year%20sentence%20in%20Fort%20Dix%20case&p_field_advanced-0=&p_text_advanced-0=%28%224%20Life%20terms,%201%2033-Year%20sentence%20in%20 Fort%20Dix%20case%22%29&xcal_numdocs=20&p_perpage=10&p_sort=YMD_date:D&xcal_useweights=no

Nader, L. (1989). Orientalism, occidentalism and the control of women. *Cultural Dynamics, 11*, 323–335.

Omar Khadr. (n.d.). In Wikipedia. Retrieved from http://en.wikipedia.org/wiki/Omar_Khadr

Ong, A. (2006). *Neoliberalism as exception: Mutations in citizenship and sovereignty*. Durham, NC: Duke University Press.

Orfalea, G. (2006). *The Arab Americans: A history*. Northampton, MA: Olive Branch Press.

Pease, D. (1993). New perspectives on U.S. culture and imperialism. In A. Kaplan, & D. Pease (Eds.), *Cultures of United States imperialism* (pp. 22–37). Durham, NC: Duke University Press.

Puar, J. (2007). *Terrorist assemblages: Homonationalism in queer times*. Durham, NC: Duke University Press.

Rashbaum, W. (2006, April 24). Terror case may offer clues into police use of informants. *The New York Times*, p. B1.

Rodríguez, D. (2006). *Forced passages: Imprisoned radical intellectuals and the U.S. prison regime*. Minneapolis: University of Minnesota Press.

Román, E. (2002). Membership denied: An outsider's story of subordination and subjugation under U.S. colonialism. In B. E. Hernández-Truyol (Ed.), *Moral imperialism: A critical anthology* (pp. 284–296). New York: New York University Press.

Razack, S. H. (2008). *Casting out: The eviction of Muslims from Western law and politics*. Toronto, ON: University of Toronto Press.

Said, E. (1981). *Orientalism*. New York: Vintage/Random House.

Said, E. (1993). *Culture and imperialism*. New York: Vintage/Random House.

Salaita, S. (2006). *Anti-Arab racism in the U.S.A.: Where it comes from and what it means for politics today*. London: Pluto Press.

Shepard, B., & Hayduk, R. (Eds.). (2002). *From ACT UP to the WTO: Urban protest and community building in the era of globalization*. London: Verso.

Shephard, M. (2009, October 28). Khadr "innocent" in death of US soldier. *The Toronto Star*. Retrieved from http://www.thestar.com/specialsections/omarkhadr/article/717885--omar-khadr-innocent-in-death-of-u-s-soldier

Smith, N. (2005). *The endgame of globalization*. New York: Routledge.

Spivak, G. (2004). Terror: A speech after 9–11. *boundary 2, 31*, 81–111.

Stoler, A. L. (2006). Intimidations of empire: Predicaments of the tactile and unseen. In A. L. Stoler (Ed.), *Haunted by empire: Geographies of intimacy in North American history* (pp. 1–22). Durham, NC: Duke University Press.

UNICEF. (n.d.). Optional protocols to the Convention on the Rights of the Child: Providing legal protection for children against the worst forms of exploitation. Retrieved from http://www.unicef.org/crc/index_protocols.html

UNICEF defends the rights of a child soldier held in Guantanamo. (2008, May 2). *United Nations Radio*. Retrieved from http:// www.unmultimedia.org/radio/english/detail/37852.html

US men charged over synagogue plot. (2009, May 21). *Al Jazeera*. Retrieved from http://english.aljazeera.net/news/americas/2009/05/200952144536467973.html

Why was a child sent to Guantanamo Bay in the first place? (2008, July 19). *World News*. Retrieved from http://www.lestout.com/article/news-society/world-news/why_was_a_child_sent_to_guantanamo_bay_in_the_first_place.html

Williams, W. A. (1980). *Empire as a way of life: An essay on the causes and character of America's present predicament*. New York: Oxford University Press.

Winton, R. (2007, November 10). Outcry over Muslim mapping. *Los Angeles Times*. Retrieved from http://articles.latimes.com/2007/nov/10/local/me-lapd10

33

CULTURAL PRODUCTION

John Broughton

The predominant tendency in social science and education is to treat culture objectively and statically, without asking where it comes from or what it means. Where cultural production is addressed, it is typically dealt with as a simple productive process, a result of collective goal-directed action, which results in a deliverable product or artifact. There is no attention here to any subjective process of the producers, any expressive dimension of the productive process, any interpretive abilities or dilemmas, or any effects that this process might have on the subjectivity of the producers. Those aspects, if considered at all, are usually taken to fall on the side of cultural consumption.

When cultural production is considered in this orthodox way, the term tends to be used to refer to the process of generating cultural forms to assert and reinforce a sense of national unity, identity, and destiny. In this case, cultural production is scarcely distinguished from cultural *re*production, the transmission of cultural information from one generation to another, for better or worse. Schooling is traditionally viewed in precisely this way, as an institution guaranteeing the passing down of the knowledge and skills of the previous generation (represented concretely by teachers) to the emergent generation (in the form of the students).

The concept of cultural production as something other than faithful transmission is foregrounded most frequently in the areas of Cultural Studies and Cultural Theory, especially their neo-marxist and post-marxist versions. In this context, it has been associated primarily with informal activities, typically in the domain of popular culture, although some educational institutions have recently attempted to incorporate the productive cultural practices of youth in their formal curricula. The radical notion of teachers as *cultural workers* has helped to foster that practice in some instances. However, the liberal hegemony in schooling has invested in a very different approach.[1]

Media Literacy in Schools

Schools have tended increasingly to reduce popular culture to mass media, building secondary school curricula around a notion of visual literacy that is modeled on the reading of text. The focus here is consumption, although youth agency has been reintroduced in the fashionable *critical media literacy* approach, where students supposedly expose implicit messages, subliminal advertising, or hidden political agendas (Macedo & Steinberg, 2007). Some educators draw on the Frankfurt School or Screen Education theory (Alvarado, Buscombe, & Collins, 1993; Broughton, 2010) to legitimate this approach.

When popular culture is denounced as surreptitious marketing or propaganda in this way, youth perception is narrowed down to a defensive and cynical debunking of media as deliberately manipulative misrepresentation. The approach is based on an inverted communications model: rather than helping kids get the message, we try to intervene to prevent that from happening. Such a model encourages moral panics, for example about the pernicious effects of commercials or violent video games on children. It tends to make paternalistic assumptions about the naivete, gullibility, and vulnerability of young people and the need for educators to step in and protect them. The condescension involved here tends to be disguised by rhetorical appeal to the supposed "agency," "voice," and "empowerment" achieved by young people who engage in the debunking of media.

While critique can be productive, the critical media literacy approach keeps such analysis private—not only confined to the school but usually to a particular classroom. It falls short of addressing capitalist commodification, tending instead toward a rhetoric of consumer advocacy, truth-in-advertising, and the right-to-choose. The focus is entirely on reading given media, not writing them, thus preempting the mobilization of any youth production.

Youth Practices

The distinction between the reading and writing of culture has been complicated by research on youth consumption, especially in cultural studies, showing that there is a productive, generative moment to the act of consuming—a previously unsuspected "postconsumption" (Willis, 1990). Thus youth are not so much pawns of the market or skeptical critics of it; rather, they are spontaneous, creative appropriators of commodities who proceed to edit, revise, repurpose, and redirect what they consume.

There has been an explosion of user-generated content on the Internet. Youth have been recording music, making videos, and devising new forms of satirical amusement, such as *mash-ups, mockumentaries,* and *literals.* However, it is not clear when or how these collective exercises qualify as cultural production. Simply doing or making something may not constitute *production.* Self-expression is often local and personal rather than being part of culture, even if it is broadcast. Moreover, informal creative activities tend to be unresponsive to current or previous cultural formations; they are arguably ways of eliding or finessing culture rather than learning about it.

Where youth creativity does connect to cultural practices, it may be quite conventional and derivative (reproduction rather than production). Young people are quite capable of spontaneously taking up the maintenance of cultural norms themselves. For example, in the hit movie, *High School Musical* (Disney Channel & Ortega, 2006), the students convene in the cafeteria to sing "Stick to the Status Quo." Such appropriation underlines the important distinction between mere passive conformity and active conventionality, the latter requiring a vigorous identification with and even enforcement of, rather than obedience to, norms (Kohlberg, 1980). On the other hand, cultural reproduction may be conducted more or less unconsciously, even in the guise of cultural production, as when youth repeat past practices without realizing it (e.g., the baggy pants revival of zoot-suit fashion). Such unintended symbolic recycling may be fostered by a lack of historical perspective.

To provide a school-based example, in media classes there is a strong tendency for students to produce only traditional documentary videos, usually of the "social justice" type, and chiefly through the use of talking heads—inadvertently imitating TV news programs (Goodman, 2003). This orientation tends to ignore the quality and creativity of video-making, minimizing cinematic aspects of both the product and the process. Attention is systematically shifted away from esthetic and cultural ambitions toward more or less unreflective liberal concern with democracy, citizenship, and social inequities. Such production is governed by an instrumental value: The deliverable must have an explicit "use." At this point, media studies converge with community service.

High and Low Cultural Production

Culture in school is almost exclusively official, national, or high culture; it is as orthodox as it is authoritative. Its affordances do not include a demand that students help to produce it. Instead, the demand is to learn about it and appreciate it, while respecting the mastery of knowledge and skills it requires. Progress through schooling implies deeper and deeper entrenchment in this set of cultural assumptions.

On the other hand, popular culture is largely marginalized in schools by even the most progressive teachers. It remains a kind of underground culture of subjectivity for the students, giving them an avenue of escape, relief, and pleasure that is conducive to the elaboration of taste, style, personal identity, and a sense of humor. This domain is not a regime of expertise or virtuosity, and does not stress knowledge or even the mastery of skills. Amateurs can join in, especially lately, with the rise of reality TV, talent shows, user-generated content on the web, social networking, and the DIY ethos. Thus popular culture stresses accessibility and participation. It offers all kinds of postconsumption activities to youth and also allows them to engage in miniemulations, like being an amateur DJ, posting a YouTube video, or tweeting back to Ashton Kutcher. Needless to say, these are all activities occurring outside of school. Progressive teachers may attempt to bring such activities into the formal curriculum, but that runs the risk of vitiating the privacy of the students' personal world and preventing the emergence of their anarchic tendencies, which typically sit alongside the conventional ones.

In both cases, low as well as high, it must be admitted that cultural production is chiefly in the hands of adults, although the production of popular culture is more likely to be under the control of young adults, and information about how it is done is readily available to the general public. However, popular culture is still perceived as low, as trivial and ephemeral, as related to body more than mind, and hence as uncensored, risqué, morally compromised, and generally disreputable (Broughton, 2008). Participating in the production of it, therefore, carries a certain stigma in the adult world, which paradoxically provides youth an additional means of distinguishing and distancing themselves from that world.

Youth may further identify and separate themselves as a generation through improvised spatial practices. Interpretations of culture, such as those borrowing from dada/surrealism, everyday life approaches, or carnivalesque literary criticism, put more emphasis on public events or places, the normal functioning of which is temporarily subverted by individual or small group interventions. Examples of such interventions are the spate of *streaking* (in the 1970s), *parkour* (in the 1990s), or *flashmobbing, happy slapping,* and *fire in the hold* (in this decade), which often have the character of performance art.[2] Other examples, less publicly enacted but eventually quite notorious, include orchestrated losses of virginity (the *yellow teddybears* of the 1960s), burnout suicide pacts (in the 1980s), and planned group teen pregnancies (in the current decade).

Discourse Approaches

Some forms of youth productivity could best be called discursive rather than practical. An example of this is *slang*: new terms (and often new underlying concepts) are invented weekly, and circulate widely before becoming conventionally accepted and eventually obsolete, only to be replaced by other, fresher terms. *Awesome, sweet, OMG, word, bling, props, mad, chav, lame,* and *hot mess* are some established examples, while *awkward, sketchy, hella, blaze, bangin, fail, sick, crunk,* and *real talk* are more recent. In the case of such slang, the provenance is often unclear, but it does appear that much of the youth vernacular is generated and distributed by youth themselves.

Discourse theory has given rise to the notion of *productivity* of discourse—its capacity to seduce and captivate such that it generates, proliferates, and disseminates new cultural regimes, orders, and identities. A number of postmodern and poststructural theorists have construed this productivity as "performative" (e.g., Butler, 1990). According to this rhetorical view, gender, subjectivity, and personal identity, as well as the conventions governing them, need to be repeatedly instantiated or acted out in order to maintain their viability. They should be expected to change unpredictably due to the contingent and improvisatory nature of performances. Youth production of slang, like extreme public practices, can be seen in this light as a way to sustain or change generational identity and historical specificity performatively. Thus positive, proactive dramatization of new youth formations can be substituted for the traditional notion of rebellious subversion of norms.

Behind attention to subtle changes in cultural practices lies a postmodern relation to political activism that is expressive and stylistic rather than instrumental in form, demanding less than total social transformation—a subliminal rather than overt insubordination. Such is more inclined to a cultural or esthetic politics rather than a sociological one, which may not result in any definable product but gives rise instead to a "structure of feeling" (Williams, 1977) that may prefigure and gesture at a more explicit cultural formation, yet to be identified or articulated. This concept suggests how culture can constellate critical affects, representing a symbolic social subjectivity, such that cultural production may then take the form of generative paradigms of identity, interiority, and authenticity. This is a far cry from treating subjects as merely mediators for the production of objective cultural artifacts.

From a poststructuralist perspective, the orientation of inquiry might profitably be turned to the study of the discourse of cultural production itself. Productionist rhetoric does seem to privilege a depoliticized and ahistorical emphasis on instrumental action, thereby ignoring more progressive approaches that include esthetic, discursive, and rhetorical forms of cultural creativity. Such alternative frameworks would not only embrace popular cultural production, youth subcultures, and informal learning outside of school but also the mosaic of linguistic and stylistic innovations, both inventive and retroactive, that already permeate school culture more or less subliminally. It may be enough to recognize, appreciate, and engage with these without institutionalizing them right away in terms of formal curricula.

Notes

1   Thanks to Reuben Castagno, Alison Matika, David Ragland, Mary Schuler, Kelvin Sealey, and Blake Seidenshaw for their helpful comments on earlier drafts.

2 Saunders (2005). See also http://www.break.com/index/fire-in-the-hole-compilation. html and http://www.associatedcontent.com/article/2628399/the_real_story_behind_ lifetimes_the.html

References

Alvarado, M., Buscombe, E., & Collins, R. (Eds.). (1993). *The screen education reader*. New York: Columbia University Press.

Broughton, J. M. (2008). Inconvenient feet: How youth and popular culture meet resistance in education. In K. Sealy (Ed.), *Film, politics and education* (pp. 1–43). New York: Peter Lang.

Broughton, J. M. (2010). Cultural studies in schools. In S. Clauss-Ehlers (Ed.), *Encyclopedia of cross-cultural school psychology* (pp. 326–336). New York: Springer.

Butler, J. (1990). *Gender trouble*. New York: Routledge.

Disney Channel (Producer), & Ortega, K. (Director). (2006). *High school musical* [Motion picture]. United States: Disney.

Goodman, S. (2003). *Teaching youth media*. New York: Teachers College Press.

Kohlberg, L. (1980). Moral development. In J. M. Broughton, & D. J. Freeman-Moir (Eds.), *The cognitive-developmental psychology of James Mark Baldwin* (pp. 277–325). Norwood, NJ: Ablex.

Macedo, D., & Steinberg, S. (Eds.). (2007). *Media literacy: A reader*. New York: Peter Lang.

Saunders, R. (2005). Happy slapping: Transatlantic contagion or home-grown, mass-mediated nihilism? *Static/London Consortium*, *1*, 1–11. Retrieved from http://static.londonconsortium.com/archive.html

Williams, R. (1977). Structures of feeling. In *Marxism and literature* (pp. 128–135). New York: Oxford University Press.

Willis, P. (1990). *Common culture*. Boulder, CO: Westview.

34

HYBRIDITY

Pam Nilan

For the past three decades hybridity has been a key concept in cultural studies, postcolonial theorizing, and youth studies. This loan term from biology informed social science and language discourses regarding the outcomes of cultural mixing. In the 18th century public opinion feared racial mixing or hybridity would lead to a weakening of White races, producing minimized distinctiveness and subsequent loss of superior status. Similarly, language hybridity threatened a country's national language through the introduction and adoption of foreign terms. At the end of the 20th century influential social theorists including Donna Haraway (1985) and Stuart Hall (1993) reinvented the concept. For Homi Bhabha (1994) hybridity implied a discursive "third space" of identity/subjectivity characterized by ambivalence in the postcolonial moment. Hybridization is how "newness enters the world" (p. 227). Currently, hybridity or hybridization describes cultural synthesis or mixing, in relation to transnational practices, identities, and diaspora, implying the conflation of culture and nation.

Hybridity critically engages with power relations between different nations and cultures in the world by acknowledging nonhegemonic or subaltern knowledges. As a mode of analysis it examines spaces of resistance and reinvention in transnational engagements, and in colonial and postcolonial encounters (Anjali, 2007). Coining the term "hybrid cultures," García Canclini (1995) maintains that all late modern identities involve border-crossings.

In youth studies, we find the somewhat romantic idea that youth are the cultural leaders of hybridity as a form of subversion and resistance. In the hybrid space of youth culture, forms, practices, identities, and meanings are "appropriated, translated, rehistoricized, and read anew" (Bhabha, 1994, p. 37). Hybrid youth cultures point to "new conceptions of subjectivity and identification that articulate the local and the global in novel and exciting patterns" (Gilroy, 1993, p. 6). The creative, dynamic nature of youth culture (Willis, 1990) means that young people are a particularly seductive population to attach to the vanguard of hybridity.

Critiques of Hybridity

The term hybridity in youth studies and elsewhere represents an analytical endeavor to move beyond binary essentialisms such as traditional and modern, local and global, and Black and White. However, attempts are not always successful (Papastergiadis, 1997; Young, 1996). Many have criticized the concept of hybridity. Friedman (1999, p. 241) maintains hybrid cultural phenomena "are only surprising and confusing if we expect to find a neatly classified world" in which much remains the same. In fact all of us are cultural hybrids. More seriously, the skewed core–periphery distinction that originally defined the term hybridity stalks the quest to analyze contemporary hybrid identities. For example, researchers studiously identify the double consciousness or hybrid "third space" (Bhabha, 1994) of immigrant youth in Western countries but never the reverse.

The term diaspora refers to any people or ethnic population who left their country of origin to live elsewhere in the world. When researching youth cultures in the Arabic-speaking diaspora, for example, there is an analytic tendency to describe the inevitable mixing of Western and Middle Eastern musical genres as hybridity, even though it may be better described as synthesis that illustrates a creative aspect of globalization.

Hybridity in Youth Studies

There are two strands of youth studies in which the concept of hybridity remains popular: empirical investigations of the cultural identity of "ethnic" youth in first-world countries (e.g., Faas, 2009; Noble, Poynting, & Tabar, 1999; Tizard & Phoenix, 2002), and studies of how local youth in their specific cultures understand, absorb, synthesize, and produce hybridized forms of global popular culture, from U.S. gangsta rap (Morelli, 2001) to Japanese manga (Consalvo, 2006). In the latter, the concept of hybridity links directly to the cultural transformations engendered by globalization.

In empirical studies, researchers often use hybridity to make sense of the myriad syncretic cultural practices in which, for example, second-generation Lebanese youth in Western Sydney constitute themselves as being both Australian and Lebanese at the same time (Butcher & Thomas, 2006). Here it seems almost impossible to avoid binaries such as "mainstream Anglo" vs. "ethnic," which implicitly load the cultural meaning of racialized hierarchical power relations into the heuristic of hybridity for explaining identity phenomena. Furthermore, interpretations of hybrid identity oscillate between positive and negative views of how young ethnic people fare in mainstream "Anglo" culture. As Anjali (2007, p. 14) points out, this is characteristic of the epistemological problem: "the rhetorical alternation between heroism . . . and victimhood . . . is one that takes center stage in constructing discourses of hybridity" for global diasporas.

In the cultural field, studies of fusion popular music genres such as Afro-trance, remix bhangra, and electro-nasyid have made extensive use of the term hybridity. For example, British bhangra music is a blend of South Asian lyrics, themes, and beats with contemporary popular music genres, many of which derive originally from African American sources. Although it developed from a Punjabi music and dance genre, in its current remix form bhangra draws on Bollywood movie sound tracks and Western genres such as reggae, R&B, rock, hip-hop, dance, house, and ska (Dudrah, 2002). However, although the genre of British bhangra itself is clearly syncretic, so are many other contemporary fusion music genres. Social analyses of bhangra that use the notion of hybridity are overtly concerned with the identification of South Asian bhangra as a resistant cultural form within a Western immigrant context (Paganoni, 2006). Although the hybrid transnational character of bhangra does illustrate the importance of youth cultures for creating "new conceptions of subjectivity and identification that articulate the local and the global in novel and exciting patterns" (Gilroy, 1993, p. 6), yet again "young people become the privileged bearers of cultural dynamism and change," in this case rescuing South Asian identity from Anglo domination. Hybridity once more reveals its roots in geophysical politics, and in the desire of adult researchers to find resistance and authenticity in the messy creativity of youth cultures.

An Illustration of Cultural Mixing

We can illustrate the benefits and drawbacks of using the concept of hybridity by looking at what happens when Indonesian teenage girls engage with popular

Japanese animé films and manga cartoons. If we use hybridity as an interpretive concept, this emphasizes power relations between rich and poor nations in the region, a productive, but also limiting, approach. One observes how the Indonesian girls reinterpret the heroic female manga cartoon styles in their own drawings of girls wearing all-concealing garments and the Muslim headscarf. Piously covered girls with faces like animé heroine Princess Monoke fly about having adventures. How can we decide whether this is indeed an instance of hybridity or just an illustration of the popularity of a certain kind of fantasy cartoon drawing reproduced locally?

Imputations of hybridity imply the mingling of foreign signifiers in a Western context, but here no Western cultural paradigm is involved. We see a mélange of Asian cultural forms and meanings. Yet this does not mean geopolitical power relations do not inhere in the syncretic practice of Indonesian Muslim girls sketching the distinctively stylized figures and showing them to their friends. The girls are engaged in appropriating, translating, rehistoricizing, and reading anew, to paraphrase Bhabha (1994, p. 37). They are in a relatively poor and populous Muslim-majority country, reworking cultural materials that come from a much smaller, but far wealthier, predominantly secular, country in the Asia-Pacific region. A previous colonial aggressor in Indonesia, Japan is now a sophisticated Asian economic world power that exports desirable style products around the globe. Conversely, Indonesia is an overpopulated, developing country moving slowly to overcome widespread poverty. Yet this is not the whole story either. Asian cartoon genres are consciously preferred over Western genres by these Muslim Indonesian girls, adding a further layer of geopolitical complexity. The concept of hybridity, as it is commonly used in youth studies, struggles to encompass such myriad layers of synthesis, consensus, and refusal.

Young People and Perceptions of Hybridity

That which casts the greatest shadow of doubt over the concept of hybridity for youth studies is that young people themselves rarely perceive their identities, their social worlds, or their popular culture preferences to be "hybrid" at all. For them it is just what is happening in their world, whether we are talking about "ethnic" identity or everyday life, or about the "new" exciting trend in music or popular culture. Interpretations of hybridity in the identities, lives, and cultural preferences of youth come from researchers much older than the young people they study.

As indicated earlier, there is a tendency to romanticize hybridity as a subversive practice of youth that challenges the dominant culture. Yet in their practices of cultural mixing and synthesis, young people may not see themselves as resisting dominant cultural authorities or saving local culture. Youth researchers should be wary not to impute hybridity as a form of resistance in the complex synthesis of youth cultures. However, at the same time it would be analytically limiting to remain within the literal worlds and concepts of youthful research participants. We need to theorize, but remain cautious of oversimplifying and romanticizing the complex cultural engagements of youth as a simple hybridity between dominant and subversive.

Conclusion

Hybridity has long implied a combination or synthesis of two influences, races, cultures, languages, styles, genres, symbolic systems, and so on, or sets of these. However, young people everywhere now use personal communication devices and information technology for communication and entertainment purposes. This further increases the awkwardness of applying hybridity to questions of contemporary youth identity and cultural preferences. If it is not clear which element dominates, if there are many more than two significant things coming together, or if influences cannot be easily separated, then phrases like "multiple hybridities" come into play, at which point a word like complexity, syncretism, or plenitude would serve. The geopolitical configurations of the world have changed markedly since hybridity first appeared in the social sciences. We must ask whether the term hybridity retains relevance if we do not return to the nuanced framings of ambivalence and transformation first offered by Haraway and Bhabha. It may even be that we need a new concept of cultural synthesis and mixing to analyze the complex practices, outcomes, and products in contemporary youth phenomena.

References

Anjali, P. (2007). *Hybridity: Limits, transformations, prospects.* Albany, NY: SUNY Press.

Bhabha, H. (1994). *The location of culture.* London: Routledge.

Butcher, M., & Thomas, M. (2006). Ingenious: Emerging hybrid youth cultures in western Sydney. In P. Nilan, & C. Feixa (Eds.), *Global youth? Hybrid identities, plural worlds* (pp. 53–71). London: Routledge.

Consalvo, M. (2006). Console video games and global corporations: Creating a hybrid culture. *New Media Society, 8,* 117–137.

Dudrah, R. K. (2002). Drum'n'dhol: British bhangra music and diasporic South Asian identity formation. *European Journal of Cultural Studies, 5,* 365–383.

Faas, D. (2009). Reconsidering identity: The ethnic and political dimensions of hybridity among majority and Turkish youth in Germany and England. *The British Journal of Sociology, 60,* 299–320.

Friedman, J. (1999). The hybridization of roots and the abhorrence of the bush. In M. Featherstone, & S. Lash (Eds.), *Spaces of culture: City-nation-world* (pp. 230–256). London: Sage.

García Canclini, N. (1995). *Hybrid cultures: Strategies for entering and leaving modernity* (C. Chiappari, & S. Lopez, Trans.). Minneapolis: University of Minnesota Press.

Gilroy, P. (1993). Between Afro-centrism and Euro-centrism: Youth culture and the problem of hybridity. *Young, 1,* 2–12.

Hall, S. (1993). Cultural identity and diaspora. In P. Williams, & L. Chrisman (Eds.), *Colonial discourse and postcolonial theory: A reader* (pp. 392–403). London: Harvester Wheatsheaf.

Haraway, D. (1985). A cyborg manifesto: Science, technology and socialist feminism in the 1980s. *Socialist Review, 15,* 65–107.

Morelli, S. (2001). "Who is a dancing hero?": Rap, hip-hop and dance in Korean popular culture. In T. Mitchell (Ed.), *Global noise* (pp. 248–257). Middletown, CT: Wesleyan University Press.

Noble, G., Poynting, S., & Tabar, P. (1999). Youth, ethnicity and the mapping of identities: Strategic essentialism and strategic hybridity among male Arabic-speaking youth in south-western Sydney. *Communal/Plural, 7*, 29–44.

Paganoni, M. C. (2006). Shaping hybrid identities: A textual analysis of British bhangra lyrics. *Culture, 19*, 231–246. Retrieved from http://www.club.it/culture/culture2005-2006/15culture.pdf

Papastergiadis, N. (1997). Tracing hybridity in theory. In P. Webner, & T. Modood (Eds.), *Debating cultural hybridity: Multicultural identities and the politics of anti-racism* (pp. 257–281). London: Zed.

Tizard, B., & Phoenix, A. (2002). *Black, white or mixed race? Race and racism in the lives of young people of mixed parentage* (2nd ed.). London: Routledge.

Willis, P. (1990). *Common culture*. Boulder, CO: Westview Press.

Young, R. (1996). *Colonial desire: Hybridity in theory, culture and race*. London: Routledge.

35

SAFE SPACES

M. Piper Dumont

As an educator, I have spent a good deal of time in faculty meetings discussing the need to create safe spaces for our students. We wanted these safe spaces to foster students' learning as they develop into actualized individuals. Some schools go to great lengths to secure safety—metal detectors, police in schools, separate schools for marginalized or otherwise "problematic" students, and so on. The recent U.S. hyperawareness of bullying, and its, sometimes, dire implications, have reinvigorated efforts to ensure both physical and psychological safety within schools. In this chapter, I interrogate the notion of *safe space* as it is used within educational practice, particularly in regard to queer youth. In order to do this I examine what is meant by safety, especially as it intersects with ideological mechanisms of regulation. Through this analysis, safe space emerges as a problematic concept warranting reevaluation.

Interrogating Safety within the Context of Schooling

The search for safe spaces in schools is borne out of a generalized concern within education to nurture students' development by providing a space that facilitates learning, exploration, and growth. Within this conceptualization, education is not a natural process, but one that must be conscientiously monitored and overseen. As Stengel (2010) asserts, "Educators take for granted the need to protect students" (p. 523). Subsequently, safe space is a dominant metaphor in education (Boostrom, 1998). Weems (2010) notes the primacy of safety in another common metaphor—that of school as home (e.g., *in loco parentis*). The ubiquity of safe space in educational talk affirms a belief in safety as an environmental precursor to successful learning. School is a place of protection (from society) to learn about society, acknowledge each other's differences, and express one's individuality. Increasingly, special attention has been paid to issues such as race, class, gender, sexual orientation, religion, and national origin as they impact a child's sense of safety.

However, the nature (and practice) of creating and maintaining safety is ambiguous. Interrogating the nature of safe space reveals narratives supported by the dominant culture. For example, Boostrom's (1998) analysis reveals that isolation and individual expression are key assumptions made about the nature of education. Within this context, safe space is conceptualized as a democratic forum to share individuals' ideas and ensure everyone's comfort in doing so. These lead to what Boostrom calls the "unintended consequences" of safe space discourse. Safe spaces protect by segregating nonnormative individuals. Safety in this context is reduced to freedom to express opinions and identity. Disagreement, critical reflection, and authentic dialogue are stifled in an effort to support and affirm every student's expression. Not only is this superficial, but, as Boler (2004) notes, such notions of equalized expression ignore the power inequalities impacting our speech and expression. Therefore, they fail to contest oppressive structures that undergird a lack of safety. Recognizing that schools are primary sites of ideological reproduction, including processes of socialization and regulation (Dewey, 1944; Shor, 1992; Soltis & Feinberg, 2004; Walkerdine, 1990), helps us interrogate the meaning of safety and the nature of safe space in these educational contexts.

In order to provide focus, the rest of this essay interrogates the notion of safe space in regard to queer youth. A quick review of the reported experiences of queer students in school contextualizes the concern for their safety. According to the Gay, Lesbian and Straight Education Network's (GLSEN) 2009 School Survey (GLSEN, 2010), nine out of ten queer students have "experienced harassment at school in the past year" (para. 2). Almost two-thirds of queer students feel "unsafe in schools because of their sexual orientation" (para. 5) and four in ten queer students feel unsafe because of their gender expression. In response, a number of advocacy and educational institutions implement safe space curricula. Safe space programs are designed to create a visible network of queer allies throughout educational institutions. After completing the training, attendees are given safe space paraphernalia to display prominently on their person (buttons, lapel pins, patches, T-shirts) and in their personal space (dorm room door, office door). Theoretically this alerts queer and questioning students to people who will provide a safe space in which to be openly queer or to explore one's sexuality or gender. Statistics like those of the GLSEN survey help justify safe space programs, because we want to believe schools are safe spaces.

According to the safe space logic, queer youth are not only looking for support, but also a reprieve from the insecurity of the dominant context. Barry (2000) contends that "[m]arginalized groups have long sought alternative venues where they can escape the pressures of a dominant society" (p. 84). However, Stengel (2010) points out "ironies" within this conception of safe space:

> (1) The need for safe space for students who experience social exclusion and harassment is the result of a political economy that was intended to create safe space for others. (2) Students who are able to articulate a need for safe space often don't need the kind of space separation offers; students who need (if only temporarily) separation, often are unable to say so. (3) "Safe space" does not always or only function to defuse fear and establish safety for students; safe space may also function to create emotional relief for adults.
>
> (p. 524)

Hackford-Peer (2010) notes that these spaces are often justified by discourses reliant on unsafe conditions for queer youth. She warns that "when efforts towards making schools safer spaces for queer youth are grounded in discourses that rely on un-safety, the possibilities for even imagining what safety might mean are constrained by the discourses" (p. 543). These discourses are derived from the dominant context, which is built on, and supports, the structures threatening nonnormative students' safety. Creating segregated spaces of relative safety does not challenge marginalizing mechanisms. Subsequently, safe spaces are problematic.

Providing safety by designating special spaces questions our actual commitment to nondominant identities. These practices of safe spaces illustrate the naturalization of cultural logics and ideological structures such that we fail to recognize the regulatory, exclusionary, and oppressive nature of them. Thompson (as cited in Stengel & Weems, 2010) argues, "[W]hat we count as 'safe' is an imaginary construction reliant on ritualized forms of control" (p. 505). The ideological mechanisms of surveillance, regulation, and control of spatiality and the people within spaces are dependent upon the embodied acceptance of these structures (Low, 2009). As ideological frameworks become embodied (Connell, 2002; Walkerdine, 1990), we self-regulate (and regulate others) to comply with social norms. Queerness, on the other hand, celebrates the *in-between spaces*, which are multiple, dynamic, and even ambiguous identities and ways of being. Subsequently, queer identities are often directly oppositional to dominant ideological structures, and queer bodies are active sites of resistance. Therefore, even as safe spaces are provided, nonnormative youth must still navigate everyday and ritualized ideological spaces and practices that cultivate the status quo, and their bodies are the focus of regulation, repression, and violence.

Given the regulatory and ideological role of schools and the problematic nature of segregated safe spaces, how do we conceptualize safety for students whose identity and expression contest dominant ideologies? Utilizing Hall's (1980) discursive examination of "dominant meanings," I attempt to conceptualize a notion of *dominant safety*. According to Hall, dominant meanings derive from and support the prevailing cultural order. Within this framework, a dominant safety prioritizes the status quo, and the dominant culture is maintained and reproduced through ideological structures that establish norms. As Walkerdine (1990) argues, these norms are asserted and defined in relation to an oppositional and pathologized "other." These norms are continuously affirmed, pervasively visible, and naturalized, while the other is denied, silenced, delegitimized, and made to seem unnatural. Social regulation through normalization also depends upon the construction of certain types of knowledge (Lesko, 1996), which embed authority into specific ways of knowing and being. In this case, heteronormativity is the naturalized and legitimized norm, whereas queer identities, histories, and ways of knowing (and being) are otherized, denigrated, and erased. Schools are crucial sites for this ideological work—they reify the knowledge supporting and justifying the status quo and its maintenance, and regulate the embodied practice of normativity. While safe spaces may provide provisional safety to marginalized youth, Rasmussen (2004) points out that these spaces also serve to "remove troublesome students" (p. 137). Because queer students transgress and challenge heteronormative boundaries and ways of being, Rasmussen questions who is being served by creating institutionalized, segregated safe spaces. Creating separate spaces for the other reinforces difference (i.e., deviation from the norm) and maintains exclusionary normativity as nonnormative identities and expression openly exist only in designated separate spaces. Subsequently, using Hall's (1980) framework, creating separate safe spaces in schools for marginalized youth constitutes a *negotiated safety*. Within this context, safe spaces allow for situational exceptions to the norm, but the dominant cultural logic is maintained and reproduced (Hall, 1980).

Making Space for Oppositional Safety

While providing safe spaces for marginalized students is an important intermediary step that gives students a space to affirm their identities and gain solidarity (Barry, 2000), these spaces are still entrenched in and validate what Hall (1980) calls the "hegemonic viewpoint." If an *oppositional safety* is one that rejects the notion that safety is achieved by enforcing normative forms of expression and identities, can we generate an oppositional concept of safe space? In the context of queer youth, oppositional safety necessitates addressing the problematic structures sanctioning violence against queer expression and identity. As exclusionary safe havens, current conceptions of safe spaces perpetuate the violence of the system because they fail to challenge the cultural norms that exclude, marginalize, punish, coerce, and violate others. The creation of oppositional safety would have to occur within oppositional structures (which fundamentally threaten the foundations of dominant ideological frameworks). In other words, enacting oppositional spaces and ways of being necessitates the breakdown of entire systems of inequity, domination, and exclusion. Oppositional safety cannot exist as isolated bubbles within a context of violence.

From our perspective fully entrenched in the dominant culture, it can be difficult to envision oppositional practices. Commensurate with this is affirming nondominant culture (i.e., nonnormative), identities, and expression and disrupting responses that penalize, remove, negate, pathologize, and perpetuate otherizing ideological mechanisms. It also necessitates fundamentally restructuring spatial arrangements, especially as they serve to categorize, segregate, and exclude. This is the challenge of conceptualizing (let alone actualizing) safe spaces, especially when, as Boostrom (1998) points out, safe space discourse stifles disagreement and challenge. Sidestepping safe spaces that disallow challenge and discomfort is important. Instead of using safe space as a forum for unquestioned tolerance, we must allow for the exploration of tensions. Achieving such safety is a long-term project of wide-ranging transformation. We cannot achieve safety as long as it is framed within and refuses to challenge dominant ideologies. In fact, learning from queerness's fluidity, resistant nature, and embrace of contradictions and tension, as well as getting comfortable with the discomfort of in-between spaces, could open up liberatory and transformative possibilities.

References

Barry, R. (2000). Sheltered "children": The self-creation of a safe space by gay, lesbian, and bisexual students. In L. Weis, & M. Fine (Eds.), *Construction sites: Excavating race, class, and gender among urban youth* (pp. 84–99). New York: Teachers College Press.

Boler, M. (2004). All speech is not free: The ethics of "affirmative action pedagogy." In M. Boler (Ed.), *Democratic dialogue in education* (pp. 3–13). New York: Peter Lang.

Boostrom, B. (1998). "Safe spaces": Reflections on an educational metaphor. *Journal of Curriculum Studies, 30*, 397–408. doi:10.1080/002202798183549

Connell, R. W. (2002). *Gender*. Malden, MA: Polity Press.

Dewey, J. (1944). *Democracy and education: An introduction to the philosophy of education.* New York: The Free Press.

Gay, Lesbian and Straight Education Network. (2010, September 14). 2009 national school climate survey: Nearly 9 out of 10 LGBT students experience harassment in school. Retrieved from http://www.glsen.org/cgi-bin/iowa/all/library/record/2624.html?state=research&type=research

Hackford-Peer, K. (2010). In the name of safety: Discursive positionings of queer youth. *Studies in Philosophy and Education, 29*, 541–556. doi:10.1007/s11217-010-9197-4

Hall, S. (1980). Encoding/decoding. In S. Hall, D. Hobson, A. Lowe, & P. Willis (Eds.), *Culture, media, language: Working papers in cultural studies, 1972–79* (pp. 128–138). London: Centre for Contemporary Cultural Studies, University of Birmingham/Routledge.

Lesko, N. (1996). Denaturalizing adolescence: The politics of contemporary representations. *Youth & Society, 28*, 139–161. doi:10.1177/0044118X96028002001

Low, S. M. (2009). Toward an anthropological theory of space and place. *Semiotica, 175*(1–4), 21–37. doi:10.1515/semi.2009.041

Rasmussen, M. L. (2004). Safety and subversion: The production of sexualities and genders in school spaces. In M. L. Rasmussen, E. Rofes, & S. Talbot (Eds.), *Youth and sexualities* (pp. 131–152). New York: Palgrave Macmillan.

Shor, I. (1992). *Empowering education: Critical teaching for social change*. Chicago: University of Chicago Press.

Soltis, J. F., & Feinberg, W. (2004). *School and society* (4th ed.). New York: Teachers College Press.

Stengel, B. S. (2010). The complex case of fear and safe space. *Studies in Philosophy and Education, 29*, 523–540. doi:10.1007/s11217-010-9198-3

Stengel, B. S., & Weems, L. (2010). Questioning safe space: An introduction. *Studies in Philosophy and Education, 29*, 505–507. doi:10.1007/s11217-010-9205-8

Walkerdine, V. (1990). *Schoolgirl fictions*. London: Verso.

Weems, L. (2010). From "home" to "camp": Theorizing the space of safety. *Studies in Philosophy and Education, 29*, 557–568. doi:10.1007/s11217-010-9199-2

36

STREET CHILDREN

Rob Pattman

What makes a child a street child? Poverty as well as abuse in home communities and families are usually cited as key contributory factors, and in Southern Africa much has been written about HIV/AIDS in loosening family ties and creating a generation of orphans, many of whom feel compelled to migrate to the cities and look for work and stability and end up living and/or working on the streets. But the term "street child" is taken for granted in this response, and the impression is created that street children constitute a relatively fixed and homogenous group.

Another way of responding to the question is to explore why some children get categorized as street children. Rather than seeking to identify push and pull factors, which might encourage children to abandon their homes to become street children, this response questions the very categories "child" and "street child." The focus in this response is not exclusively on "street children" but "children" in general and how these are constructed in relation to each other as different and contrasting categories.

A History of the Category

The naming of certain children with the prefix "street" came to prominence in the mid to late 19th century. These children were not, however, "street children" but "street Arabs." Constructions of "street Arab" were part of an Orientalist discourse (Said, 1978) which produces the Orient by juxtaposing it to the West and making the West the moral standard against which to judge the deficiencies imputed to the Orient. These include, as illustrated in depictions of "street Arabs" in popular fiction at that time, unreliability, untrustworthiness, lack of self-discipline, and immaturity. For example, in *Household Words Volume 10*, Charles Dickens describes "a wretched, ragged, untaught Arab boy" and Horatio Alger's book *Tattered Tom: Or the Story of a Street Arab* focuses on a homeless girl who lives on the streets of New York (Street Children, n.d.). Associations of children with Arabs and the street reflected assumptions about Arabs as child-like, nomadic, and problematic. They implied, too, that poor children in Western cities belonged to an inferior species. In her study of representations of poor children in late 19th-century England, Lynda Murdoch (2006, p. 25) argues that "poor children" constructed as "street Arabs" were seen and treated as "a separate race from the English," as "savages . . . as distinct from civilised English people." The popularity of the term "street Arab" in England, she suggests, "signified fears of domestic decline" at a time of rapid imperial expansion.

The term "street children" was actually introduced and adopted by child welfare agencies and nongovernmental organizations in response to concerns about the stigmatization of children given the racist epithet "street Arab" as well as other abusive names such as "street urchins" and "vagrants" (Williams, 1993). "Street child" seemed more neutral and descriptive. Indeed it is precisely because of this that the term "street child" has been criticized as a particularly insidious category which conceals its pejorative connotations.

Unlike the term "street Arab," "street child" is not overtly racist but is used selectively in ways which reproduce racial stereotypes. Contemporary uses of the term "street child" tend to be restricted to children living outside Western countries. Of course, given higher levels of poverty and rural urban migration in these countries, children without parental support, who sleep in shelters or live rough and spend much of their time on the streets trying to support themselves, may be more numerous and visible than, for example, in London. However, children in London in similar situations have rarely or ever been called street children. Indeed, as if responding to a tendency not to think about street children as a European phenomenon, the Council of Europe (n.d.) introduces its *Building a Europe for and with Children* program with the assertion that "every city in Europe has street children." "Street children" is not only a term which stigmatizes certain children and their home backgrounds, but also so-called "third-world" countries; in the construction of societies as "third world," street children are important constituents.

Constructions of Children, the Street, and "Street Children"

The question "How are children constructed as street children?" has been raised by academics and activists who have taken issue with the term "street children" precisely because of its tendency to patronize and stigmatize children who may be living in cities and spending much of their time on the streets without parental support (Connolly & Ennew, 1996; Glauser, 1997; Moura, 2002). Such writers argue it is the label "street children" and "the frequency" of its use which "seems to suggest that such a group exists as a homogeneous phenomenon in reality" (Glauser, 1997, p. 146). Labeled as street children, young people are denied individuality and agency and rendered one-dimensional; their behavior and their views are simply explained in terms of this deviant "master status" which is ascribed to them. In the construction of street children, "the venue for their actions" becomes "the essence" (Hecht, 1998, p. 103) and the street defines the child as opposed to the home. According to Moura (2002), discourses on street children tend to "naturalise social deprivation and stigmatise poor families and children," with "street life" being "presented as the outcome of an organic and linear chain of adverse factors including migration, economic hardship, family dysfunction and child abuse" (p. 353).

An affection for and identification with the street is often invoked in Western countries, with the street being experienced and remembered, certainly in traditional working-class communities, as a space where families socialized and supported each other and formed strong communal bonds and identities (Young & Willmott, 1957) and where childhood was lived through play (see, e.g., Twist, 2010). Yet in spite of the significance attached to the street in such nostalgic accounts of childhood in the United Kingdom, the children who grew up in these communities were not called street children.

The prefix "street" in "street children" does not operate as an adjective like clever or happy to describe a particular child but combines with "child" to imply deviation from childhood. The term "street children" draws attention to those who are labeled as such by constructing them as different. The "street" in "street children" does not represent an ideal where childhood fantasies are realized; on the contrary, it is, in the symbolic imagination, a cold and hostile space that denudes childhood. Significantly, nostalgic fantasies about street life and childhood in towns and cities in the West are usually juxtaposed to depictions of contemporary streets as anonymous, unfriendly, and unsafe spaces for children. Street children then are both children and not children.

This symbolic opposition of street and home is fundamental and (usually) implicit, with the home associated with parental protection and normality and the street with a lack of this and abnormality. As Glauser (1997, p. 152) notes, "The street contradicts . . . dominant ideas about situations suitable for children to grow up in." "Street children" then tend to elicit sympathy as children denied parental protection and care, but also fear/hostility as children who lack what are seen as normal childlike qualities such as deference to adult authority. The "concern with street children," Glauser argues, arises not only because "they may suffer" from various kinds of abuses and dangers but also "because they disrupt the tranquillity, stability and normality of society." They are highly visible markers and constant reminders of social breakdown and "perceived as a physical menace, as they roam the shopping districts and the residential neighbourhoods of towns, either by themselves or in gangs" (pp. 152–153) as if they are children gone "feral" (Moura, 2002, p. 359).

Contemporary concerns about "street children" came to the fore in the build up to the 2010 football World Cup in South Africa. Eurocentric denigrations of Africa framed intense introspective debates in South Africa about how the country, as the first African nation to host the football World Cup in 2010, should present itself to the world, and prompted questions about what to do with "street children." For not only were "street children" understood as posing a threat to the safety and well-being of international tourists and fans but also as signifying the failure of South Africa to modernize. Responding to this, many children were rounded up by police in cities and dumped in places outside. There was considerable opposition to this, which stemmed in part from popular discourses about the World Cup as a vehicle for promoting unity between diverse cultural groups. On the one hand street children represented the publicly conspicuous Other who needed to be hidden from world view, yet on the other, they were the Other who needed to be embraced.

Significantly the "round-ups" of street children were never publicized by the police or by politicians and were given a highly critical slant by exposés in local and national media, with street children represented as the abused. The Street Children's World Cup held in Durban and organized by Umthombo, a Street Children's project, in which teams of "street children" (girls and boys) were invited to participate from different countries, was celebrated as a way of making visible the reality of the lives of vulnerable and marginalized children, in opposition to campaigns to "sweep the streets" (Street Children Aim for World Cup Victory, 2010).

"Street" features not only to delineate and stigmatize a category of children but also of women. The name "street girl" not only refers to a female "street child" but also to a female who practices as a sex worker (the two may or may not coincide), and like the category "street child" is constructed as deviant in opposition to the home traditionally seen as a nurturing and caring female space. Indeed, in Harare, Zimbabwe, police round-ups have been targeted at women walking alone on the streets at night. Girls who are called "street children" are doubly stigmatized not only as children but as girls, and often constructed, as Lucchini (1994) found, as prostitutes and experience moral opprobrium as well as sexual abuse. The acute problematization of (girl) street children may deflect attention from other children deserving care, and notably girls, who are not as visible as street children, and who may be confined to homes working as unpaid domestic servants or sex workers (Glauser, 1997, p. 154).

"Taking the Side" of "Street Children"

"Taking the side" of "street children" has often meant turning them into objects of pity, in ways, ironically, which deny agency, and presenting their lives through a unidimensional lens which emphasizes their impotence and victimhood in the face of negative social forces compounded by living and working on the street. In this construction of street children, "even as [they] are characterised by reprehensible behaviour, they are also partially exonerated from blame for their faults" (Moura, 2002, p. 359).

"Taking the side" of "street children" in this sense entails a series of identifications and disidentifications, as exemplified in the recently acclaimed South African movie *Izulu Lami* (Frederikse, Nathan, & Ncayiyana, 2008). The movie tries to depict the difficult and dangerous worlds the "street children" inhabit through the eyes of two recently orphaned children, an older sister and brother, who have migrated to Durban from their rural homestead.

In contrast to popular stigma models of "street children," the movie presents a refreshingly rounded and empathetic view of their lives and identities. We acquire nuanced and complex understandings of the lives of street children, the hardships they suffer, as well as the pleasures they derive from their companionship and play, their conflicts, and also the care they show for each other. But the "street children" with whom they mix also serve, by contrast, to highlight the moral authority and commitment of the older sister. While the former rely on petty theft and occasional sex work to eke out a living, she secures legal and long-term employment. Unlike them, she does not show violence nor does she sniff glue, but uses glue to make curios from wire and sweet papers which she sells to an African Arts Centre. Such dramatic contrasts may reinforce the stigma attached to street children, especially when taken in conjunction with the movie's powerful rescue narrative. Though the older sister mixes and makes friends with other "street children," the movie ends with her rescuing her brother, who had started to reject her in favor of his (male) "street children" friends, extricating both him and her from "street life," and returning to their rural homes with the proceeds made from her work.

How to take the side of "street children" without reinforcing the stigma implied by the label and reifying and objectifying the children is a concern which has come to prominence in recent years, especially following the publication in 1990 of the United Nations Convention of the Rights of the Child. Influenced by this, many child welfare organizations such as UNICEF have come to recognize that "promoting the best interests of children is not just a matter of protecting and providing for them but listening to them and fostering child participation" (Panter-Brick, 2002, p. 156). Ways of working with (and researching) so-called street children, which are participatory and engage with them as experts about their lives and identities, are implied by a social constructionist theory which questions and problematizes not the children themselves but the discourses which construct them as street children.

An example of one such initiative in which street children (and in this case female street children) were given an opportunity and a platform to discuss and present issues of concern to them was "the manifesto for change" which the girls, who were participating in the Street Children's World Cup, were asked by Umthombo to collectively construct. The demands the girls made in their manifesto were not only informed by protection rights, such as the right to safety and protection from sexual abuse and other forms of violence, but also by participatory rights such as the right "to speak and be heard" and to be "treated with dignity" (Street Child World Cup, 2010). In participatory studies and interviews with street children, sexuality, which in popular discourses about street children is usually associated with "promiscuity," exploitation, and abuse, is discussed in much more nuanced ways, sometimes associated with abuse but also with warmth, companionship, and security (e.g., Kariuki, 2007). Redefining street children as experts rather than treating them as objects of pity or disgust may open up possibilities of challenging predominantly negative associations with street life. "Growing up in the streets," Glauser (1997) speculates, may even become "a new paradigm for children's lives and growing up in disintegrating societies" (p. 163).

To point to the socially constructed nature of street children does not necessarily mean abandoning the category. Grouping particular children and calling them street children may be important politically to raise concerns about the living conditions or treatment of certain children. Baker, Panter-Brick, and Todd (1996) found that "street children" might, themselves, subscribe to the label as a source of collective identity, while conversely rejecting it because of its pejorative implications. Rather than taking it for granted as a descriptive category, the focus then becomes how and why the term "street child" is used and invoked and the consequences of this for "street children" and others.

References

Baker, R., Panter-Brick, C., & Todd, A. (1996). Methods used in research with street children in Nepal. *Childhood: A Global Journal of Child Research, 3,* 171–193.

Connolly, M., & Ennew, J. (1996). Introduction: Children out of place. *Childhood, 3,* 131–146.

Council of Europe. (n.d.). Building a Europe for and with children. Retrieved from http://www.coe.int/t/transversalprojects/children/violence/streetchildren_en.asp

Frederikse, J., Nathan, J. (Producers), & Ncayiyana, M. (Director). (2008). *Izulu lami* [Motion picture]. South Africa: DV8 Films.

Glauser, B. (1997). Street children: Deconstructing a construct. In A. James, & A. Prout (Eds.), *Constructing and reconstructing childhood* (pp. 145–164). London: Falmer Press.

Hecht, T. (1998). *At home in the street: Street children in northeast Brazil.* Cambridge: Cambridge University Press.

Kariuki, J. (2007). The voices of street children in Durban shelters. In R. Pattman, & S. Khan (Eds.), *Undressing Durban* (pp. 182–189). Durban: Madiba Press.

Lucchini, R. (1994). *The street girl: Prostitution, family and drugs.* Fribourg: University Fribourg Press.

Moura, S. (2002). The social construction of street children: Configuration and implications. *British Journal of Social Work, 32,* 353–367.

Murdoch, L. (2006). *Imagined orphans: Poor families, child welfare and contested citizenship in London.* New Brunswick, NJ: Rutgers University Press.

Panter-Brick, C. (2002). Street children, human rights, and public health: A critique and future directions. *Annual Review of Anthropology, 31,* 147–171.

Said, E. (1978). *Orientalism.* New York: Pantheon.

Street Children. (n.d.). In Wikipedia. Retrieved from http://en.wikipedia.org/wiki/Street_children

Street Children Aim for World Cup Victory. (2010). Retrieved from http://news.bbc.co.uk/2/hi/8567522.stm

Street Child World Cup. (2010). Girls living on the streets. Retrieved from http://streetchildworldcup.org/blog/we-the-girls-living-on-the-streets/

Twist, G. V. (2010, October 3). Nostalgia: Remembering the childhood games in the streets of Aston. *Sunday Mercury.* Retrieved from http://www.sundaymercury.net/news/

midlands-news/2010/10/03/nostalgia-remembering-the-childhood-games-in-the-streets-of-aston-66331-27387761/

Williams, C. (1993). Who are "street children"? A hierarchy of street use and appropriate responses. *Child Abuse and Neglect, 17,* 831–841.

Young, M., & Willmott, P. (1957). *Family and kinship in East London.* London: Routledge and Kegan Paul.

37

STYLE

Kristen Luschen

Style has been an integral concept to youth studies from its early emergence within cultural studies. At its core, style is a key arena through which cultural studies scholars have examined the intersections of social structure and production of collective identities by young people. In its earliest expression, cultural theorist Dick Hebdige developed the concept of "style" in his text, *Subculture* (1979). In his well-referenced discussion of punks, mods, and teddyboys, Hebdige identified a crucial relationship between youth subcultures, resistance, and style. In order to understand the significance of "style," readers must first become familiar with the concept of subculture, for in Hebdige's work style was a key expression of resistance to dominant social norms and practices by the subculture. Writing over 20 years later, Maira (2002) emphasized the earlier theorist's assertion that subculture was not just different from dominant culture, but it presumed an active resistance to dominant cultural practices via style. Hence, youth style continues to be a key aspect of the demarcation between the dominant and subculture.

Subculture, Style, and Resistance

Theorists from the Birmingham Centre for Contemporary Cultural Studies (est. 1964, closed 2002) pioneered the study of youth subcultural style and explained that youth contribute to a shared subculture when there is

> a set of social rituals which underpin their collective identity and define them as a "group" instead of a mere collection of individuals. They adopt and adapt material

objects—goods and possessions—and reorganise them into distinctive "styles" which express the collectivity of their being-as-a-group.

(Clarke, Hall, Jefferson, & Roberts, 1976, p. 47)

Illustrative of their theoretical symbiosis, other writers have articulated style and subculture as mutually defining concepts.

A subculture is understood as a shared aesthetic or preferred style, including dress, accessories, speech and demeanor. Subcultures grow out of multiple structures of inequality, though class has usually been analytically privileged, and are generally understood as simultaneously resistances to and reproductions of those inequities.

(Bettie, 2003, p. 45)

Quite simply, within subcultural theory, style is a key arena through which youth cultivate identity and seek visibility within a larger cultural context.

When theorizing subculture as a group that coheres around values opposi-tional to dominant ideologies, understanding how ideology operates is key to making sense of the relationship of resistance to style. Concisely, ideology works to make the connection between sign (object/practice) and meaning seem natural. The effect is that the constructedness of the relationship—and its potential for disruption—are then invisible. Hebdige (1979) noted that this relationship is secured within a broader system of power in which some groups have more access to the dissemination of ideas and the production of meaning associated with various signs than do other groups. Subcultural style, then, is predicated on inverting or disrupting the "naturalness" of the sign/object-meaning system established within dominant relations of power. Within youth studies, Hebdige and many cultural studies scholars have emphasized the mean-ings ascribed to symbolic cultural products and practices—music, clothing, and so on—and they read these expressions by young people as indicators of their resistance to cultural norms. Interestingly, Hebdige noted that, even as subcul-tures position themselves in opposition to dominant cultural practices and meanings, subcultures must draw on popular signs/style in ways that are recog-nized, but inverted. As Hebdige explained in *Subculture*, punks first had to be recognized as alienated before their style could be read as disruptive or threat-ening to conventional practices.

Youth style is negotiated within a terrain of struggle over meaning. Subcultural theory asserts that subcultures use commodities to construct their style, though the intended use of a commodity often is in opposition to the particular sub-culture's values. Yet, within a capitalist context, producers seek to recuperate subcultural style and draw it back into a mainstream framework of understand-ing. As Hebdige (1979) identified, one can see this in T-shirts that emphasize the likeness of Che Guevara or Malcolm X sold at popular department stores. In a similar vein, Disney gift shops selling T-shirts positioning the image of Mickey Mouse next to text about environmental consciousness is a co-optation of the environmental justice movement for the benefit of big business. Through appropriation of resistant styles in the interest of profit, the radical aspects of subcultural style effectively are depoliticized when drawn back into the mainstream. Malcolm Gladwell (1997) has written his *The New Yorker* article about "cool hunters," people who are hired by companies to seek out innovative, "edgy" styles from the cultural margins, to light the way for the next "new" look for youth. Because of the ongoing revision of the meaning of stylistic practices, the work of subcultures, similar to the mainstream, involves constant innovation of style that coheres to the values of the subculture.

While Hebdige's writing on subculture and style has reverberated through youth studies, subcultural theory emerged from a margin-center paradigm and did not account for different negotiations of identity within subculture. Much scholarship in the 1990s retained a mainstream-subculture paradigm, though scholarship increasingly has called attention to ways participants were variously positioned within and by subcultural practices. Lorraine Leblanc's study of gender and punk culture, *Pretty in Punk* (1999), is a notable contribution to the ethnographic literature on subcultural style. Published in 1999, Leblanc's study built on the groundbreaking feminist cultural studies work begun earlier by Angela McRobbie and Jenny Garber (1976). Together they offered a meaningful departure from early youth cultural studies, arguing that while subcultural theory explained an important relationship between symbolic resistance and youth subcultures, it failed to explore how groups were differently positioned and embued with authority within subcultures. Leblanc's study explored what a masculinist subculture offered female punks such that they would continue to endure the harassment from people outside the subculture as well as constricting expectations from inside the subculture. Her ethnographic research detailed the difficulties faced by girl punks and argued that they had a different investment in the subculture than did their male counterparts. A key implication of Leblanc's work was that, while resistance may be read by cultural theorists through the stylization of bodies within a particular subculture, the meaning of that resistance to subculture participants was not uniform.

An Emancipatory Politics of Style?

Hebdige and other cultural studies scholars speak about subcultures as involved in a war over meaning through style, yet the debate as to what is at stake in a politics of style continues to rage. Does the reorganization of signs in the interests of the disruption of dominant ideology and practices change inequitable political and economic structures? Does resistance at the level of identity change the material experiences of those engaged in the resistant cultural practices? Fundamentally, such scholars are asking whether resistance at the level of sign can be effective resistance. McRobbie warned against a kind of "cultural populism to a point at which anything which is consumed and is popular is also seen as opposition" (1994, p. 39). Maira (2002) noted that, while McRobbie supported a cultural studies analysis of symbols and rituals, she and other cultural studies scholars worried that "early subcultural theory often overinterpreted social action in terms of resistance and symbolic resolution" (p. 40).

Tricia Rose's (1994) work is relevant to this discussion of a liberatory politics of style. Her essay, "A Style Nobody Can Deal With," explored hip hop within the context of Black urban renewal. She demonstrated that the deindustrialized, decaying urban landscape of the 1970s and 1980s gave life and shape to the creative practices and styles of hip hop artists. Hip hop, she argued, became a community of renewal and resistant cultural practices that sustained and even enlivened communities of color living in conditions of poverty and shrinking social resources.

While Rose did not speak explicitly of hip hop artists as a subculture, in many ways hip hop was a subcultural movement of marginal and resistant actors who, in alignment with Hebdige's work, actively worked against mainstream cultural meanings to reveal fissures within dominant ideological assumptions. Yet Rose asserted that, beyond symbolic politics and hip hop artists' creative mixing, borrowing, and sharing of ideas and practices enlivened communities of color in the South Bronx in ways that created the conditions for political agency. If one understands Rose's study of hip hop to be a study of subcultural style, then hip hop artists were engaged in a politics of style that was linked to political and economic change.

Alvarez's book, *The Power of the Zoot* (2008), presents additional complexity to earlier theorizing about the connection between subcultures, style, and resistance. Writing about zoot culture among Black and Latino youth during World War II, Alvarez dislodged style from its dependence on subculture and located it more generally in the relationships of youth culture. Exploring style as a process and ongoing negotiation within and against mainstream cultural practices, Alvarez argued that both non-White male and female zoot style was a way to publicly demand attention and dignity in what was otherwise a dehumanizing cultural context of poverty and, for many Japanese Americans, internment.

Zoot style was excessive in a context where clothing, spending, and cultural practices more generally were conservative. Zoot style, including language, music, comfort with leisure, and careful attention to the self, located the zoot suiter in the public eye as counter to middle-class values and dominant understandings of patriotic practices. Offering a different analysis than Rose, Alvarez argued that, despite stylistic resistance, zoot suiters colluded with mainstream norms of World War II, with some contributing significantly to wartime effort in many ways. While zoot cultural practices were a politics of the body that represented efforts to define one's own style/body in ways that were nonnormative and resistant to all that normativity encapsulated, the consumer practices of zoot suiters entered money into the wartime economy, with zoot suiters often accepting low pay or employment with no growth possibilities in order to fund their style. Alvarez demonstrated that, though otherwise alienated from the dominant, White, middle-class culture, zoot suiters participated in the wartime economy on their own terms when other things (like job choice, etc.) were not under their control, and effectively blurring the neat borders separating subculture/mainstream culture.

Interrogating Subculture/Exploring Youth Styles

While the notion of subculture as a coherent, resistant group of youth who position themselves in relation to the mainstream has been disintegrating slowly over the last few decades, style remains fertile analytic ground for the exploration of how identity, affiliation, and resistance is crafted within youth culture. In Maira's ethnography, *Desis in the House* (2002), she importantly shifts from a rigid depiction of subculture to an exploration of scenes. She notes that scenes are spaces where ethnic identities are negotiated within and against dominant cultural ideologies, style is not understood simply in relation to class politics (see also Harris, 2008), and that racially dominant ideologies are contested and reorganized. Maira's study examined the meaning of style among second-generation Indian American youth in the Desi party scene in New York City in a manner that explored the liminal—betwixt and between—position of Desi youth. Examining the mediated gendered and racialized performance of identities, Maira's ethnography succeeded in disrupting the notion of a unified Desi subculture by discussing the regional borders created through affiliation with various musical forms and sounds.

While the notion of subculture has shifted and fairly dissipated over the past 30 years, attention to style within youth studies has remained robust. Explorations of style point us to the ways in which youth make sense of their experiences, negotiate identities, and move within and across various communities. Whereas early ideas of style were bounded by clearer delineations of subculture/dominant culture, Leblanc, Alvarez, and Maira's and others' work has highlighted the splintering within subcultural identities, alerting us to the constant negotiation that goes on within youth cultures around racial, ethnic, and gendered identities, and has drawn our attention to the spaces in which identities and resistance are crafted.

References

Alvarez, L. (2008). *The power of the zoot: Youth culture and resistance during World War II.* Berkeley: University of California Press.

Bettie, J. (2003). *Women without class: Girls, race and identity.* Berkeley: University of California Press.

Clarke, J., Hall, S., Jefferson, T., & Roberts, B. (1976). Subcultures, cultures and class: A theoretical overview. In S. Hall, & T. Jefferson (Eds.), *Resistance through rituals: Youth subcultures in post-war Britain* (pp. 9–79). London: Hutchinson & Co.

Gladwell, M. (1997, March 17). The coolhunt. *The New Yorker*, p. 78. Retrieved from http://www.newyorker.com/archive/1997/03/17/1997_03_17_078_TNY_CARDS_000378002

Harris, A. (2008). Introduction: Youth cultures and feminist politics. In A. Harris (Ed.), *New wave cultures* (pp. 1–13). New York: Taylor and Francis.

Hebdige, D. (1979). *Subculture: The meaning of style.* New York: Methuen.

Leblanc, L. (1999). *Pretty in punk: Girls' gender resistance in a boys' subculture.* New Brunswick, NJ: Rutgers University Press.

Maira, S. (2002). *Desis in the house.* Philadelphia: Temple University Press.

McRobbie, A. (1994). New times in cultural studies. In A. McRobbie (Ed.), *Postmodernism and popular culture* (pp. 24–43). London: Routledge.

McRobbie, A., & Garber, J. (1976). Girls and subculture. In S. Hall, & T. Jefferson (Eds.), *Resistance through rituals: Youth subcultures in post-war Britain* (pp. 209–229). London: Hutchinson & Co.

Rose, T. (1994). A style nobody can deal with: Politics, style and the post industrial city in hip hop. In A. Ross, & T. Rose (Eds.), *Microphone fiends* (pp. 71–88). New York: Routledge.

38

YOUTH VIOLENCE

Todd R. Ramlow

In the summer of 2010, Washington, DC was seemingly beset by youth violence, particularly on the securitized spaces of the DC Metro. In the breathless prose that has become common in news of youth violence, the *Washington Post* reported:

> It was bad enough when Kimberly Hay's family, riding the Metro to the Kennedy Center on Friday night to watch "Mary Poppins," saw three youths assault a terrified young rider reading "To Kill a Mockingbird." . . . But the brawl they witnessed on the way home several hours later, which involved at least 70 youths fighting each other in a frenzy, left Hay's nieces "freaked out" and the 43-year-old wary of riding the Metro in off-peak hours.
>
> (Strauss & Lucas, 2010)

Explicit in the newspaper's construction are the normative, regulatory, and moralizing discourses that characterize mass media spectacles and public sphere discussions of "youth violence." There is its ubiquity; twice in "several hours" are the Hay family witness to and affected by violent youth. There is the reconstruction of the normative spaces of violence; here the Metro is aligned with urban spaces where "violence," and particularly "youth violence," in the dominant cultural imaginary is endemic, while the Hays are aligned with the "safety" of suburban spaces. This proscription of the spaces of violence also participates in the reconstruction of the normative "victims" and "perpetrators" of violence; "urban" youth are the perpetrators, suburban youth and adults the victims.

For those of us familiar with the demographics of Washington, DC and the communities served by the variously color-coded lines of the Metro system, this story of the eruption of youth violence reiterates and reconsolidates the racial and class segregations of the DC metropolitan area, further elaborating in less explicit ways stereotypical understandings of the perpetrators and victims of youth violence. The "brawl" occurred at the Gallery Place/Chinatown station, a transfer point for the Red Line (which serves the predominantly White and privileged NW quadrant of DC) and the Green and Yellow Lines (which serve the predominantly Black and Latino working-class communities of the SE and NE quadrants of DC). The *Washington Post*'s reportage thus reinforces the racialization of spectacles of youth violence; while the youth involved in the "brawl" aren't explicitly marked, the reader will understand that the perpetrators of violence here are Black and underclass, either because of familiarity with local demographics, or because of the ways in which the descriptor "urban" has come to signify racially fraught encounters and contexts. The *Washington Post* makes this distinction clearer: "The melee highlights the difficulties authorities have in dealing with teen violence and how it can encroach on a Metro system that routinely carries commuters, families, tourists and late-night revelers." Violent teens are directly juxtaposed to the normal, normative, and desirable Metro riders and are identified as subjects who must be "dealt" with through disciplinary management and surveillance. In fact, in order to "manage" the threat of youth violence, the owners of the Gallery Place commercial strip that sits atop the Metro station installed an "antiloitering" "Mosquito" device at the subway entrances that omits a high pitched noise that either can only be heard by or that disproportionately affects teens (Prince of Petworth, 2010).[1]

The *Washington Post*'s reportage is typical of the "moral panics" regularly constructed in mass media and public sphere discourses over the threat posed by violent youth to normative social orders. In his foundational study *Folk Devils and Moral Panics*, Stanley Cohen (2002) identified the "three elements needed for the construction of a successful moral panic." First, a "suitable enemy" must be identified; one that is "easily denounced" and with little social position or power. Second, a "suitable victim" must be similarly identified; "someone who could have been and one day could be anybody." And third, there must be a "common-sense" consensus that the actions performed or beliefs expressed have become or may become common unless "something is done" (p. xi). In *Policing the Crisis: Mugging, the State, and Law and Order*, Hall, Critcher, Jefferson, Clark, and Roberts (1978) concur, asserting that moral panics are "a reaction by the control agencies and the media to the *perceived or symbolic* threat to society" (p. 29).

Figures of youth and acts of youth violence are particularly impacted sites around which such moral panics are constructed and circulated. As minors, youth are positioned (morally, materially, legally) as having few or no civil rights and little access to social or political power. Youth, their beliefs, and (violent) actions are easily juxtaposed to an imagined normative citizenry, the values and social organizations of which are threatened by "immature" youth who have not fully learned or might directly reject the norms of the dominant social order. Critical scholarly analyses over the course of the development of the field of youth studies have demonstrated how youth and in particular youth violence are perennially central to moral panics. *Folk Devils and Moral Panics* (Cohen, 2002) takes the "mod" and "rocker" subcultures of Great Britain in the late 1960s as exemplary, while *Policing the Crisis* (Hall et al., 1978) locates the object of moral panic in Great Britain in the violent assaults perpetrated by young, underprivileged Black men in the early 1970s. Similarly, Dick Hebdige's *Subculture: The Meaning of Style* (1993) examines the "threat" of punk subcultures in late-1970s London, and Charles Acland, in *Youth, Murder, Spectacle: The Cultural Politics of "Youth in Crisis"* (1995), draws attention to a wide-ranging set of mass-mediated panics over violent and apathetic youth in the United States in the 1980s. As Hall et al. (1978) assert, there is a "succession of 'moral panics' focused on the deviance and anti-social behavior of youth which spiral through the whole post-war period" (p. 182), and which continues today.

This "succession" demonstrates that, rather than a series of discrete or thinly connected moral panics, what we have is a perpetual crisis of youth and youth violence constructed and circulated in the interest of maintaining normative social orders and against the material and civil rights interests of youth. The public dimension of social anxieties over "youth violence" suggests that rather than narrowly focus on sociological theories of "moral panics" we might more productively consider the cultural politics of "youth violence" through the lens of Guy Debord's "society of the spectacle." In *Comments on the Society of the Spectacle* (1998), Debord assigns the role of the spectacularization of society to mass media. Debord argues that "the spectacle would be nothing other than the excesses of the mediatic" (p. 6), by which he means the proliferation and infiltration of mass media into every aspect of our lives. RETORT (2005) further argues that the society of the spectacle represents the "colonization of everyday life" by the interests, values, and protocols of Capital, and they examine the "means modern societies have at their disposal . . . to subject the texture of day-to-day living to a constant barrage of images, instructions, [and] slogans" (pp. 19–20) that reproduce the hegemony of the ruling order.

Within the society of the spectacle is a constant barrage of images, instructions, and slogans about the "threat" of violent youth. Of course, concern over youth violence is never about any broad-based interest in real youth of whatever demographic, their lives, or any structural transformation of the conditions of their oppression and exploitation. As Hall et al. (1978) assert, "these panics are about other things than crime, per se" (p. vii).

The figure of youth violence in the society of the spectacle should be read as a cipher for "other" anxieties that arise in relation to changing norms and forms of social life, and perceived "threats" to the perpetuation of dominant class power. In their discussion of the similar metaphorical function of representations of disability, David T. Mitchell and Sharon L. Snyder (2000) argue that in literature (and we can add mass media and popular culture here) disability is circumscribed by "overheated symbolic imagery" (p. 16) in which what is at stake in such representation is hardly if ever about disability rights, enfranchisement, or people with disabilities themselves. Like representations of youth and youth violence, disability representations always gesture to other anxieties about social and bodily normativity. And yet, such representations have direct effects on the lives of people with disabilities: "Literature serves up disability as a repressed deviation from cultural imperatives of normativity, while disabled populations suffer the consequences of representational association with deviance and recalcitrant corporeal differences" (Mitchell & Snyder, 2000, p. 8).

We can consider spectacles of youth violence in relation to this history of disability representation, as violent youth are excoriated in public sphere discourses that express anxieties over the threatened or perceived failure of "cultural imperatives [to] normativity" that have little to do with the real lives and structural positions of populations of youth, even while those youth "suffer the consequences" for their perceived challenge to the hegemony of the dominant social order.

The perpetual crisis of youth violence in the society of the spectacle is both strikingly static in its representations and eminently flexible in how "youth violence" figures other social and political concerns. The spectacle is static insofar as it is always some X group of youth and their violent actions that threatens the safety, security, and normality of a fantasized mainstream culture. The spectacle of youth violence is at the same time flexible enough to encompass a wide range of perceived threats to cultural norms.

One recent example of the flexibility of the spectacle of youth violence has been cultural hand-wringing over the "rise" in girl youth violence. The "truth" of this current crisis of girl youth violence is attested to throughout the mediascape of the society of the spectacle. It can be found in books like James Garbarino's *See Jane Hit: Why Girls Are Growing More Violent and What We Can Do About It* (2007) and Deborah Prothrow-Stith and Howard R. Spivak's *Sugar and Spice and No Longer Nice: How We Can Stop Girls' Violence* (2006), in the informational and educational materials on "girl violence" disseminated over the internet by public interest organizations like Keys to Safer Schools (n.d.), and in newspaper headlines like this one from the *Orlando Sentinel*: "All-Girl Gang Gaining Ground in Daytona, Authorities Warn" (Taylor, 2009).

Even when mainstream media outlets like *Good Morning America* (*GMA*) challenge the perception that girl youth violence is increasing, and acknowledge the role of mass media in producing social anxieties over girl violence, their reporting often reproduces the symptom they reject. *GMA*'s report from April 10, 2008, "Mean Girls' Fights Haven't Increased Teen Violence" (Chang, Kazdin, Hagan, & Ibanga), opens with a rejection by the Centers for Disease Control and Prevention (CDC) of an increase in teen violence; in fact, the CDC reports that teen violence has decreased over the past 10 years. Nonetheless, immediately afterward, *GMA* rehashes a litany of stories from "violent" girls that leave the viewer with the perception that the CDC is mistaken, that girls are indeed increasingly violent, and "we" must do something about it. If we consider this "rise" of girl violence in relation to concurrent spectacles over the sexualization and promiscuity of young girls, we can see how both crises are connected to and expressive of dominant cultural anxieties about changing gender and sexual norms. Media spectacles over young girls' violence and promiscuity go hand in hand with the disciplinary regulation of gender and sexuality under neoliberalism that Lisa Duggan (2003) has described as a simultaneous hetero-and-homo-normalization (p. 50).

If the ubiquity, consistency, and flexibility of "crises" of youth violence are primarily about shoring up of dominant social orders, class privilege, and power, and only marginally about the material realities facing specific groups of youth, even while such spectacles have directly repressive effects on the lives of youth, how might the field of youth studies proceed in its engagement with spectacles of "youth violence"? One way, as I have tried to do here, is to unpack the dominant cultural norms and values that are reasserted in the spectacle of youth violence. That is to say, we must look beyond the "youth" of youth violence to see other cultural politics at work. In this way we might challenge the hegemony of normative social orders by demonstrating how the attempt is made to reassert dominant class power through the demonization of youth, and at the same time afford the real youths whose lives are directly affected by such public anxieties a break from their perpetual exploitation by and subordination within our society of the youth violence spectacle.

Note

1   The antidevice did not, thankfully, stay in place for long, and on October 6, 2010, Theresa Vargas reported in the *Washington Post* that the device was silenced after the National Youth Rights Association challenged its use as age discrimination.

References

Acland, C. (1995). *Youth, murder, spectacle: The cultural politics of "youth in crisis."* Boulder, CO: Westview Press.

Chang, J., Kazdin, C., Hagan, K., & Ibanga, I. (2008, April 10). Mean girls' fights haven't increased teen violence: Bullies use internet as way of winning bragging rights for exploits. *Good Morning America*. New York: ABC.

Cohen, S. (2002). *Folk devils and moral panics* (3rd ed.). New York: Routledge.

Debord, G. (1998). *Comments on the society of the spectacle*. London: Verso.

Duggan, L. (2003). *The twilight of equality? Neoliberalism, cultural politics, and the attack on democracy*. Boston: Beacon Press.

Garbarino, J. (2007). *See Jane hit: Why girls are growing more violent and what we can do about it*. New York: Penguin.

Hall, S., Critcher, C., Jefferson, T., Clark, J., & Roberts, B. (1978). *Policing the crisis: Mugging, the state, and law and order*. New York: Palgrave Macmillan.

Hebdige, D. (1993). *Subculture: The meaning of style*. New York: Routledge.

Keys to Safer Schools. (n.d.). Violence among teen girls on the increase. Retrieved from http://www.keystosaferschools.com/girlviolence.htm

Mitchell, D., & Snyder, S. (2000). *Narrative prosthesis: Disability and the dependencies of discourse*. Ann Arbor: University of Michigan Press.

Prince of Petworth. (2010, August 30). Dear PoP: Anti-teen noise weapon hits DC at Chinatown Metro [Web log comment]. Retrieved from http://www.princeofpetworth. com/2010/08/dear-pop-noise-intimidation-outside-chinatown-metro-station/

Prothrow-Stith, D., & Spivak, H. (2006). *Sugar and spice and no longer nice: How we can stop girls' violence*. San Francisco: Jossey-Bass.

RETORT (Boal, I., Clark, T. J., Matthews, J., & Watts, M.). (2005). *Afflicted powers: Capital and spectacle in a new age of war*. London: Verso.

Strauss, V., & Lucas, P. (2010, August 9). Amid Metro brawl, family's night out turns into "pandemonium." *Washington Post*. Retrieved from http://www.washingtonpost.com/wp-dyn/content/article/2010/08/08/AR2010080802755.html

Taylor, G. (2009, August 16). All-girl gang gaining ground in Daytona, authorities warn. *Orlando Sentinel*. Retrieved from http://articles.orlandosentinel.com/2009-08-16/news/girl_1_chitwood-girl-gang-gang-members

Vargas, T. (2010, October 6). "Mosquito" noisemaker silenced in Chinatown after youth rights group complains. *Washington Post*. Retrieved from http://www.washingtonpost.com/wp-dyn/content/article/2010/10/06/AR2010100602792.html

SECTION VII

Enchantment

Nancy Lesko and Susan Talburt

> Ideologies happen. Power snaps into place. Structures grow entrenched. Identities take place. Ways of knowing become habitual at the drop of a hat. *But it's ordinary affects that give things the quality of a **some**thing to inhabit and animate.*
>
> (Stewart, 2007, p. 15; emphasis added)

Kathleen Stewart's ideas orient us toward the *ordinary affects* at work in youth studies that help make particular kinds and methods of research and activism, as well as particular kinds of narratives and portraits of youth, into *some*thing desirable. Feelings shape a field of study and members' engagement, as do classic texts and must-read theoretical accounts. Thus we ask, toward what feelings does research on youth direct us? And toward what research on youth do feelings direct us? In exploring the ordinary feelings toward which we are directed, we also draw on the idea of "proper pleasures" as a way of deconstructing normative conventions. Erica McWilliam (1999) interrogates the contingent pleasures of teaching and claims that historically recorded pleasures are no longer intelligible. Proper pleasures in youth studies might include the voyeuristic thrill of "being one of them" and the satisfaction of "helping" young people with an insider's knowledge about school, health, internet use, or the world of work. Proper pleasures undoubtedly include smirks about the clownish, freaky, or exotic aspects of watching and interacting with youth (Lesko, 2001; Ramlow, 2005). Such pleasures are taken along the way of narrative accounts that emphasize subcultural agency, structural barriers, and cultural creativity, among others.

Narrative pleasures are produced through an interplay of past–present–future, in which

> Fantasies about the future are always, at least in part, projections, images, hopes, and horrors extrapolated from the present, though not simply from the present situation but from its cultural imaginary, its self representation, its own latencies or virtualities. … [T]hese fantasies represent neuralgic points of present investment and anxiety, loci of intense vulnerability, anxiety, or optimism.
>
> (Grosz, 2001, p. 44)

Where we feel we are now keeps us looking backward and forward in order to imagine *some*thing good for youth and society. Consider, for example, a recent term to describe one of the latest generations of youth, "millennials." Hailing them as "America's next great generation," Howe and Strauss (2000) proclaimed a decade ago:

> The Millennials, born in or after 1982, . . . are unlike any other youth generation in living memory. They are more numerous, more affluent, better educated, and more ethnically diverse. More important, they are beginning to manifest a wide array of positive social habits that older Americans no longer associate with youth, including a new focus on teamwork, achievement, modesty, and good conduct. Only a few years from now, this can-do youth revolution will overwhelm cynics and pessimists. Over the next decade, the Millennial generation will entirely recast the image of youth from downbeat and alienated to upbeat and engaged—with potentially seismic consequences for America.
>
> (p. 4)

We are waiting.

Toward What Feelings Does Research on Youth Direct Us?

Pan-Optimism

Since youth are by definition about the future and becoming, they are co-constructed with progress and positive development. At a feeling level, we emphasize the "pan-optimism" of studies of youth, the desire to feel good about the outcomes of youth projects and studies. Pan-optimism involves a belief in the power of correct knowledge, rationally implemented, to effect desired outcomes and fantasizes escaping loss and other bad feelings, and avoiding rupture or misrecognition (Berlant & Edelman, 2009). Vulnerabilities of youth and the "in between" years may be acknowledged, but they can be avoided by following expert dictates. Courses on youth studies typically describe problems, conflicts, and inequalities, which are followed by articles offering theories and practical interventions that enable "corrections," which end the course on an upbeat note. Pan-optimism merges a belief in the power of correct knowledge (arrived at using innovative methodologies, youth participation, youth-centric epistemologies, etc.) being applied energetically and sensitively to problems to produce proper sociality, happiness, and orderliness (Berlant & Edelman, 2009). Pan-optimism foresees good outcomes of research and activism and directs adults to adopt the same can-do attitude they desire in youth. Youth are expected to be upbeat, forward-looking, and optimistic, even though such a posture may enhance their surveillance by educators and family members (Miyazawa, 2010), who put into place mechanisms (such as test prep or leadership academies) to ensure the "right behavior" for success. Pan-optimism employs different registers, from religious "redemptions" to neoliberal "turnarounds" of low-performing, typically urban, schools to "safe spaces" for vulnerable youth populations. Shadowed by nostalgia, pan-optimism relies on stable knowledge to secure a stable future.

Stable Knowledge

Knowledge of youth natures and youth worlds circulate as confident characterizations in the media, among teachers, in research, in youth organizing, and among parents. Whether the focus is new—teens' emotional brains or cyber-bullying—or old—raging hormones or peer pressures—such phrases, endlessly repeated, have solidified into stable knowledge spoken about with assurance, sometimes even by young people themselves. Valerie Walkerdine's (1990) criticism that context is generally pasted on to studies of children and youth remains current; sociohistorical and political knowledge of youth that might destabilize these certainties is generally a last thought. Furthermore, the history and politics of the production of knowledge about youth are almost never described, analyzed, or interrogated. Youth studies knowledge thereby performs with certainty in a spatiotemporal abstraction of "here-today." The problems are always current and pressing: youth are troubled (e.g., by transitions, labor markets, limited futures); youth are influenced by popular culture and media (with issues for education, literacy, higher education); youth have identity issues (unrealistic expectations, nonacademic, too-creative, low self-esteem); or young people seem headed toward bad citizenry (political apathy, sexual excess, freaks, or gangstas). The young are never okay; and youth studies contributes to such understandings, positioning its expertise as both necessitated by problems in the world and in youths' lives and as responsive to those situations. Gay-bullying, adolescent brains, slum dogs—each crafty new phrase worries, intoxicates, and simultaneously offers assurances (at minimum that "we" are no longer "youth").

Confident characterizations suggest "an unrelenting epistemological will to power" (Puar, 2007, p. 216), and also invoke a nostalgia for "simpler" times in the quality of family relations, in language, meaning, and authority (Boym, 2001; Gilbert, 2004). The nostalgia embedded in circulations of stable knowledge reflects cultural desires for an original meaning to pass on, or a transmission of parental and institutional norms to the next generation, to ensure a particular future. Stuart Hall (1997) claims that commonsense categories, ones that are irrefutably *visible*, as are youth's development, "otherness," and precariousness, allow us to sleep at night. We are comforted because we know how to think of youth (in psychological, developmental, or sociological terms), to foreground their strangeness and moodiness, and to want to help them. If modernity involves "life lived in fragments," asserting a stable, unchanging view of knowing and knowledge refuses the loss of universal, abstract meanings (Pickering & Keightley, 2006, pp. 923–924); it is a perpetually staged "back to the future." This future regulates social and political relations in the present through what Edelman (2004) calls "reproductive futurism," which always promises the realization of wholeness, meaning, and identity through the development of the child. But this future is perpetually deferred.

Impossible Fictions

Our use of the term "impossible fiction" invokes the understanding that unfeasible narratives, say of a single teacher attending to and nurturing the unique, perfect development of each child/student (Walkerdine, 1990), are repeated and fueled by theoretical supports as well as by ordinary feelings to be *some*thing recognizable, a "good teacher." Such impossible fictions are also maintained by nostalgic ideas of classrooms, reading, and books, as well as by reform platforms that already know what is to come (Rajchman, 2000, p. 6).

Narrative genres in youth studies are either stories of equal opportunity (attempted, reached, or denied), youth as social problems, youth as redeemable, or youth as critical transformers (overcoming adversity and seizing opportunities). Such narrative genres were well established at the beginnings of mass public schooling, juvenile justice, and playground reforms (Lesko, 2001). Mass-mediated images of youth, such as those in classic teenpics of the 1950s, *Rebel Without a Cause* and *Blackboard Jungle*, consolidated the narratives with soundtracks, dialogue, and youthful Hollywood stars along with renewed panic over youth (Bulman, 2005; Gilbert, 1986).

Narrative pleasures inhere in each of the genres' promise of *some*thing. For example, youth studies researchers and activists take pleasure in discovering agency that is often invisible to adults, whether detailing the young girl's resistance to hyperfeminine uses of Barbie (Rand, 1995) or locating new sites of agency, such as the rural gay youth empowered to develop a gay identity and community through internet contact. This may be a search for agency that adults wish they had possessed as young people themselves, a satisfaction of gaining an "insider's view" of "subversive moments" that outsiders don't quite grasp, or a reliving of one's own youthful resistances (see Biklen, 2007, on adult memory in youth studies).

The thrill of creating knowledge that has not been previously identified by experts spatializes young people as existing in another, unknown world. These narrative pleasures rely on boundary-breaking efforts in which adults learn to enter a new space to connect with youthful "others," seeing, hearing, or documenting new voices, perspectives, and practices. Researchers romance the self as the one who will interpret or represent young people better by reflecting on "the role of adult researcher as they work to gain access to youth worlds, break through 'fronts,' and develop meaningful rapport" (Best, 2007, p. 8). Whether they narrate themselves as crossing a "great Gulf" (Raby, 2007, p. 39), securing "entry to peer cultures" (Hadley, 2007, p. 160), or gaining "access to previously marginalized cultures" (Driver, 2007, p. 29), researchers imagine they can create previously undisclosed insights into youth. One tactic for minimizing this "distance" is that of researchers adopting "a least adult role" (Best, 2007; Hadley, 2007), or acting as much like one of the natives as possible in order to lessen adult status and power. These fantasies of creating more intimate knowledge obscure the very power relations they pretend to undo, imagining that youth "overcome their objectified status" (Best, 2007, p. 15) through authentic representation created by ever-more-sensitive researchers.

Researchers' fantasies of self-redemption via assisting youth directly or representing young people's ideas and voices sympathetically also "stick" (Ahmed, 2004b) to youth studies materials, particularly those that claim to move from adult- to youth-centered research (e.g., Best, 2007; Leonard, 2007). These are roving, sticky feelings of wanting youth to become like "us," and imagining ourselves as "them." Researchers imagine blurring "boundaries between researcher and researched" (Best, 2007, p. 14) as research relationships create adult–youth bonds that offer intergenerational support, advocates, or allies (Driver, 2007). A sticky pleasure inheres in youth studies researchers' optimism that they can "provide children with the tools to realize their own political agendas or to participate in the production of their own culture" (Jenkins, 1998, p. 30) or construct "research that empowers youth and children to find ways to improve the conditions under which their lives unfold" (Best, 2007, p. 9). Research that brings adults and youth together promises better researchers, better research, and better youth. In particular, participatory, action, and collaborative genres of research, which "get close," imagine that "insider youth researchers" serve as "important sounding boards" (p. 14) or "native anthropologists" (p. 16). This process promotes youths' abilities to represent themselves, to become civically engaged, or to become "social agents" (Raby, 2007, p. 54), *and* redeems the researchers by overcoming "the disappointment of academics longing for theories to reinvigorate our own sense of political efficacy" (Maira & Soep, 2005, p. xxxi).

These impossible fictions determine the field of youth studies and what kinds of ideas, logic, and initiatives are intelligible. Even though adults want to help, their emotional attachments to "problem kids" and redemptive futures, as well as their unwillingness to consider the relative power and position of themselves and young people, shape and constrain new research and projects (Alonso, Anderson, Su, & Theoharis, 2009).

Affective Economies of Youth Studies

Emotions do not reside in persons/objects nor in the social world exclusively, nor are they drives or automatic responses. Following Sara Ahmed, we consider emotions relationally, as "affective economies" in which the accumulation of affective value (or intensification of feeling) is an effect of the circulation of objects and signs. "Emotion does its work by 'reading' the object" (Ahmed, 2004b, p. 13). For example, when a journalist claims "the nation mourns," the nation becomes a shared "object of feeling" through the orientation that is taken toward it. Tracking how words for feeling (mourn) and objects of feeling (nation) circulate and generate effects means to examine how "they move, stick, and slide" (p. 13). Especially intriguing is Ahmed's metaphor that emotions are sticky. "Stickiness is an effect of the histories of contact between bodies, objects, and signs" (p. 90). Objects, people, narratives, and a whole host of other signs "amass affective associations that embody and stand for the object" (Micciche, 2007, p. 27). For example, a Hummer accumulates affective valuations that "transform the car into an object of disgust and wildly immoral excess . . . and an object synonymous with American-inflected feelings linked to liberty, freedom, affluence, and choice" (p. 27). Circulating and sticking to objects such as youth through affective economies, "emotions *do things*, and they align individuals with communities . . . through the very intensity of their attachments" (Ahmed, 2004a, 119).

In our thinking about the affective economies of youth studies, we also emphasize the spatial dimension of performatives and speech acts that circulate sticky emotions. J. L. Austin's example of "I dare you" as a speech act ostensibly involves a singular first and a singular second person; however, it "effactually depends on the tacit demarcation of the space of a third-person plural, a 'they' of witness—whether or not literally present" (Sedgwick, 2003, p. 69). The "they of witness" constitutes the membership of youth studies and indicates how stories implicate us as writers, readers, and researchers. The circulation of sticky objects and signs, such as "subcultural resistance," "at-risk youth," "youth civic engagement," or "girl power," creates a community—of responsible, agentic, and hopeful citizens. We use two iconic films about the problems of youth, *Blackboard Jungle* and *Born into Brothels*, to trace the sticky emotions that circulate and how witnesses are likely to be enchanted by and stuck to particular representations, narratives, and emotions.

Blackboard Jungle (Berman & Brookes, 1955) tells the story of a White teacher, Mr. Dadier, just out of the Navy and hired by an all-male, inner-city high school, who struggles to wrest the allegiance of a Black student, "a potential leader," away from an interracial gang of juvenile delinquents led by an Irish boy. The film aims to "provide adults with the social knowledge they require in order to tackle the problem of juvenile delinquency effectively" (Medovoi, 1997, p. 144). Mr. Dadier at one point turns down a job offer at an all-White, orderly, suburban school because "his duty" directs him to help his inner-city students. The film recruits witnesses to the moral economy of redeemable and unredeemable youth and to the triumphant "good teacher" who leads his non-White students to cross-identify with his masculinity, whiteness, and maturity. The unredeemable Irish boy, Artie West, terrorizes Dadier's wife, is unpatriotic, and believes that crime does pay. The White hero-teacher succeeds in separating Artie from the rest of the redeemable boys. Multiracial, inner-city education can succeed when young committed teachers redouble their efforts and non-White students come to accept adults' wisdom, values, and authority.

The affective economy of *Blackboard* recruits viewers as witnesses of the rightness of the school order, of Mr. Dadier's goodness, and of the weakness of the other teachers and administrators. We witness the moral economy and invest Mr. Dadier with our fantasies of being simultaneously loved and feared, and compassionate and tough, and in his rescue of inner-city young men.

Born into Brothels (Briski & Kauffman, 2004) exemplifies the rescue narrative that creates authentic youth and unique individual youths from Brown masses, who have voice and the ability to name and photograph their world. The film, which won the 2005 Academy Award for Best Documentary Feature, raises adult and international consciousness through knowledge, a recognizable narrative, and emotionally wrenching scenes. The back of its DVD case describes the following:

> A tribute to the resiliency of childhood and the restorative power of art, *Born into brothels* is a portrait of several unforgettable children who live in Calcutta's red light district, where their mothers work as prostitutes. Spurred by the kids' fascination with her camera, Zana Briski, a New York-based photographer living in the brothels and documenting life there, decides to teach them photography. As they begin to look at and record their world through new eyes, the kids, who society refused to recognize, awaken for the first time to their own talents and sense of worth. Filmmakers Ross Kauffman and Zana Briski capture the way in which beauty can be found in even the seemingly bleakest and most hopeless of places, and how art and education can empower children to transform their lives.

Born into Brothels thus "reiterate[s] a very old story of heroic white westerners saving poor brown children, who don't know any better than to persist in their dead-end lives" (Shah, 2005, para. 1). The film also spins a recognizable tale about prostitution, "a tale in which prostitution and violence are synonymous, sex workers are unfit parents, and the only hope for children living in red light districts with their families is to be taken away from them by non-sex worker adults, who necessarily know better" (para. 1). The film omits the history of Indian sex workers' own struggles to organize for political power. Indian children/youth have been the object of unprecedented policy attention as their lives have been cast into "categories of problems such as 'child labour,' 'street children' and 'child prostitution' from which real, living children may seem quite impossible to extricate" (Nieuwenhuys, 2009, p. 147). The stories of Indian children/youth allude to the inadequacy of government, the ignorance of parents, the callousness of the public, and the lack of educational opportunities, and they construct Indian society as lacking in a fully developed conception of childhood (Nieuwenhuys, 2009).

The film's doubled foci of helping youth and enlightening adults portrays the filmmaker/activist as humanitarian and the children's lives as hopeless without her help (Smith, 2009). Viewers bear witness to "'incorrect' images of children" lacking presumed "basic necessities of life" (p. 163), a witnessing that confirms the construction of a humanitarian space, which culminates in a Sotheby's auction of the children's photos and Amnesty International's use of them in its 2003 calendar.

In both of these films, young people become "shared objects of feeling" in that the orientation taken toward youth reads them as needy, as not knowing any better, and as needing help if disaster is to be avoided. There is also a sense of danger in the portrayal of youth, for they may subvert society through crime or by perpetuating the status quo. The agentic adults—a White teacher and a White photographer—collect knowledge about the youths' lives, persist in their goals to educate them, and refuse to give up hope, as other adults have done.

The perilous circumstances, of a mixed-race inner-city school in the 1950s and of Calcutta's brothels in 2000, help *stick* these youth to responsible-and-courageous adult witnesses who are able to "penetrat[e] the children's physical space" (Smith, 2009, p. 162). The intentions of the films to educate and incite viewers recruit and revive the community of youth studies. Young people are "othered," yet redeemable; hope and responsibility stick to us as receptive, sympathetic viewers–witnesses.

Toward a Different Youth Studies Vocabulary of Affect, Moving, Becoming

Youth as an Assemblage

If youth are constituted by the circulation of emotions that stick or adhere to figures such that "emotions *involve* subjects and objects, but without residing positively within them" (Ahmed, 2004a, p. 119), who are the youth of youth studies? Rather than figures of a discrete time and space and embodiment, we might consider youth as an assemblage. Assemblages "allow us to attune to movements, intensities, emotions, energies, affectivities, and textures as they inhabit events, spatiality, and corporealities" (Puar, 2007, p. 215). Assemblages are considered crucial conceptual tools for social formations in transition in order to "acknowledge and comprehend power beyond disciplinary regulatory models," where "particles, and not parts, recombine, where forces, and not categories, clash" (p. 215).

Deleuze and Guattari (1987) conceptualize assemblages as multiplicities rather than singular, enclosed entities, subjects, or objects that have fixed identities. Although forces can make an assemblage appear as "a kind of organism, or signifying totality, or determination attributable to a subject," an assemblage does not bear its own meaning, but is comprised of and connects with other assemblages, intensities, forces, and convergences (p. 4). As Deleuze and Guattari explain, the idea of assemblage does away with divisions between such fields as "reality" (the world), representation (the book), and subjectivity (the author) (p. 23). We extrapolate these terms to erase strict divisions between youth, youth studies, and researchers to suggest that each of these fields connects with the others with varying intensities, assembling and reassembling in such a way as to sometimes appear to create something stable and sometimes to become something else. Youth as assemblage, then, is a multidimensional *some*thing that is in motion: "Assemblage, in its debt to ontology and its espousal of what cannot be known, seen, or heard, or has yet to be known, seen, or heard, allows for becoming beyond or without being" (Puar, 2007, p. 216). In other words, youth need not stay "stuck."

Stewart's (2007) "thrown togetherness" echoes many aspects of assemblage but places it in the realm of the ordinary rather than a theoretical tool:

> The ordinary throws itself together out of forms, flows, powers, pleasures, encounters, distractions, drudgery, denials, practical solutions, shape-shifting forms of violence,

daydreams, and opportunities lost or found. Or it falters, fails. But either way we feel its pull.

(p. 29)

"Vermontness," for example, exists in "the differences and repetitions of a grab bag of qualities and technologies that can be thrown together into an event and a sensation. . . . It is fall colors, maple syrup, tourist brochures, calendars, snow, country stores; liberalism and yet the fight over gay marriage; racial homogeneity and yet everywhere white lesbian couples with babies of color" (p. 30). Vermontness is a list of incommensurate yet mapped elements that throws itself together into something. Again. Through a fast sensory relay that is different each time yet "the repetition leaves a residue like a track or a habit" (p. 30).

Youth as thrown togetherness might include acne, fast-moving limbs, sexual jokes, cruelty, idealism, too big, too small, awkwardness, laughter, threatening, familiar, physical ease, and disinterest. "Youth-ness" sometimes throws itself together and sometimes fails. These failures may constitute new connections, new assemblages.

Backward Futures

"Backwardness means many things here: shyness, ambivalence, failure, melancholia, loneliness, regression, victimhood, heartbreak, antimodernism, immaturity, self-hatred, despair, shame" (Love, 2007, p. 146). Heather Love is trying to "imagine a future apart from the reproductive imperative, optimism, and the promise of redemption," a "backward future" (p. 147). Without redemptive and optimistic fantasies, how might adults know, represent, and relate to youth?

Bad feelings are part of such a backward future. Bad feelings include uncertainties, mistakes, misrecognitions, messiness, and knowledge without "next steps" or "best practices." Bad feelings involve "unactionable conclusions," knowledge without discrete deliverables, vulnerabilities, unfamiliar longings, doubts, anxieties, and regrets. Sara Ahmed claims that happiness (and other good feelings, such as a sense of certainty) "direct" us to long for certain emotional states and outcomes and to shrink back from surprise, mistakes, loss, and other bad feelings. Being directed toward happiness, certainty, and safety constrains "our ability to long in open-ended ways" (Ahmed, 2008b). Thus, the intentional or "end orientated" (Ahmed, 2008a, p. 11) nature of happiness and of narratives of success and redemption constrains our knowledge and affective imaginaries and abilities.

What feelings and pleasures might be invoked, for example, by noncelebratory stories of youth? What affective economies might develop around nonderogated youth lives? What kinds of feelings might stick to youth as thrown togetherness, and could different "tracks or habits" be carved out and new assemblages formed? If youth scholars and activists are uncertain or ambivalent or ashamed by knowledge of youth, what kinds of "nows" might be possible?

Sedgwick (2003) claims that it is likely only in the middle ground, in the local, that theory and practice can come together in effective ways. She invokes the location "beside" for readers seeking a broader range of affects including surprise, misrecognition, and mistakes. If youth studies scholars and activists are *beside* youth, rather than above or ahead, positions named as mature, powerful, developed, and redeeming/enforcing, what objects might we read and with what kinds of affects?

Can research, youth studies, and youth who do not fit an agentic, optimistic, can-do world have a place in "our" future? What would we see, represent, or research if we were not remembering an imagined past or curing the present via the future? Our thinking is that a "backward future" offers a way of proceeding in the world and with youth "for those who want to *do* something with respect to new uncommon forces, which we don't quite grasp, who have a certain taste for the unknown, for what is not already determined by history or society" (Rajchman, 2000, p. 6). Such experimentation may allow for more interesting futures.

References

Ahmed, S. (2004a). Affective economies. *Social Text, 22,* 117–139.
Ahmed, S. (2004b). *The cultural politics of emotion.* New York: Routledge.
Ahmed, S. (2008a). Sociable happiness. *Emotion, Space, and Society, 1,* 10–13.
Ahmed, S. (2008b). *On being directed by happiness.* Lecture presented at Center for Gender & Sexuality Studies, New York University, New York.
Alonso, G., Anderson, N. S., Su, C., & Theoharis, J. (2009). *Our schools suck: Students talk back to a segregated nation on the failures of urban education.* New York: New York University Press.
Berlant, L., & Edelman, L. (2009). *Sex without optimism.* Lecture presented at Rethinking Sex: Gender and Sexuality Studies State of the Field Conference, University of Pennsylvania, Philadelphia, Pennsylvania.
Berman, P. S. (Producer), & Brooks, R. (Director). (1955). *Blackboard jungle* [Motion picture]. United States: Metro-Goldwyn-Mayer.
Best, A. L. (2007). Introduction. In A. L. Best (Ed.), *Representing youth: Methodological issues in critical youth studies* (pp. 1–36). New York: New York University Press.
Biklen, S. K. (2007). Trouble on memory lane: Adults and self-retrospection in researching youth. In A. L. Best (Ed.), *Representing youth: Methodological issues in critical youth studies* (pp. 251–268). New York: New York University Press.
Boym, S. (2001). *The future of nostalgia.* New York: Basic Books.
Briski, Z., & Kauffman, R. (Producers & Directors). (2004). *Born into brothels: Calcutta's red light kids* [Motion picture]. United States: Red Light Films.
Bulman, R. C. (2005). *Hollywood goes to high school: Cinema, schools, and American culture.* New York: Worth.
Deleuze, G., & Guattari, F. (1987). *A thousand plateaus: Capitalism and schizophrenia* (B. Massumi, Trans.). Minneapolis: University of Minnesota Press.
Driver, S. (2007). *Queer girls and popular culture: Reading, resisting, and creating media.* New York: Peter Lang.
Edelman, L. (2004). *No future: Queer theory and the death drive.* Durham, NC: Duke University Press.
Gilbert, J. (2004). Between sexuality and narrative: On the language of sex education. In M. L. Rasmussen, E. Rofes, & S. Talburt (Eds.), *Youth and sexualities* (pp. 109–130). New York: Palgrave.

Gilbert, J. B. (1986). *A cycle of outrage: America's reaction to the juvenile delinquent in the 1950s.* New York: Oxford University Press.

Grosz, E. (2001). *Architecture from the outside: Essays on virtual and real space.* Cambridge, MA: MIT Press.

Hadley, K. G. (2007). Will the least-adult please stand up? Life as "older sister Katy" in a Taiwanese elementary school. In A. L. Best (Ed.), *Representing youth: Methodological issues in critical youth studies* (pp. 157–181). New York: New York University Press.

Hall, S. (1997). Race, the floating signifier. Retrieved from http://www.mediaed.org

Howe, N., & Strauss, W. (2000). *Millennials rising: The next great generation.* New York: Vintage.

Jenkins, H. (1998). Introduction: Childhood innocence and other modern myths. In H. Jenkins (Ed.), *The children's culture reader* (pp. 1–40). New York: New York University Press.

Leonard, M. (2007). With a capital "G": Gatekeepers and gatekeeping in research with children. In A. L. Best (Ed.), *Representing youth: Methodological issues in critical youth studies* (pp. 133–156). New York: New York University Press.

Lesko, N. (2001). *Act your age! A cultural construction of adolescence.* New York: RoutledgeFalmer.

Love, H. (2007). *Feeling backward: Loss and the politics of queer history.* Cambridge, MA: Harvard University Press.

Maira, S., & Soep, E. (2005). Introduction. In S. Maira, & E. Soep (Eds.), *Youthscapes: The popular, the national, the global* (pp. xv–xxxv). Philadelphia: University of Pennsylvania Press.

McWilliam, E. (1999). *Pedagogical pleasures.* New York: Peter Lang.

Medovoi, L. (1997). Reading the blackboard: Youth, masculinity, and racial cross-identification. In H. Stecopoulos, & M. Uebel (Eds.), *Race and the subject of masculinities* (pp. 138–169). Durham, NC: Duke University Press.

Micciche, L. R. (2007). *Doing emotion: Rhetoric, writing, teaching.* Portsmouth, NH: Heinemann.

Miyazawa, K. (2010). *Home away from home: Paradoxes of nostalgia in the lives of first generation immigrant girls.* Unpublished doctoral dissertation, Teachers College, Columbia University.

Nieuwenhuys, O. (2009). Is there an Indian childhood? *Childhood, 16,* 147–153.

Pickering, A., & Keightley, P. (2006). The modalities of nostalgia. *Current Sociology, 54,* 919–941.

Puar, J. K. (2007). *Terrorist assemblages: Homonationalism in queer times.* Durham, NC: Duke University Press.

Raby, R. (2007). Across a great gulf? Conducting research with adolescents. In A. L. Best (Ed.), *Representing youth: Methodological issues in critical youth studies* (pp. 39–59). New York: New York University Press.

Rajchman, J. (2000). *The Deleuze connections.* Cambridge, MA: MIT Press.

Ramlow, T. R. (2005). Bad boys: Abstractions of difference and the politics of youth "deviance." In S. Maira, & E. Soep (Eds.), *Youthscapes: The popular, the national, the global* (pp. 192–214). Philadelphia: University of Pennsylvania Press.

Rand, E. (1995). *Barbie's queer accessories.* Durham, NC: Duke University Press.

Sedgwick, E. K. (2003). *Touching feeling: Affect, pedagogy, performativity.* London: Duke University Press.

Shah, S. P. (2005). Born into saving brothel children. *SAMAR, 19,* n.p. Retrieved from http://www.samarmagazine.org/archive/article.php?id=190

Smith, D. J. (2009). Big-eyed, wide-eyed, sad-eyed children: Constructing the humanitarian space in social justice documentaries. *Studies in Documentary Film, 3,* 159–175.

Stewart, K. (2007). *Ordinary affects.* Durham, NC: Duke University Press.

Walkerdine, V. (1990). *Schoolgirl fictions.* London: Verso.

39

THE EROTIC

Jen Gilbert

In youth studies, there is little talk about the erotic. Instead, the field is concerned with understanding teen pregnancy, the reduction of sexually transmitted disease and infection, the perils of masculinity and femininity, and the various manifestations of youth's sexual cultures. The concepts we bring to our study of youth work to constitute our object of study and the scope of our inquiry, and "the erotic," if youth studies were to use that concept, pushes our understanding of sexuality past the current focus on identities, sexual practices, and either the management or liberation of youth's sexualities. Indeed, the erotic belies our attempts to pin down its essence, to circumscribe its scope, or to catalogue its effects. The term feels both specific and unwieldy: it envelops sexuality but not all sexual acts and it can include supposedly nonsexual experiences, ideas, and affects that brush up against pleasure and desire. The erotic is both profoundly subjective and highly social, made in the collision between selves and the world, and this ambiguity and movement, far from being a definitional failure, is constitutive of the concept itself. The erotic gathers its libidinal force from its capacity to reach out and touch anything. The world, including the world of youth–adult relations, is enlivened by its touch. It is exactly this fluidity and capaciousness that causes trouble for the field of youth studies.

In youth studies, the young person is made to occupy a paradoxical position in relation to the erotic; at once constructed as vulnerable to the exploitative, conventional, and conflicted discourses of sexuality that circulate through the social and especially the media, youth are also touted as holding the potential to disrupt the normalizing effects of those discourses. Youth both need adult protection from adult versions of sexuality and are hailed as potential erotic warriors, doing battle with the stale, heterosexist assumptions of adult sexuality. In the recent debates on the sexualization of girls, for instance, young women are constructed as both subject to the predatory, sexist, and racist messages of the mainstream media, and paradoxically invested with an almost omnipotent agency to speak back to these narrow messages. The adult, having escaped adolescent vulnerability, is endowed with the ability to tell the difference between girls' victimization and resistance and so is able to protect youth from the corruption of other people's sexuality while identifying with youth's revolutionary desire. The field of youth studies bears the trace of these contradictory desires.

Schools, as well, inherit these paradoxical desires. Here the institution, designed in part to regulate the erotic lives of teachers and youth, confronts the impossibility of its mission. In schools, adults and youth touch and are touched by each other. And despite and because of this danger, this erotic touch is the frisson of teaching and learning. While schools are organized by timetables, outcomes, and measures of accountability, the erotic can erupt unexpectedly, arriving like an uninvited guest, disrupting the desire for order and predictability (Taubman, 2009). Indeed, a robust and speculative body of scholarship critiques this culture of accountability and measurement, in part, by reimagining the productive place of the erotic in teaching and learning (e.g., Gilbert, 2006; McWilliam, 1999; Phelan, 1997; Simon, 1995; Todd, 1997). In this work, the Eros of pedagogical relations bumps up against the institutional regulation of adult and youth desires. Sharon Todd (2003) argues that the rigid codification of Eros in schools, including the panoptic regulation of teacher–student relationships, is an institutional response to the ambiguity of the erotic. Jane Gallop (1997) describes how the relationship between teacher and student is often, and at its best, charged with Eros, even while educational institutions, including the university, increasingly regulate the boundaries of appropriate relations between teachers and students. Gallop notices that while there is no learning without Eros—our relationship with ideas springs from Eros—schools interpret most forms of erotic life as an obstacle to learning. Below, I follow this irony through a discussion of the ambiguous qualities of the erotic that cause trouble for youth studies and then conclude with some comments on the antierotic nature of sex education—one institutional site to which the erotic lives of youth are routinely and ineffectively exiled.

The Erotic as a Relation

The erotic is a relation, not an identity. It belongs neither to the self in the form of some irreducible kernel of desire that hardens into a sexual identity, nor to the world and its surplus of representations of erotic life. Instead, the erotic is made when our interior lives are animated by our living in the world with others. This relation is not without conflict. Britzman (1998) describes how the ego, our emissary into the world, is "caught somewhere between the desire to attach to the world and the desire to ignore all that stands in the way of attachment" (p. 5). Borrowing from the Greeks, Freud names this desire to attach to the world, "Eros."

This desire to attach to the world is frustrated not only by social norms and conventions which regulate sexual desires and practices, but also by Eros' coming into conflict with the death drive. The death drive aims at regression, undoing, and destruction, while the life instincts, or Eros, bind things together: it "[brings] about a more and more far-reaching combination of the particles into which living substance is dispersed, aims at complicating life and at the same time, of course, at preserving it" (Freud, 1920, p. 40). The push and pull of Eros and the death drive creates ambivalence—the erotic is constituted in relation to the world and to an internal aggression that seeks to undo our ties to others.

Freud has some confidence that, where Eros meets social and psychical prohibition, those instincts can, through the process of sublimation, be channeled into socially acceptable activities: "the erotic instincts appear to be altogether more plastic, more readily diverted and displaced than the destructive instincts" (1920, pp. 44–45). The erotic travels—it moves from its original objects to new, disguised pursuits: art, literature, industry, and religion, for instance, but also romantic love, kissing, and other sexual practices. For Freud, Eros is not synonymous with sexual activity, and indeed, the sex we have is not the sex we want. Yet, despite the optimism that Eros would tie us to others in love and be sublimated for social and personal gain, Freud also understands Eros as causing trouble for the ego. He laments, "And from the struggle against Eros! . . . —the force that introduces disturbances into the process of life" (1920, pp. 46–47). Even as Eros pushes us forward into the world and into relations with others, it also invites disturbances. Our erotic attachments, however enduring, are unruly.

Todd (2003) echoes this contradiction and suggests that because Eros is a relation with both the other and one's own otherness, and so cannot be fully known, erotic life demands an openness and a willingness to encounter surprise in both the self and the other, what she calls, citing Jane Gallop, "the pedagogical excess" (p. 35). While the erotic binds the self to others, we cannot determine the nature of that relation in advance.

The Erotic as Loss

While erotic life brings us into often ecstatic contact with others, including perhaps our own otherness, this relation confronts us with our susceptibility to and dependence on others. The erotic causes us pain. Eros is made from loss: we desire what we cannot or do not have, erotic satisfaction is fleeting, and we long for what has already been lost. Eros, then, is a confrontation with the limits of the self. Anne Carson (1998) describes the "bittersweet" contradiction that Eros, in its fleetingness, can both tie us to others while also painfully estranging us from ourselves and the world. Carson returns to Greek poetry to argue that where there is the sweet promise of love there is also a threat to the couple. She names this threat "a triangulation" (p. 18): the threat of a third—the world, another lover, distance or separation—interrupts and ruins the fantasy of the united couple. This threat, rather than being extraneous to love, constitutes love's loveliness. Eros is marked always by its ruin.

This is a story of Eros that psychoanalysis inherits and elaborates through the Oedipal myth. According to Freud, at first the baby loves her mother with an omnipotent appetite, but this love affair is soon interrupted and the baby learns that she must give up her mother as a love object as a condition of entering civilization. Thus, this Oedipal story is also a story of triangulation. The dyad of the mother–baby is broken when the world intrudes, often through the figure of the father, and the mother comes to exist as a separate person for the baby. While this development brings its compensations, it is experienced as a profound loss. For Freud, any finding of a love object is, in fact, an attempt at refinding that original love object. Significantly, our erotic lives are inaugurated through this loss.

If the erotic is a relation inaugurated through loss, then we might notice the echoes of this construction in the field of youth studies. The study of youth is, in part, a study of adults' lost or forgotten selves refound in contemporary youth cultures. The worry about youth's susceptibility to damaging discourses of sexuality or the championing of youth's refusal of adult authority betrays adults' desire for and identification with not just contemporary youth, but the youth we once had or wish we once had. This nostalgic relation, saturated with erotic longing, animates the academic field of youth studies.

Erotic Education

Sex education would seem an ideal site for adults and youth to have conversations with each other about problems of relationality, our susceptibility to loss, and the reach of the erotic in our lives. Charged with preparing youth to enter sexual relationships in a responsible and "healthy" way, sex education gathers around itself all manner of hopes and worries related to erotic life. However, a cursory glance at the history of sex education reveals a profound distrust of erotic life. Indeed, most often, sexuality is conceptualized as an obstacle to sex education (Gilbert, 2010). Instead, sex education is organized by the management of youth sexualities. In an act of projective identification, youth are constructed as dangerous, reckless, and sexually irresponsible by adults who, having thus evacuated themselves of those dangerous contents, can lay claim to maturity, responsibility, and safety. It is a fraught construction: when youth serve as a container for threatening ideas and feelings, adults also hold youth close and meticulously monitor that evacuated content as a way of keeping in contact with those parts of adult selves projected into youth. In this additional way, youth become objects of erotic longing for adults.

In a powerful critique of the ways youth are ordinarily positioned as the objects of this sex education pedagogy, and thus, slyly, as erotic objects for concerned adults, Michelle Fine (1988), Louisa Allen (2004), and others have extended a call to introduce a "discourse of erotics" into sex education. The wish is that a narrative of pleasure and desire could remedy the implicit positioning of girls, especially, as subject to other people's often predatory erotic desires and instead offer a resource for youth to articulate their own agentic sexual subjectivities (Fields, 2008; Tolman, 2002).

This call for a discourse of erotics in sex education interrupts, in part, the way this construction of youth as sexually dangerous disenfranchises young people who are constructing sexual lives for themselves. What if youth, and girls in particular, could claim their right to their own sexual pleasure? What if youth had access, in school, to a narrative of sexuality that included pleasure, excitement, responsibility, and hope? How would youth enter into the work of imagining and living their sexual lives with such discursive resources available to them? It is a bold call.

And yet, in an effort to rescue the field of sex education from those who would cruelly restrict youth from access to information and resources about their sexual lives, we have constructed a discourse of sexuality as positive, healthy, normal, and pleasurable, forgetting in the meantime that erotic life springs from loss and brings with it considerable, ordinary suffering. One does not need psychoanalysis or Greek poetry to remember that our erotic lives often teeter on the edge of disaster and that this risk constitutes the thrill of Eros. This is a problem for sex education: how to represent, as openly as possible, the contradictions of erotic life. If we are to let Eros instruct the field of youth studies, we will need to remember that a discourse of erotics, a well-planned intervention into the risky sexual practices of youth, or an idealization of youth's rebellion, cannot contain the wildness of Eros. Eros does not want an education. But strangely, and this may be what Gallop means by the "pedagogical excess," it will be Eros that spurs us on, in youth studies, to invent new research practices, new styles of thinking, and new forms of relationality.

References

Allen, L. (2004). Beyond the birds and the bees: Constituting a discourse of erotics in sexuality education. *Gender and Education, 16*(2), 151–167.

Britzman, D. (1998). Why return to Anna Freud? Some reflections of a teacher educator. *Teaching Education, 10*, 3–16.

Carson, A. (1998). *Eros: The bittersweet.* Normal, IL: Dalkey Archive Press.

Fields, J. (2008). *Risky lessons: Sex education and social inequality.* New Brunswick, NJ: Rutgers University Press.

Fine, M. (1988). Sexuality, schooling and adolescent females: The missing discourse of desire. *Harvard Educational Review, 58*, 29–53.

Freud, S. (1920). The ego and the id. In J. Strachey (Ed.), *The standard edition of the complete psychological works of Sigmund Freud, 1953–1974* (pp. 3–68). London: Hogarth Press and Institute for Psychoanalysis.

Gallop, J. (1997). *Feminist accused of sexual harassment.* Durham, NC: Duke University Press.

Gilbert, J. (2006). "Let us say yes to what or who shows up": Education as hospitality. *Journal of the Canadian Association of Curriculum Studies, 4*, 35–44.

Gilbert, J. (2010). Ambivalence-only? Sex education in the age of abstinence. *Sex Education: Sexuality, Society, and Learning, 10*, 233–237.

McWilliam, E. (1999). *Pedagogical pleasures.* New York: Peter Lang.

Phelan, A. (1997). Classroom management and the erasure of teacher desire. In J. Tobin (Ed.), *Making a place for pleasure in early childhood education* (pp. 76–100). New Haven, CT: Yale University Press.

Simon, R. (1995). Face to face with alterity: Postmodern Jewish identity and the Eros of pedagogy. In J. Tobin (Ed.), *Pedagogy: The question of impersonation* (pp. 90–105). Bloomington: Indiana University Press.

Taubman, P. (2009). *Teaching by numbers: Deconstructing the discourse of standards and accountability in education.* New York: Routledge.

Todd, S. (Ed.). (1997). *Learning desire: Perspectives of pedagogy, culture and the unsaid.* New York: Routledge.

Todd, S. (2003). A fine risk to be run? The ambiguity of Eros and teacher responsibility. *Studies in Philosophy and Education, 22*(1), 31–44.

Tolman, D. (2002). *Dilemmas of desire: Teenage girls talk about sexuality.* Cambridge, MA: Harvard University Press.

40

INNOCENCE

Elizabeth Marshall

An ideological concept used in academic and nonacademic contexts to describe a state of being, the word "innocence" comes from the Latin *in-nocere* which "meant either 'not to hurt' or 'not to be hurt,' thus embracing both the active and passive voices of the verb 'to harm'" (Gittins, 1998, p. 146). Its contemporary association with naïveté, ignorance, and vulnerability originates in the 14th century and continues to mark contemporary discourses about youth in North America, the United Kingdom, and Australia. In the *Oxford English Dictionary*, innocence (n.d.) is defined as: (1) A state of "freedom from sin, guile or moral wrong in general; state of being untainted with, or unacquainted with, evil; moral purity." (2) "Freedom from specific guilt; the fact of not being guilty of that with which one is charged." (3) "Freedom from cunning or artifice; guilelessness, artlessness, simplicity; hence, want of knowledge or sense, ignorance, silliness."

Ideas about innocence organize the ways in which adults talk about youth and are used to justify the management of adolescents by state, institutional, and domestic entities. The claim to protect the innocence of youth is carried out through such diverse activities as deciding what materials are appropriate for reading, viewing, and/or listening; when youth should "know" about sex; when it is legal to prosecute a teen as an adult in criminal proceedings; what rights are granted to youth; and so on. The meanings and usages of innocence in youth studies are dynamic and even unpredictable because the arbitrary line between childhood and adolescence continues to shift. Thus, it is more constructive to think about innocence as a relational term that gains meaning in its pairing with "experience." Through experience rather than reaching a particular chronological age, youth lose their innocence. Adult anxieties, fears, and/or fantasies about the ways in which this loss of innocence might play out surface in numerous popular cultural texts created by adults about adolescents from *Lord of the Flies* (Golding, 1954) to *Blackboard Jungle* (Berman & Brooks, 1955) to *Kids* (Vachon, Van Sant, Woods, Konrad, & Clark, 1995) to the more recent *Thirteen* (Levy-Hinte, London, & Hardwicke, 2003). These cultural texts not only display the dangers and pleasures of innocence lost, but also reaffirm the idea that youth need adult guidance and regulation to achieve normal, responsible adulthood.

Regulating Innocence

The idea of childhood innocence has been studied and critiqued in various ways (Cross, 2004; Higonnet, 1998; Kincaid, 1992; Rose, 1992; Walkerdine, 1997); however, most scholars agree that innocence operates in less obvious or direct ways for youth than for young children. The "discovery" of adolescence in the United States in the last two decades of the 19th century and the publication of G. Stanley Hall's (1904) *Adolescence* offered the teenage years as a state of prolonged childhood. Hall defined adolescence as a precarious period of physical and psychological change. Like childhood, adolescence is commonly assumed to be a vulnerable space and adults must carefully guide the coming-of-age process by limiting youth's exposure to toxic culture or harmful media. Mary Pipher's (1995) *Reviving Ophelia: Saving the Selves of Adolescent Girls* details a "girl poisoning culture" in which young (predominately White middle-class) North American-teen girls are in need of saving by concerned adults. Protecting youth from "a loss of innocence" translates in public and private spaces to regulating sexual activity (safe sex/abstinence) and/or media, violence, and drug/alcohol abuse.

Innocence is an elastic term that is stretched and retracted as it tags different ideas and evokes varied associations in relation to youth. Innocence, then, implicitly informs youth studies both as it tracks these associations (and often reproduces them) and also as it undergirds the focus on how to protect or help youth protect themselves against harm, "how young people should be schooled, policed, housed, employed, or prevented from becoming involved in any number of risky (sexual, eating, drug abusing or peer cultural) practices" (Kelly, 2000, p. 303).

Theorizing youth as innocents in need of protection plays out in the larger cultural scene in the form of social panics about youth. The concept of innocence has allowed adults to focus on "the best interests of the child" (Gordon, 2008, p. 332) and to make policies and laws to protect youth from harm; and, yet, these policies and practices have different outcomes and often-contradictory effects that do not necessarily make the lives of youth better (Gordon, 2008). In the United States, late 19th-century purity reformers sought to protect White working-class teenage girls by campaigning to raise the age of consent from 10 or 12 years to 16 or 18 years (Odem, 1995). The 1954 Senate hearings on graphic and violent comic books prefigured The Parent Music Resource Center's attempts in the late 1980s to label violent and/or sexually explicit music recordings. More recently, the Parental Television Council's campaigns against video games and television continues the practice by adults of launching campaigns to protect youth that seek to rearticulate the childlike innocence of adolescents. These campaigns in turn allow adults to theorize harm as something that comes from outside the presumed safety of the home.

The Myth of Innocence

Numerous academics debunk innocence as a myth that functions to sustain adult power over youth (Giroux, 2000; Gittins, 1998; Higonnet, 1998; Jenkins, 1998). These scholars ask questions about how the idea of innocence disenfranchises youth from political, social, and economic life. Questions about youth's sexuality and/or adult preoccupations with it are central to studies of innocence. The idea of innocence as an attribute of youth requires continuous maintenance and is often challenged by the realities of teens' lives and actions. How can youth remain innocent when confronted with sexual violence, bullying, and a range of other "adult" concerns? The Columbine Massacre on April 20, 1999, made it clear that innocence wasn't a "natural" trait of youth. A public outcry in the United States sought to reaffirm innocence as a right of adolescence and rushed to represent the shooters as deviants who had succumbed to the violence they had been exposed to in music and video games, rather than address the possibility that teens weren't inherently good. Headlines such as "The Day Innocence Died" (O'Driscoll, 1999) reaffirmed that this was an exception rather than the norm. Conceptions of innocence retain a strong hold on North American ideas about youth, and examples of youth violence—especially those perpetrated by White middle-class youth—are often blamed on the images of sex and violence that kids are exposed to in video games and other popular cultural outlets.

Politics of Innocence

James Kincaid (1992) asks provocative questions about how the innocent figure of the child provides an empty screen for adults to project their own erotic pleasures and in turn continually eroticize youth. This adult gaze regulates innocence and simultaneously defines the erotics of the youthful body through its positioning in front of the camera and the appropriateness of certain representations. In a North American context, innocence is also a gendered concept often associated with and used to police and eroticize White middle- and upper-middle-class heterosexual girls. For instance, in 1998, 16-year-old Britney Spears caused a major controversy when she left behind her image as innocent Disney Mouseketeer in favor of a titillating Catholic schoolgirl. In the video "Baby One More Time" Spears (2003) sports ponytails and knee-length socks but dances in a physically mature body that moves with knowledge of not so innocent female sexuality.

This innocence is only afforded to certain subjects as these protections and sympathies are enacted around worthy victims. Youth of color, immigrant children, poor kids, LGBT youth, and others are often marked as "knowing" subjects whose inherent violence and/or knowledge about sexuality preclude them from being considered either worthy victims of sympathy (Jiwani, 1999) or subjects who are innocent until proven guilty. As Henry Giroux (2000) writes, "The rhetoric of innocence and its guarantee of support and protection typically have not applied to kids who are poor, black, and brown" (p. 9). To be considered "innocent" or untainted one must also fit into the normative dimensions of the seeming universal categories enshrined in the definition of innocence in the *Oxford English Dictionary* (Innocence, n.d.).

In 1997 14-year-old Reena Virk, a girl of South Asian background, was brutally murdered by a group of eight teens (seven girls and one boy) in Victoria, British Columbia. Scholar Yasmin Jiwani (1999) argues that the media coverage of the case ignored the racial motivations behind Virk's murder and instead focused on Virk's inability to fit in. In this way, Virk was not considered an innocent victim, but one who asked for it. "Thus, the issue of racism was erased from the dominant discourse, and Reena Virk's identity as a racialized young woman has been similarly erased in terms of its significance and contribution to her vulnerability and marginality" (Jiwani, 1999, p. 182). The use of innocence to mark and protect only certain youthful bodies has numerous effects across many different institutions. Cindy Patton (1996), for instance, points out how notions of "innocence" have led to racist and homophobic sex education campaigns that fail to mark White heterosexual youth as sexually active while refusing to save those youth who have already been presumed to have lost their innocence, LGBT youth and teens of color.

Conclusion

Alternative ways of thinking about innocence might include the recognition that adolescence is itself a historical and cultural construct, the meanings of which shift across time and location (Lesko, 2001). The idea that innocence is an innate attribute of youth hides from view the ways in which children and adolescents, like adults, are situated in particular historical, political, and social contexts, as well as the adult manufacture of the category of innocence. Innocence is hardly a universal experience for youth, and the ways in which this term gets used creates an idealized and normative category that tends to be White, middle class, and heterosexual. It also makes it difficult for adults to see the ways in which youth take up and/or talk back to innocence in their everyday experiences (Driver, 2007; McRobbie, 2007). Innocence and its vision of angelic White heterosexual youth is a form of violence that keeps us from confronting the ways in which race, ethnicity, ability, and/or sexuality are as important (if not more so) than chronological age as a key marker of "innocence." A critique of innocence asks us to challenge idealizations of youth, which celebrate the misplaced desires, fantasies, fears, and/or nostalgia of adults.

References

Berman, P. S. (Producer), & Brooks, R. (Director). (1955). *Blackboard jungle* [Motion picture]. United States: Metro-Goldwyn-Mayer.

Cross, G. (2004). *The cute and the cool: Wondrous innocence and modern American children's culture.* New York: Oxford University Press.

Driver, S. (2007). *Queer girls and popular culture: Reading, resisting and creating media.* New York: Peter Lang.

Giroux, H. (2000). *Stealing innocence: Youth, corporate power, and the politics of culture.* New York: St. Martin's Press.

Gittins, D. (1998). *The child in question.* New York: St. Martin's Press.

Golding, W. (1954). *Lord of the flies.* London: Faber and Faber.

Gordon, L. (2008). The perils of innocence, or what's wrong with putting children first. *Journal of the History of Childhood and Youth, 1*(3), 331–350.

Hall, G. S. (1904). *Adolescence: Its psychology and its relations to physiology, anthropology, sociology, sex, crime, religion, and education.* New York: D. Appleton and Company.

Higonnet, A. (1998). *Pictures of innocence: The history and crisis of ideal childhood.* New York: Thames and Hudson.

Innocence. (n.d.) In *Oxford English Dictionary.* Retrieved from http://www.oed.com/innocence

Jenkins, H. (1998). Introduction: Childhood innocence and other modern myths. In H. Jenkins (Ed.), *The children's culture reader* (pp. 1–37). New York: New York University Press.

Jiwani,Y. (1999). Erasing race:The story of Reena Virk. *Canadian Women's Studies/Les Cahiers De La Femme, 19*(3), 178–184.

Kelly, P. (2000).Youth as artifact of expertise: Problematizing the practice of youth studies in an age of uncertainty. *Journal of Youth Studies, 3*, 301–315.

Kincaid, J. (1992). *Child-loving: The erotic child and Victorian culture*. New York: Routledge.

Lesko, N. (2001). *Act your age! A cultural construction of adolescence*. New York: Routledge.

Levy-Hinte, J., London, M. (Producers), & Hardwicke, C. (Director). (2003). *Thirteen* [Motion picture]. United States: Fox Searchlight Pictures.

McRobbie, A. (2007). Top girls? *Cultural Studies, 21*, 718–737.

Odem, M. E. (1995). *Delinquent daughters: Protecting and policing adolescent female sexuality in the United States, 1885–1920*. Chapel Hill: University of North Carolina Press.

O'Driscoll, P. (1999).The day innocence died: It began with a chilling prophecy. *USA Today*, p. 4 A.

Patton, C. (1996). *Fatal advice: How safe-sex education went wrong*. Durham, NC: Duke University Press.

Pipher, M. (1995). *Reviving Ophelia: Saving the selves of adolescent girls*. New York: Ballantine.

Rose, J. (1992). *The case of Peter Pan: Or the impossibility of children's fiction*. Philadelphia: University of Pennsylvania Press.

Spears, B. (2003). *Baby one more time* [Music video]. Retrieved from http://www.youtube.com/watch?v=C-u5WLJ9Yk4

Vachon, C.,Van Sant, G.,Woods, C., Konrad, C. (Producers), & Clark, L. (Director). (1995). *Kids* [Motion picture]. United States: Shining Excalibur Films.

Walkerdine,V. (1997). *Daddy's little girl: Young girls and popular culture*. Cambridge, MA: Harvard University Press.

41

NGOs

Dana Burde

The term nongovernmental organization, or NGO, originated with the passing of a United Nations resolution in February 1950 to officially recognize certain "organizations with no governmental affiliation that had consultative status" within the U.N. system (Vakil, 1997, p. 2068). They evolved rapidly. Since the 1970s and the growth of the neoliberal state, NGOs and governments have shifted roles, with governments decentralizing and devolving their powers to nongovernmental organizations (Edwards & Hulme, 1996; Reimann, 2006; Steiner-Khamsi, 1998). NGOs, in turn, have grown and assumed many responsibilities (education, health care) that were managed formerly by the state.The end of the Cold War magnified this trend. Support to NGOs grew again both to distribute and manage much of this aid and to support an emerging civil society.

As the end of the Cold War magnified the growth of NGOs and diversified them, September 11, in turn, had the effect of refocusing many of these organizations on development issues linked to security and youth. Western governments looked at "youth bulges" around the world and attributed new significance to these populations. Sharon Stephens' (1995) prescient essay, "Children and the Politics of Culture in 'Late Capitalism,'" forecasted the melding of development and security into one paradigm (Duffield, 2001) featuring both the protection and danger of children as twin problems. In this paradigm, street children and child soldiers are regarded as living in social worlds "*outside* the normative socializing control of adult society" (Stephens, 1995, p. 11). These children and youth are no longer perceived only as *at risk*, but they are also increasingly perceived as *the risk* (Stephens, 1995). Likewise, aid donors are beginning to view underdeveloped countries as slipping beyond the socializing control of world society.

As the neoliberal state grew throughout the past several decades, strong states in the global north expanded the way they work with NGOs and harnessed civil society to address these issues. I trace the burgeoning of NGOs through the trends of privatization, democratization, and the more recent move toward a humanitarian security paradigm. The dual focus on youth as "at risk" and "the risk" is not new. Yet early trends produced a sufficient "coincidence of interests" that allowed NGOs to work toward their needs-driven missions without questioning their role in the neoliberal project, despite their relationship to strong states' foreign policy. The current emphasis on development as security, however, particularly in relation to youth, ties civil society to strong states' interests in new ways, changing the structure of international development work.

Situating International NGOs within a Sea of Organizations

The Union of International Associations (UIA), which catalogs and tracks NGOs, uses the term to refer to any association, agency, or organization that is private, nonprofit, and not controlled or managed by a government. According to the UIA, by 2010 there were "63,912 civil society organizations in 300 countries and territories, in every field of human endeavour" (UIA, 2010). Despite the diversity included under the NGO label, the kind that is best known and well established in the collective imagination of U.S. and global citizens is the transnational nonprofit aid organization—for example, CARE, the International Rescue Committee, or Save the Children. Service delivery activities such as providing food and shelter, livelihood training, health care, and education typically form the bulk of their mandates. They receive significant funds from bilateral government organizations such as the U.S. Agency for International Development (USAID) or multigovernmental organizations (e.g., United Nations, World Bank), often totaling more than 50% of their budgets. Although youth are not the sole focus of these organizations, young people are often included among the populations these aid programs are intended to reach.

Privatization and Democratization

As the neoliberal state expanded in the mid-1990s, two movements strengthened NGO prominence around the world: privatization and democratization. NGOs played a key role in both. First, states around the world were encouraged to increase their reliance on markets and the private sector as the best and most efficient way to achieve economic growth and provide services (Edwards & Hulme, 1996; Kamat, 2004). This included reducing the role of the state in service provision and cutting back what were seen as bloated governments. NGOs benefitted from a shift in values away from state involvement and toward individual responsibilities (Inglehart & Abramson, as cited in Anhier & Themudo, 2002, p. 198). As policymakers cut state budgets and trimmed bureaucracies, NGOs assumed the role of providers of formerly state-managed services in education and health care. They often initiated programs based on the U.S.-deficit model of youth at risk, identifying and addressing issues such as marginalization and poverty that were thought to increase the likelihood of exploitation or risky behavior (Hull, Zacher, & Hibbert, 2009).

Second, a strong push toward democratization awarded NGOs a critical role in this process. NGOs were considered key components for a strong civil society serving as a critical "counterweight to state power, opening up channels of communication and participation, providing training grounds for activists and promoting pluralism" (Edwards & Hulme, 1996, pp. 961–962). In this context, NGOs, backed by bilateral funders, supported youth organizations with civic education and empowerment programs. The youth organization Otpor, which was credited with peacefully overthrowing Slobodan Milosevic in Serbia, serves as a dramatic example of this effort.[1] Yet Serbia was an exception. In the neoliberal model of democratization, the role of civil society as the counterweight to the state was eroded in favor of the more benign view of civil society as a complement to the state. In this view, civic-minded citizens participate actively in their communities and perpetuate the smooth functioning of the state. To date, whether youth were viewed as beneficiaries of aid, key catalysts of social change, or potential threats to social order, NGOs benefitted from incorporating young people into their programs.

Aid, Security, and the Youth Bulge

If the 1980s and 1990s were about privatization and democratization, the new millennium launched the security decade. After September 11, bilateral aid agencies such as USAID maintained their relationship with NGOs while at the same time tightening the link between development goals and security. Institutional restructuring placed development and humanitarian activities under direct control of the U.S. State Department. The revised relationship was intended to integrate foreign assistance across government institutions and align development aid more closely with political priorities. As part of the restructuring, aid recipient countries were reorganized into categories designated according to political urgency and importance. Those representing the most significant security concerns were referred to as "Critical Priority Countries," including, for example, Afghanistan, Iraq, Pakistan, and Sudan. Linking development goals tightly to security outcomes aims to protect wealthier countries in the north by deterring threats, and to contain populations in the global south by improving economic indicators (Duffield, 2001). Youth are a central focus of this shift.

The phrase "youth bulge" refers to a generation of youth usually described as between 15 and 24 years old that is disproportionately large compared to the adult population in the same country or region (Urdal, 2006). Scholars argue that an unusually large cohort of youth is associated with a number of social ills including revolutions (Goldstone, 1991), political extremism (Huntington, 1996), and increased likelihood of civil conflict (Urdal, 2006). The danger youth are thought to pose has captured the imagination of many bilateral aid agencies, including, for example, USAID, and has led to programs that are intended to target the problem of youth. For example, in the early 2000s, USAID launched a new series of projects under the banner "Educational Quality Improvement Program 3" (EQUIP3) to focus on youth development. Likewise, in 2010, the World Bank invested $2.3 billion in youth programs, a 15-fold increase over investments from 2000 (World Bank, 2010). As is the case with privatization and democratization, NGOs are key partners in managing and implementing these programs.

The Melding of the Aid and Security Paradigms

Failed states with their youth bulges no longer pose a danger only to the people living within their borders; in the post-September 11 world, they pose a mortal danger to many living comfortably beyond those limits. Aid programs in these states are intended to promote stability via education, livelihood development, health, civic engagement, and economic empowerment for marginalized, uneducated, and undereducated youth (USAID, 2006). In eastern Afghanistan, for example, apprenticeship programs teach "job skills to at-risk youth," specifically providing training in "tailoring, carpentry, metalwork, mobile phone repair, and car body repair" (USAID, 2009, p. 1). NGOs implement these programs and play a key role in this process. According to former U.S. Secretary of State Colin Powell, "just as surely as our diplomats and military, American NGOs . . . are out there serving and sacrificing on the frontlines of freedom. NGOs are such a force multiplier for us, such an important part of our combat team" (as cited in Falconer, 2008). At first glance, aid appears to serve both the security concerns of the neoliberal state as well as the development aims of international NGOs.

Using NGOs as vehicles for channeling bilateral aid in conflict-affected countries, however, presents new contradictions and threats. First, because aid is used to stabilize a state, funders direct it to restive areas. Worldwide, therefore, the United States channels resources to Critical Priority Countries. Likewise, in Afghanistan, the Taliban-dominated south and east (otherwise known as the "Pashtun belt") receive the lion's share of foreign aid in the hope of winning over destabilizing actors (i.e., young men). Thus, counterterrorism and humanitarianism work in close partnership, with international NGOs serving as key agents in hearts and minds strategies (Barnett, 2009). Yet awarding aid based on need is one of the fundamental principles of NGOs. Basing aid decisions on security concerns rather than on need violates this principle.

Second, Oxfam International (2010) and 28 other aid agencies denounce the militarization of humanitarian aid, saying that using aid to win hearts and minds puts Afghan and foreign civilians at risk and undermines development. If the population is the prize, they argue, civilians become a military target. Indeed, NGOs have suffered significant loss of life under the new security paradigm. Close to 100 aid workers were killed in Afghanistan in 2010. NGOs are neither prepared nor willing to serve as "force multipliers," yet continuing to work in critical priority regions requires that they do so.

In sum, the role of youth programs in the post–September 11 security paradigm reflects a fundamental restructuring of development. Privileging security over development appropriates aid efforts to serve war aims and creates a perverse system of rewards for conflict. Youth living in conflict-affected regions may benefit in the short term, but only at the expense of youth who are denied aid elsewhere. At the same time, NGOs who object to their role in this system risk losing their central position in the aid paradigm.

Note

1 Later news of Otpor's heavy support from the U.S. government and U.S.-funded NGOs undermined its grassroots image.

References

Anhier, H., & Themudo, N. (2002). Organizational forms of global civil society: Implications of going global. In M. Glasius, M. Kaldor, & H. Anheier (Eds.), *Global civil society* (pp. 191–216). Oxford: Oxford University Press.

Barnett, M. (2009). Evolution without progress? Humanitarianism in a world of hurt. *International Organization, 63*, 621–663.

Duffield, M. (2001). *Global governance and the new wars: The merging of development and security.* London: Zed.

Edwards, M., & Hulme, D. (1996). Too close for comfort? The impact of official aid on non-governmental organizations. *World Development, 24*, 961–973.

Falconer, B. (2008, May 18). Armed and humanitarian. *Mother Jones.* Retrieved from http://motherjones.com/politics/2008/05/armed-and-humanitarian

Goldstone, J. (1991). *Revolution and rebellion in the early modern world.* Berkeley: University of California Press.

Hull, G., Zacher, J., & Hibbert, L. (2009). Youth, risk, and equity in a global world. *Review of Research in Education, 33*, 117–159.

Huntington, S. (1996). *The clash of civilizations and the remaking of world order.* New York: Simon & Schuster.

Kamat, S. (2004). The privatization of public interest: Theorizing NGO discourse in a neo-liberal era. *Review of International Political Economy, 11*, 155–176.

Oxfam International. (2010). *Nowhere to turn: The failure to protect civilians in Afghanistan.* Joint briefing paper for NATO heads of government summit, Lisbon. Retrieved from http://www.oxfam.org/sites/www.oxfam.org/files/bn-nowhere-to-turn-afghanistan-191110-en.pdf

Reimann, K. (2006). A view from the top: International politics, norms, and the worldwide growth of NGOs. *International Studies Quarterly, 50,* 45–67.

Steiner-Khamsi, G. (1998). Too far from home? "Modulitis" and NGOs' role in transferring prepackaged reform. *Current Issues in Comparative Education, 1,* 35–41.

Stephens, S. (1995). Children and the politics of culture in "late capitalism." In S. Stephens (Ed.), *Children and the politics of culture* (pp. 3–48). Princeton, NJ: Princeton University Press.

Union of International Associations (UIA). (2010). Yearbook of international organizations. Retrieved from http://www.uia.be/yearbook

Urdal, H. (2006). A clash of generations? Youth bulges and political violence. *International Studies Quarterly, 50,* 607–629.

USAID. (2006). Illustrative program description—Youth development in fragile states. Program document. EQUIP3/Youth Trust. Retrieved from http://www.equip123.net

USAID. (2009). Success story: Apprenticeships provide jobs to at-risk youth. Retrieved from http://afghanistan.usaid.gov/en/Article.616.aspx

Vakil, A. C. (1997). Confronting the classification problem: Toward a taxonomy of NGOs. *World Development, 25,* 2057–2070.

World Bank. (2010). Youth worldwide risks becoming a "lost generation." Children and Youth. Retrieved from http://go.worldbank.org/HVCA3FYRO0

42

NOSTALGIA

Kaoru Miyazawa

The original meaning of nostalgia—*nost* (returning home) and *algia* (painful condition), which refers to acute longing for familiar surroundings—was at one time an illness, a type of depression that occurs due to the loss of home. Today, nostalgia is commonly known as a romantic sentiment. Rarely has the relationship between youth and nostalgia been discussed nor the connection between them been clarified. Although it is implicit, nostalgia has always been an undercurrent in the discourse of youth. Individuals have grieved over their losses and fantasized their lost objects. Simultaneously they have been absorbed into a nationalistic movement of reconstructing a stable homeland. This has resulted in producing various subjects ranging from adolescents to loyal citizens, future-oriented disciplined youths, and hybrid youths.

Construction of Adolescence and Nostalgia

Adolescence, which is a "naturalized" concept today, is a construct developed within the discourse of developmental psychology in the late 1800s and early

1900s (Lesko, 1996). Adolescents are viewed as confused and uncontrollable as they are located within the problematic time period between childhood and adulthood in a Darwinistic notion of development. A link between adolescence and nostalgia became possible as they both became temporal concepts that indicated a linear transition from the past to the present and to the future. Nostalgia, which was viewed as a reaction to a loss of home, was originally a spatial concept, but by the 19th century it had become a temporal concept; nostalgia came to refer to a loss of a particular cherished moment in the past. By the 20th century a popular notion of nostalgia came to mean longing for one's own childhood (Boym, 2001). The shift of nostalgia from a spatial to a temporal concept made the transposition of nostalgia to human development (another temporal concept) possible. Just as one who is driven by nostalgia fantasizes one's past as ideal and problematizes the present, developmental psychologists saw childhood (past) as a stable time in individuals' life course while viewing adolescence (present) as the time of problems and confusions. The conceptualization of the present as a problematic period seems to reflect the anxieties that dominated society in the 19th and 20th centuries, an era marked by loss of stabilities in individuals' lives due to industrialization, urbanization, and structural change in the family system joined by the desire to recreate an orderly and stable society. The problematization of the present and romanticization of the past that is reflected in the concept of adolescence overlaps with a key symptom of nostalgia, such that the projection of these scholars' nostalgia universalized the definition of adolesence as a problematic phase in one's life, and this idea continues to circulate widely in our society.

Re/constructing "National" Bodies and Minds

The idea of adolescence further became normalized in the discourse of the modern nation-state. This discourse itself is another form of nostalgia—restorative nostalgia, which is a collective recreation of the past (Boym, 2001). Modern nation-states created official collective memories of homeland that articulate the nations' origin of place, people, and culture and instilled those memories in the bodies and minds of their citizens (Hall, 1992). This practice allowed nations to construct national loyal citizens. Adolescents, who were viewed as being in the process of becoming adults, became popular targets of transformation in this project. In carrying out the project, schools played a significant role. Schools instilled official memories of the nation into the bodies and minds of young people by having them salute a national flag, sing a national anthem, learn the nation's official history, and speak the official national language. In addition, reconstruction of national bodies, based on the memories of the nation, was conducted by having youths engage in national sports. In the United States, for example, invitations for boys to play American football became rampant in the early 20th century, based on the belief that American football would enhance physical and personality traits such as rigor, stamina, vigor, and endurance that are considered as essential traits of American males (Gagen, 2004). In fact, American football continues to occupy a significant position in the United

States even today. In addition to creating American masculine bodies, American football has also served as a space for community members to integrate their national collective narrative into their personal memories. The spectacle of America, through the repetitive presentation of youthful American male bodies juxtaposed with national symbols such as the American flag and national anthem at football games, led citizens to internalize the national memories in a personally meaningful way (Berg, 2006). Personalization of a collective memory through participation in public events promoted individuals' active and voluntary engagement in the discourse of nation. This collective and repetitive enactment of nostalgia has become naturalized to the extent that the questioning of the authenticity of collective memories, symbols, and rituals came to signify disloyalty to the nation-state.

Future-Oriented Nostalgia and Youth

Although reconstruction of the past through the reiteration of nationalistic memories of homeland continues today, recent practices of nostalgia within the national discourse have gained a new quality of future orientedness. In future-oriented nostalgia, individuals project their cherished memories of the past to the future, and collectively move toward the future, instead of recreating the past in the present. This type of nostalgia has become more active in a neoliberal society, which operates on free-market principles. Financial uncertainty, deconstruction of alliances and communities, increasing competition, and responsibilization of individuals caused by neoliberalism have increased many subjects' longing for a society when things were stable, predictable, and communal. Neoliberalism further increased their desire and commitment for reconstruction of such a perfect society in the future.

Similarly to the national discourse in the past, youths' bodies, again, play a significant role in future-oriented nostalgia. The use of youths' bodies is carried out, first, by paralleling the problematic condition of the nation-state with the decreasing quality of adolescents. For instance, the emphasis on a decline in adolescents' academic skills, morality, and poor physical conditions within the current condition of the nation-state, especially in comparison to the state of other nations, is common in the discourse of education, health, social work, business, and media. Based on the problem, adults—such as teachers, social workers, and youth activists—who are concerned about youths' decreasing conditions as well as the weakened condition of the nation, attempt to rescue the future of the nation by empowering youth.

In future-oriented nostalgia, individuals' longing for the vanished society of the past is used as a driving force to motivate individuals. Reflecting this characteristic, young people in future-oriented nostalgia are expected to embody traditional values and traits. At the same time, they are expected to invest in themselves for their healthy and financially stable future. One area where future-oriented nostalgia manifests clearly today is sexuality education, such as Abstinence Only Until Marriage (AOUM) programs and comprehensive sexuality education programs. For instance, in AOUM in the United States, neo-conservative adults' fantasies of creating a better collective future is enacted by instilling young people with conservative Christian sexuality and family values, which they consider to be essentially American. While instilling traditional values in the bodies and minds of young people, AOUM also propagates young people to become future-oriented and self-invested individuals by teaching them to plan their lives linearly, especially by abstaining from acting on their desires for intimacy in the present in order to ensure their future success. The implementation of this program shows how future-oriented nostalgia produces future-oriented active citizens, who reappropriate their actions and desires toward the "better future" (i.e., a future just like the past) (Petersson, Olsson, & Popkewitz, 2007).

Youth Space and Nostalgia

While nostalgia has been a major driving force to construct young citizens in modern nation-states, the presence of nostalgia has been naturalized within the discourse of adolescence and nationalism. Only recently has scholarship highlighted the productive nature of nostalgia in relation to the construction of youths' subjectivities and spaces. One of the studies that captures the productive nature of youths' nostalgia is Maira's (2002) study of second-generation Indian American youths. By exploring the subcultural spaces and subjectivities youths' nostalgia creates within those spaces, the study uncovers the collective and flexible nature of nostalgia. The type of nostalgia that the youths in the study perform differs from previously described collective nostalgias that rearticulates a stable nation and moves its citizens toward a fixed future. Unlike other nostalgia that is a projection of anxieties caused by the loss of the familiar on the bodies of young people, the youths in the study show that youths themselves create new spaces and identities led by their own nostalgia, which is combined with other sentiments they currently have. The creative effects of nostalgia emerge, for example, through genres of music such as Bhangra, Reggaeton, and Oriental rap, in which traditional ethnic music's beat, rhythm, and lyrics are infused with those of rap, hip-hop, techno, and/or reggae (Huq, 2006).

Reflective nostalgia runs through these spaces (Boym, 2001). Unlike restorative nostalgia, reflective nostalgia does not produce a single narrative based on an official collective memory of homeland. Reflective nostalgia, instead, sporadically produces multiple stories of the past, and individuals dwell on the past. Sometimes, individuals' memories of homeland are infused with other sentiments derived from their current social, political, and cultural locations. For example, in Oriental rap, Turkish immigrant youths in Europe express their longing for homeland together with aggression and counter-hegemonic messages grounded in their urban experiences as the marginalized (Kaya, 2002). In that sense, the nostalgia expressed through their music is not a simple rearticulation of their memories; their nostalgia is often fictional and hybrid—a remix of fantasies about their homeland, which they have never been to, and their current urban sentiment. In that sense, their nostalgia is not bounded by their origins. In addition, their nostalgia, unlike restorative nostalgia, does not simply reconstruct a static past space. Instead, it moves individuals constantly and produces new multiple spaces and subjects. Reflective nostalgia is a creative process in which pleasure rather than despair or anxiety drives individuals. This quality of nostalgia, the experience of pleasure through the highlighted fantasization of lost objects, including fictional ones, seems to overlap with a symptom of nostalgia in the medical discourse of nostalgia. However, they are different in a sense that youths today are aware of the crafted nature of their nostalgia while they are dwelling on those romanticized memories of homeland.

Concluding Thoughts

Nostalgia, or longing for home—whether individual or collective, imagined or real, pleasure or anxiety oriented—has moved various individuals in the modern era. Originally, nostalgia, which was categorized as a form of pathology in medical discourse, produced "depressive" patients who suffered from losses of the cherished. Nostalgia has also been creating loyal national citizens, adolescents, and future-oriented citizens, as well as new genres of music that recreated one's fantasies of his/her homeland. Understanding that the knowledge we have been familiar with, in fact, is something constructed as an effect of nostalgia makes us wonder whether such knowledge should be legitimate or not. The response to this question may depend on the discourse one is in. The medical discourse, which is an original founder of this concept, pathologizes nostalgia, and this discourse would invalidate the knowledge that is produced by individuals' mourning over loss. However, the pathologization of nostalgia is no longer universal in the contemporary society in which individuals must live with constant unpredictable changes and the accompanying losses. We must live with nostalgia. The mixture of pain of loss and pleasure of being reconnected to the lost object in one's fantasy will continue to move us. And if that is indeed the case, we must dwell on our multiple personal memories of home, while casting a critical eye on power that normalizes our memories of home and moves us collectively to reconstruct a particular past.

References

Berg, P. (Producer). (2006). *Friday night lights* [Television series]. New York: NBC Universal.

Boym, S. (2001). *The future of nostalgia.* New York: Basic Books.

Gagen, E. A. (2004). Making America flesh: Physicality and nationhood in early twentieth-century physical education reform. *Cultural Geographies, 11*(4), 417–442.

Hall, S. (1992). The question of cultural identity. In S. Hall, D. Held, & T. McGrew (Eds.), *Modernity and its futures* (pp. 273–326). Oxford: Oxford University Press.

Huq, R. (2006). European youth cultures in a post-colonial world: British Asian underground and French hip-hop music scenes. In P. Nilan, & C. Feixa (Eds.), *Global youth? Hybrid identities, plural worlds* (pp. 14–31). New York: Routledge.

Kaya, A. (2002). Aesthetics of diaspora: Contemporary minstrels in Turkish Berlin. *Journal of Ethnic and Migration Studies, 28*(1), 43–62.

Lesko, N. (1996). Denaturalizing adolescence: The politics of contemporary representations. *Youth & Society, 28*, 139–161.

Maira, S. (2002). *Desis in the house: Indian American youth culture in New York City.* Philadelphia: Temple University Press.

Petersson, K., Olsson, U., & Popkewitz, T. S. (2007). Nostalgia, the future, and the past as pedagogical technologies. *Discourse: Studies in the Cultural Politics of Education, 28*(1), 49–67.

43

TEACHER MOVIES

Rebecca Stanko

Teacher movies—movies about teachers and, implicitly, about the students they teach—are texts which instruct us in ways to read youth. Particularly in relation to teachers and schooling, youth as students have been re/produced through film as troubled, yet salvageable; as misguided, but talented; as vulnerable, but ultimately independent. The re/production of youth through film has re/inscribed the ways in which society has come to know youth, in relation to role, power, knowledge, and pleasure, all of which re/present effects of desire in relations between teacher and student.

Recognizing (Youth in) Teacher Movies

Early teacher movies, like Britain's 1939 classic *Goodbye, Mr. Chips*, appeared internationally, but the genre of teacher movies in America can be traced to *Blackboard Jungle* (1955), which coincided with panic over the "emergence of teenage culture" in the United States (Bulman, 2005, p. 36). Though it has grown considerably since the 1980s, the "genre" of teacher movies remains relatively small; the genre numbers in the low hundreds, including international and other types of school films (Bulman, 2005). Still, remarkably, several British and American teacher movies have garnered critical acclaim, notably in the form of Academy Awards and nominations, frequently for Best Actor or Actress for the role of the teacher. Some contemporary teacher movies, such as *Dead Poets Society* (1989) and *Dangerous Minds* (1995), have also achieved small-scale popular success in the United States and abroad, speaking to a global interest in cinematic re/presentations of teachers and students. In 1967, the title track from *To Sir, with Love* won a Grammy, and songs from several other teacher films have made the Billboard charts.

The popularity of the genre, Bulman (2005) has argued, is re/produced by the pleasures audiences derive from a *"collective* experience" of "the same cultural product" (p. 2). Teacher movies have re/produced familiar and pleasurable categorizations of "teacher" and "student," founded conventionally on age and position, as "filmmakers play on recognized tropes . . . to correspond to the knowledge of a particular audience" (Coleman, Ehrenworth, & Lesko, 2004, p. 157). Apart from film-specific contexts and storylines, teachers and youth, as categories with identifiable characteristics, have been re/presented within the genre in ways that are "remarkably consistent" (Keroes, 1999, p. 4). "Teacher" has meant adult, one who knows and who exercises power in order to redeem or re/form youth. Relationally, "student" has meant youth who need to know in order to "become" (Lesko, 2001) what they are not yet: educated, civilized, employable, not at risk.

In one recognizable narrative of teacher movies, the teacher-hero demonstrates new ways of knowing that are alluring to students, for the ways in which they interrupt or disrupt academic and institutional pedagogical norms. In this particular narrative structure, schools and administrators are positioned as powerless to control youth, while youth are positioned as in need of redemption or reform. In *To Sir, with Love* (1967), Mr. Thackeray resolves to treat his unmanageable students like adults, taking them on field trips and abandoning textbooks as sources of knowledge. In *Conrack* (1974), our hero transforms mainstream cultural traditions and rituals of personal hygiene into school knowledge for his impoverished pupils. John Keating (*Dead Poets Society*, 1989) instructs his conformist prep-school students to stand on his desk to demonstrate the value of a new perspective. To engage their underprivileged, urban students, Louanne Johnson (*Dangerous Minds*, 1995) dons a leather jacket and performs karate moves, and Jaime Escalante (*Stand and Deliver*, 1988) takes a theatrical approach—props included—to teaching math.

The personalities and pedagogies of these teacher-heroes are seductive to their students and to audiences for the ways of knowing they re/present and make possible for particular students in particular contexts. The students in these films "learn" to depend on their teachers, and to imitate or recapitulate the knowledge transmitted to them through their teachers' pedagogical performances, such that the desires of student and teacher are met, at least in part: "for the student the promise of a more powerful self, for the teacher not just the further exercise of power already claimed but also . . . the desire for intellectual partnership" (Keroes, 1999, p. 3). Perhaps accounting for the popularity and recurrence of this narrative in the genre of teacher movies are the pleasures for audiences in knowing that the students have been, in some sense, re/formed by the teacher-hero, and that society, too, has been saved from the peril of undisciplined youth (Bulman, 2005).

"Within/Against": "Troubling" Performances of Desire

While working within the genre's recognizable constructions of teacher and student, two recent films, *Half Nelson* (2006) and *The History Boys* (2006), interrupt and suggest alternatives to conventional ways of knowing youth as in need and teachers as heroes, particularly in relation to one another. Disrupting the clear categorical distinctions re/presented in other teacher movies, performances of teacher and student in these films invite audiences to consider the ways in which teacher and student are *not* "unitary subjects occupying predictable power positions" (Mac an Ghaill, 1994, p. 11).

Dan Dunne, the presumptive teacher-hero of *Half Nelson*, teaches middle school history in an urban school. Throughout the film, the White, middle-class, crack-addicted Dunne violates the boundaries of adult and youth, teacher and student, as he develops a complex, intimate relationship with Drey, a Black, female student, who knows about his secret drug habit.

Even as the film disrupts conventional boundaries between teacher/adult and student/youth by articulating visceral desires, whether for drugs or companionship, it paradoxically re/inscribes dominant perceptions of urban schools and the youth they serve—even those, like Drey, who are "promising"—as doomed or unsalvageable, without a teacher who is also a hero, as in other popular teacher movies about urban youth: *Stand and Deliver* (1988), *Dangerous Minds* (1995), *Freedom Writers* (2007).

The teacher-hero of *The History Boys* is Irwin, the newest and youngest addition to the faculty at an all-male prep school in England, where he is charged with inspiring and reforming the banal college admission essays of a small group of Oxford- and Cambridge-bound high-school students. Dakin, leader of the student/"boys" is seduced by Irwin's "reckless, impulsive, immoral" interpretations of history, and perceives Irwin's body as the physical manifestation of an alluring way of thinking about history. *The History Boys* recalls the scandalous Miss Jean Brodie (*The Prime of Miss Jean Brodie*, 1969), who projects her romantic and sexual desires onto her students, encouraging one student to engage in the affair Miss Brodie herself longs to have; this degree of separation between teacher and student does not exist in *The History Boys*, as Dakin propositions Irwin. Irwin hesitates before conceding, attempting to maintain boundaries, but they are—he is—undone by his desire for Dakin.

Half Nelson and *The History Boys* operate within the familiar hero narrative of the teacher movies genre, as the teacher-hero is positioned, at least at first, to rescue students from the dysfunctional establishment. But students in these films demonstrate competence and independence, and in so doing, exercise power via physical performances of ways of knowing not conventionally attributed to youth: Drey rescues her teacher from a crack-house, and Dakin propositions his. In this way, these two films function "within/against" the genre of teacher movies, "both 'doing it' and 'troubling it' simultaneously" (Lather, 2007, p. 38).

Experiencing Pleasure through Performances of Knowledge

In *Half Nelson* and *The History Boys*, desires become manifest in sexual tensions made explicit between teacher and student, interrupting conventional performances of power, knowledge, desires, or pleasures in teacher movies. Keroes (1999) has claimed, "Teaching is an exchange, a relationship that involves giving and receiving, the pleasures of which . . . are basically erotic" (p. 2). *Half Nelson* and *The History Boys* demonstrate the *exchange* of knowledge—or the possibilities for exchange—between teachers and students, in physical ways, rather than the recapitulation or mimicry of knowledge by students for teachers, as in earlier teacher movies like *Dead Poets Society* (1989), when students protest Keating's departure by standing on *their* desks, calling out "O Captain! My Captain!" as Keating had encouraged them to do, or in *Stand and Deliver* (1988), when students perform their knowledge of Calculus by acing the AP exam, or in *Mr. Holland's Opus* (1995), when students perform, well, Mr. Holland's opus. Rather than the familiar pleasures in these examples of students' conventional performances of knowledge, it is the threat of transgression of categorical and physical boundaries between teacher and student in *Half Nelson* and *The History Boys* that makes these films pleasurable for viewers, as students' performative ways of knowing become seductive to their teachers. Pleasure, in these films, begins with the recognition of what is familiar, but the departure into what is unfamiliar, uncertain, evokes a different kind of pleasure—in that which is illicit, unexpected, unconventional, and risky.

Within the discursive confines of teacher movies, students as youth are re/constructed and re/produced in relation to teachers as adults, and audiences bring to films conceptions of what those categories mean and have meant. Through cinematic re/presentations of teacher, student, and performances of knowledge, we re/learn what pleasures are "*thinkable* . . . for the present generation of teachers" (McWilliam, 1999, p. 1), youth, and viewing audiences. Thus, while they work recursively within traditional, normalized expectations set forth by the genre, repeating in such a way that is recognizable, new iterations of teacher films interrupt and work against the genre in ways that introduce new possibilities for desire and pleasure such that we might re/consider in what ways of understanding youth and teachers these films instruct us to believe, and what ways of knowing are seductive to us.

References

Bulman, R. C. (2005). *Hollywood goes to high school: Cinema, schools, and American culture.* New York: Worth Publishers.

Coleman, A., Ehrenworth, M., & Lesko, N. (2004). Scout's honor: Duty, citizenship, and the homoerotic in the Boy Scouts of America. In M. L. Rasmussen, E. Rofes, & S. Talburt

(Eds.), *Youth and sexualities: Pleasure, subversion, and insubordination in and out of schools* (pp. 153–176). New York: Palgrave Macmillan.

Keroes, J. (1999). *Tales out of school: Gender, longing, and the teacher in fiction and film.* Carbondale, IL: Southern Illinois University Press.

Lather, P. (2007). *Getting lost.* Albany, NY: State University of New York Press.

Lesko, N. (2001). *Act your age! A cultural construction of adolescence.* New York: Routledge.

Mac an Ghaill, M. (1994). *The making of men: Masculinities, sexualities and schooling.* Philadelphia: Open University Press.

McWilliam, E. (1999). *Pedagogical pleasures.* New York: Peter Lang Publishing, Inc.

Filmography

Berman, P. S. (Producer), & Brooks, R. (Director). (1955). *Blackboard jungle* [Motion picture]. United States: Metro-Goldwyn-Mayer.

Boden, A., Howell, L., Korenberg, R., Orlovsky, A., Patricof, J., & Walker, J. K. (Producers), & Fleck, R. (Director). (2006). *Half nelson* [Motion picture]. United States: ThinkFilm.

Clavell, J. (Producer & Director). (1967). *To sir, with love* [Motion picture]. United Kingdom: Columbia Pictures.

Cresson, J., & Fryer, R. (Producers), & Neame, R. (Director). (1969). *The prime of Miss Jean Brodie* [Motion picture]. United Kingdom: 20th Century Fox.

DeVito, D., Shamberg, M., & Sher, S. (Producers), & LaGravenese, R. (Director). (2007). *Freedom writers* [Motion picture]. United States: Paramount Pictures.

Duncan, P. S. (Producer), & Herek, S. (Director). (1995). *Mr. Holland's opus* [Motion picture]. United States: Hollywood Pictures.

Haft, S., Witt, P. J., & Thomas, T. (Producers), & Weir, P. (Director). (1989). *Dead poets society* [Motion picture]. United States: Touchstone Pictures.

Jones, D., Loader, K., & Hytner, N. (Producers), & Hytner, N. (Director). (2006). *The history boys* [Motion picture]. United Kingdom: Fox Searchlight.

Musca, T. (Producer), & Menendez, R. (Director). (1988). *Stand and deliver* [Motion picture]. United States: Warner Bros.

Ritt, M. (Director). (1974). *Conrack* [Motion picture]. United States: 20th Century Fox.

Saville, V. (Producer), & Wood, S. (Director). (1939). *Goodbye, Mr. Chips* [Motion picture]. United Kingdom: Metro-Goldwyn-Mayer.

Simpson, D., & Bruckheimer, J. (Producers), & Smith, J. N. (Director). (1995). *Dangerous minds* [Motion picture]. United States: Hollywood Pictures.

44

YOUTH ACTIVISM

Noel S. Anderson

Activism is a term with multiple meanings and interpretations. A common definition of activism is individuals engaged in activities, such as direct action and community organizing, to foster some form of social change. The attempts at social change can range from concerns about the environment, racism, and gay rights to school reform in urban centers. Yet, like the multiplicity of social issues undertaken by people around the world, what is viewed as activism can vary from country to country, context to context, and from one end of the political spectrum to the other.

Youth activism is also a problematic term. "Youth is a historically contingent category and its boundaries are neither solely biological nor cultural. Therefore, it is often hard to clearly define the age boundaries of youth, and in fact, it is often the historian's task to narrate the shifting nature of youth over time" (Ides, 2009, p. 8). Youth is not static, unchanging. So what classifies *youth*, like activism, can vary from one historical period to another (Ides, 2009).

In the United States, organized youth activism emerged from the Progressive era of the 19th century, when labor strikes became the means by which young people engaged those in power to correct working conditions in factories, adopt child labor laws, and bring in a livable wage (Freeman, 2000). Well into the 1960s, civil rights, antiwar, feminist, and gay rights movements helped to shape what was defined as *student movements*. In these student movements, youth activism was led by young people themselves, such as in the case of the Student Nonviolent Coordinating Committee (SNCC), which helped to desegregate lunch counters during the civil rights era and spawn the youth-led Black Power movement of the late 1960s and early 1970s (Anderson & Kharem, 2009).

There is currently a robust youth activist movement, utilizing social media and other technologies, to organize around issues of injustice, locally and globally. The most visible is the diverse youth movement against global dominance of big business on international trade policy, the environment, and human rights. This youth movement was evident in protests and clashes with police at World Trade Organization (WTO) meetings, most notably in Seattle in 1999, also called "the Battle in Seattle."

Adult Nostalgia and Youth Activism

Much of the popular discourse on youth activism in the United States today, ·unfortunately, is shaped by the nostalgia for a bygone era of the 1960s, a period usually characterized as the golden age of youth engagement. As Hasian and Shugart (2001) argue, nostalgia is a special type of individual and collective mourning involving a form of bereavement for objects or events that are considered lost or displaced. Dwelling on a romanticized past helps some people fill a void in their lives (Hasian & Shugart, 2001). It also allows individuals to relive their experience and simultaneously propagate the next generation of activists.

In fact many of the leaders of the 1960s youth movements have become the present day adult leaders of major civil rights institutions, powerful elected officials, noted journalists, professors, and public intellectuals. Further, their prolific output of memoirs, books, lectures, and public appearances reflecting on their work in youth movement and their work to foster social change have come to shape the commonsense of how youth activism should look.

An example is evident in the edited text, *From ACT UP to the WTO: Urban Protest and Community Building in the Era of Globalization*. The authors, the majority of whom were key leaders in social movements decades ago, assert "the text does not attempt to create a nostalgic tribute to past activism" (Shepard & Hayduk, 2002, p. xi). Nonetheless, the book presents youth activism as a direct outgrowth of earlier movements, such as ACT UP, which was the leader in the HIV/AIDS awareness campaigns of the 1980s. It fails to give the WTO movement its own identity, as something that could have evolved independent of prior movements. A number of these authors tend to view activism as a youthful rite of passage, while others errantly analyze present day circumstances as simply an extension of the past. This collection has also become a key text for the development of studies in youth activism.

Jena 6: Youth Activism vs. "A New Civil Rights Movement?"

An illustrative case of how adult nostalgia and power can shape present day youth activism was evident in the "Jena 6" movement. The Jena 6 movement emerged from the events that took place in Jena, Louisiana, in 2006, when a Black student at Jena High School, Kenneth Purvis, asked the principal if he could sit under the "white tree," an area in the schoolyard where White students congregated during breaks. When the principal stated that Purvis could "sit wherever he liked," Purvis and his cousin Bryant, also a student at Jena High School, stood under the tree. The following morning three nooses were hanging from the tree, a presumed warning to students who crossed the racial line in the school.

Subsequently, Jena High School exploded in racial violence between Black and White students. In fact, one of the six young Black men who engaged in a school-yard fight was arrested and then sentenced to 25 years in prison for "assault with a deadly weapon," which was determined by the judge to be the "tennis shoes" he wore when he stomped on a White male student (Maxwell & Zehr, 2007, para. 3).

The Jena criminal case harkened back to the early days before civil rights, when White judges and all White juries doled out excessive jail sentences to

Black defendants. And although the subsequent events led youth in Jena and youth activist groups around the country to hold national student walkouts and solidarity strikes to protest the treatment of Black young people, adults seized on the event, with youth-led protests being rendered silent. Adult activists soon became the center of attention and began speaking "on behalf" of youth.

For instance, youth activist-turned-elder statesman Reverend Jesse Jackson promoted the term Jena 6 to evoke the "Scottsboro 9"[1] and stated that it was a "defining moment, just like Selma [Alabama] was a defining moment" (Mooney, 2007, para. 8). Reverend Al Sharpton (Schapiro, 2007, para. 5) stated, while leading his own rally, that the Jena 6 case "could be the beginning of the 21st century's civil rights movement."

In fact, what started out as a school-yard fight became a national civil rights issue. The acceleration of harsh school discipline practices and zero tolerance policies affecting young people in many school systems around the country fell out of the discussion, and larger issues of civil rights reframed the national conversation and protest. Jena High School, as the institution that allowed a white tree to exist in the first place and that allowed young people to be in harm's way to "integrate" a social space for White students, was not scrutinized on its own, but quickly disappeared into discussion about the criminal justice system and civil rights in the United States. According to Beverly Daniel Tatum, president of Spelman College, an historically Black institution in Atlanta, "educators have a tremendous responsibility to not only know what the academic needs of their students are, but to know what the social climate is in their school, because those are not unrelated . . . It seems to me that school leaders in Jena lost several opportunities to address these incidents before things became physically violent" (Maxwell & Zehr, 2007, para. 5).

When adults began to speak for the Jena 6 in the media, youth activists attempted to reclaim the movement from adults. For instance, Reginald McKinley, a 21-year-old student from Morehouse, expressed his dismay that "generationally speaking . . . this is the youth of America speaking out [against Jena 6]. My collaborators [college students] have worked hand-and-hand with me with the understanding that this is the youth's voice and this is the social consciousness of us. And—I mean, we built upon that" (Chideya, 2007, para. 15).

Moreover, the young men of Jena were refashioned by adults to become typologies, model youth citizens, likened to the Scottsboro boys. Historian Robin Kelley asserts that from the social science research on Blacks during the civil rights era emerged typologies of Black youth as one-dimensional characters. These typologies were shot through with class assumptions as well. In many cases poor youth were viewed as "lames" and middle-class youth as "strivers" (Kelley, 1997). These typologies, according to Kelley, have persisted in studies of urban youth. In most media coverage of the Jena 6, adults spoke on their behalf, and the young men were always presented as middle-class strivers, dressed in Oxford shirts or suits, not the common clothing worn by young men who are a part of hip-hop culture.

Yet some months later, when two of the young men from the Jena 6 group appeared on the Black Entertainment Television (BET) awards show, wearing clothing that evoked their connection to hip-hop culture, there was public criticism. The young men walked on stage, with low-slung pants, basketball sneakers, and sunglasses, thanked the audience for supporting their case, and left the stage holding their fingers in the air in the shape of the number 6. Soon after, those in the mainstream civil rights groups, like the National Association for the Advancement of Colored People, were critical of their appearance. Some media outlets referred to them as "thugs and gangstas" because they wore the attire generally associated with urban underclass youth (Bennett, 2007).

Youth Activists: Still Speaking Truth to Power

Like in the Jena 6 example, youth concerns are not static but shaped by the current milieu. Technologies and youth culture, such as hip-hop, make the lives of young people distinctively different than in the 1960s and 1970s. Young activists are blogging, text messaging, videotaping, and using social media to create community, strategize, and rapidly respond to present day injustice like police brutality and segregated school conditions (Alonso, Anderson, Su, & Theoharis, 2009).

Young people's use of virtual media to address harsh social realities through activism is a testament to their innovation and belief in social justice. In turn, adult activists must see themselves in solidarity with young people to address concerns that young people identify as important, not the other way around.

Note

1   "Scottsboro 9," also known as the "Scottsboro Boys," referred to a group of teenage boys who were wrongfully convicted of gang raping two White women on a train through Scottsboro, Alabama, in the 1930s. Their case became an example of racial injustice in southern court systems.

References

Alonso, G., Anderson, N., Su, C., & Theoharis, J. (2009). *Our schools suck: Students talk back to a segregated nation on the failures of urban education*. New York: New York University Press.

Anderson, N., & Kharem, H. (2009). *Education as freedom: African American educational thought and activism*. Lanham, MD: Lexington Books.

Bennett, G. (2007, October 15). Jena 6 the latest rap group? *National Public Radio*. Retrieved from http://www.npr.org/blogs/newsandviews/2007/10/jena_6_the_latest_rap_group.html

Chideya, F. (2007, September 20). Thousands rally for the "Jena 6." *National Public Radio*. Retrieved from http://www.npr.org/templates/story/story.php?storyId=14567418

Freeman, J. (2000). *Working class New York: Life and labor since World War II*. New York: The New Press.

Hasian, M., & Shugart, H. A. (2001). Melancholic nostalgia, collective memories and the cinematic representation of nationalistic identities in Indochine. *Communication Quarterly*, 49, 329–350. Retrieved from http://www.tandf.co.uk/journals/RCQU

Ides, M. (2009). *Cruising for community: Youth culture and politics in Los Angeles, 1910–1970*. Doctoral dissertation, University of Michigan, Ann Arbor.

Kelley, R. (1997). *Yo mama's disfunktional: Fighting the culture wars in urban America.* New York: Beacon Press.

Maxwell, L., & Zehr, M. A. (2007, October). "Jena 6": Case study in racial tensions. *Education Week, 27,* 1–19. Retrieved from http://www.edweek.org/ew/articles/2007/10/03/06jena.h27.html

Mooney, A. (2007, September 19). Jesse Jackson: Obama needs to bring more attention to Jena 6. *CNN.* Retrieved from http://www.cnn.com/2007/POLITICS/09/19/jackson.jena6/index.html?iref=allsearch

Schapiro, R. (2007, September 21). Rev. Al Sharpton leads "Jena 6" protest in Louisiana. *NY Daily News.* Retrieved from http://www.nydailynews.com/news/national/2007/09/21/2007-09-21_rev_al_sharpton_leads_jena_6_protest_in_-3.html

Shepard, B., & Hayduk, R. (Eds.). (2002). *From ACT UP to the WTO: Urban protest and community building in the era of globalization.* New York: Verso.

45

YOUTH PARTICIPATORY ACTION RESEARCH

Michelle Fine

As a form of democratic science, youth participatory action research (yPAR) grows out of a vibrant lineage of social inquiry crafted in the soil of radical social movements. Reflecting the commitments of Paolo Freire (1982), Orlando Fals-Borda (1979), and Ignacio Martín-Baró (1994), yPAR projects are generally taken up by activist research collectives of elders, adults, and youth critically documenting conditions of structural inequality, excavating pools of collective resistance, and contesting scientific imaginings of youth that circulate in popular culture, such as the unformed adolescent brain.

Drawing on critical race, feminist, queer, disability, neo-Marxist, indigenous, and/or poststructural theory, yPAR contests structural violence that youth endure, the symbolic violence of demonizing representations, and the scientific violence through which they are studied. That is, these inquiry projects document the grossly uneven structural distributions of opportunities, resources, and dignity; trouble the ideological categories projected onto youth (delinquent, at risk, promiscuous, damaged, innocent, victim); and contest how "science" has been recruited to legitimate dominant policies and practices. Whether Black babies are displayed as "endangered" to mobilize antiabortion

That Frustrating Teen Brain

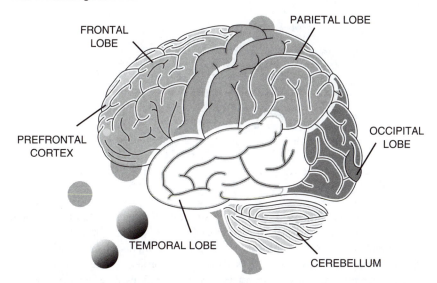

While you may have heard about some of the research regarding the development of the adolescent brain, the folks at the *MIT Young Adult Development Project* (2008) are collecting the research data in one place for us. You can learn about how the adolescent brain develops from back to front. That means that the prefrontal cortex, the part of the brain responsible for judgment, managing emotions, and complex thinking, doesn't fully develop until the mid-twenties.

sentiments in communities of color, or images of young sexual innocence are celebrated on billboards to bolster an abstinence-only campaign, the deliberate deployment of youth imagery seduces, distorts, and deflects in public discourse, policy, and the production of mainstream science. Across fields, there is growing scholarship on the scientific consequences of demonizing and/or diminished representations of adolescents (see, e.g., Geronimus & Thompson, 2004; Lesko, 2001; Males, 2001; McClelland & Fine, 2008). yPAR projects are designed, by multi-generational research collectives taking up social struggle, to expose these conditions, deconstruct these images, and engage a democratic public science.

The Praxis of Critical Participatory Science

Cammarota and Fine (2008) catalogue a set of critical yPAR projects launched in schools, communities, activist youth organizations, and prisons. These projects seek to document varied circuits of dispossession and privilege (Fine & Ruglis, 2009) across a wide range of issues, for example food justice, the school to prison pipeline, violence against girls and women, police harassment of youth of color, sexuality/abstinence education, push out practices in high school, harassment of and organizing by LGBT youth, the racial consequences of high

(Campaign for Our Children, Inc., n.d.)

stakes testing, tracking and school closings, the rights of undocumented students, charters, and critical youth media (see also Ginwright, 2009).

The practice of yPAR relies upon varied embodiments of expertise, coming together, to cultivate new knowledges. Participatory projects gather often a diverse collective of sometimes dissenting voices, across generations, race/ethnicity, sexuality, stance, class, and zip codes (see Chávez & Soep, 2005; Gutiérrez, Baquedano-Lopez, & Tejeda, 1999; Torre, 2005; Torre & Ayala, 2009). Within these contact zones, a notion migrated into yPAR by Maria Elena Torre (2005) of the Public Science Project, differently situated youth and adults stretch to collaborate in sometimes contentious or awkward dialogue to sculpt research questions of meaning, design research with sharp edges, spin analyses, and develop products of use to feed public action. By so doing, yPAR projects explicitly queer prevailing notions of expertise, objectivity, and neutrality; trouble, as we stumble through, simple victim-blaming explanations; interrogate how State policy and structural formations induce social injustice; and lift up stories of how young people survive, resist, collapse, and/or organize under the weight. A few images of yPAR may help.

YRNES

The YRNES (Youth Researchers for a New Education System) project was designed as a rhizomatic undertaking, inspired by Deleuze and framed through indigenous theory, facilitated by critical education scholar Eve Tuck (2009). The youth-led research collective set out to document the structural violence exacerbated once public education in New York City was placed under mayoral control. The YRNES report chronicles the redlining of education, the accumulation of dignity violations, and the normalization of both in many public schools.

> On April 16, 2005, parents, students, teachers, and advocates met at the Education Action Summit to call for a new system of public education in NYC based on human rights. As a result of that conference the Education is a Human Right Campaign officially launched on Sept 28, 2005 on the steps of City Hall. Over twenty organizations joined the lead organizer, the Independent Commission for Public Education (iCOPE) and endorsed the campaign . . . In November 2006, iCOPE invited youth

researchers to independently design and conduct a participatory action research project; this group became YRNES. During 2007, the campaign conducted two tribunals, met with various community, youth and parent organizations, and held a day-long retreat to envision a human rights-based school system. The purpose of the Education is a Human Right Campaign is twofold: 1) To show that a more just, democratic, and effective education system is possible; 2) To encourage a citywide dialogue, so that all stakeholders can knowledgeably share their views before a legislative decision is made in Albany about the sun-setting of the current governance law, which gave the Mayor total control of the system. The campaign insists that this decision, which affects the education of 1.1 million students, can be made only after open, public dialogue.

(YRNES, 2008, p. 1)

YRNES produced a powerful monograph of evidence gathered from youth in and out of schools, a monograph of science and outrage, displaying a politically and aesthetically compelling Problem Tree of the roots, the trunks, and the blossoming manifestations of oppression within public education. The report has been list-serve distributed across the United States and internationally to progressive educational sites, while the elegant, gorgeous, infected Problem Tree has been on display at the Schomburg Center for Research on Black Culture in Harlem.

Fed Up Honeys

While YRNES was a research team of young people from across New York City, the Fed Up Honeys (Cahill, 2010) was born as a place-based Lower East Side research collective dedicated to cataloguing symbolic violence and the demeaning representations of young women of color that circulate in policy, schools, on the streets, and in the popular imagination. Initially interested in how young women navigate public space, these young researchers were reading policy documents when they encountered crude stereotypes about young women of color represented in the policy analyses. Fed Up Honeys initiated a systematic analysis of floating stereotypes and launched a counter-hegemonic sticker campaign about young women on the streets of the Lower East Side (Fed Up Honeys, n.d.).

With a creative blend of photography, mapping, interviews, census data, and critical excerpts from policy documents, Fed Up Honeys have presented their findings nationally and designed a participatory website that enjoys much traffic in the United States and globally.

Polling for Justice

A city-wide participatory poll of New York City youth experiences of (in)justice in education, criminal justice, and health care, Polling for Justice (PFJ) was designed to challenge the scientific framing of youth "at risk" (Fine & Ruglis, 2009). Inspired by the theorizing and meticulous research of W. E. B. DuBois' (1898) Philadelphia Negro, PFJ set out to reverse the gaze away from

Young Urban Womyn of Color are...

Likely to Become Teen Moms

Stereotype #1
www.fed-up-honeys.org

Young Urban Womyn of Color are...

In Abusive Relationships

Stereotype #3
www.fed-up-honeys.org

Young Urban Womyn of Color are...

Promiscuous

Stereotype #5
www.fed-up-honeys.org

Young Urban Womyn of Color are...

Lazy and on Welfare

Stereotype #2
www.fed-up-honeys.org

Young Urban Womyn of Color are a ...

Burden To Society

Stereotype #4
www.fed-up-honeys.org

Young Urban Womyn of Color are...

Uneducated

Stereotype #6
www.fed-up-honeys.org

Stereotype Sticker Campaign, © Fed Up Honeys 2011, www.fed-up-honeys.org

"problematic youth" and map instead the geography and footprints of neoliberal policies (e.g., high stakes testing, criminalization, gentrification, abstinence education, etc.) on young people's social health (for a detailed description of PFJ, see Fox, Mediratta, Ruglis, Stoudt, Shah, & Fine, 2010).

In a series of participatory "research camps," researchers, activists, and youth came together to learn methods, read critical theory, and engage Stats for the People and Participatory Analysis Strategies. Designed by a wide-ranging collective of youth and adult researchers, the project speaks back to popular framings of "youth at risk." PFJ has gathered data from more than 1,100 young people across NYC, and is now distributing and performing, through Theatre of the Oppressed and Playback Theatre, zip-code-level analyses of dispossession for a number of human rights campaigns, for example for queer youth, schools not prisons, gender safety, alternatives to high stakes testing, mobilizations against police harassment, and community actions against school closings.

Enabling Conditions of PAR: Epistemology and Action

Relying upon varied methodologies—quantitative surveys, interviews, focus groups, archival analyses, memoir, visual methods, and ethnography—participatory projects enact a critical epistemology that draws upon democratic expertise; cultivates deep participation as a practice of strong objectivity; and insists on politically mobilized actions informed by critical inquiry (see Fals-Borda, 1979; Freire, 1982; Harding, 1995). Indeed, democracy, critique, and action are the foundational enabling conditions of PAR.

Research products and actions are central to participatory work, theorizing throughout how the research will invite and provoke varied audiences, fueling campaigns for educational policies, and informing social theory. Findings from all three projects have been fed back to movements for educational justice; folded into legal battles and policy struggles; glued onto street lights in sticker campaigns challenging dominant stereotypes; kneaded into youth testimony and radio shows; displayed in museums; and choreographed into spoken word, dance, theatre, graffiti walls, and other forms of performance to provoke community engagement with issues that may seem distant, but are intimate to our collective well-being.

★★★

Before I close, I should comment on what has been called the "tyranny of participation." Participatory action research as a methodology has, of recent times, become a fashionable technology of capitalism and imperialism, appropriated by the Right, the International Monetary Fund, the U.S. military, the for-profit charter movement, and varied development organizations to reframe hegemonic interests as if they were the interests of "the people"—in this case, "the youth" (see Cooke & Kothari, 2001).

In contrast to the neoliberal appropriation of participatory methods, yPAR seeks to take up critical questions of power, history, participation, representation, science, and the difficult intimacies of collaboration. When practiced by young and old critical theorists and activists engaging often awkward conversation and spicy inquiry sustained over time, yPAR is anything but enchanting. Long day/late night arguments about what justice might look like emerge from difficult negotiations across theory, practice, generation, race/ethnicity, gender, sexuality, immigration status, (dis)abilities, place, and biographies. Embedded in deeply reflexive methods and equally precarious social movements with adult allies, yPAR insists that young people have a "right to research" (Appadurai, 2006). Standing in opposition to academic research done on, for, but without youth, yPAR is a humble, trying, and often clumsy effort to carve a messy space where youth and adults inquire critically and creatively about sites of dispossession and possibility, struggling to reframe today as they craft a radical reimagination of tomorrow.

References

Appadurai, A. (2006). The right to research. *Globalization, Societies, and Education, 4*, 167–177.

Cahill, C. (2010). Negotiating grit and glamour: Young women and urban economic restructuring. In L. Lees, T. Slater, & E. Wyly (Eds.), *The gentrification reader* (pp. 299–314). New York: Routledge.

Cammarota, J., & Fine, M. (2008). *Revolutionizing education: Youth participatory action research in motion.* New York: Routledge.

Campaign for Our Children, Inc. (n.d.). Retrieved from http://www.cfoc.org

Chávez, V., & Soep, E. (2005). Youth Radio and the pedagogy of collegiality. *Harvard Educational Review, 75*, 409–434.

Cooke, B., & Kothari, U. (2001). *Participation: The new tyranny?* London: Zed.

DuBois, W. E. B. (1898). The study of the Negro problems. *The Annals of the American Academy of Political and Social Science, 11*, 1–23.

Fals-Borda, O. (1979). Investigating the reality in order to transform it: The Colombian experience. *Dialectical Anthropology, 4*, 33–55.

Fed Up Honeys [Authors]. *Stereotype stickers* [Photograph]. (n.d.). Retrieved from http://www.fed-up-honeys.org/mainpage.htm

Fine, M., & Ruglis, J. (2009). Circuits of dispossession: The racialized and classed realignment of the public sphere for youth in the U.S. *Transforming Anthropology, 17*, 20–33.

Fox, M., Mediratta, K., Ruglis, J., Stoudt, B., Shah, S., & Fine, M. (2010). Critical youth engagement: Participatory action research and organizing. In L. Sherrod, J. Torney-Puta, & C. Flanagan (Eds.), *Handbook of research and policy on civic engagement with youth* (pp. 621–650). Hoboken, NJ: Wiley Press.

Freire, P. (1982). Creating alternative research methods: Learning to do it by doing it. In B. Hall, A. Gillette, & R. Tandon (Eds.), *Creating knowledge: A monopoly* (pp. 29–37). New Delhi: Society for Participatory Research in Asia.

Georgia Right to Life [Sponsor]. Black children are an endangered species [Advertisement]. (2010). Retrieved from http://www.jillstanek.com/genocide/black-children.html

Geronimus, A. T., & Thompson, J. P. (2004). To denigrate, ignore, or disrupt: Racial inequality in health and the impact of a policy-induced breakdown of African American communities. *Du Bois Review: Social Science Research on Race, 1*(2), 247–279.

Ginwright, S. (2009). *Black youth rising: Race, agency and radical healing in urban America.* New York: Teachers College Press.

Gutiérrez, K., Baquedano-Lopez, P., & Tejeda, C. (1999). Rethinking diversity: Hybridity and hybrid language practices in the third space. *Mind, Culture, & Activity: An International Journal, 6*, 286–303.

Harding, S. (1995). Strong objectivity: A response to the new objectivity question. *Synthese, 104*, 331–349.

Lesko, N. (2001). *Act your age! A cultural construction of adolescence.* New York: Routledge.

Males, M. (2001). *"Kids & guns": How politicians, experts, and the press fabricate fear of youth.* New York: Common Courage Press.

Martín-Baró, I. (1994). *Writings for a liberation psychology.* Cambridge, MA: Harvard University Press.

McClelland, S., & Fine, M. (2008). Embedded science: The production of consensus in evaluation of abstinence-only curricula. *Cultural Studies<=>Critical Methodologies, 8*, 50–81.

MIT Young Adult Development Project [Author]. *Teen brain* [Illustration]. (2008). Retrieved from http://journeytomanhood.blogspot.com/2008/08/that-frustrating-teen-brain.html

Pratt, M. L. (1991). Arts of the contact zone. *Profession, 91*, 33–40.

Torre, M. E. (2005). The alchemy of integrated spaces: Youth participation in research collectives of difference. In L. Weis, & M. Fine (Eds.), *Beyond silenced voices* (pp. 251–266). Albany, NY: State University of New York Press.

Torre, M. E., & Ayala, J. (2009). Envisioning participatory action research entremundos. *Feminism and Psychology, 19*, 387–393.

Tuck, E. (2009). Suspending damage: A letter to communities. *Harvard Educational Review, 79*, 408–429.

Youth Researchers for a New Education System (YRNES). (2008). *The YRNES report.* Retrieved from http://www.icope.org/documents/yrnes.pdf

CONTRIBUTOR BIOGRAPHIES

Noel S. Anderson is Acting Chairperson in the Department of Political Science and Associate Professor in the Department of Political Science and School of Education (affiliated) at Brooklyn College, City University of New York. His research centers on urban politics, urban school reform, and college access. Dr. Anderson has coauthored *Our Schools Suck: Students Talk Back to a Segregated Nation on the Failures of Public Education* (New York University Press, 2009) and *Education as Freedom: African American Education Thought and Activism* (Lexington Books, 2009).

Benjamin Baez is an Associate Professor in the Department of Leadership and Professional Studies at Florida International University. His recent books include *The Politics of Inquiry: Education Research and the "Culture of Science"* with Deron Boyles (SUNY Press, 2009), winner of the 2009 CHOICE Award for Outstanding Title and 2010 American Educational Studies Association Critics Choice Selection, and *Understanding Minority-Serving Institutions: Interdisciplinary Perspectives* (SUNY Press, 2008) with Marybeth Gasman and Caroline Turner. His teaching and research interests include economic policies on education, knowledge and its production, and the law of education.

Stephen J. Ball is Karl Mannheim Professor of Sociology of Education at the Institute of Education, University of London. He works in policy sociology and has conducted a series of ESRC-funded studies which focus on issues of social class and policy. His recent books include *The Education Debate* (Policy Press, 2008), *Education Plc* (Routledge, 2007), *Education Policy and Social Class* (Routledge, 2006), and *Childcare Choice and Class Practices* (Routledge, 2005) with Carol Vincent. He has an honorary doctorate from Turku University. He is a Visiting Professor at the University of San Andres, Buenos Aires and a Fellow of the British Academy.

John Broughton teaches courses on cultural studies in the Department of Arts & Humanities at Teachers College, Columbia University, where he also runs the Film and Education Research Academy (http://blogs.tc.columbia.edu/fera). His research is about youth culture, gender, illness, violence, and trauma, with an emphasis on the educational role of visual media. He is coeditor of *Cultural Studies, Education and Youth* (Lexington Books, 2011), and founding coeditor of *Cultural Formations*, an online journal on cultural theory, schooling, and subjectivity. He is working on a collection of his papers on war and on a manuscript about critical media literacy and popular culture.

Mary K. Bryson is a Professor in the Faculty of Education at the University of British Columbia. She is the Director of the Centre for Cross-Faculty Inquiry in Education and Director, Network of Centers and Institutes in Education (http://ubc.academia.edu/MaryKBryson). Bryson's current research in critical cultural studies of gender and sexuality concerns the networked technologies that constitute health informatics and their role in the mobilization of knowledge, citizenship, and accessible publics. Bryson has published on gender/sexuality and pervasively networked media, queer theory, and the politics of democratization and difference/s, including *Radical In(Ter)Ventions* (SUNY Press, 1997). In 2000, Bryson received the Canadian Pioneer in New Technologies and Media award. She is also the recipient of a Stanford University Senior Research Fellowship (for 2010–2011) at the Clayman Institute for Gender Research.

Dana Burde is Assistant Professor of International Education at New York University and a research affiliate at the Saltzman Institute of War and Peace Studies, Columbia University. Her research and teaching focus on education, political violence, international organizations, and humanitarian action in countries at war. With the support of the Spencer Foundation, NSF, USIP, and the Weikart Family Foundation, she examined the impact of community-based schools on children, households, and villages in Afghanistan. She received her PhD in Comparative Education and Political Science from Columbia University, EdM from Harvard University, and BA from Oberlin College.

M. Piper Dumont, an educator and agrarian, cultivates connections with the land and the people living on it. Equipped with a BA in Human Ecology from College of Atlantic and an enduring sense of wonder, Piper's passions led her to Teachers College, Columbia University, to earn a master's in International Educational Development with a focus on peace education. As a doctoral student at TC, she's pursuing a self-designed interdisciplinary program integrating peace education and cultural studies around food. She's applying her studies as the supervisor of Union Theological Seminary's initiative to incorporate ecological and food justice into their programming, including converting parts of their grounds and roofs into organic growing spaces.

Carles Feixa holds a PhD from the University of Barcelona and a Doctorate *Honoris Causa* from the University of Manizales (Colombia). He teaches at the University of Lleida. He has been a Visiting Scholar at universities in Rome, Mexico, Paris, California at Berkeley, Buenos Aires, Santiago de Chile, and Newcastle. He is the author of *De jovenes, bandas y tribus* (Barcelona, 1998, 4th edition, 2008), *Jovens na America Latina* (São Paulo, 2004), and *Global Youth?* (London, 2006) with Pam Nilan. He is the coeditor of the journal *Young* (London/Delhi) and a member of the international board of *Nueva Antropología* (Mexico), *Revista Latinoamericana de Ciencias Sociales, Niñez y Juventud* (Colombia), *Mondi Migranti* (Milan), and *Analise Social* (Lisboa), among others. He has been advisor for youth policies of the United Nations and Vice President of the International Sociological Association Research Committee "Sociology of Youth."

Beth A. Ferri is an Associate Professor at Syracuse University. She has published on the intersection of race and disability, including articles in *Teachers College Record, International Journal of Inclusive Education, Gender & Education, Disability Studies Quarterly*, and *Disability & Society*. Her book, *Reading Resistance: Discourses of Exclusion in Desegregation and Inclusion Debates* (Peter Lang, 2006), with David J. Connor, examines how rhetorics of race and dis/ability were used to maintain and justify segregated education after the historic *Brown* v. *Board of Education* decision. She is currently working on two books, *Opting Out*, on homeschooling, and *Righting Educational Wrongs*, coedited with Arlene Kanter.

Michelle Fine is Distinguished Professor of Social Psychology in Women's Studies and Urban Education at the Graduate Center, City University of New York. She has been teaching at CUNY since 1992 and is a founding member of the Participatory Action Research Collective.

Jen Gilbert is Associate Professor of Education at York University, Toronto. Her research interests include LGBTQ issues, sexuality education, and psychoanalytic theories of teaching and learning.

Anita Harris is a mid-career research fellow at the Centre for Critical and Cultural Studies at the University of Queensland. Her research interests include youth identities and cultures, citizenship, participation and new politics, and globalization and multiculturalism. She is the author of a forthcoming book, *Young People and Multicultural Living* (Routledge). Her recent books include *Next Wave Cultures: Feminism, Subcultures, Activism* (edited, Routledge, 2008), *Young Femininity: Girlhood, Power and Social Change* (Palgrave, 2005) with Sinikka Aapola and Marnina Gonick, *Future Girl: Young Women in the Twenty First Century* (Routledge, 2004), and *All About the Girl: Culture, Power and Identity* (edited, Routledge, 2004).

Valerie Harwood is a Senior Lecturer in the Faculty of Education, University of Wollongong, Australia. Her research interests include the production of knowledge on psychopathology, critical disability studies, and youth exclusion.

Her work examines child and youth psychiatric disorders and associated diagnostic practices as they impact education.

Julian Henriques has worked for London Weekend Television and BBC Television, Music and Arts Department, and run his own production company, Formation Films. He is writer–director of the feature film, *Babymother*. Henriques ran the film and television department at CARIMAC at the University of the West Indies, and is currently Senior Lecturer in the Department of Media and Communications, at Goldsmiths, University of London. He is the coauthor of *Changing the Subject* (Routledge, 1998), a founding editor of the *Ideology & Consciousness* journal, and has written chapters and articles in *Auditory Culture Reader, Sonic Interventions, Sonic Synergies, African and Black Diaspora*, and *Body & Society*. His monograph *Sonic Bodies* was published in 2011.

Tommi Hoikkala is a Research Professor at the Finnish Youth Research Society. He has conducted ethnographic field studies among youth gangs, conscripts in the Finnish army, and school classes. Hoikkala is a sociologist whose interests include praxis-orientated youth research, generations, health, and the networking of scientific organizations. He has over 120 scientific publications, four monographs, and *The Known Soldier: The Experience and Health Sense of the Finnish Conscript* (2009) with Mikko Salasuo and Anni Ojajärvi.

Rupa Huq is a Senior Lecturer in Sociology at Kingston University. Her research interests include youth culture, pop music, and urban/suburban relations. Her *Beyond Subculture: Pop, Youth and Identity in a Postcolonial World* (Routledge, 2005) is a study of youth culture and popular music. Her forthcoming book will chart representations and realities of suburbia. Her interests outside work include DJ-ing, being a mum, and active involvement in local politics. She served as Deputy Mayoress of the London Borough of Ealing from 2010–2011. She has studied at Cambridge, Strasbourg, and East London universities.

Amira Jarmakani is Associate Professor of Women's Studies at Georgia State University. She is the author of *Imagining Arab Womanhood: The Cultural Mythology of Veils, Harems, and Belly Dancers in the U.S.* (Palgrave Macmillan, 2008), which won the National Women's Studies Association Gloria E. Anzaldúa book prize. She has also published chapters in *Arabs in the Americas, Arab and Arab American Feminisms*, and *The Cultural Politics of the Middle East in the Americas*; as well as articles in *Signs: Journal of Women in Culture and Society* and *Critical Arts: A South-North Journal for Cultural and Media Studies*.

Mary Jane Kehily is a Senior Lecturer in Childhood and Youth Studies at the Open University, UK. She has a background in cultural studies and education. She has published widely on gender and sexuality, narrative and identity, and popular culture. Her books include *Gender, Sexuality and Schooling: Shifting Agendas in Social Learning* (Routledge, 2002), *An Introduction to Childhood Studies*

(Open University Press/McGraw Hill, 2009), *Understanding Youth: Perspectives, Identities and Practices* (The Open University/Sage, 2007), and *Gender, Youth and Culture: Young Masculinities and Femininities* (Palgrave, 2008), with Anoop Nayak.

Aaron Koh is an Assistant Professor in the Department of English at Hong Kong Institute of Education, Hong Kong, China. He is the author of *Tactical Globalization* (Peter Lang, 2010). His current research is on youth and popular culture and the teaching of English in Hong Kong.

Julie Kubala is Director of Undergraduate Studies and Senior Lecturer in the Women's Studies Institute at Georgia State University. She teaches courses on queer theory, Foucault, social class, girls, and historical and theoretical perspectives on activism. She recently coedited a special issue of *The Scholar & Feminist Online* that brings together art, activism, and academia. She is working on a project that explores histories of queer and antiracist activism in Atlanta to investigate current strategies of community organizing.

Nancy Lesko teaches curriculum studies and gender and education at Teachers College, Columbia University. She has been researching affective aspects of curriculum and developing new research around immigrant youth's feelings of belonging and teachers' affective agency around LGBTQ students and issues. Recent articles include "Feeling abstinent? Feeling comprehensive? Touching the affects of sexuality curricula" in *Sex Education: Sexuality, Society and Learning* and "Feeling jumpy: Teaching about HIV/AIDS" in *International Journal of Qualitative Studies in Education*. A second edition of her book, *Act Your Age! A Cultural Construction of Adolescence*, is due out in 2011.

Allan Luke is Professor of Education at Queensland University of Technology, Brisbane, Australia. His most recent book is *Pierre Bourdieu and Literacy Education* (Routledge, 2008). He is currently studying Aboriginal and Torres Strait Islander policy and school reform in Australia.

Kristen Luschen is Associate Professor of Education Studies at Hampshire College and faculty in the School of Critical Social Inquiry and the Critical Studies of Childhood, Youth, and Learning Program. She teaches courses in gender studies, youth studies, and qualitative research methods. Her published research explores how cultural conceptions of youth shape educational policies, practices, and school culture and how young people negotiate identity within these contexts. Luschen recently edited a special issue of *Educational Studies* (2010), "Youth, New Media and Education."

Lori B. MacIntosh is a doctoral candidate in the Department of Educational Studies at the University of British Columbia. Her research focuses on media production, youth culture, sexuality, gender, and the politics of media and education. Lori's current work explores how youth-produced film and digital media are pedagogically employed in the interests of social justice education.

Her scholarly publications address antihomophobia pedagogies and youth media culture.

Meg Maguire is Professor of Sociology of Education at King's College, London. Her work is in the area of policy and social justice, with a particular concern for policy enactments in urban settings. She recently published *Changing Urban Education* (Continuum, 2010) with Simon Pratt-Adams and Elizabeth Burns. Currently, she is working with Annette Braun and Stephen Ball on an ESRC-funded project "Policy Enactments in the Secondary School: Theory and Practice." She is lead editor of the *Journal of Education Policy*.

Sunaina Maira is Professor of Asian American Studies at the University of California, Davis. She is the author of *Desis in the House: Indian American Youth Culture in New York City* (Temple University Press, 2002) and coeditor of *Youthscapes: The Popular, the National, the Global* (University of Pennsylvania Press, 2005) and *Contours of the Heart: South Asians Map North America* (Asian American Writers' Workshop, 1996), which won the American Book Award in 1997. Her most recent book, *Missing: Youth, Citizenship, and Empire after 9/11* (Duke University Press, 2009), is on South Asian Muslim immigrant youth in the United States and issues of citizenship and empire after 9/11.

Martha Marín Caicedo is an independent Colombian researcher, documentarist, and conceptual director of educational TV series for youth. She has shared her research about youth cultures, specifically related to the Aesthetic Dimension, through seminars in various universities and NGOs. She also publishes on the knowledges constructed by youth cultures to resolve conflicts peacefully and on the sexual and reproductive rights of young women and men. She is the coauthor of *Secretos de Mutantes* (Bogotá: Siglo del Hombre Editores-Central University, 2002) and the author of numerous articles and documentaries.

Elizabeth Marshall is an Assistant Professor in the Faculty of Education at Simon Fraser University. Her research on the representation of girls and girlhood in popular cultural texts has been published in *College English, Feminist Studies, Gender and Education, Girlhood Studies, Reading Research Quarterly,* and *Rethinking Schools.*

Claudia Matus is an Assistant Professor at the Pontifical Catholic University of Chile. She received her PhD from the University of Illinois in Urbana-Champaign. Her research interests include subjectivities and representation, place and movement theories, curriculum theory, and policy. Her recent work has focused on meanings of internationalizing higher education institutions, as well as issues of difference in universities and schools. Theories of space and time, feminist approaches, and cultural studies frameworks infuse her analyses.

Julie McLeod is an Associate Professor in Curriculum, Equity, and Social Change, Graduate School of Education, University of Melbourne. Her research areas are youth and gender studies, curriculum history and feminism, and subjectivity, inequality, and schooling. She is currently working on a cultural history of adolescence and schooling, 1930s–1970s. Her publications include *Researching Social Change: Qualitative Approaches* (Sage, 2009), with R. Thomson, *Troubling Gender and Education* (Routledge, 2009), edited with J. Dillabough and M. Mills, *Learning from the Margins: Young Women, Social Exclusion and Education* (Routledge, 2007), edited with A. Allard, and *Making Modern Lives: Subjectivity Schooling and Social Change* (SUNY, 2006), with L. Yates.

Erica R. Meiners teaches, writes, and organizes in Chicago. She is a participant in local and national justice work, specifically antimilitarization campaigns, prison abolition, reform movements, and queer and immigrant rights organizing. She is the author of *Flaunt It! Queers Organizing for Public Education and Justice* (Peter Lang, 2009) and *Right to Be Hostile: Schools, Prisons and the Making of Public Enemies* (Routledge, 2009), and of articles in *AREA Chicago*, *Journal of International Women's Studies*, *Meridians*, *Academe*, and *Upping the Anti*. Meiners is a 2010 Lillian J. Robinson Scholar at the Simone de Beauvoir Institute, a beekeeper, and an intermittent *Ms Magazine* blogger.

Kaoru Miyazawa is Assistant Professor in the Education Department at Gettysburg College, Pennsylvania. Her research interests include immigration, youth, gender, sexuality, popular culture, language, curriculum, and secondary school education. Her recently completed dissertation, *Home away from Home: Paradoxes of Nostalgia in the Lives of First-Generation Immigrant Girls in the U.S.*, is based on her study of immigrant girls' nostalgia and future aspirations in New York City.

Pam Nilan is Associate Professor of Sociology at the University of Newcastle, Australia, and Treasurer of the Asia-Pacific Sociological Association. She has conducted research on youth in Australia, Indonesia, and other countries in the Asia-Pacific region. She has coauthored two books and published numerous articles in the field of youth studies. She is writing a book on ambivalent adolescents in Indonesia with coresearcher Lyn Parker. Her current research project is on masculinity and violence in Indonesia and India.

Rachel Oppenheim is a core faculty member in the School of Education at Antioch University, Seattle. Her current research focuses on the lives and educational experiences of incarcerated women. In her most recent study she employed feminist poststructural theories to analyze discourses surrounding incarcerated women and examine the ways they have been positioned as women, inmates, and learners. Other areas of research include participatory action research, disability studies, queer theory, and the complex circulation of power and surveillance in educational spaces.

Bill Osgerby is Professor of Media, Culture, and Communications at London Metropolitan University. His research focuses on 20th-century British and American cultural history. His books include *Youth in Britain Since 1945*

(Blackwell, 1998), *Playboys in Paradise: Youth, Masculinity and Leisure-Style in Modern America* (Berg/New York University Press, 2001), *Youth Media* (Routledge, 2004), and a coedited anthology, *Action TV: Tough-Guys, Smooth Operators and Foxy Chicks* (Routledge, 2001).

Rob Pattman is Associate Professor of Sociology at Stellenbosch University. He is interested in youth and social identities, including race, gender, and sexuality; HIV/AIDS education in Southern Africa; and developing self-reflexive research methods which position young people as experts. His recent publications include *Young Masculinities* (Palgrave, 2002) with Stephen Frosh and Ann Phoenix, *Finding Our Voices: Gendered and Sexual Identities and HIV/AIDS in Education* (UNICEF, 2003) with Fatima Chege, and *Undressing Durban* (Madiba, 2007), edited with Sultan Khan. Rob describes himself as a subordinate male when it comes to dress but fairly hegemonic when it comes to sport.

Cindy Patton holds the Canada Research Chair in Community, Culture, and Health and is Professor of Sociology and Anthropology at Simon Fraser University, Vancouver, Canada. She works in the areas of media studies, social studies in medicine, and social theory with special attention to race, gender, and sexuality. Her most recent work is the edited volume *Rebirth of the Clinic* (University of Minnesota Press, 2010).

Wanda S. Pillow is an Associate Professor jointly appointed in Education, Culture, and Society and Gender Studies at the University of Utah. Her research and teaching interests cover qualitative methodologies, educational policy, and gender/race/sexuality studies. She is continuing research on the educational rights of pregnant/mothering students while completing work on cultural and historical representations of Sacajawea and York of the 1804 Corps of Discovery expedition.

Thomas S. Popkewitz is a Professor in the Department of Curriculum and Instruction at the University of Wisconsin-Madison. His historical, ethnographic, and comparative research examines systems of reason that govern policy, research, and practices related to pedagogy and teacher education. His recent publications include *Cosmopolitanism and the Age of School Reform* (Routledge, 2008), *Globalization and the Study of Education* (The National Society for the Study of Education, 2009), edited with F. Rizvi, and *Schooling and the Making of Citizens in the Long Nineteenth Century: Comparative Visions* (Routledge, 2011), with Daniel Tröhler and David Labaree.

Stuart Poyntz's research interests include children; youth and media cultures; theories of the public sphere, with specific concern for the work of Hannah Arendt; and young people's historical thinking, particularly in relation to digital media technologies. He has extensive background in the history of media literacy, nationally and internationally, and recently coauthored *Media Literacies: Between Past and Future* (Wiley-Blackwell). Currently, he is undertaking a three-year project examining youth digital media ecologies in Canada.

Todd R. Ramlow teaches courses in the Women's Studies Program at George Washington University that intersect mass media and popular culture, feminist theories, queer theory, disability studies, and youth studies. His work has appeared in *GLQ: A Journal of Lesbian and Gay Studies*, *Rhizomes*, and *MELUS*, and in the anthologies *Youthscapes: The Popular, the National, the Global* and *The Ashgate Research Companion to Queer Theory*.

Mary Louise Rasmussen is a Senior Lecturer in the Faculty of Education at Monash University, Victoria, Australia. Her research is in the area of sexualities, gender, and education. She is the author of *Becoming Subjects: Sexualities and Secondary Schooling* (Routledge, 2006) and coeditor, with Susan Talburt and Eric Rofes, of *Youth and Sexualities: Pleasure, Subversion and Insubordination in and out of Schools* (Palgrave, 2004). In 2010 she coedited a special issue of the *International Journal of Qualitative Studies in Education* on "'After-queer' tendencies in queer research." Currently she is working on a project related to secularism and sexuality education in Australia and the United States.

Andrew J. Reisinger is a doctoral student in the History Department at George State University, staff member of the Women's Studies Institute, and freelance public historian. His dissertation explores the meanings and experiences of sexual liberation in the social movements and countercultures of Atlanta, Georgia, during the long sixties.

Emma Rich is a Senior Lecturer in Sport and Education at the University of Bath. Rich has published broadly in areas of sociology of education, pedagogy, the body, and physical culture. Her recent research examines the impact of new health imperatives associated with obesity on health policy, embodied identities, and eating disorders. She is the coauthor of *The Medicalization of Cyberspace* (Routledge, 2008), with Andy Miah, and *Education, Disordered Eating and Obesity Discourse: Fat Fabrications* (Routledge, 2008), with John Evans. She is the coeditor of *Debating Obesity: Critical Perspectives* (Palgrave, 2010).

Fazal Rizvi is a Professor at the University of Melbourne, former editor of *Discourse: Studies in the Cultural Politics of Education*, and a past President of the Australian Association for Research in Education. His recent research focuses on identity and culture in transnational contexts, global mobility of students, theories of globalization, and the internationalization of education. His current projects include an examination of the ways Indian universities are negotiating pressures of globalization and the knowledge economy, as well as a theoretical exploration of the cosmopolitan possibilities of education. His recent books include *Youth Moves: Identities and Education in a Global Era* (Routledge, 2007), *Globalization and the Study of Education* (Wiley, 2009), and *Globalizing Educational Policy* (Routledge, 2010).

Mikko Salasuo is a Senior Researcher in the Finnish Youth Research Society. His doctoral thesis (2004) dealt with drug subcultures in Finland from the

1960s onwards. Salasuo has published books on youth culture, youth work, Finnish military culture (with Hoikkala and Ojajärvi), and drug-related deaths. Salasuo has edited several publications on drugs and youth cultures in Nordic countries, history of Finnish marginality, social activism, counter cultures, sports, and alcohol education. Currently, Salasuo is studying recreational doping use, cultural addictions, street cultures, and sports.

Elizabeth Seaton is a Canadian scholar of cultural and communication studies who specializes in questions concerning the ideology and political economy of media and consumer cultures, and issues regarding the human body and social identity. While her published work is interdisciplinary and far-ranging, one consistent factor is its interest in the dialectical relationships of humans to their changing social, cultural, and natural (nonhuman) environments. A former Associate Professor of Communication Studies at York University, Toronto, Seaton is currently Research Associate and Faculty Associate in the undergraduate and graduate programs of Women's and Gender Studies at the University of British Columbia.

Noah W. Sobe is Associate Professor and Graduate Program Director of Cultural and Educational Policy Studies in the School of Education at Loyola University, Chicago. His work examines the transnational circulation of educational policies and practices in historical and contemporary settings. He has published articles in *Educational Theory, Paedagogica Historica, European Education, Revista Brasileira de História da Educação, Current Issues in Comparative Education*, and *Harvard Education Review*. He is the author of *Provincializing the Worldly Citizen: Yugoslav Student and Teacher Travel and Slavic Cosmopolitanism in the Interwar Era* (Peter Lang, 2008) and the editor of *American Post-Conflict Educational Reform: From the Spanish-American War to Iraq* (Palgrave, 2009).

Elisabeth (Lissa) Soep is Research Director and Senior Producer at Youth Radio, a national youth-driven production company in Oakland, CA. She holds a PhD from Stanford and has published widely on youth discourse and digital media culture, including *Drop that Knowledge* (University of California Press, 2010) with Vivian Chávez, and *Youthscapes* (University of Pennsylvania Press, 2004) with Sunaina Maira. The Youth Radio stories Lissa has produced for NPR have been recognized with honors including the Peabody Award, three Murrow Awards, and the Robert F. Kennedy Journalism Award. With NSF support, Lissa cocreated the *Brains and Beakers* series—interactive dialogues between youth and inventors. She is the Principal Investigator for a 2010 winning entry in the MacArthur Foundation's Global Digital Media and Learning Competition.

Rebecca Stanko is a doctoral student in Curriculum & Teaching at Teachers College, Columbia University. Her dissertation research, engendered by her own experiences as a high-school English teacher, explores the ways of knowing of secondary English teachers. Rebecca holds undergraduate degrees in English and American Studies from Wellesley College and an MPhil in Anglo-Irish Literature from Trinity College, Dublin, Ireland. This is her first publication.

Gordon Tait is a Senior Lecturer in the School of Cultural and Language Studies in Education at the Queensland University of Technology. His research interests include the philosophy of education, education and the law, youth and governance, the sociology of death, and the rise of behavior disorders and schooling.

Susan Talburt is Director of the Women's Studies Institute at Georgia State University. She has published in the fields of curriculum studies, qualitative research, higher education, youth studies, and gay and lesbian studies. Her books include *Subject to Identity: Knowledge, Sexuality, and Academic Practices in Higher Education* (SUNY Press, 2000), *Thinking Queer: Sexuality, Culture, and Education* (Peter Lang, 2000) with Shirley R. Steinberg, and *Youth and Sexualities: Pleasure, Subversion, and Insubordination in and out of Schools* (Palgrave, 2004) with Mary Louise Rasmussen and Eric Rofes. She is currently thinking about neoliberalism, affect, sexualities, and spatialities.

Carolyn Vander Schee is Assistant Professor of Education at Northern Illinois University. Her research focuses on the intersections of sociology of education, curriculum studies, and educational policy, specifically as these relate to school health policies and practices. Her work explores the ways in which contemporary school health policies are justified, negotiated, and experienced by students and school personnel. A central theme of her research is the relationship between discourse and social dynamics as this bears on understandings of health, illness, and the body, and influences the responsibilities and obligations of public schools.

Alejondro Venegas-Steele hails (and interpellates) from Atlanta, Georgia. He has published before in *Left Turn* magazine as A.V. Venegas-Steele. He is in his final year of undergraduate work at the Women's Studies Institute at Georgia State University. His academic interests include queerness, transness, feminism, Deleuze, Foucault, Spanish-language theory, structural and post-structural social thought, critical race and ethnic studies, and Internet cultures.

Lisa Weems is Associate Professor of Cultural Studies and Curriculum at Miami University. She holds a joint appointment in the Western Program for Interdisciplinary Studies and the Department of Educational Leadership. Weems teaches courses in qualitative research methodology, gender and sexuality studies, and feminist transnational cultural studies. Her current research focuses on historical and contemporary discourses of girls and "development." In 2009, she cofounded the DIVA Institute, a program to increase awareness and activism for social justice among minoritized young women in Southwest Ohio.

Yen Yen Woo is an Associate Professor in the Department of Curriculum and Instruction, College of Education and Information Sciences at Long Island University, C. W. Post, where she teaches Curriculum Development, Action Research for Teachers, and Social Foundations of Education. She wrote and directed *Singapore Dreaming*, a feature film that has won several international awards. She is currently working on *Dim Sum Warriors*, a graphic novel and animated movie about anthropomorphic kung-fu fighting Chinese snacks.

Johanna Wyn is Professor of Education in the Melbourne Graduate School of Education and Director of the Youth Research Centre at the University of Melbourne. Her research focuses on young people's experiences of education and work, health, and wellbeing. She leads the Life-Patterns research program, a comparative longitudinal panel cohort study of young people comparing two generations of young Australians. Her recent books include *Youth Health and Welfare: The Cultural Politics of Education and Wellbeing* (Oxford University Press, 2009), *Touching the Future: Building Skills for Life and Work* (ACER, 2009), and *The Making of a Generation: The Children of the 1970s in Adulthood* (University of Toronto Press, 2010).

INDEX